Anomalistic Ps

Exploring Paranormal Belief and Experience

Christopher C. French

and

Anna Stone

palgrave
macmillan

First published 2014 by
PALGRAVE MACMILLAN

Palgrave Macmillan in the UK is an imprint of Macmillan Publishers Limited, registered in England, company number 785998, of Houndmills, Basingstoke, Hampshire RG21 6XS.

Palgrave Macmillan in the US is a division of St Martin's Press LLC, 175 Fifth Avenue, New York, NY 10010.

Palgrave Macmillan is the global academic imprint of the above companies and has companies and representatives throughout the world.

Palgrave® and Macmillan® are registered trademarks in the United States, the United Kingdom, Europe and other countries.

ISBN 978–1–4039–9571–1

This book is printed on paper suitable for recycling and made from fully managed and sustained forest sources. Logging, pulping and manufacturing processes are expected to conform to the environmental regulations of the country of origin.

A catalogue record for this book is available from the British Library.

A catalog record for this book is available from the Library of Congress.

Typeset by MPS Limited, Chennai, India.

To Anne, with love and thanks (for putting up with me!) – CCF

To Peter, for endless tea and sympathy – AS

Contents

List of Table, Figures, and Boxes

Table

Figures

Boxes

Preface

One way or another, anomalistic psychology has been around for a long time even if it is only relatively recently that the actual term *anomalistic psychology* has begun to be used more widely. Two centuries ago, Dr John Ferriar argued that reports of ghosts were based upon optical illusions and several other examples could be cited of thinkers down the centuries who have tried to account for ostensibly paranormal experiences in non-paranormal terms, albeit that such attempts were rather sporadic. It was not until the early 1980s that the term *anomalistic psychology* was coined. Since that time, the number of books and scientific papers on topics in this area has gradually increased to the point where we felt that it was timely to produce a volume that attempts to provide a comprehensive overview of thinking and findings in this field. The result is the volume that you now hold in your hands.

There are a number of ways in which we could have covered our chosen subject. One would be to have taken a topic-based approach with chapters on particular paranormal phenomena such as ghosts, mediums, telepathy, precognition, and so on. Alternatively, we might have organized the book in terms of psychological rather than paranormal topics, describing the relevance of, say, memory, perception, and reasoning in different chapters (to give but a few examples). Instead, we have adopted a novel approach by devoting most chapters to a consideration of the insights and understanding of our chosen field that is provided by one of the major sub-disciplines of psychology: developmental, social, cognitive, clinical, evolutionary, individual differences, and psychobiological. We think this approach has served us well in organizing the material that we wished to cover and we hope that you agree.

This book will be of use to lecturers and students on courses in anomalistic psychology, parapsychology, and critical thinking. The number of such courses is currently increasing year by year. However, we also hope that the book will appeal to the general reader who has an interest in trying to understand what lies behind the paranormal claims that so pervade the world in which we live. Presentation of such claims in the media is often sensationalistic and uncritical, pandering to the belief that allegedly paranormal phenomena make life more exciting and interesting. We believe that a proper understanding of the psychological factors that might lead someone to believe that they have had a paranormal experience when in fact they have not is just as exciting and interesting. Furthermore, given the fact that such experiences and beliefs have been reported in every known society since records began, such understanding can provide great insight into an important aspect of what it means to be human.

Christopher C. French and Anna Stone
17 May 2013

Acknowledgements and Publisher's Acknowledgements

We would like to take this opportunity to thank Jamie Joseph, Paul Stevens, and Jenny Hindley of Palgrave Macmillan for their endless patience, support, and encouragement. We would also like to thank four anonymous reviewers for their constructive criticism of earlier drafts of this text. Finally, our gratitude goes out to innumerable colleagues, students, and friends over the years for their interest, ideas, and input relating to the topics covered in this volume. You know who you are.

The authors and publisher would like to thank the following for permission to reproduce copyright material:

Box 1.1 Reprinted from Thalbourne, M., The 18-item Australian Sheep-Goat Scale (Forced-Choice Format). *Journal of the American Society for Psychical Research*, 89(3), 245–6, first published by the American Society for Psychical Research 1995. Reprinted with kind permission from Michael Thalbourne's family.

Box 1.2 Reprinted from Tobacyk, J., A Revised Paranormal Belief Scale. *International Journal of Transpersonal Studies* 23, p. 96, 2004 with permission from Jerome Tobacyk and the Institute of Transpersonal Studies

Box 2.1 Reprinted from Merckelbach, H. Horselenberg, R., Muris, P., The Creative Experiences Questionnaire (CEQ): a brief self-report measure of fantasy proneness. *Personality and Individual Differences*, volume 31, issue 6, pages 987–995, copyright 2001, with permission from Elsevier and Harald Merckelbach

Introduction

1

What is anomalistic psychology?

Psychology is defined by Eysenck (1998, p. 3) as 'the science which uses intro-spective and behavioural evidence to understand the internal processes which lead people to think and to behave as they do'. In practice, psychologists consider their subject matter from a variety of related perspectives and bring to bear evidence from a wide range of different sources in order to address these issues. They may, for example, consider the ways in which individual differences between people – such as age, gender, cultural background, and personality – affect thought and behaviour. Developmental psychologists focus upon understanding the psychological changes that occur across the lifespan, from birth to old age. Social psychologists concentrate upon the way in which an individual's mental processes and actions are influenced by others with whom they interact. Cognitive psychologists devise experiments to probe the ways in which we process information when performing such complex opera-tions as perceiving the world around us, remembering previous events, and making judgements. The psychobiological approach attempts to describe the underlying biological processes at the level of activity in the brain and central nervous system that allow us to achieve such everyday miracles. Clinical psy-chologists have a particular interest in understanding those patterns of thought and behaviour which result in distress on the part of the person experiencing them. Evolutionary psychologists consider the human mind in terms of the adaptations that have shaped it over the millennia in order for us to survive as a species. Needless to say, although each of the sub-disciplines has its own particular focus, each draws upon insights from the others in attempting to understand precisely what makes us tick.

What then is the newly emerging sub-discipline of **anomalistic psychology**? French (2001a, p. 356) states that anomalistic psychology

> attempts to explain paranormal and related beliefs and ostensibly par-anormal experiences in terms of known (or knowable) psychological and

1

physical factors. It is directed at understanding bizarre experiences that many people have, without assuming that there is anything paranormal involved. While psychology, neurology and other scientific disciplines are rich with explanatory models for human experiences of many kinds, these models are rarely extrapolated to attempt to explain strange and unusual experiences.

As we shall see, anomalistic psychologists attempt to understand their subject matter by considering the phenomena to be explained from the varying perspectives of all of the traditional sub-disciplines of psychology. Before discussing the nature of anomalistic psychology in more detail, the following section describes a number of typical scenarios that illustrate the types of bizarre experiences that come within the remit of anomalistic psychology.

Just imagine ...

Imagine yourself as the central character in each of the following scenarios.

* * *

You have been trying for a long time to get to sleep after a long evening of revising for an exam the next day but so far without success. The sounds of street life outside your window keep grabbing your attention every time you start to drift off. You can't help thinking that you will be getting up again in a few hours and you still need to do some last-minute preparation before the exam starts at 10 am. You are worried that you have not really had time to prepare properly. Things have just been so hectic recently. You are now beginning to regret those cups of coffee you consumed earlier in order to keep yourself awake so that you could cram in a few more hours of revision.

Eventually, after hours of tossing and turning, you feel the warm and welcome onset of sleep gradually beginning to creep over you – but suddenly you are aware that something is not right. You can feel the fear building up in the pit of your stomach as you realize that you are not alone. At first, you simply get a very strong impression that someone is standing in the shadows at the foot of your bed. A chill runs up your spine as you lie there, paralysed with fear, and concentrate on the sounds you can hear. Although you can still clearly hear the night-time traffic on the road outside, you can also hear the unmistakable sound of breathing. You feel as if your pounding heart is going to burst out of your chest as you force yourself to open your eyes.

There is no doubt in your mind that someone – or *something* – is lurking in the shadows. Whatever it is, you instinctively know that it is evil. As you watch, to your horror the dark shadows take shape into the form of a grotesque old hag, with a wizened face and stooped body. Most terrifyingly of all, she is staring intently at you with red eyes that seem to glow in the dull light.

She shuffles slowly towards where you lie. You want to flee but you cannot move. You want to scream for help but no sound emerges from your mouth. The monstrous figure leans over the bed and stares into your face as you lie immobile on your back, so close that you can smell her warm, stinking breath. She continues to stare into your eyes as she climbs onto the bed and sits astride your chest. You can feel her filthy clothes against your skin and her greasy hair on your face as she puts her cold strong hands around your neck and begins to squeeze. You feel her weight pressing you down into the bed and your panic reaches new heights as you try in vain to gasp for breath.

You know that if you cannot escape from her vice-like grip, you will die. Despite your terror, you summon all your strength into one final attempt to move your arms. After what seems like an eternity, you manage to move your left arm a fraction of an inch – and, suddenly, the spell is broken. The hag is gone. You can move again. Shaking and drenched with sweat, you turn on your bedside light and leave it on until the morning. You are too frightened to go back to sleep.

You do not perform at your best in your exam the next day.

*   *   *

You watch a TV documentary on the topic of **alien abduction**. The programme features interviews with many people who claim that, against their will, they have been taken on board spaceships by extraterrestrials and subjected to medical examination. The claimants appear to be sane and intelligent people and the commentary clearly implies that their claims should be taken seriously and, in all likelihood, are probably true. A couple of sceptical scientists are briefly featured expressing their doubts about the evidence put forward in support of such claims but there appear to be a lot more scientists who seem to be convinced, including professors and doctors at respectable universities.

According to the programme, there is lots of evidence to support the idea that our planet is frequently visited by aliens. Apparently, the governments of the world are well aware of this. In fact, they have even recovered crashed flying saucers and stored them away in top-secret military bases (such as Area 51 in the USA). The advanced technology from these ships has been used to develop our own military technology. It is claimed that the reason people are being abducted is so that they can be used as guinea pigs in alien experiments to produce human–alien hybrids. It is happening on a much grander scale than anyone would imagine. This is because the aliens are able to wipe the memories of their unfortunate victims following the abduction so that they usually do not remember the event. Luckily for us though, there are often telltale signs that expert **UFOlogists** claim indicate that an abduction has taken place. These include things like strange marks and scars appearing on people's bodies with no obvious explanation or episodes of so-called **missing time**, when individuals realize that they have no memories whatsoever for a period of time despite being, as far as they know, fully conscious throughout.

To be absolutely sure that an abduction really has taken place, potential victims often have to undergo hypnotic regression. Following a hypnotic induction procedure, the subject is taken back mentally to the time and place of the possible abduction in the belief that hypnosis will provide the key to recover any repressed or blocked memories. It was clear from the documentary that when people were regressed in this way, they appeared to be reliving the whole bizarre episode. Not only were they able to describe the aliens that had abducted them and the operations they had performed, they showed an appropriate emotional response to their treatment, often crying and shaking. Unless these people were trained actors, they certainly did not appear to be faking it.

* * *

You are staying with your old Uncle Bob and his wife for a few days. You never really used to like spending time with him very much. He always seemed to you to be rather unfriendly and abrupt, always too busy with his business, and a little bit too obsessed with money and possessions for your liking. All that changed a couple of years ago when, shortly after his retirement, he had a heart attack and almost died. Since then, he has been like a different person. He has become much more caring about friends and family, and even people that he does not know personally. He does voluntary work for a number of charities and has even given away a substantial proportion of his personal wealth, built up through hard work over many decades. His wife, Vera, while generally approving of the transformation that has occurred to her husband of over 40 years, has found it hard to accept his high level of generosity in this regard. He is also now actively involved in the green movement, despite having for years dismissed green campaigners as interfering 'do-gooders'. All in all, you now find him to be one of the nicest people you know and always enjoy his company.

One evening, sitting by the fire talking to Uncle Bob after your evening meal, the conversation turns to matters **paranormal**. You tell your uncle about the occasional weird experiences that have happened to you personally, some of the things that you have heard from friends, and things that you have read about in books and magazines and seen on TV. Uncle Bob is very interested and appears to want to tell you about an experience of his own but he is hesitant to do so. 'The only other person I've told about this is Vera – and I think it worried her a lot. I think she thought I was losing my marbles!' he eventually confides. 'She told me not to mention it to anyone else … but you've told me about your own weird experiences, so I'm going to take a chance and tell you about mine.'

Uncle Bob tells you the most remarkable story. Apparently, the day he almost died from his heart attack, he 'saw heaven' with his own eyes – and now that he knows that there really is life after death, he no longer has any fear of dying. When he had collapsed in the supermarket that day, he had suddenly realized that, to his great surprise, he was watching events unfold from a vantage point about 5 metres above the ground ('I could see the tops of the supermarket shelves as I looked down!'). He saw a concerned middle-aged man kneeling on the floor next to him asking him if he was alright and the man's wife hurrying to the checkout counter to raise the alarm. He saw the ambulance men arrive. He was vaguely amused at all the fuss. 'I wanted to tell them not to worry, that I was OK, but no one could hear me. In fact, I was better than OK – I'd never felt so calm and peaceful as I did then.'

The next thing Uncle Bob remembered was that he was floating gently down a long dark tunnel and he could see a light at the end. He was aware of two other beings guiding him down the tunnel. They communicated with him telepathically, reassuring him that everything was going to be alright. As he approached the light, it became brighter and brighter ('But it didn't hurt my eyes'). He entered into the light and felt an all-consuming love and acceptance. 'It was God,' says Uncle Bob simply.

Uncle Bob was then presented with scenes from his life ('Like watching a film'), from his childhood right up through to his old age. Although it seemed like his whole life was replayed before his eyes, the whole experience was over very quickly. It was as though each scene was presented for him to learn from it, but he was not being judged in any way. For both acts of kindness and acts of selfishness, he was simply made aware of how his actions had had repercussions for himself and for those around him.

He then found himself walking through an idyllic landscape, still accompanied by his two spirit guides. They came to a bridge over a river. On the other side, he could see many people standing in a beautiful garden, all waving and smiling at him. At the front of the group were his parents, both of whom had died many years earlier. They both looked happy and healthy, and he noticed that his mother was no longer confined to the wheelchair that she had used during the final years of her life. He desperately wanted to join them but as he approached the bridge, one of the spirit guides gently told him, 'Your time will come, but it is not now. You must go back.' With that, he felt himself suddenly jerked back into his own body and he opened his eyes to find himself lying in a hospital bed. 'But I'll never forget it,' he says. 'It was the most beautiful experience I have ever had – and it wasn't just a dream!'

*   *   *

Although the previous scenarios have been invented for illustrative purposes only, they typify the kind of evidence that convinces many people that paranormal forces really do exist. A surprisingly high proportion of the population report frightening sleep-related experiences similar to that described in our first scenario. The media frequently present claims of alien abduction supported by university-based scientists with PhDs. Many thousands of people around the world have had so-called **near-death experiences** (**NDEs**), similar to that described by old Uncle Bob. Are such experiences only explicable in terms of the operation of paranormal forces – forces not currently recognized by conventional science? Or might there be other explanations?

Paranormal belief and experience

Results from public opinion polls and other sources consistently reveal high levels of belief in the paranormal among the general public in modern Western societies. For example, Moore (2005) reported, on the basis of a telephone survey of 1002 American adults, that around three-quarters of the adult American population endorses at least one paranormal belief, a figure in line with previous surveys of that population. Breaking those figures down, the levels of endorsement for different types of paranormal claim were are follows: **extrasensory perception (ESP)**, 41%; haunted houses, 37%; **ghosts**, 32%; telepathy (defined as 'communication between minds without using traditional senses'), 31%; **clairvoyance** (defined as 'the power of the mind to know the past and predict the future'), 26%; **astrology**, 25%; communication with the dead, 21%; **witches**, 21%; **reincarnation**, 20%; and **channelling** (defined as 'allowing a 'spirit-being' to temporarily assume control of body'), 9%. Note that the figures presented here refer to the percentages of the sample that positively endorsed each belief item. In all cases, there was also a substantial percentage of the sample (between 12% and 27%) that reported that they were 'not sure about' each paranormal phenomenon. Similar levels of endorsement have been found among the British adult population.

Clearly, if you have personally had what you regard to be a paranormal experience, you will believe in the paranormal. Previous research shows that personal experience of ostensibly paranormal phenomena is the most common reason that people give for paranormal belief (Blackmore, 1984; Clarke, 1995; Palmer, 1979). However, many people believe in the paranormal not on the basis of direct personal experience, but instead because of the testimony of trusted others and/or on the basis of information presented by the media (Clarke, 1995).

In modern Western societies, the media regularly deal with paranormal topics. Publishers of books, newspapers, and magazines are well aware that the public appetite for such material is virtually insatiable. Television and radio programmes regularly deal with the paranormal in both science and religion documentaries, as well as highly successful fictional series, such as the *X-Files* and so-called reality TV series such as *Most Haunted*. In the digital age, there are TV channels devoted entirely to the paranormal. Paranormal topics are also a staple subject of talk shows and of successful films such as the *The Exorcist*, *The Sixth Sense*, and *White Noise*.

Many people make a good living upon the basis of New Age practices such as astrology, **tarot cards**, and **aura** readings. For those who cannot find the time for a face-to-face reading, readings can be provided over the telephone by companies specializing in this lucrative practice. The digital age has fully embraced the paranormal industry with the Internet providing both paranormal services and information with little by way of quality control.

Similarly, the providers of **complementary and alternative medicine (CAM)** are also an important and profitable part of the general trend in the West towards New Age practices. These alternative therapies typically have little or no scientific evidence to support them (Singh & Ernst, 2008) and yet millions of people around the world prefer to spend their money on such unproven remedies than opt for conventional medicine.

It goes without saying, however, that paranormal beliefs are not only to be found in modern Western societies. In fact, there is no known society, either historically or geographically, where paranormal experiences are not reported and paranormal beliefs cannot be found. This near-universality of paranormal belief and experience would initially appear to support the idea that paranormal forces actually do exist. If this is the case, the wider scientific community should accept the reality of paranormal forces and subject them to the same type of scientific scrutiny that would be applied to any other phenomenon of nature.

But it is at least possible that the study of paranormal beliefs and ostensibly paranormal experiences will reveal answers which suggest that in fact paranormal forces do not exist. If this is the case, the study of paranormal belief and experience promises to reveal a great deal about what it means to be human. It will inform us about the ways in which our beliefs and wishes can influence the way we perceive and remember events, how we make decisions and come to conclusions about how the universe operates. So, whether paranormal forces actually exist or not, it is certainly worth taking such claims seriously.

Problems with defining the paranormal

It is appropriate at this point to take a step back and ask the question, what exactly do we mean by the word *paranormal*? It is important in science to be clear about exactly what is meant by the use of particular words and phrases but it is clear from the discussion so far that the word *paranormal* is applied to a very wide range of phenomena indeed. Is it acceptable to simply use the term to refer to anything that we deem 'weird and wonderful'? The simple answer to this question is: it depends who you ask.

A good place to start is the website of the Parapsychological Association (PA), who describe themselves on their home page (http://www.parapsych.org/) as 'the international professional organization of scientists and scholars engaged in the study of "psi" (or "psychic") experiences, such as **telepathy**, clairvoyance, **psychokinesis, psychic healing,** and **precognition**'. The PA has been an affiliated organization of the American Association for the Advancement of Science (AAAS) since 1969 and the *Journal of Parapsychology* is an affiliated publication of the PA. Issues of the *Journal* sometimes include a glossary of terms used in parapsychological research 'borrowed or adapted from' a glossary produced by Thalbourne (2003).

One such authoritative glossary appears in Volume 71, pp. 201–5. Here we find the word *paranormal* defined as follows: 'Term for any phenomenon that in one or more respects exceeds the limits of what is deemed physically possible according to current scientific assumptions.' **Parapsychology** itself is defined as

'The scientific study of certain paranormal or ostensibly paranormal phenomena, in particular, ESP and PK' (psychokinesis; if you are unsure what any of the terms used in this and other chapters actually mean, refer to the Glossary at the end of this book). Even if we include in this definition the area of evidence relating to the possibility of life after death, widely regarded as being within the remit of parapsychological investigation, we can immediately see that some of the phenomena we have mentioned so far might well be considered to be beyond that remit on the basis of the strict definition provided.

For example, if it were to be shown that aliens really were abducting people as claimed, this would not directly require the overturning of any currently accepted scientific assumptions. We may wonder at the means used by the aliens to transport themselves to Earth given our current understanding of what is and is not physically possible, but plausible scenarios based upon superior technology (e.g. suspended animation) could be developed. The mere presence of extraterrestrials on Earth would not, in and of itself, be deemed paranormal using the strict definition employed by parapsychologists. Similarly, the existence of a variety of other postulated extraordinary life forms – such as the Loch Ness monster, **Bigfoot**, and so on – would not directly violate any accepted scientific assumptions and would therefore not be deemed to be paranormal phenomena if we accept the strict definition offered. However, it is clear that people in general, and the media in particular, often do deal with such scientifically controversial claims under the umbrella heading of 'the paranormal'.

The area of traditional religious belief is also problematic. This time, the problem is not that something which is typically thought of as being paranormal (such as alien abduction) does not fit our strict definition but that some claims which are usually *not* thought of as being paranormal (i.e. religious claims) actually do fit the definition in many instances. By defining the paranormal as phenomena which are outside the currently accepted paradigm of scientific explanation, we can see that there are aspects of many religions that would fall under the 'paranormal umbrella'. For instance, most of the world's religions maintain that we survive bodily death, and reported miracles from a variety of traditional religions routinely involve the violation of currently accepted scientific assumptions, including examples of apparent psychokinesis (e.g. from Christianity, Jesus turning water into wine and miracle healing, and Moses parting the Red Sea) and precognition (e.g. dreams foretelling of future events). The psychology of religion is a recognized sub-discipline in its own right (Fontana, 2003; Loewenthal, 2000; Wulff, 1997) but it clearly overlaps with both anomalistic psychology and parapsychology.

Belief in systems of **divination** such as astrology and tarot cards, or the reading of palms and tea leaves, would also present problems, as would traditional superstitious beliefs, such as it being unlucky to walk under ladders or lucky to find a four-leaf clover. These beliefs certainly fit the definition of *paranormal* offered by the PA in that they involve practices which, if valid, could not be explained in terms of currently accepted scientific assumptions, but they do not involve ESP, PK, or life after death, and therefore fail to meet the strict defini-tion of *parapsychological*.

There are many other phenomena which would also be problematic insofar as they are often considered to be 'paranormal' by the media and the general public but do not involve in any obvious way either ESP, PK, or life after death. A partial list (taken from Carroll, 2003) could arguably include **angels**, the **Bermuda Triangle**, the **Bible Code**, **crop circles**, **crystal power**, **dermo-optical perception**, **dowsing**, **fairies**, **Feng Shui**, **glossolalia**, the **'hundredth monkey' phenomenon**, **hypnosis**, *I Ching*, **Kirlian photography**, **ley lines**, **lycanthropy**, **Men in Black (MIBs)**, **prana**, **reflexology**, **runes**, the **Shroud of Turin**, **spontane-ous human combustion**, **vampires**, and **zombies**! Again, if you are unsure what some of these terms mean, refer to the Glossary at the back of this book for brief descriptions and to Robert Todd Carroll's (2003) *The Skeptic's Dictionary* for further detail. The latter can be found online at www.skepdic.com.

In practice, parapsychologists do in fact sometimes publish papers on topics other than ESP, PK, and life after death, but the vast majority of their investiga-tions do indeed deal with these three central concepts. Anomalistic psycholo-gists, however, tend to adopt the looser definition of paranormal as preferred by the media: that is, anything weird and wonderful (even occasionally topic areas that no one would consider to be paranormal). The reasons for this approach are discussed later in this chapter, but for now we should simply note that these different conceptions of the paranormal will influence the top-ics researchers choose to investigate. The previous discussion on how we define the paranormal has illustrated that it is simplistic to think of paranormal belief as if it were unidimensional, when in fact it is complex and multidimensional. This in itself should serve as a warning that explaining the psychology of para-normal beliefs and experiences is unlikely to be a simple affair; it seems much more probable that different types of paranormal belief and experience will each be influenced by different factors, sometimes interacting with each other in complex ways.

Measuring paranormal beliefs

How then have social scientists, and psychologists in particular, gone about measuring levels of paranormal belief? We have already referred to pub-lic opinion poll data which over recent decades have routinely shown high levels of belief in a wide range of paranormal phenomena in various countries around the world. Such data are of great interest in their own right but they are often rather crude indices, typically just asking respondents if they believe or disbelieve in a number of different phenomena and usually including a 'don't know' option.

Psychologists typically measure beliefs, attitudes, and personality character-istics using carefully constructed scales which ideally go through a meticulous process of standardization (Anastasi & Urbina, 1997). Among other things, it is important that scales are reliable (e.g. the results are similar if the scale is used on different occasions if one is measuring a stable trait) and valid (i.e. the scale really is measuring what one wants to measure).

A number of different measures of paranormal belief are in common use but, as one might expect, the content of these scales reflects the conception of the paranormal held by those constructing the scale. Similarly, the choice of scale on the part of users will reflect the particular experimental aims of individual researchers (Goulding & Parker, 2001). One of the most commonly used scales is the so-called Australian Sheep–Goat Scale (ASGS) developed by Australian parapsychologist Michael Thalbourne (Thalbourne & Delin, 1993; Thalbourne, 1995; Thalbourne, 2001, 2010a). Within parapsychology, believers in the paranormal are referred to as 'sheep' and sceptics are referred to as 'goats', hence the rather unusual name for this scale (this terminology is based upon a Biblical reference). The original version of the scale asked respondents to indicate their level of belief in various psi phenomena by marking a line. However, a simpler version of the test with three response options per item was subsequently developed. This version is reproduced in Box 1.1. You should complete the questionnaire before continuing.

As you can see, this scale focuses very much on beliefs and experiences relating to the three core concepts of the paranormal: ESP, PK, and life after death. The scale is very easy to administer and score. To calculate your total score on the scale, simply add together all of your responses (i.e. no points for every 'false' response, one point for every 'uncertain' response, and two points for every 'true' response). The most extreme sceptic would have a score of zero, having responded 'false' to all items, whereas the most extreme believer would have a score of 36, having responded 'true' to all items. What score did you get? For comparison purposes, you might like to note that Thalbourne (1995) administered the scale to 247 psychology students at the University of Adelaide. Their mean score was 14.90 (with a standard deviation of 7.61). How does your score compare? Are you a sheep or a goat? Or are you somewhere in between? You might like to complete this scale again once you have finished reading this book to see if your views have changed.

Whereas the ASGS focuses very much on the core concepts of parapsychology, other scales in common use are based upon a much broader conception of the paranormal. The most commonly used of these is the Revised Paranormal Belief Scale (RPBS) developed by Jerome J. Tobacyk (2004). A great deal of research was carried out using the original Paranormal Belief Scale (PBS) published by Tobacyk and Milford (1983), but Tobacyk revised the scale in 1988. It was widely used in its unpublished form for many years prior to its eventual publication in 2004. This scale is reproduced in Box 1.2. Once again, you may find it instructive to complete the scale before continuing.

In addition to obtaining a full-scale score by summing the responses for all items (after reverse scoring Item 23), the RPBS also allows the calculation of seven subscale scores. Scoring instructions for the subscales are presented beneath the scale items in Box 1.2. For comparison purposes, the means (and

---

Box 1.1   Australian Sheep-Goat Scale (Thalbourne, 1995)

For each item indicate your attitude using the following scale:

0 = False
1 = Uncertain
2 = True

1. I believe in the existence of ESP.
2. I believe I have had personal experience of ESP.
3. I believe I am psychic.
4. I believe that it is possible to gain information about the future before it happens, in ways that do not depend on rational prediction or normal sensory channels.
5. I have had at least one hunch that turned out to be correct and which (I believe) was not just a coincidence.
6. I have had at least one **premonition** about the future that came true and which (I believe) was not just a coincidence.
7. I have had at least one dream that came true and which (I believe) was not just a coincidence.
8. I have had at least one vision that was not a hallucination and from which I received information that I could not have otherwise gained at that time and place.
9. I believe in life after death.
10. I believe that some people can contact spirits of the dead.
11. I believe that it is possible to gain information about the thoughts, feelings or circumstances of another person, in a way that does not depend on rational prediction or normal sensory channels.
12. I believe that it is possible to send a 'mental message' to another person, or in some way influence them at a distance, by means other than the normal channels of communication.
13. I believe I have had at least one experience of telepathy between myself and another person.
14. I believe in the existence of psychokinesis (or 'PK'), that is, the direct influence of mind on a physical system, without the mediation of any known physical energy.
15. I believe I have personally exerted PK on at least one occasion.
16. I believe I have marked psychokinetic ability.
17. I believe that, on at least one occasion, an inexplicable (but non-recurrent) physical event of an apparently psychokinetic origin has occurred in my presence.
18. I believe that persistent inexplicable physical disturbances, of an apparently psychokinetic origin, have occurred in my presence at some time in the past (as, for example, a poltergeist).

---

standard deviations) of the RPBS full scale and subscale scores for 217 university students in the southern United States, as presented by Tobacyk (2004), are as follows – Full Scale: 89.1 (21.9); Traditional Religious Belief: 6.3 (1.2); Psi: 3.1 (1.5); Witchcraft: 3.4 (1.7); Superstition: 1.6 (1.2); **Spiritualism:** 2.8 (1.4); Extraordinary Life Forms: 3.3 (1.3); Precognition: 3.0 (1.3). (Note that

---

Box 1.2   Revised Paranormal Belief Scale (Tobacyk, 2004)

Please put a number next to each item to indicate how much you agree or disagree with that item. Use the numbers as indicated next. There are no right or wrong answers. This is just a sample of your own beliefs and attitudes. Thank you.

1 = Strongly disagree; 2 = Moderately disagree; 3 = Slightly disagree; 4 = Uncertain; 5 = Slightly agree; 6 = Moderately agree; 7 = Strongly agree

1. The soul continues to exist though the body may die.
2. Some individuals are able to levitate (lift) objects through mental forces.
3. Black magic really exists.
4. Black cats can bring bad luck.
5. Your mind or soul can leave your body and travel (astral projection).
6. The abominable snowman of Tibet exists.
7. Astrology is a way to accurately predict the future.
8. There is a devil.
9. Psychokinesis, the movement of objects through psychic powers, does exist.
10. Witches do exist.
11. If you break a mirror, you will have bad luck.
12. During altered states, such as sleep or trances, the spirit can leave the body.
13. The Loch Ness monster of Scotland exists.
14. The horoscope accurately tells a person's future.
15. I believe in God.
16. A person's thoughts can influence the movement of a physical object.
17. Through the use of formulas and incantations, it is possible to cast spells on persons.
18. The number '13' is unlucky.
19. Reincarnation does occur.
20. There is life on other planets.
21. Some psychics can accurately predict the future.
22. There is a heaven and hell.
23. Mind-reading is not possible.
24. There are actual cases of witchcraft.
25. It is possible to communicate with the dead.
26. Some people have an unexplained ability to predict the future.

Note: Item 23 is reverse scored. Traditional Religious Belief = Mean of Items (1, 8, 15, 22); Psi = Mean of Items (2, 9, 16, 23); Witchcraft = Mean of Items (3, 10, 17, 24); Superstition = Mean of Items (4, 11, 18); Spiritualism = Mean of Items (5, 12, 19, 25); Extraordinary Life Forms = Means of Items (6, 13, 20); Precognition = Mean of Items (7, 14, 21, 26)

---

the subscale scores are means which must therefore be between one and seven, whereas the Full Scale score is simply the total score across all items. Therefore, the Full Scale score will not equal the sum of the subscale means.)

As you can see, this scale provides a profile of a person's paranormal beliefs and not just an overall score. Thus, although you may have a similar full-scale score to someone else, your actual profile may be quite different. This highlights the fact that it is a mistake to think of 'paranormal belief' as if it were a unidimensional entity. One person may express high levels of belief in, say, ESP, PK, and extraordinary life forms but low levels of belief in those aspects of the paranormal tapped by the RPBS subscales dealing with, say, traditional religious belief and superstitions. Another person may show the opposite profile but end up with a similar full-scale score.

Exactly how many different dimensions of paranormal belief there are is a controversial and unresolved issue, dependent to some extent upon whether one starts with the strict definition of the paranormal preferred by experimental parapsychologists (ESP, PK, and life after death) or the much broader conception as employed by the media, the general public, and anomalistic psychologists (i.e. pretty much anything weird and wonderful). Identification of the factorial structure of paranormal belief depends upon complex statistical analysis of data from large samples of respondents to the various scales in use. As one might expect, analyses of data from different scales based upon different conceptions of the paranormal produce different factor structures, but that is not the sole determining factor. There is even disagreement over the number of factors involved when data from the same scale are analysed. For example, Tobacyk and Milford (1983) felt that seven main factors could be identified in response data for the Paranormal Belief Scale and also for the revised version of this scale (Tobacyk & Thomas, 1997), corresponding to the seven subscales listed previously. Although some researchers have replicated this factor structure (Haraldsson & Houtkooper, 1996), many have failed to do so (Davies, 1988; Johnson, de Groot, & Spanos, 1995; Lange, Irwin, & Houran, 2000; Persinger & Richards, 1991; Thalbourne, 1995; Thalbourne, Dunbar, & Delin, 1995), with the number of factors produced ranging from one to six.

The actual details of the statistical procedures used to analyse the data are important in determining the factor structure produced and this undoubtedly explains to some extent the wide range of solutions proposed. A number of commentators have criticized the approach taken by Tobacyk and colleagues in this respect (Hartman, 1999; Lawrence, 1995; Lawrence & de Cicco, 1997; Lawrence, Roe, & Williams, 1997; Thalbourne, 1995; see also, Tobacyk, 1995; Tobacyk & Thomas, 1997). Both Lawrence (1995) and Hartman (1999) have pointed out that the number of items in this scale is insufficient from a statistical perspective to adequately sample seven independent dimensions of paranormal belief. The details of this controversy are beyond the scope of this book but it may be concluded that the available data generally do support the common-sense notion that paranormal belief is a multidimensional entity even if the precise details of that dimensionality remain to be determined. Furthermore, despite the criticisms levelled against the RPBS in terms of its apparent failure to definitively reveal the dimensionality of paranormal belief, it has proven to be an extremely useful and popular research tool.

Most researchers with an interest in paranormal beliefs do employ standardized scales of the type described earlier in their research. One of the main advantages of such scales is that the scales are known to be valid and reliable thanks to the standardization procedures employed in their construction. Also, the use of standard scales allows results from different studies using the same scales to be compared. However, even those scales which allow for the calculation of subscale scores may sometimes be deemed to be too general in terms of what is being measured. For this reason, researchers will sometimes use one (or a very small number) of specifically worded Likert-type items instead of (or in addition to) the standardized scales. In this way, belief in (and possibly experience of) specific paranormal phenomena can be targeted more precisely.

The previous discussion should be borne in mind when considering studies which investigate psychological differences between 'believers' and 'disbelievers'. Although it is often a convenient shorthand to refer to experimental participants in this way and, indeed, they will often be referred to in this way throughout this book, one always needs to be aware of the fact that the terms may be referring to a global measure of overall paranormal belief or to a very specific paranormal belief, depending upon how the beliefs were assessed. Furthermore, one would not expect necessarily to find the same psychological mechanisms underlying different types of paranormal belief and ostensibly paranormal experience.

The relationship between anomalistic psychology and parapsychology

Whereas parapsychologists typically restrict their subject matter to the core topics of ESP, PK, and life after death, anomalistic psychologists are interested in a much wider range of phenomena, many of which would often be labelled as 'paranormal' (if one adopts a broad definition of this term). One reason for this is that the same psychological processes may well underlie different phenomena, some of which clearly fit the strict definition of 'paranormal' preferred by parapsychologists, while others clearly fall outside that definition. For example, a reading by a **medium** clearly falls within the strict definition, being as it is an alleged communication with the spirits of physically dead people. Astrological readings, on the other hand, are not within that strict definition. However, readings given in both contexts appear to be very similar in some ways. In both situations, the reading involves the apparent presentation of information from some external source relating to the sitter's life and personality. As discussed in Chapter 7, the underlying psychological processes involved in readings in both contexts may well be identical. It makes sense, therefore, for anomalistic psychologists to study both.

Similarly, whereas claims of alien abduction do not fit into the strict definition of the paranormal, claims of past-life memories most certainly do. In both cases, however, a strong case can be made (see Chapters 6 and 7) that both involve **false memories,** as do claims relating to allegedly 'recovered' memories of ritualized satanic abuse. Thus, the psychology of false memories is relevant to all of these phenomena and it would be arbitrary and pointless to artificially restrict attention to only those phenomena which related to the central areas of interest to parapsychologists.

Thus insight into understanding paranormal claims can often be gained by considering similar claims that arise in a non-paranormal context. This can be further illustrated by considering David Oates's (1991) pseudoscientific claims relating to reversed speech. Oates alleges that normal human speech actually contains two simultaneous messages. The first is that which the listener consciously perceives, this message being produced by the left cerebral hemisphere of the speaker. However, Oates claims that there is a hidden message in speech that can only be heard consciously if the message is played backwards. He claims that the right cerebral hemisphere of the speaker produces this message and that the message is readily understood by the listener's unconscious mind even though consciously they remain unaware of it. It is further claimed that this message reveals the speaker's true intentions and feelings even if the consciously perceived message does not. To illustrate this, Oates claims that part of President Clinton's testimony during the Lewinsky scandal sounds like 'Kiss the lying ass' when played backwards. Oates claims that his technique would be an invaluable aid to police investigators, therapists, interviewers, and negotiators, and offers training seminars at high prices.

Such claims have no validity whatsoever for reasons discussed by Byrne and Normand (2000) and Langston and Anderson (2000). Essentially, the 'messages' that are heard in reversed speech are the result of what psychologists refer to as 'top-down processing' (French, 2001b). It is generally accepted by cognitive psychologists that when we interact with the outside world, we do so by referring to a 'mental model' of that world and our current position within it. We do this on the basis of two sources of information. The first is 'bottom-up' information in the form of raw sensory data coming in through our eyes, ears, and other sensory systems. In order to make sense of this input, we also make use of top-down processing. This refers to our knowledge, belief, and expectations about the world. As you might expect, top-down influences have their strongest effect when the sensory input is ambiguous or degraded in some way.

When Oates and his followers listen to **reverse speech**, they are expecting to hear a message in the speech-like sounds they hear. Their own expectations are sufficient to ensure that they often do so. The subjective nature of the supposed message is powerfully illustrated by the fact that one typically cannot hear the alleged message until one knows what it is that one is supposed to hear (and even then, it's not always easy!). You can experience this for yourself by visiting David Oates's website at http://www.reversespeech.com/. Try listening to the sounds without knowing what it is that you are supposed to hear. You will almost certainly not be able to discern the message that Oates claims is present. Once you do know what the message is supposed to be, the expectation produced is such that you will probably hear the message.

Once again, the psychology of a non-paranormal, albeit pseudoscientific, claim is directly relevant to understanding the psychology behind a paranormal claim. In this case, the paranormal example is the so-called **electronic voice phenomenon (EVP)**. The idea that spirit voices could be recorded by leaving a tape recorder in record mode in empty rooms or by recording the noise produced when a radio tuner is set between stations was popularized by Konstantin Raudive (1971). It is probable that some of the recordings actually have inadvertently recorded genuine (living) human voices and at other times have recorded transient radio signals. But this body of work has received most criticism because of the entirely subjective nature of the interpretations of the unclear sounds recorded (Banks, 2001, 2012; Baru*š*, 2001; Ellis, 1975; Smith, 1972). There are many websites where you can access examples of EVP samples for yourself (just type 'EVP' into a search engine). You will find that in the majority of cases you will not be able to hear the alleged message until you know what it is you are supposed to hear.

The power of top-down processing is also demonstrated by the phenomenon of so-called backward masking (also known as 'backmasking'). This is the idea that rock music contains hidden backwards messages, a claim widely accepted among American Christian fundamentalists who believe that these messages are satanic in nature. By similar reasoning to that employed by David Oates, they believe that although the messages cannot be consciously perceived when the music is played forwards, they can still have a powerful unconscious influence on the listener. There is no evidence whatsoever to support such beliefs other than the subjective impression on the part of those pushing this idea that these messages are real. In one famous case, the rock band Judas Priest was taken to court over such claims (McIver, 1988). Two American teenage boys had shot themselves, one of them fatally, and the parents of the boys claimed that they had done so because the backwards message 'Do it' was hidden in one of the tracks by the band. Fortunately, the judge found in favour of the defendants.

There are many websites that will allow you to listen to examples of these alleged messages. Once again, try listening to them initially without knowing the message you are supposed to hear and then again when you do know the message. The most stunning example we have personally come across is a clip from Led Zeppelin's classic track *Stairway to Heaven* (just type 'Stairway to Heaven backwards' into a search engine). The first time you play the backwards clip, you may pick up a word or two. But when you play it again having read what you are supposed to hear, you will hear a message running to some 35 words of coherent English. You will hear the message as clear as a bell and wonder how you missed it the first time. But the truth is that the message is not really there at all.

As these examples vividly illustrate, it is often fruitful to consider psychological explanations of non-paranormal phenomena when attempting to explain ostensibly paranormal phenomena. Topics of potential interest to anomalistic psychologists cover a wide range, from those topics which would fall within the strict definition of the paranormal preferred by parapsychologists to many topics which would not be classed by anyone as paranormal, such as urban myths, hypnosis, and placebo effects. Along the way, anomalistic psychology would also encompass all of those topics which the media would describe as 'paranormal' even if parapsychologists would not.

But why should psychologists devote valuable research time to attempting to explain ostensibly paranormal experiences at all? There are a number of very good reasons. As we have already seen, the majority of adults in Western societies do believe in the paranormal and a sizeable minority claim to have had direct personal experience of it. In fact, as stated, there is no known society, either historically or geographically, where such beliefs and experiences are not common. Until fairly recently, with a few notable exceptions, psychologists have had little to offer by way of explanation for such beliefs and experiences which clearly constitutes an important aspect of what it means to be human.

Furthermore, people make important decisions on the basis of such beliefs. Many people consult astrologers, tarot card readers or psychics for guidance relating to important life decisions concerning relationships, finances, and health. Millions of pounds are spent annually in the UK alone on complementary and alternative therapies, many of which are based upon paranormal notions. Making the wrong decisions regarding one's health can have serious repercussions both financially and medically.

As stated, the models put forward by anomalistic psychologists are often derived from and informed by theories developed in other sub-disciplines within psychology. Indeed the organization and structure of this book is based upon this fact as explained in the next section. However, it is important to emphasize that the relationship between anomalistic psychology and psychology as a whole is reciprocal. Many of the findings from anomalistic psychology have implications that go well beyond explaining unusual experiences. To take but one example, much recent work has been directed towards investigating memory for anomalous experiences (French, 2003; French & Wilson, 2006). While such research clearly helps us to understand how memory for unusual experiences can be influenced by one's level of paranormal belief, many of the conclusions drawn are likely to generalize in the sense that memory biases are likely to be influenced by beliefs held in other contexts as well (e.g. political and religious beliefs). Thus, this body of research can be seen as one particular example of the study of the effects of belief upon memory.

Anomalistic psychologists typically assume as a working hypothesis that paranormal forces do not exist and attempt to explain ostensibly paranormal experiences in non-paranormal terms. Wherever possible, it is important that anomalistic psychologists produce empirical evidence in support of their proposed explanations as opposed to simply putting forward explanations that may sound plausible but have not actually been subjected to any empirical testing. The appropriate attitude for anomalistic psychologists to adopt is one of scepticism in the true sense of the word (French, 2005a). Scepticism should involve an attitude of open-minded doubt, a willingness to examine the available evidence and to admit that one may be wrong. It should not involve dismissing claims on the basis of pure prejudice without fairly assessing the evidence put forward in support of those claims.

For this reason, anomalistic psychology should not be thought of as being opposed to parapsychology. The assumption on the part of most anomalistic psychologists that paranormal forces do not exist is simply a working hypothesis and should be treated as such. It is open to revision should parapsychologists (or other types of researchers for that matter) ever manage to produce compelling evidence that paranormal forces really do exist (see Chapter 10 for an assessment of the current state of parapsychology). If this point is ever reached, anomalistic psychologists would still have performed a valuable service for parapsychologists by helping them to distinguish between what is genuinely paranormal and what just looks like it is on the surface.

The structure of this book

The structure of this book is based upon the structure of the discipline of psychology as a whole. Psychology is divided into a number of sub-disciplines each with a characteristic perspective and approach to its subject matter. Inevitably, these sub-disciplines overlap each other considerably, and any reasonably comprehensive explanation of a particular psychological phenomenon will usually involve considering that phenomenon from more than one such perspective. In practice, however, most topics in psychology have traditionally been investigated within one particular sub-discipline or another and psychology textbooks and courses are traditionally taught in terms of these sub-disciplines. It therefore makes sense to consider what each of these perspectives might offer in terms of providing insight into the topics of interest to anomalistic psychologists. Having outlined in this introductory chapter the general domain and approach of anomalistic psychology, there now follows a summary of the contents of the remaining chapters of this book. It should be noted that the early chapters of the book tend to be more focused upon paranormal beliefs whereas the latter chapters focus more on ostensibly paranormal experiences. As already stated, these two areas are obviously related by the fact that anyone who has had a potentially paranormal experience is much more likely to believe in the paranormal than someone who has not.

Chapter 2   Individual differences

Chapter 2 will summarize the considerable body of research that has investigated various individual differences associated with paranormal beliefs (Irwin, 1993a, 2009; Irwin & Watt, 2007). Much of the research in this area has been driven by the desire to test particular hypotheses related to the possible functions of paranormal belief. For example, a case has been made that levels of paranormal belief may be higher among those with relatively less power and influence within society. This is referred to by Irwin and Watt (2007) as the **social marginality hypothesis**. Differences in levels of belief associated with gender, age, socio-economic status, race, and marital status will be considered with respect to this hypothesis. Consideration will also be given to cross-cultural differences in paranormal beliefs. Chapter 2 will also discuss the evidence relating to possible differences between believers and non-believers in the paranormal in terms of personality.

Chapter 3   Clinical perspectives

Uninformed sceptics often assert that anyone who believes in the paranormal or claims to have had a paranormal experience is probably psychologically maladjusted. There is, in fact, reasonably consistent evidence that paranormal beliefs and the tendency to report ostensibly paranormal experiences do correlate significantly with a number of measures of psychological maladjustment, including manic-depressive (**bipolar**) tendencies, magical ideation (**schizotypy**), and **dissociativity**. However, as will be discussed in Chapter 3, these findings are open to a variety of interpretations. A useful framework to apply here is that of the **reality monitoring** approach. Reality monitoring refers to the psychological processes which underlie our ability to distinguish between events taking place in the external world and our internal mental events (resulting from imagination, fantasy, dreams, and so on). Among the consequences of poor reality monitoring one might expect to find greater susceptibility to suggestion, tendency to hallucinate, and susceptibility to false memories. Evidence suggests that believers in the paranormal may indeed demonstrate such proclivities. However, it is certainly not the case that all believers would fit such a psychological profile and that no sceptics would. These factors may play some role in explaining ostensibly paranormal beliefs and experiences but they only account for part of the observed variance.

Chapter 4   Developmental perspectives

Chapter 4 considers developmental aspects of paranormal beliefs and experience. It is often claimed that childhood is characterized by **magical thinking**, a tendency which supposedly disappears as one matures into adulthood. In fact, a reasonable case can be made that examples of magical thinking can be observed in both children and adults. The available evidence is assessed in this chapter. Picking up on the themes of **fantasy-proneness** and reality monitoring developed in Chapters 2 and 3, this chapter will also outline one particular model of the development of paranormal beliefs first proposed by Harvey Irwin (1992) which links the development and maintenance of paranormal belief to **fantasy-proneness** and the tendency to dissociate, both of which may themselves have developed as psychological defence mechanisms to cope with childhood trauma.

Chapter 5   Psychobiological perspectives

It is a central assumption of modern neuroscience that all experiences, including ostensibly paranormal experiences, are mediated by the central nervous system. It is certainly the case that neuroscience can provide valuable insights into many such experiences and Chapter 5 illustrates this by outlining neuroscientific approaches to understanding two commonly reported altered states of consciousness. The first of these is known as **sleep paralysis** (French & Santomauro, 2007; Santomauro & French, 2009), as illustrated by the fictional scenario with which this chapter opened. Sleep paralysis in its most basic form is commonly reported among the general population. It involves the realization, either as one is drifting off to sleep or as one emerges from sleep, that one is paralysed. The experience is often accompanied by frightening visual and auditory **hallucinations,** a strong **sense of presence,** difficulty breathing, and intense fear. Such experiences are often interpreted in paranormal terms.

The fictional account of Uncle Bob's experience presented earlier illustrates many of the common features of another vivid altered state of consciousness known as a *near-death experience* (Blackmore, 1993; French, 2005b, 2009b). Such experiences are surprisingly common among people who have had a close brush with death. As described, they often involve a profound sense of peace, an **out-of-body experience** (OBE), travelling down a tunnel towards a light, entering the light, meeting spirits of deceased loved ones and/or religious figures, a life review, reaching a point of decision, and returning back to the physical body. The transformational effects of such experiences can be long lasting. From a scientific point of view, the issue is whether the experience is best conceived of as a glimpse of an afterlife or, to put it simply, the visions of a dying brain. Plausible neuropsychological explanations for the different components of NDE will be presented. The involvement of the temporal lobes of the brain in a variety of ostensibly paranormal experiences will also be discussed.

Chapter 6   Cognitive perspectives

Cognitive psychology is another sub-discipline which has a great deal to offer in terms of insights into ostensibly paranormal experiences. Chapter 6 summarizes research into cognitive biases that may underlie a range of subjective psi experiences, including telepathy, clairvoyance, and precognition (French, 1992a; French & Wilson, 2007). The possible roles of non-conscious processing in ostensibly paranormal experiences will also be discussed. The central importance of the reliability of memory in assessing reports of anomalous experiences is emphasized, drawing upon the vast research literature relating to the inaccuracy of eyewitness testimony and the generation of false memories (French, 2003; French & Wilson, 2006).

Chapter 7   Social perspectives

Chapter 7 considers the valuable contribution that social psychology makes to our understanding of paranormal belief and ostensibly paranormal experiences. Although much of this book deals with psychological explanations of personal experiences that are interpreted as involving paranormal forces, a large proportion of the population believe in the paranormal despite never having had any such personal experiences themselves. Among the most common reasons given for believing in the paranormal among such people is the personal testimony of trusted friends and relations as well as media coverage of the paranormal, as described in this chapter.

Many people believe in the paranormal because they are impressed by the readings given by psychics, astrologers, and other fortune tellers, either as personally experienced or as seen on TV. Chapter 7 describes the social psychology of **cold reading**, a technique used by deliberate con artists to give the impression that they know everything about complete strangers that they have never even met before (Hyman, 1977). This should not be taken as implying that all individuals who claim to possess such a gift are deliberate frauds, but it is plausible that they may be drawing upon the same sources of information in their readings as the intentional cold reader but without realizing that they are doing so. This chapter will also present recent research into the psychology of psychic–sitter interactions that has employed a social constructionist approach, which considers the ways in which anomalous experiences are mediated through language and social interaction.

The sociocognitive perspective on a range of ostensibly paranormal phenomena is also considered in this chapter (Spanos, 1996). In attempting to understand the phenomena associated with hypnosis, two main opposing schools of thought have emerged. The first school of thought maintains that the hypnotic trance is a unique altered state of consciousness, as different to the normal waking state as, say, dreaming is. In the hypnotic state, the mind is said to operate differently to the way it operates during normal consciousness and the individual may be able to perform tasks that would not normally be possible. This is known as the **state theory of hypnosis**. Non-state theorists, on the other hand, maintain that all of the so-called hypnotic phenomena can be explained in much more mundane terms, involving such factors as compliance, role enactment, and imagination, without the need to invoke any unique altered state of consciousness (Wagstaff, 1999). The **non-state theory of hypnosis** is one example of the sociocognitive perspective but this perspective can also be applied to a wide range of ostensibly paranormal phenomena including mediumship, **possession, exorcism**, and reincarnation claims (Spanos, 1996).

Chapter 8 Evolutionary perspectives

Like the rest of the animal and plant kingdoms, human beings are the products of evolutionary history. It is reasonable to assume that psychological and behavioural traits that are found widely within human populations both across time and space have become so prevalent because they confer some kind of advantage in terms of survival. This chapter will consider whether such reasoning can be applied to paranormal beliefs and supernatural beliefs more generally. At first glance, it may seem odd that beliefs which may well be untrue could actually confer any kind of survival advantage, but deeper consideration reveals that in fact this may well be the case. It is possible that such beliefs are to some extent a by-product of a cognitive system that has evolved to make quick decisions that are usually right as opposed to slower decisions that are right a little more often. In evolutionary terms, the former may be preferable to the latter.

Chapter 9   Integrating the different approaches: Alien contact claims

Chapter 9 attempts to explain alien contact and abduction claims as an example of the way in which any reasonably comprehensive explanation of a particular ostensibly paranormal phenomenon is likely to draw upon a number of different perspectives (French, 2001c; Holden & French, 2002). It will be demonstrated in this chapter that individuals who claim to have been contacted by aliens tend to have a particular personality profile (Chapter 2) and developmental history (Chapter 4) consistent with tendencies towards being susceptible to hallucinations and false memories (Chapter 3). The role of sleep paralysis and the possible role of unusual neural activity in the temporal lobes (Chapter 5) will be outlined. Ultimately, it will be argued that reports of alien abduction experiences are almost certainly generally based upon false memories (Chapters 6 and 7).

Chapter 10   Parapsychological perspectives

As stated earlier, anomalistic psychologists generally adopt the working hypothesis that paranormal forces do not exist but genuine scepticism requires that the possibility that paranormal forces do exist is recognized. For that reason, many anomalistic psychologists devote some of their research effort to directly testing paranormal claims. Chapter 10 presents an overview of parapsychology (Irwin & Watt, 2007), emphasizing that some of the findings presented from researchers carrying out experimental investigations under apparently well-controlled conditions do appear to support the claim that psi exists. It will be argued that although the parapsychological research literature taken as a whole falls well short of providing definitive proof of the existence of paranormal forces, some of the current avenues of research are worthy of being taken seriously by the wider scientific community and merit further investigation.

Chapter 11   Philosophical perspectives

This chapter will consider some of the philosophical aspects of anomalistic psychology and parapsychology. Two main issues will be addressed. First, the scientific status of parapsychology will be discussed. Critics of parapsychology often condemn it as being nothing more than a **pseudoscience**. Such assessments depend upon the means used to differentiate true science from non-science, a topic that has exercised philosophers of science for well over a century. The position taken here is that, regardless of whether or not paranormal forces actually exist, parapsychology at its best can legitimately be described as a true science. The second issue to be addressed relates to the implications for our understanding of consciousness if certain paranormal claims were proven to be true. If it turned out that consciousness really can be separated from the physical brain, this would prove that some form of **dualism** is required to fully understand consciousness.

Chapter 12 Future prospects for anomalistic psychology and parapsychology

The final chapter of the book will consider the current status and future prospects for the fields of anomalistic psychology and parapsychology, paying particular attention to the implications for parapsychology of current concerns within psychology relating to poor replication rates and publication bias.

Suggested further reading

For general discussion of anomalistic psychology:

Cardeña, E., Lynn, S. J., & Krippner, S. (eds). (2013). *Varieties of anomalous experience: Examining the scientific evidence.* 2nd edn. Washington, DC: American Psychological Association. (NB: Readers will find several references in the current volume to chapters in the first edition of this book. We only learned that an updated second edition was being produced as the current volume went to press.)

French, C. C. (2009a). 'Anomalistic psychology'. In M. Cardwell, L. Clark, C. Meldrum, & A. Wadeley (eds), *Psychology A2 for AQA A.* 4th edn (pp. 472–505). London: Collins.

Holt, N., Simmonds-Moore, C., Luke, D., & French, C. C. (2012). *Anomalistic psychology.* Basingstoke: Palgrave Macmillan.

Zusne, L. & Jones, W. H. (1989). *Anomalistic psychology: A study of magical thinking.* 2nd edn. Hillsdale, NJ: Lawrence Erlbaum Associates.

For discussion of the measurement of paranormal belief:

Irwin, H. J. (2009). *The psychology of paranormal belief: A researcher's handbook.* Hatfield, UK: University of Hertfordshire Press. Chapter 3, pp. 35–50.

Individual Differences

2

Introduction

In one sense, this whole book is directed at one question: why do people believe in paranormal and related phenomena? It is possible, of course, that some people believe in the paranormal because paranormal forces really do exist and these people have had direct personal experience of them. This is a possibility that has been taken seriously by many of the finest intellects in the history of science and a considerable amount of time and effort has been spent in trying to prove that paranormal forces really do exist. After well over a century of serious scientific research investigating this possibility, however, the wider scientific community remains unconvinced by the evidence produced to date. Chapter 10 of this book will present an overview of parapsychology that will conclude that although some current approaches appear to at least merit further research, the wider scientific community is fully justified in its scepticism.

Anomalistic psychologists, as described in Chapter 1, generally adopt the working hypothesis that paranormal forces do not exist. They attempt to explain belief in and experience of such phenomena in psychological terms. If they are correct in adopting this working hypothesis, we might expect to find evidence of psychological differences between those who do believe in the paranormal and those who do not, as well as between those who claim to have had direct personal experience of the paranormal and those who have not. As we shall see, there is a great deal of evidence to show that such differences do indeed exist. However, it should always be borne in mind that such differences do not in themselves prove that paranormal forces do not exist. It is always possible to argue that genuine paranormal forces really do exist, but that an individual is more likely to experience them if they happen to have a certain type of psychological profile.

This chapter will start by considering demographic differences in paranormal belief, including gender, age, socioeconomic status, race, and marital status. We will examine some cross-cultural differences and consider the **social marginality hypothesis** (e.g. Irwin, 2009) as an explanation for many forms of paranormal belief. The evidence relating paranormal belief to the personality factors of **extraversion, openness to experience, sensation seeking,** intuitive-feeling personality type, and **locus of control** will be considered. The fantasy-prone personality will be given special attention as it has been strongly linked to several types of subjective paranormal experience.

Other individual difference variables will be considered in depth in later chapters. Chapter 3 will consider the relationship between psychological health and paranormal belief and Chapter 4 will discuss developmental aspects of paranormal belief. In each case, this more detailed coverage is justified by the amount of attention that each topic has received within anomalistic psychology. Chapter 5 will present evidence that susceptibility to many ostensibly paranormal experiences may reflect underlying variations in brain function and Chapter 6 explores the idea that differences in cognitive functioning play a major role in explaining why some people believe in the paranormal while others do not. Chapter 6 will also discuss Michael Thalbourne's **transliminality** model of paranormal experiences (e.g. Thalbourne, 2000) which attempts to explain the underlying relationship between many of the psychological factors discussed in Chapters 2, 3 and 4.

Before starting to examine individual differences in paranormal beliefs, it is worth taking a quick preview of the functions that may be served by belief or disbelief in various phenomena. Different functions may be valued by different people and this may explain some of the variations in levels of belief. For example, Kennedy (2007) proposes that belief in psi may confer a sense of control and efficacy, especially in social situations. It may help to foster a sense of meaning or purpose in life and may generate mystical and spiritual experiences offering transcendence, a sense of self-worth, and feelings of connectedness with others. It is worth noting that the functions served by paranormal belief should plausibly relate to the specific areas of belief and individual personality characteristics.

The review of the literature concentrates on works published in the last 25 years or so plus earlier works of particular significance and influence. The size of the literature on individual differences in paranormal belief necessitates some decision about selection criteria and the more recent works are likely to be more accurate today, given that the content of paranormal belief varies somewhat from generation to generation. Works are referenced mainly from the psychology literature with the occasional sidestep into sociology or anthropology.

It should be noted that the research papers described here have used a variety of different measures of paranormal belief. Although these scales may be generally comparable, it is possible that different findings may stem from the use of different measures, and this should be borne in mind.

The literature reviewed concentrates on paranormal belief, rather than paranormal experience, although it must be recognized that there is a relationship between the two. Prior paranormal belief makes it more likely that a particular experience will receive a paranormal explanation, while an experience that is interpreted as paranormal will logically demand a level of paranormal belief.

Gender

Women, despite the advances brought about by the feminist movement and other social forces, are still recognized as being generally less powerful than men within modern society. According to the notion that belief in the paranormal may compensate for feelings of powerlessness (e.g. Kennedy, 2007) therefore, they would be expected to show higher levels of belief in the paranormal than men. The empirical evidence suggests that for most paranormal beliefs, this is in fact the case, but the effects reported tend to be fairly small even when they are statistically significant.

A number of studies have reported higher levels of *global paranormal belief* among women compared to men (e.g. Blackmore, 1994b; Canetti & Pedahzur, 2002; Göritz & Schumacher, 2000; Irwin, 1993a, 2001; McGarry & Newberry, 1981; Orenstein, 2002; Randall, 1990, 1997; Randall & Desrosiers, 1980; Rogers *et al.*, 2006; Saher & Lindeman, 2005; Schulter & Papousek, 2008; Tobacyk & Tobacyk, 1992; Williams, Francis, & Robbins, 2007). A number of studies, however, have failed to find any sex differences in *global paranormal belief* (e.g. Donovan, 1998; Dudley & Whisnand, 2000; Fox & Williams, 2000; Gaynard, 1992; Houran & Thalbourne, 2001; Houran & Williams, 1998; Kumar, Pekala, & Cummings, 1993; McClenon, 1994; Peltzer, 2002; Rattet & Bursik, 2001; Sjöberg & Wåhlberg, 2002).

Turning to specific aspects of the paranormal, there is substantial evidence that women believe more strongly than men in spiritualism and life after death, psi abilities, witchcraft, precognition, astrology, psychic healing, reincarnation, and in superstitions and omens of luck. Men believe more strongly than women in UFOs (unidentified flying objects), alien visitations, and extraordinary life forms (e.g. Bigfoot, the Yeti, the Loch Ness monster). The numerous studies supporting these assertions are listed in Table 2.1.

It is interesting to note that the beliefs held more strongly by men, that is extraordinary life forms and UFOs, though not scientifically proven, are not contrary to basic principles of science – rather they remain as unproven possibilities. The tendency of men to have higher belief in scientifically possible phenomena, while women have higher belief in scientifically implausible phenomena, may have something to do with gender roles that men and women are encouraged to assume. Perhaps the greater popularity of science as a subject of study and as a general interest among men than among women may be a relevant factor. If men have greater knowledge and understanding of science this would make it harder for them to believe in scientifically implausible phenomena. In this case, whatever psychological function is served by paranormal belief would have to be satisfied by those beliefs that do not contradict our scientific understanding. Women may feel less obliged to pay attention to the laws of science as currently understood and are thus more able to believe in scientifically implausible phenomena. The gender difference in specific aspects of paranormal belief will be relevant to the discussion of analytical versus intuitive **thinking styles** later in this chapter.

Table 2.1 Studies showing gender differences in specific types of paranormal belief

Spiritualism and life after death (F > M)
Aarnio & Lindeman (2005); Clarke (1991, 1993); Fox (1992); Haraldsson & Houtkooper (1996), in Iceland but not USA; Heard & Vyse (1998–9); Hollinger & Smith (2002); Houran et al. (2002); Irwin (2000a); Messer & Griggs (1989); Persinger & Richards (1991); Rice (2003); Sjödin (2002); Vitulli, Tipton, & Rowe (1999); Wolfradt (1997).

Psi abilities (F > M)
Aarnio & Lindeman (2005); Auton, Pope, & Seeger (2003); Blackmore (1997); Clarke (1991, 1993); Emmons & Sobal (1981); Fox (1992); Gray (1990); Haraldsson (1981); Heard & Vyse (1998–9); Hollinger & Smith (2002); Houran et al. (2002); Irwin (2000a); Kennedy (2003); Lange & Thalbourne (2002); Persinger & Richards (1991); Rice (2003); Sjödin (2002); Spinelli, Reid, & Norvilitis (2001–2); Thalbourne, Dunbar, & Delin (1995); Tobacyk & Milford (1983); Vitulli, Tipton, & Rowe (1999); Wolfradt (1997).

Witchcraft (F > M)
Aarnio & Lindeman (2005); Heard & Vyse (1998–9); Persinger & Richards (1991); Wolfradt (1997); note that Tobacyk & Pirttila-Backman (1992) found belief in witchcraft to be higher among men).

Precognition (F > M)
Aarnio & Lindeman (2005); Clarke (1991, 1993); Haraldsson & Houtkooper (1996) in Iceland but not USA; Heard & Vyse (1998–9); Irwin (2000a); Lange, Irwin, & Houran (2000); Sjödin (2002); Spinelli, Reid, & Norvilitis (2001–2); Tobacyk & Milford (1983); Wolfradt (1997).

Astrology (F > M)
Clarke (1991); Emmons & Sobal (1982); Fichten & Sunerton (1983); Gray (1990); Hollinger & Smith (2002); Kim (2005); Messer & Griggs (1989); Rice (2003); Sjödin (2002); Torgler (2007); Wuthnow (1976).

Psychic healing (F > M)
Gray (1990); Rice (2003).

Reincarnation (F > M)
Gray (1990); Rice (2003).

Superstitions and omens of luck (F > M)
Aarnio & Lindeman (2005); Blum (1976); Clarke (1993); Dag (1999); Dagnall, Parker, & Munley (2007); Haraldsson & Houtkooper (1996), in Iceland but not USA; Lange, Irwin, & Houran (2000); Scheidt (1973); Sjödin (2002); Torgler (2007); Wiseman & Watt (2004); Wolfradt (1997); Zebb & Moore (2003).

Extraordinary life forms and UFOs (M > F)
Aarnio & Lindeman (2005); Clarke (1991, 1993); Dag (1999); Gaynard (1992); Gray, (1990); Haraldsson & Houtkooper (1996), in the USA but not Iceland; Heard & Vyse (1998–9); Houran (1997); Irwin (2000a); Messer & Griggs (1989); Patry & Pelletier (2001); Pekala, Kumar, & Cummings (1992); Persinger & Richards (1991); Rice (2003); Sjödin (2002); Thalbourne, Dunbar, & Delin (1995); Tobacyk & Milford (1983); Tobacyk & Pirttila-Backman (1992); Tobacyk, Pritchett, & Mitchell (1988); Vitulli & Luper (1998); Wolfradt (1997).

Key: F > M = Females show higher levels of belief than males. M > F = Males show higher levels of belief than females.

Interestingly, in Blackmore's (1997) study of over 6000 respondents, more women than men believed in ESP in every age group except in the youngest group of under-25s. A study of this magnitude suggests the interesting possibility that perhaps the gender gap is diminishing, although some caution must be exercised in generalizing from Blackmore's sample as they were self-selected and may not therefore be representative of the population as a whole. Maybe the observed gender differences in paranormal belief are a product of past gender roles, and the increase in the social and economic power of women (in Western Europe, Canada, Australia, USA) or other social changes are bringing about a decrease in the excess of paranormal belief in women relative to men. Indeed, Vitulli and Luper's (1998) study of 125 college students aged 17–33 found higher levels of experience of, and belief in, psi abilities, UFOs, and contact with the spirits of dead people, in men than in women. Further support comes from McClenon's (1994) study of college students that found no sex differences in paranormal belief.

Overall it appears that there is a broad, though not universal, consensus that women have higher levels of belief in a range of paranormal phenomena (excepting extraordinary life forms and UFOs) than do men. This may be less apparent in young adults, college and university students, than in adults from older age groups.

A word of caution should be sounded, however, before proceeding. Lange, Irwin, and Houran (2000) have reported a problem with **differential item functioning** in the most popular measure of paranormal belief – the Revised Paranormal Belief Scale (Tobacyk, 2004; Tobacyk & Milford, 1983) presented in Chapter 1. Differential item functioning means that different demographic groups – for example, men versus women or older versus younger groups – may interpret questions differently so that answers to questionnaire items do not necessarily mean the same thing from all respondents. This raises the possibility that observed differences in levels of paranormal belief may not mean what they appear to mean, and what is really being measured is a difference in interpretation of a questionnaire item rather than a difference in belief. This renders comparisons of levels of paranormal belief between different demographic groups somewhat unreliable. It should be noted that the impact of differential item functioning has not been conclusively established, so it remains possible that the reported differences are all genuine. We simply cannot be certain.

Some studies have taken account of this problem. Lange, Irwin, and Houran (2000) created two new scales that were free from differential item functioning, termed *Traditional Paranormal Belief* and *New Age Philosophy*. Irwin (2001) used these new scales to verify that the higher levels of belief in women than in men on both scales persisted even after controlling for differential item functioning, though the new effects were small. Houran and Lange (2001) and Houran and Thalbourne (2001), using the same new scales, did not find gender differences. More studies would be required to establish whether or not gender differences persist separately from the potential issue of differential item functioning. It should also be noted that the new scales do not distinguish between belief in UFOs and extraordinary life forms, on which men usually score higher, and other beliefs, on which women usually score higher. Thus, the ability to compare these different types of belief in order to learn about the underlying factors may be lost.

Age

The evidence for age-related differences in paranormal belief is not very strong. Göritz and Schumacher (2000) reported that levels of general paranormal belief were positively correlated with age but other studies have found that the relationship with age may depend on the type of belief. Aspects of the paranormal that emphasize the mental powers of the individual, particularly ESP and mental healing, have been observed to increase with age (e.g. Blackmore's, 1997, study of over 6000 respondents; Clarke, 1991; Lange & Thalbourne, 2002; Rice, 2003). In contrast, belief in ghosts, precognition, and extraordinary life forms (Clarke, 1991; Rice, 2003) or astrology and superstition (Torgler, 2007) were more common in the young.

There are several studies reporting that young people have higher levels of belief in paranormal phenomena overall than the old, though effect sizes are typically small. Higher levels of paranormal belief have been observed in young adults, typically college and university students, compared to elderly adults (e.g. Heintz & Baruss, 2001; Lange, Irwin, & Houran, 2000; Tobacyk, Pritchett, & Mitchell, 1988) or adults in their 40s (Irwin, 2001). Other studies have found a general decline in paranormal belief with age (e.g. Emmons & Sobal, 1981; Randall, 1990; Sjödin, 2002). Irwin's (2001) study found that the higher levels of paranormal belief in the young compared to people in their 40s persisted even after controlling for differential item functioning. Also of relevance, the personality trait of **absorption**, that has been frequently associated with paranormal belief (see later in this chapter), has been reported to decline with age (e.g. Wolfradt, 1997), although Myers *et al.* (1983) found no relationship between age and absorption.

A large number of studies have found no relationship between paranormal belief and age. Some of these examined a restricted range of ages, mainly college and university students (e.g. Aarnio & Lindeman, 2005; Donovan, 1998; Dudley & Whisnand, 2000; Groth-Marnat & Pegden, 1998; Houran & Thalbourne, 2001; Peltzer, 2002; Randall, 1990; Williams, Francis, & Robbins, 2007). More to the point, age was not related to paranormal belief in several studies in which the age range of participants and the sample sizes seem adequate to detect even a fairly small effect of age (e.g. Fox, 1992: over 1000 adults of all ages; Haraldsson, 1981: over 1000 Icelandic participants of all ages; Houran & Williams, 1998: 107 participants aged 18 to 60; Rogers *et al.*, 2006: 250 participants aged 18 to 82; Thalbourne, 1994a: 402 participants aged 17 to 91; Wuthnow, 1976: 1000 respondents aged 16 to over-60).

Perhaps a possible association of paranormal belief with youth should not be too surprising, considering the general increase in interest in all matters paranormal beginning with the counterculture movement of the 1960s. Those aged 70 or over would have grown up before this time and so would have been less exposed to New Age ideas in general. This analysis does not fit, though, with Irwin's (2001) finding of more paranormal belief in the young than in adults in their 40s who would have been in their formative years when the counterculture movement was at its height and so would be expected to have higher levels of paranormal belief.

An alternative explanation was advanced by Torgler (2007) who noted that the young typically face an uncertain future, have less control over their circumstances, and are searching for meaning and a place in life, to a greater extent than older adults. To the extent that belief in paranormal phenomena offers comfort and a sense of security and predictability this could explain the observed patterns of greater belief in the young. This reasoning is consistent with Irwin and Watt's (2007) description of the **social marginality hypothesis** in which the people most susceptible to paranormal belief are those who are experiencing deprivation and alienation associated with their marginal status in society.

There are limitations of this research that should be noted before drawing any firm conclusions. In particular, most of the research is **cross-sectional** (i.e. studying different groups of adults at the same point in time) rather than **longitudinal** (i.e. following one group of adults as they grow older). This means that we cannot be sure whether any observed effects are due to the aging process, or whether they are due to the decade in which people were born, educated, and formed their spiritual and philosophical views (known as the *cohort effect*). If levels of paranormal belief are seen to be lower in a group of the over-60s compared to a group of university students, this could be a result of aging, or it might depend on the general cultural representations of the paranormal at a time when people were in their adolescence and deciding for themselves what to believe. There is also the problem of differential item functioning (e.g. Irwin, 2000a; Lange *et al.*, 2000) that may render any observed differences in levels of paranormal belief among different age groups unreliable (recall that differential item functioning means that people of different ages may interpret questions differently).

In summary, the consensus is that paranormal belief tends to decline rather than increase with age, although effects are typically small. Limitations of the research, including possible cohort effects and differential item functioning, render even the weak relationships that have been observed unreliable and hard to interpret.

Socio-economic status

The evidence relating socio-economic status, along with related factors such as income, level of education, and employment status to paranormal belief is ambiguous and not straightforward.

Regarding education, some researchers have found that belief in the paranormal in general declines with increasing education (e.g. Donovan, 1998; Schulter & Papousek, 2008) while others have reported a decline in specific areas of paranormal belief (e.g. Plug, 1976, superstition; Rice, 2003, ghosts and astrology; Sjöberg & Wählberg, 2002, new age beliefs; Torgler, 2007, astrology and superstition; Wuthnow, 1976, astrology). In contrast, Rice (2003) found that higher education was associated with higher levels of belief in ESP and psychic healing; Haraldsson (1985a) found that belief in ESP increased with education level in the USA and Germany, while belief in contact with the dead increased with education in the USA. Finally, Fox (1992) found no relationship between education level and paranormal belief in an analysis of over 1000 adults in the USA. The effect of education level, and choice of subject area, is covered in more depth in Chapter 6.

With respect to income, Rice (2003) observed that higher income was associated with lower levels of belief in astrology and superstition, but more belief in psychic healing, though relationships were small. Fox (1992) found no relationship between paranormal belief and income. Wuthnow (1976) and Torgler (2007) found that belief in astrology was higher among those unable to work (disabled or ill) or looking for work than among those currently employed, but Emmons and Sobal (1981) found no such relationship, noting that the unemployed generally showed lower levels of paranormal belief than the employed.

Considering socio-economic status in general, Plug (1976) reported that superstition declines with socio-economic status, and McClenon (1994) observed that paranormal experiences were more likely to be reported by people experiencing social stress or deprivation. In contrast, Torgler (2007) reported that higher socio-economic status was related to higher levels of belief in astrology and superstition (although this was after income and education levels had been taken into account).

These studies collectively suggest that perhaps different aspects of paranormal belief are related in different ways to socio-economic status. Belief in mental powers – for example, ESP and psychic healing – may increase with education level and income (Haraldsson, 1985a; Rice, 2003). Belief in aspects of the paranormal that suggest the influence of external forces on individual outcomes (e.g. superstition and astrology) seems to be higher with unemployment, low income, and poorer education (Plug, 1976; Rice, 2003; Torgler, 2007; Wuthnow, 1976; but see Emmons & Sobal, 1981). The studies reviewed here do not wholly correspond to this pattern, but nonetheless it seems plausible that if different types of paranormal beliefs serve different functions, then they will be of particular interest to different demographic groups. Perhaps those with higher levels of education and income are seeking self-actualization and transcendent spiritual experiences, and hence are attracted to mental powers. Those with lower levels of income and education, or who are unable to work, are at the mercy of external powers and so are more attracted to aspects of the paranormal that offer some understanding or predictability of life events. This speculative hypothesis must await the results of further research.

Race

Several studies in the USA have examined the impact of race on paranormal belief, with very mixed results. Higher levels of belief in blacks than in whites have been reported in some studies (e.g. Wuthnow, 1976) while others have reported higher belief in whites (e.g. Emmons & Sobal, 1981; Rice, 2003) or a mixed pattern depending on the particular aspect of paranormal belief (e.g. Tobacyk et al., 1988).

There have also been reports of no differences according to race. Caucasian versus non-Caucasian ethnicity was not related to paranormal belief in Rogers et al.'s (2006) study, although 80% of their 250 participants were Caucasian. Race was not related to paranormal belief in Fox's (1992) study of over 1000 adults in the USA. Tobacyk et al. (1988) reported that black and white university students showed similar levels of belief in a range of paranormal phenomena, and a similar rank ordering of the most common aspects of the paranormal.

In summary, it appears that there is no clear evidence for different patterns or levels of paranormal belief depending on race. However, like the pattern regarding socio-economic status, there was an indication that perhaps belief in mental powers – for example, ESP and psychic healing – is more likely in white US Americans (Emmons & Sobal, 1981; Rice, 2003) while belief in external forces controlling individual outcomes – for example, astrology, precognition, spiritualism, superstition, and witchcraft – is more likely in black US Americans (Tobacyk et al., 1988; Wuthnow, 1976). Belief in UFOs was stronger in whites than blacks (Emmons & Sobal, 1981; Rice, 2003; Tobacyk et al., 1988), and while no obvious reason presents itself, it is interesting to note that belief in UFOs has also been frequently observed to be stronger in men than in women.

Marital status

Wuthnow (1976) reported greater interest in, and belief in, astrology among the separated, divorced, and widowed than among the married, though these differences may not have survived the increase over the decades in the number of marriages ending in divorce, or the increase in the number of couples deciding not to get married. Unmarried status is no longer an index of social marginality as it may once have been. Emmons and Sobal (1981) found more belief in the paranormal in the unmarried than in the married, but again, this study is too dated to permit a strong conclusion for today. Fox (1992) found no relationship between marital status and paranormal belief in the analysis of data from over 1000 adults in the USA. However, Torgler (2007) found higher belief in superstition and astrology in people who were widowed, divorced, or separated, than in those who were married. This limited set of studies suggests that perhaps those who are in a less settled state may entertain more paranormal belief than those who have followed the traditional route of marriage. Of course, the question of causality cannot be easily answered, and it is just as plausible to say that those who have chosen to follow the more conventional path of marriage are less likely to be attracted to paranormal beliefs compared to those who have chosen less conventional lifestyles.

Cross-cultural comparisons

Members of different cultures may demonstrate different levels of belief in a range of paranormal phenomena for a variety of reasons. Some cross-cultural variations will depend on the different traditions of belief regarding particular paranormal phenomena. For example, spiritualism may be accepted as fact in some cultures (as in the UK and USA in the nineteenth century). Other variations may depend on the proportion of people in a country who feel socially alienated and deprived and who may, therefore, be more susceptible to paranormal belief that provides a sense of comfort, consolation, or personal efficacy. In countries where there is a high level of social and economic inequality, there will be large numbers of people feeling social insecurity, a sense of economic deprivation, and feelings of alienation from the dominant forces in society. Levels of paranormal belief may be higher in such countries. Of course, we should always be careful to consider that any observed differences may have an alternative explanation based on average levels of education.

There is not sufficient space to consider all of the cross-cultural research on paranormal belief and so we will offer some examples of each of the major factors underlying cross-cultural variations.

Individuals are generally rewarded for showing socially desirable patterns of belief and commitment, so some cross-cultural differences are expected to be based on political systems, levels of traditional religious belief, intellectual traditions, and popular culture. People will often tend to endorse beliefs for which they are rewarded which will tend to be the dominant beliefs in a society. According to Tobacyk and Tobacyk's (1992) study, Poles and US Americans reported similarly high levels of traditional religious belief, attributed to the strength and prominence of the Christian churches in each country. This was accompanied by low levels of belief in spiritualism, superstition, and witchcraft, attributed to the opposition of traditional Christian churches to alternative forms of belief in the supernatural. Poles had a somewhat higher level of belief in psi abilities, consistent with psi forming a more mainstream part of intellectual culture in Poland than in the USA. The strongest contrast was that paranormal beliefs were more relevant, involving, and important to the sense of self in Poland compared to the US. In Poland, both the church and the state were opposed to belief in paranormal phenomena in general, and so anyone espousing such belief would need a strong personal level of commitment. This pressure was weaker in the USA where there was less state interference in personal interests.

Turning to the issues of relative wealth, social inequality, and alienation, Hollinger and Smith (2002) conducted a large-scale questionnaire study in four regions of the world: Latin America (Argentina, Brazil, Columbia, and Uruguay); the USA; North-Western Europe (Austria, Germany, and Great Britain); and Southern Europe (Italy and Portugal). Participants were 3500 university students. The levels of belief in fairies, contact with the dead, psychic healers, and astrology showed similar patterns, being highest in Latin America (24/30/44/31%) followed by the USA (24/32/30/25%), then Southern Europe (18/17/28/24%), and lowest in North-Western Europe (14/12/23/20%). Please refer to Figure 2.1. The other two factors of clairvoyance and telepathy also had higher levels of belief in Latin America (28/54%) and the USA (26/52%), but had higher levels of belief in North-Western Europe (22/47%) than in Southern Europe (17/41%).

Hollinger and Smith (2002) suggested that paranormal belief appears to be highest where standard of living, literacy, average educational level, and general quality of life are the lowest. The pattern of belief increasing from North-Western Europe to Southern Europe to Latin America fits this theory, but there would appear to be too much belief in the USA. They attributed the high levels of paranormal belief in the USA to the instability and insecurity of living conditions, noting that geographical mobility is higher, with consequently looser family ties and less stability of the nuclear family, and also that there is a relatively weak social security system with higher levels of crime and physical violence. In a way this supports the **social marginality hypothesis** in that citizens of the USA might feel insecure and vulnerable in their society, and so turn to belief in concepts that offer an **illusion of control**.

Similar comparisons between countries and between continents have been observed by other researchers. An interesting case is the comparison of Finland

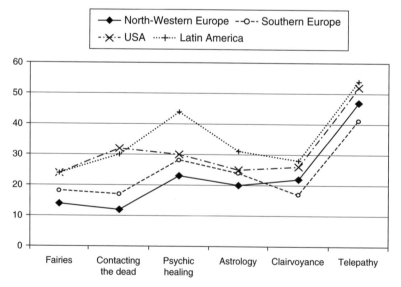

Figure 2.1   Percentage belief in paranormal phenomena in North-Western Europe, Southern Europe, USA, and Latin America, from Hollinger and Smith (2002)

versus USA performed by Tobacyk and Pirttila-Backman (2002). Both these countries have a high standard of living and are roughly equal in literacy, economic and social standing, and general quality of life. There was an overall higher level of paranormal belief in the USA, especially belief in witchcraft and superstition, which fits with the proposition of Hollinger and Smith (2002) explaining that citizens of the USA may be seeking a sense of control over the major events in their lives. Belief in extraordinary life forms was higher in Finland, which is harder to understand, though it has been seen that this belief is often stronger in a socially dominant group: men more than women, white rather than black US Americans, people of higher socio-economic status, and the young rather than the old. Orenstein (2002) and Rice (2003) also showed that Finnish students hold less paranormal belief than students in the USA and Canada. Haraldsson and Houtkooper (1996) reported that Icelandic people have higher belief in spiritualism than is found in USA, but lower levels of belief in psi, witchcraft, superstition, extraordinary life forms, and precognition, which is generally consistent with Hollinger and Smith (2002) except for the position of extraordinary life forms. McClenon (1990) reported that Chinese students had higher levels of belief in ESP and contact with the dead than US American students, also consistent with Hollinger and Smith given recent changes in Chinese society that have resulted in greater inequality of income and opportunity.

Torgler (2007) reported a high level of superstition, specifically belief in lucky charms, astrology, and fortunetelling, in former Eastern Bloc communist countries. It was suggested that this was related to current high levels of social uncertainty and insecurity compared to other European countries. It may also have been related to the suppression of church religion under communist rule that in other countries has been antagonistic to superstition and may have fulfilled the same emotional need thus acting as a substitute for superstition.

These cross-cultural comparisons must be interpreted with caution: questions may have different meanings, and terms convey different understandings, in different countries. The picture is, however, quite consistent, and suggests that paranormal belief flourishes in countries where people feel a sense of social insecurity, lack of stability, fear of what the future may hold, and a sense that personal outcomes are at the mercy of wider social and economic forces. This offers support for the **social marginality hypothesis** that is considered later in this chapter.

Ideas to think about

What is the relationship between cross-cultural differences in various aspects of paranormal belief, measures of wealth and equality within nations, and locus of control (see later in this chapter)?

The social marginality hypothesis

Irwin and Watt (2007, p. 225) describe the social marginality hypothesis as follows:

> [P]eople most susceptible to paranormal belief are members of socially marginal groups, that is, groups such as the poorly educated or the unemployed that possess characteristics or roles that rank low among dominant social values. The deprivation and alienation associated with marginal status in society is held to encourage such people to appeal to magical and religious beliefs, presumably because these beliefs bring various compensations to the lives of their adherents.

If this hypothesis is correct, it would imply that demographic factors indicating lower social status should be associated with higher levels of paranormal belief. An interesting corollary of the social marginality hypothesis is that scepticism would be more associated with men than with women and there does seem to be some evidence for this. The Committee for the Scientific Investigation of Claims of the Paranormal (CSICOP; now known as the Committee for Skeptical Inquiry, CSI) is the world's leading sceptical organization. As Blackmore (1994b) pointed out, the founding board of CSICOP was entirely male and the leadership has been dominated by white males.

Wuthnow (1976) analysed data from 1000 respondents in the San Francisco Bay Area regarding belief in astrology. His analysis showed that 'it was the more poorly educated, the unemployed, non-whites, females, the unmarried, the overweight, the ill, and the lonely, who were most taken with astrology' (Wuthnow, 1976, p. 167). Thus, the social marginality hypothesis was strongly supported with respect to belief in astrology in this particular sample, but that does not necessarily mean that it would be supported across a wider range of beliefs and respondent groups.

In fact, looking back at the previous sections, although it is an intuitively appealing idea, support for the social marginality hypothesis is patchy at best when considered in a wider context. The strongest and most consistent evidence is the finding, for the majority of studies and the majority of aspects of paranormal belief, of an excess of female over male believers. There is also evidence for stronger belief in astrology in those who are widowed, separated, or divorced. For the other demographic factors, the evidence is much weaker and for the factor of age there is a consensus that the young have higher levels of belief than the old.

However, before passing final judgement on the social marginality hypothesis, it is worth considering whether the predictions of the social marginality hypothesis have been correctly posed, that is, whether social marginality can be determined by simple demographic properties. It may be that complex interactions would be needed to define social marginality rather than simple age, sex, race, or socio-economic comparisons. Maybe we should be looking at the interaction of demographic factors rather than at simple main effects. For example,

Emmons and Sobal (1981) and Vitulli, Tipton, and Rowe (1999; psi abilities, life after death, and UFO visitations) found an interaction between age and sex such that older women and younger men had higher levels of paranormal belief than older men and younger women. This could make sense from an evolutionary point of view. Men value their social status and wealth and these are properties more of the old than the young, not diminishing much even with retirement for the more successful members of the current generation. Women place higher value on beauty and youth and this fits well with the observations of reduced or absent sex differences in paranormal belief in young adults. If young women perceive themselves to be of high social value, and not marginalized, then there is no reason to expect higher levels of paranormal belief compared to young men. In contrast, elderly women are traditionally seen as possessing lower social value, and are more likely to be widowed, and therefore particularly marginalized for this age group. Also, consider that young men may feel marginalized by a society than treats them as potential criminals, drunks, or generally problematic, that gives them a hard time in the media, and that tolerates high levels of unemployment. Young women have overtaken young men as college and university students and are getting better academic results, so maybe young men do feel a sense of social marginalization. They may not be actually marginalized compared to other groups to a great degree, but belief in the paranormal would depend on what they feel, not what actually occurs.

Another type of interaction is that between age and income. Those people retiring now are from the 'baby boom' generation, who enjoyed more security of employment, lower house prices, and better pensions, compared to adults currently entering the labour market or in mid-career. It may be too simplistic to assume that the elderly and retired are socially marginalized without considering their income. Studies that have looked at age and gender have not typically reported the income of participants, but this is of key relevance to the social marginality hypothesis. Related to this is the issue that studies have not asked people how they felt, in terms of social inclusion-exclusion or social value, only recorded their basic demographic status. But it is logically the perception of the individual that determines to what extent they will adopt paranormal beliefs. As Vitulli, Tipton, and Rowe (1999) put it, membership of a marginalized group in society might lower the threshold of belief in the possibility of powers and abilities that might offer compensatory feelings of power and worth. The degree to which the individual desires compensatory feelings of power and worth will depend on their perception of their current social situation. Someone retiring now with an ample pension and owning their own home has no reason to feel socially marginalized compared to an 18-year-old school leaver with poor employment prospects for whom the chances of ever owning their own home are slender.

Future studies should take into account that simple demographic main effects may be insufficient to capture the essence of social marginality. In particular, any group of university students may feel themselves to be more socially connected than a group of unemployed and poorly educationally qualified adults of similar ages. Future studies could concentrate on soliciting from participants their perceptions of their degree of social marginality and examine the predictive value of this measure.

Another complication is that people who feel themselves to be socially marginalized may compensate with religious affiliation (e.g. Fox, 1992), and religious organizations may frown on paranormal belief. Then there would be two pressures on paranormal belief: a positive motivation from social marginality and a negative motivation from religious teaching. The net effect might be no overall relationship with paranormal belief. An analysis that takes into account paranormal belief, religious affiliation and social marginality, would be needed to fully understand the relationships.

Ideas to think about

It is interesting to speculate that different types of paranormal belief may have different relationships with demographic factors. A distinction could be drawn between three types of paranormal phenomena: those that imply that the individual may possess superior mental powers, including ESP and psychic healing; those that imply that the individual is at the mercy of external forces with little personal control over their own outcomes; and belief in UFOs and extraordinary life forms. There is some evidence that belief in superior mental powers is associated with higher social status, that is, with white over black US Americans, and with people of higher educational level and higher income. It may also be associated with older rather than younger adults, but as we have discussed, age on its own is not a good measure of social marginality. Recall that Kennedy (2007) proposes that belief in psi may confer a sense of control and efficacy in social situations, may help to foster a sense of meaning or purpose in life, and may generate a sense of self-worth and feelings of connectedness with others. Would these outcomes appeal to the demographic groups expressing stronger belief in psi?

It appears that belief in external forces or fate controlling one's outcomes (e.g. astrology, superstition, precognition, ghosts, and spiritualism) is associated with socially excluded groups, including the unemployed and those unable to work; the divorced, separated, and widowed; black rather than white US Americans; and the young rather than the old. Perhaps, as suggested by Torgler (2007), groups who experience uncertainly about their future and their place in society are more vulnerable to types of belief that may suggest to them that outcomes are already decided and that the individual has little power over events.

Belief in UFOs occurs more strongly in men rather than women, in white rather than black US Americans, in people of higher socio-economic status, and in the young rather than the old (but age alone is a poor indication of social status).

Any ideas?

Return to gender differences in paranormal belief

Aside from relative social status and lower income in comparison to men, there are several other factors associated with gender that might be responsible for the observation of higher levels of paranormal belief in women than in men. These include thinking style, gender role, prenatal brain development, and the desire for social connection and social support. Each of these will be considered briefly.

Thinking styles

Aarnio and Lindeman (2005) reported that **analytical thinking style** was negatively related to paranormal belief whereas **intuitive thinking style** was positively related and appeared to be a causal factor. The two thinking styles were not related to each other. In their study, women's higher levels of paranormal belief were partially attributed to their higher preference for intuitive thinking. Hollinger and Smith (2002) also attributed higher levels of paranormal belief in women to a greater interest in intuitive thinking and in matters spiritual. Other researchers have reported a positive correlation of paranormal belief with intuitive thinking style (Epstein *et al.*, 1996; Genovese, 2005; Irwin & Young, 2002; Marks *et al.*, 2008; Wolfradt *et al.*, 1999) but only Irwin and Young (2002) found a negative relationship with analytical thinking. Epstein *et al.* (1996) did not find any differences in thinking styles between men and women in a large study of nearly 1000 undergraduates, although Pacini and Epstein (1999) reported higher levels of intuitive thinking and lower levels of analytical thinking in women. Please refer to Chapter 8 for more discussion of thinking styles and of the dual-process model of System 1 and System 2 thinking. See also Chapter 6 for a fuller discussion of critical thinking and reasoning skills in relation to paranormal belief.

It is interesting to note that men have higher levels of belief in extraordinary life forms and in UFOs, which are not scientifically proven but not contrary to basic mainstream scientific principles, while women have higher belief in other paranormal phenomena that do contradict our current scientific knowledge. Earlier in this chapter, this was tentatively attributed to men's greater interest in, and knowledge of, science in general. The tendency in men to use an analytical thinking style and women an intuitive thinking style, may also be related. An analytical thinking style would be less likely to permit a belief unjustified by evidence to continue. On the other hand, an intuitive thinking style would allow a scientifically unsupported belief as long as it was well integrated with other beliefs. So intuitive thinking style, and to a lesser extent analytical thinking style, are possible candidates to explain the higher level of paranormal belief in women than in men, though the connection is still to be firmly demonstrated.

Gender role

Simmonds-Moore and Moore (2009) reported that female participants who self-rated their gender role as feminine or androgynous had higher levels of paranormal belief than those who self-rated their gender role as masculine or undifferentiated (using the Bem Sex Roles Inventory). So belief in paranormal phenomena seems to depend not simply on sex but also on gender role, implying something at least partly socially constructed and not entirely genetically determined. Blackmore (1994b) notes that women report more paranormal experiences than men, speculating that perhaps a feminine **worldview** or style of thinking renders the individual predisposed to accept a strange event as paranormal. It is worth pointing out that in the Bem Sex Roles Inventory the definition of feminine gender role includes *gullible* while the definition of masculine gender role includes *analytical* so there is some relationship with thinking style. There is also an implication that wider acceptance of all manner of unproven beliefs may be higher in those who identify with a feminine gender role. Similarly, Coleman and Ganong (1987) reported that irrational beliefs were associated with a feminine gender role, while Blackmore (1994b) suggested that possibly women's richer fantasy life might be a factor underlying higher levels of paranormal belief.

However, Spinelli, Reid, and Norvilitis (2001–2) reported that paranormal belief was negatively associated with femininity, that is, a more feminine gender role was related to lower levels of belief in psi abilities and precognition, while masculinity was associated with higher levels of belief in the same phenomena. In this study the mean age was only 22 so perhaps this reflects the absence in the younger generation of the frequently reported trend towards stronger paranormal belief in women than in men. Similarly, Tobacyk *et al.* (1988) reported that men had stronger levels of belief than women in psi, witchcraft, and precognition, while there was no difference in superstition and spiritualism. This study also employed university students (with a mean age of 19.5).

Ideas to think about

The relationship between analytic versus intuitive thinking and belief in paranormal phenomena – does this fully explain the higher levels of paranormal belief in women? Where does the difference originate? Does it have anything to do with the widespread cultural notion that women are better than men at intuitive thinking? Is it only this cultural expectation? Are women being sold short by being told that their particular strength is intuitive thinking?

Prenatal brain development

Although Chapter 5 deals with psychobiological perspectives on anomalous experience, one particular line of neuropsychological reasoning will be considered here as a possible explanation of gender differences in levels of paranormal belief. Voracek (2009) found that men with a higher 2D:4D ratio had higher levels of paranormal belief. The 2D:4D digit ratio is the ratio of the length of the index finger to the length of the ring finger and is reliably found to be higher in women than in men, that is, women have, on average, a longer index finger compared to the ring finger than men. There is evidence that this is related to prenatal levels of male hormones (androgens) and, of particular interest to the topic of paranormal belief, evidence that prenatal androgens have permanent organizing effects on the development of the human brain (evidence cited in Voracek, 2009). Hence, one might expect that the 2D:4D digit ratio could be higher in paranormal believers than in non-believers and this would indicate an influence of prenatal hormones on levels of paranormal belief. Voracek (2009) studied over 1000 Austrian heterosexual adults aged 17 to 72 and observed that the 2D:4D ratio was positively correlated to level of paranormal belief but only in men; there was no significant relationship in women. This suggests that those men with a lower level of prenatal androgens were more likely to believe in the paranormal as adults. The absence of a significant relationship in women is understandable if one assumes that levels of prenatal androgens were generally low. The relationship between 2D:4D digit ratio and level of paranormal belief was quite small and accounted for only around 1–3% of the variance in paranormal belief, though this is roughly equivalent to the other known correlates of age, socio-economic status, and gender.

Desire for social connection and social support

Kennedy (2007) notes that women generally tend to have a higher need for a sense of interconnectedness and community. This is held to be one of the major functions of traditional religions so accounting for the higher levels of participation sometimes observed in women than in men. The desire for social connection and support could also promote a tendency to belong to groups espousing paranormal beliefs in general. The need to feel connected with others might even dispose towards belief in aspects of the paranormal that emphasize connection with others – for example, spiritualism, clairvoyance, telepathy, and even witchcraft. Kennedy (2003) proposes that the existing data are consistent with the idea that belief in psi is motivated by a sense of interconnectedness and spirituality, which appeals more to women than to men. From a slightly different angle, Torgler (2007) notes that New Age spirituality and astrology occupy areas that are traditionally the province of women rather than men – that is, spirituality, connectedness, and counselling are all areas where women more than men are traditionally regarded as experts.

Kennedy (2003) notes that the most common aftermath of a paranormal experience is an increase in feelings of spirituality, rather than a feeling of control over life events and circumstances. Indeed, a strong characteristic of research into psi phenomena is the difficulty of controlling these phenomena and this is often taken to imply that psi powers are inherently hard to control. This reasoning challenges the idea that belief in psi offers the individual a sense of control. If women more than men desire connectedness, and men more than women desire control, then the higher levels of psi belief in women are consistent with the data from experimental investigations of psi and with the reported long-term effects of psi experiences.

Another relevant aspect is that women, more than men, appear to be actively involved in commercial psychic practices (e.g. Blackmore, 1994b). One of us (AS) conducted a survey of the first ten websites retrieved from the Internet using the search engine Google with the keyword 'psychic' on the 26 January 2010. A total of 118 unique individuals were identified offering psychic consultations (including tarot, astrology, **mediumship**, angel readings, and nonspecific psychic consultations), of whom 99 were women compared to 19 men. (For statisticians: the difference in the numbers of men and women listed on the ten websites was significant in a paired-samples t-test, $t(9) = 4.26$, $p < 0.005$.) It seems likely that offering psychic consultations to the public offers the valuable benefit to women of providing a profession and an income. This could certainly appeal to women who may feel frustrated with their employment prospects, such as perhaps single mothers working from home. New Age groups in general may give women a stronger voice, being less male-dominated than traditional work places and traditional hierarchies. You might like to try a similar survey yourself.

Personality and related variables

In the following section, a number of widely studied personality factors will be examined to determine their relationship to various aspects of paranormal belief. In general, discussion of the relationship between personality factors that are clearly associated with psychological maladjustment (e.g. **neuroticism**, positive/negative affect, etc.) and paranormal belief and experience will be deferred until Chapter 3. It must be emphasized, however, that this is purely done in the interest of organizational convenience. In reality, all of these traits are found to a greater or lesser extent in the so-called normal population not just in clinical samples. Other specific personality factors that are thought to depend on differences in brain structure and function will be considered in Chapter 10 which deals with psychobiological perspectives.

Extraversion

Extraverts tend to be gregarious, sociable, and assertive, and enjoy thrills and excitement. Introverts, on the other hand, are less outgoing and more reserved. The continuum from extreme extraversion to extreme **introversion** is considered to be one of the main dimensions of personality. There is no consistent relationship between belief in paranormal phenomena and the personality trait of extraversion. Reports of a positive association between extraversion and *global paranormal belief* (Göritz & Schumacher, 2000; Peltzer, 2002) are contradicted by null results (Francis, Williams, & Robbins, 2010; Gallagher, Kumar, & Pekala, 1994; Haraldsson, 1985b; Lester, Thinschmidt, & Trautman, 1987;

Sjöberg & Wåhlberg, 2002; Thalbourne, Dunbar, & Delin, 1995; Willging & Lester, 1997; Williams, Francis, & Robbins, 2007). Regarding individual aspects of the paranormal, there are reports of positive associations with *belief in ESP* (e.g. Peltzer, 2002; Thalbourne, 1981; Thalbourne & Haraldsson, 1980), *precognition* (Rattet & Bursik, 2001), and *extraordinary life forms* (Willging & Lester, 1997). On the other hand, there are reports of no relationship with belief in *ESP* (Haraldsson, 1985b), *the existence of other beings in the universe* (Lester, 1993), and *psychic phenomena* (Willging & Lester, 1997).

Openness to experience

The personality trait of openness to experience involves having an active imagination, being open to new aesthetic experiences, having a desire for variety, and an intellectual curiosity and desire for new ideas. People who are low in openness to experience are generally happy with routine and have a narrow range of interests, and tend to be more conventional in ideas.

A couple of studies have reported that this trait is related to paranormal beliefs (Eudell & Campbell, 2007; Smith, Johnson, & Hathaway, 2009). These studies yielded a different pattern of relative importance among the six facets of openness to experience. Smith, Johnson, and Hathaway (2009) found that the fantasy facet was most strongly related to *global paranormal belief*, while Eudell and Campbell (2007) found a relationship with the aesthetics, actions, and values facets, though not the fantasy facet. The latter study is particularly interesting as it could be argued that since the fantasy facet relates to having a rich fantasy life and vivid imagination, this facet would naturally be related to paranormal belief. The observation of a relationship with other facets of openness to experience but not the fantasy facet suggests that there is some relationship between openness to experience and paranormal belief apart from fantasy-proneness (more about which later).

Sensation seeking

As defined by Zuckerman (e.g. 1994), this personality trait includes the tendency to seek out novel, varied, exciting, or intense experiences, and the willingness to take risks in pursuit of these experiences. It includes a tendency to be interested in unusual ideas that are not part of the scientific mainstream and to be motivated to explore strange, and maybe mystical, forces. Zuckerman reports that people high in sensation seeking tend to hold nonconformist beliefs. It would seem plausible on the face of it that sensation seeking might relate to belief in the paranormal, which offers opportunities to satisfy the sensation seeker.

Some researchers have found relationships of the whole sensation seeking scale with *global paranormal belief* (Smith, Johnson, & Hathaway, 2009), or with individual aspects including *psi* and *spiritualism* (Tobacyk & Milford, 1983). In contrast, other researchers have found no relationship between sensation seeking and *global paranormal belief* (Curtis & Wilson, 1997). Other researchers have proposed that the subscales of thrill and adventure seeking (TAS) and experience seeking (ES) were particularly relevant, and these were indeed found to be associated with reports of belief in *anomalous* or *psi-related phenomena* (e.g. Gallagher, Kumar, & Pekala, 1994; Groth-Marnat & Pegden, 1998, experience seeking only; Kumar, Pekala, & Cummings, 1993). A slightly different pattern of association between boredom susceptibility, experience seeking, and disinhibition seeking and *global paranormal belief* has also been reported (Smith, Johnson, & Hathaway, 2009). Sensation seeking is also discussed in Chapter 5 when we consider psychobiological perspectives.

Myers-Briggs intuitive-feeling personality type

The **Myers-Briggs Type Indicator®** is a commonly used instrument, based upon the theorizing of psychoanalyst Carl Jung, for measuring a person's preferences using four basic scales with opposite poles. Two of these poles are of particular relevance here: sensing/intuitive and thinking/feeling. The intuitive-feeling personality type has been linked by several researchers to belief in, and the search for, paranormal phenomena. Researchers have theorized that people with the intuitive-feeling personality type would have a mystical outlook and would seek knowledge of the paranormal. Intuition refers to how the individual prefers to gather information and perceive patterns. An intuitive person (as opposed to sensing) is not strongly tied to the data and observation, but prefers connections with other ideas, future possibilities, hunches, and insights that can arise from the unconscious mind. A feeling person (as opposed to a thinking person) likes to empathize with a situation, consider the needs of all the people involved, and achieve balance and harmony. On the assumption that paranormal experiences are not real, it would be harder for a person to believe in the paranormal if they have a sensing approach to data gathering that emphasizes observation of present, tangible data, and a thinking approach to decision-making, and that emphasizes logic and reason and rule-bound decision-making. An intuitive-feeling person might have higher levels of paranormal belief arising from a holistic sense of what is possible and consistent with other beliefs.

The intuitive-feeling personality type has been empirically linked to belief in the paranormal (e.g. Lester, Thinschmidt, & Trautman, 1987; Murphy & Lester, 1976). This personality type has also been related to the likelihood of an experimentally induced sense of contact with a person who had died; a facilitated reunion experience (Arcangel, 1997), although in this study the unequal sample sizes and the small number of participants of the diametrically opposed sensing-thinking types precluded formal statistical testing. Gow, Lane, and Chant (2003) and Gow, Lang, and Chant (2004) reported that people who claimed to have experienced an NDE and those who believed in the NDE were higher on the Intuitive-Feeling scale than those who did not believe in the NDE. Fox and Williams (2000) found that the preference for perception over judgement, and to a lesser extent the preference for feeling over thinking, was correlated with paranormal belief. Altogether, it seems that there is good evidence that the intuitive-feeling personality type is linked to reports of paranormal experiences and paranormal belief.

Locus of control

Locus of control refers to the perceived source of major influences on the events and outcomes in one's life and is conceived of as either internal or external (e.g. Rotter, 1975). An internal locus of control is associated with the belief that events and personal outcomes are caused by one's own actions and behaviours. An external locus of control is associated with the belief that destiny, fate, luck, powerful external forces, or other people determine one's outcomes. A related concept is that of self-efficacy, the belief that one can achieve personal goals by one's own actions and efforts. A high level of self-efficacy is associated with confidence that one has the ability to deal successfully with situations.

External locus of control is sometimes related to higher levels of global paranormal belief (e.g. Irwin, 1993a; Newby & Davis, 2004; Scheidt, 1973) though there are exceptions – for example, no relationship between paranormal belief and locus of control was found by Haraldsson (1981). Kennedy (2007) discusses how the need for control in an uncertain world can predispose towards belief in aspects of paranormal phenomena, especially those that offer some promise of control, or at least understanding, of the seemingly random forces that influence the events in our lives.

However, closer examination of the definitions suggests that we should not expect a straightforward association of external locus of control with all aspects of paranormal belief. In particular, levels of belief in psi powers may be related to internal rather than external locus of control. External locus of control is expected to be related to levels of belief in other paranormal phenomena: precognition and superstitions imply that powerful forces have influence over the events in one's life, while witchcraft, spiritualism, and extraordinary life forms suggest that other people or beings can exert control over one's personal outcomes. A substantial body of evidence supports the association between these particular aspects of paranormal belief and external locus of control. As a corollary, internal locus of control (or personal efficacy control, or personal or interpersonal control, depending on the measure used) is related to lower levels of these aspects of paranormal belief.

Greater external locus of control, or lower internal locus of control, was associated with belief in *extraordinary life forms* (Allen & Lester, 1994; Tobacyk & Milford, 1983), *precognition* (Dag, 1999; Groth-Marnat & Pegden, 1998; Thalbourne, Dunbar, & Delin, 1995; Tobacyk & Tobacyk, 1992), *spiritualism* (Allen & Lester, 1994; Davies & Kirkby, 1985; Groth-Marnat & Pegden, 1998; Thalbourne, Dunbar, & Delin, 1995; Tobacyk & Tobacyk, 1992), *superstition* (Allen & Lester, 1994; Dag, 1999; Davies & Kirkby, 1985; Groth-Marnat & Pegden, 1998; Irwin, 2000b; Peltzer, 2002; Randall & Desrosiers, 1980; Thalbourne, Dunbar, & Delin, 1995; Tobacyk, Nagot, & Miller,

1988; Tobacyk & Shrader, 1991; Tobacyk & Tobacyk, 1992; Todd & Brown, 2003), and *witchcraft* (Allen & Lester, 1994; Dag, 1999; Peltzer, 2002; Tobacyk & Milford, 1983; Tobacyk, Nagot, & Miller, 1988; Tobacyk & Tobacyk, 1992).

Stronger internal locus of control was related to belief in psi (Davies & Kirkby, 1985; Irwin, 2000b) but external locus of control has also been associated with belief in psi (Allen & Lester, 1994; Dag, 1999; Thalbourne, Dunbar, & Delin, 1995). Altogether, the evidence for internal locus of control being related to belief in paranormal mental powers is ambiguous at best.

Another interesting observation was made by McGarry and Newberry (1981) who discovered that in their sample of students with little involvement or interest in the paranormal, external locus of control related to higher levels of paranormal belief. In contrast, among participants who were actively involved in the paranormal, the higher levels of paranormal belief were related to internal locus of control, suggesting that paranormal involvement may help to generate a greater sense of mastery and control over life events. A similar line of reasoning may explain the observation made by Davies and Kirkby (1985) that internal locus of control was related to belief in witchcraft, and by Peltzer (2002), in a study of African students, that internal locus of control was related to superstition, precognition, and witchcraft.

The fantasy-prone personality

One personality type in particular has been the focus of much research and speculation with respect to paranormal beliefs and reports of paranormal experiences. This section will discuss the relationships among several related concepts of fantasy-proneness, absorption, and **hypnotic susceptibility**, and their relationship to paranormal belief and experiences. Belief in, and reports of, alien abduction, OBEs, and NDEs are particularly linked with this cluster of personality traits.

Before reading on, complete the questionnaire in Box 2.1.

The questionnaire that you have just completed is a brief self-report measure of fantasy-proneness developed by Merckelbach, Horselenberg, and Muris (2001) for use with adults. The scale is scored by simply counting up the number of 'yes' responses. For comparison purposes, Merckelbach *et al.* reported that a sample of 116 students (93 of whom were female) had a mean score of 8.3 (S.D. = 3.9). How does your score compare with theirs? Are you relatively more or less fantasy prone? Or is your score about the same as their mean score?

The concept of fantasy-proneness was first discussed by Wilson and Barber (1983). They interviewed a group of participants who were high in hypnotic susceptibility and discovered various features prevalent in this group that were termed part of the fantasy-prone personality. Fantasy-proneness is generally associated with having a rich fantasy life and frequently being able to construct a vivid daydream that seems like reality. People high in fantasy-proneness

Box 2.1   Creative experiences questionnaire (Merckelbach, Horselenberg, & Muris, 2001)

Below is a list of personal statements. Please answer each question by circling either 'Y' (yes) or 'N' (no).

1. As a child, I thought that the dolls, teddy bears, and stuffed animals that I played with were living creatures.   Y/N
2. As a child, I strongly believed in the existence of dwarfs, elves, and other fairy tale figures.   Y/N
3. As a child, I had my own make-believe friend or animal.   Y/N
4. As a child, I could very easily identify with the main character of a story and/or movie.   Y/N
5. As a child, I sometimes had the feeling that I was someone else (e.g. a princess, an orphan, etc.).   Y/N
6. As a child, I was encouraged by adults (parents, grandparents, brothers, sisters) to fully indulge myself in my fantasies and daydreams.   Y/N
7. As a child, I often felt lonely.   Y/N
8. As a child, I devoted my time to playing a musical instrument, dancing, acting, and/or drawing.   Y/N
9. I spend more than half the day (daytime) fantasizing or daydreaming.   Y/N
10. Many of my friends and/or relatives do not know that I have such detailed fantasies.   Y/N
11. Many of my fantasies have a realistic intensity.   Y/N
12. Many of my fantasies are often just as lively as a good movie.   Y/N
13. I often confuse fantasies with real memories.   Y/N
14. I am never bored because I start fantasizing when things get boring.   Y/N
15. Sometimes I act as if I am somebody else and I completely identify myself with that role.   Y/N
16. When I recall my childhood, I have very vivid and lively memories.   Y/N
17. I can recall many occurrences before the age of three.
18. When I perceive violence on television, I get so into it that I get really upset.   Y/N
19. When I think of something cold, I actually get cold.   Y/N
20. When I imagine I have eaten rotten food, I really get nauseous.   Y/N
21. I often have the feeling that I can predict things that are bound to happen in the future.   Y/N
22. I often have the experience of thinking of someone and soon afterwards that particular person calls or shows up.   Y/N
23. I sometimes feel that I have had an out-of-body experience.   Y/N
24. When I sing or write something, I sometimes have the feeling that someone or something outside myself directs me.   Y/N
25. During my life, I have had intense religious experiences which influenced me in a very strong manner.   Y/N

admit to sometimes being confused between their imagination and real events. They feel that they can actually see, hear, smell, and feel things discussed in conversations or on television. They typically had imaginary friends during childhood who seemed very real to them. Among the participants interviewed by Wilson and Barber, there was a high proportion having OBEs or waking dreams (88% of the participants interviewed), seeing apparitions (73% of the participants interviewed), and having various types of psychic experiences. They often claim to have psychic abilities (92% of the participants interviewed saw themselves as psychic) and they tend to report telepathic or precognitive experiences. They believe that they can heal people by touching them (67% of the participants interviewed). In addition, all of the fantasy-prone participants interviewed by Wilson and Barber reported that sometimes their fantasies had an involuntary quality and seemed to take on a life of their own ('self-propelling'). It should be stressed that this group of participants appeared to be functioning well in society and enjoying relationships, varying in 'emotional stability or mental health across the entire range of the normal curve' (Wilson & Barber, 1983, p. 365).

Lynn and Rhue (1988) came up with a slightly different picture in their summary of an extensive programme of research into fantasy-proneness and associated personality traits. They note that their fantasy-prone participants as a group were more hypnotisable, more imaginative, more suggestible, more creative, more prone to **hallucination**, and more likely to have had childhood experiences of abuse. However, fantasy-prone individuals were not an entirely homogenous group; not all were easily hypnotisable, and most were relatively well adjusted. In addition, the fantasy-prone individuals were not able to fantasize events as real as real life, rather their fantasies were lacking in vividness and detail. Perhaps expectations, and a lax criterion, have led to previous reports that fantasy-prone individuals can create vivid, lifelike imaginings. Lynn and Rhue noted that fantasy-proneness, absorption and imaginative involvement are not truly discriminable, but converge on the idea that some people are better able to construct vivid, believable, and absorbing fantasies.

As we will see in Chapter 9, there is considerable debate regarding whether or not fantasy-proneness is related to the tendency to report various types of alien contact, with the answer appearing to depend to some extent upon the particular methodology employed in order to address the issue. Turning to related experiences, Gow, Lane, and Chant (2003) and Gow, Lang, and Chant (2004) reported higher levels of fantasy-proneness in their participants who claimed to have experienced an NDE compared to participants who had not, and also in those who believed in NDEs compared to controls. Wilson and Barber (1983) noted that their fantasy-prone group were more likely than their non-fantasy-prone group to report OBEs.

Other studies have used questionnaire methods for measuring of fantasy-proneness and paranormal belief. Relationships with *global paranormal belief* have been reported (e.g. Auton, Pope, & Seeger, 2003; Gow, Lane, & Chant,

2003; Gow, Lang, & Chant, 2004; Irwin, 1990, 1991a; Lawrence *et al.*, 1995; Rogers, Qualter, & Phelps, 2007). Myers *et al.* (1983) reported positive relationships between fantasy-proneness and OBEs, apparitions, precognition, psi, astrology, and reincarnation.

Absorption

A concept related to fantasy-proneness is that of absorption. Tellegen and Atkinson (1974, p. 268) define the personality trait of absorption as 'openness to absorbing and self-altering experiences, a trait related to hypnotic susceptibility'. Absorption is the disposition to have episodes of total immersion in an experience that occupies all of one's senses, thoughts, and imagination. Total attention would be commanded by the experience and there would be a resistance to distraction. One can be absorbed in an experience based upon external reality – for example, a film, a play, or a book, or in an internally generated fantasy.

The trait of absorption seems to be strongly associated with fantasy-proneness. Indeed, there is some overlap in their definitions (as noted by Myers & Austrin, 1985). Strong correlations between fantasy-proneness and absorption have been reported by several researchers (Kennedy, Kanthamani, & Palmer, 1994; Lynn & Rhue, 1988; Myers & Austrin, 1985; Rhue & Lynn, 1989; Tellegen *et al.*, 1988).

Absorption has also been correlated with *paranormal belief* (e.g. Glicksohn & Barrett, 2003; Nadon & Kihlstrom, 1987); belief in *psi abilities, precognition*, and *superstition* (Wolfradt, 1997); reports of *psychic or mystical experiences* (e.g. Glicksohn & Barrett, 2003; Kennedy, Kanthamani, & Palmer, 1994; Palmer & van der Velden, 1983; Spanos & Moretti, 1988); and reports of *OBEs* (Myers *et al.*, 1983).

Hypnotic susceptibility

Hypnotic susceptibility is the ease with which a person can be induced to enter a hypnotic trance. Several studies have reported that hypnotic susceptibility is related to *fantasy-proneness* (e.g. Lynn & Rhue, 1986; Nickell, 1996; Rhue & Lynn, 1989; Wilson & Barber, 1983) and to *absorption* (e.g. Glicksohn & Barrett, 2003; Rhue & Lynn, 1989).

Hypnotic susceptibility has also been related to reports of *paranormal experiences* or *paranormal beliefs* (e.g. Atkinson, 1994; Council & Huff, 1990; Glicksohn & Barrett, 2003; Green & Lynn, 2009; Hergovich, 2003, only the superstition scale; Nadon & Kihlstrom, 1987; Pekala, Kumar, & Cummings, 1992; Pekala, Kumar, & Marcano, 1995; Richards, 1990; Thalbourne, Dunbar, & Delin, 1995; Wagner & Ratzeburg, 1987; Wickramasekera, 1989; but not Saucer, Cahoon, & Edmonds, 1992). For example, OBEs have been observed to be more common in highly hypnotically suggestible participants (Pekala, Kumar, & Cummings, 1992; Pekala, Kumar, & Marcano,

1995; Spanos & Moretti, 1988), as have NDEs (Pekala, Kumar, & Cummings, 1992) and communication with the dead (Pekala, Kumar, & Cummings, 1992; Pekala, Kumar, & Marcano, 1995).

Atkinson (1994) noted that the relationship between hypnotic susceptibility and belief in the paranormal may be mediated by the skill of absorption. The skill of absorption is conceptually linked to the ease of entering a hypnotic trance, the ease of imagining what the hypnotist asks one to imagine and in genuinely believing what one is asked to experience. Hypnotic susceptibility is related to the cognitive skills involved in imaginative involvement and to the ability to focus attention (Tellegen & Atkinson, 1974). So there is a clear conceptual similarity between hypnotic susceptibility and absorption. It is suggested that these skills in active imagining and in entering the world of the imagination are clearly conducive to creating a believable memory of a paranormal experience, and the suspension of reality testing involved in both hypnotic susceptibility and absorption could lead to belief in paranormal phenomena or memory of paranormal experiences (Atkinson, 1994).

There is a core of features that appear to exist in the definitions of fantasy-proneness, absorption, and hypnotic susceptibility, including imaginative involvement, vivid imagery, the ability to suspend reality testing, and focused attention (e.g. Atkinson, 1994). These are all conceptually conducive to paranormal experiences, and thus linked to paranormal belief, as has been demonstrated by a substantial literature.

This section has discussed a number of closely related concepts: fantasy-proneness, absorption, and hypnotic suggestibility (the related clinical concept of **dissociation** is discussed in the next chapter). All of these have been related to belief in paranormal phenomena and the tendency to report personal paranormal experiences, especially OBEs and NDEs (as well as alien contact experiences, as we will see in Chapter 9). It appears that the ability to enter a world of imagination and sense it strongly, without distraction, occurs in the same people who are most likely to report paranormal experiences that have a strong component of physical sensation. Although none of the research can establish a causal connection, it does seem plausible that some of the reports of paranormal experience may at least be exaggerated by the fantasy-prone, hypnotically susceptible individual, who is high in absorption.

Conclusion

We have examined demographic and personality factors and their relationship to paranormal belief. Women, compared to men, believe more strongly in most aspects of paranormal belief (but not UFOs and extraordinary life forms), though the difference is generally rather small. There are several alternative explanations for the higher levels of paranormal belief in women compared to men: preference for intuitive over analytical thinking style, prenatal level of testosterone in women, feminine gender role, or a desire for social connectedness and social support. New Age spirituality in general, and astrology, tarot card reading, psychic consultation, and similar practices seem likely to appeal particularly to people who desire a sense of interconnectedness and community; this is traditionally women rather than men.

Regarding age, race, and socio-economic status, the evidence is mixed and it seems different types of paranormal belief may have different relationships with these demographic variables. Cross-cultural studies suggest that levels of paranormal belief may be higher in countries where people feel a sense of social insecurity, lack of stability, and fear of what the future may hold, but data are limited.

Irwin's social marginality hypothesis receives only variable support and it is worth noting that the research to date has looked at only broad demographic factors, ignoring the wide variation that exists within any social group. It seems that a full assessment of the social marginality hypothesis will have to await the outcome of research that includes people's subjective experience of social engagement and empowerment.

Paranormal belief has been observed to be higher in people who are strong in the personality traits of openness to experience, sensation seeking, and the Myers-Briggs personality type of intuitive-feeling. There are small and inconsistent relationships of paranormal belief with the personality trait of extraversion.

Complex relationships between locus of control and paranormal belief have been observed. It seems that external locus of control may be associated with belief in superstitions, extraordinary life forms, witchcraft, and precognition, which all suppose that powerful forces or other beings may influence one's personal outcomes. However, among those who are most heavily involved in the paranormal, including practitioners, paranormal belief may be related to internal locus of control.

The concepts of fantasy-proneness, absorption, and hypnotic susceptibility, all overlapping to some degree with each other, are all associated with higher levels of paranormal belief. These concepts have in common the ability to become involved in imaginary worlds, to construct vivid imagery, to suspend reality testing, and to focus attention. In particular, these concepts are associated with reports of alien abduction, OBEs, and NDEs.

Suggested further reading

For demographic factors and personality traits related to paranormal belief:

Irwin, H. J. (2009). *The psychology of paranormal belief: A researcher's handbook.* Hatfield, UK: University of Hertfordshire Press. Chapter 4, pp. 51–66.

For cross-cultural comparisons:

Hollinger, F. & Smith, T. B. (2002). 'Religion and esotericism among students: A cross-cultural comparative study'. *Journal of Contemporary Religion*, 17, 229–49.

For a discussion of the particular engagement of women with the paranormal:

Blackmore, S. J. (1994b). 'Are women more sheepish? Gender differences in belief in the paranormal'. In L. Coley & R. A. White (eds), *Women and parapsychology* (pp. 68–89). New York: Parapsychology Foundation.
Kennedy, J. E. (2007). 'Personality and motivations to believe, misbelieve, and disbelieve in paranormal phenomena'. *Journal of Parapsychology*, 71, 263–92.

Clinical Perspectives

Introduction

Uninformed sceptics often accuse those who claim to have had direct personal experience of the paranormal of being either dishonest, stupid or 'crazy'. However, the sheer prevalence of such claims, as well as the available psychological literature, strongly suggests that only a small minority of such claimants are deliberately lying. Having said that, the history of paranormal research is peppered with many famous examples of fraudsters and hoaxes and therefore this possibility must always be considered.

For example, the origins of the Spiritualist movement can be specified very precisely to a small house in Hydesville, New York, in March, 1848, where two young sisters by the names of Kate and Margaret Fox reported hearing strange rapping noises and eventually discovered that they could communicate with the spirits of the dead using a simple code based upon the number of raps produced in response to questions. Soon others claimed also to be able to communicate with the dead and **séances** spread like wildfire across America and Europe.

Séances eventually came to involve other phenomena too, including movement of tables and objects; the playing of musical instruments by unseen hands and lips; strange lights in the dark; levitation of objects or even the medium herself (mediums were usually women); the disappearance or materialization of objects; the materialization of hands, faces, or even complete spirit forms; disembodied voices; spirit paintings and photographs; and written communications from the spirit world.

Although many people, including some of the finest scientific minds of the day, were convinced that the miracles that they had witnessed under the dim illumination of the séance room were genuine, many others were convinced that the effects were all produced by deliberate trickery (see, for example, Brandon, 1983; Hyman, 1985a). Indeed, it was a very rare medium indeed who was not actually caught red-handed at one time or another engaged in such deceit. In 1888, some 40 years after the sisters' initial claim, Margaret Fox admitted that the original rapping noises were not in any way psychic

(Kane, 1888/1985). They were produced in a variety of ways, but mainly by cracking her toe and ankle joints, a skill that she demonstrated in public. What had begun as a prank had got out of hand and the sisters had then felt unable to own up. Typically, Spiritualists simply refused to believe the confession and the movement continues to this day.

Many further examples of proven or probable fraud could be provided (see, e.g. Kurtz, 1985a; Marks, 2000; Markwick, 1985; Nicol, 1985; Randi, 1982a, 1982b, 1987; Rogo, 1985). For all that, it is widely accepted by serious scholars on both sides of the psi debate that the vast majority of those who claim to have personally experienced the paranormal are sincere in making such claims. It goes without saying that sincerity is no guarantee of accuracy, of course, but there is no convincing evidence that those who claim to have experienced the paranormal are any less honest than those who do not.

With respect to the suggestion that those who believe in the paranormal are less intelligent than those who do not, there is surprisingly little research directly addressing this basic question. Several early studies assessing the relationship between intelligence and superstitiousness reported weak negative correlations between the two variables (Belanger, 1944; Emme, 1940, 1941; Ter Keurst, 1939; Zapf, 1945). More recently, Killen, Wildman, and Wildman (1974) and Thalbourne and Nofi (1997) reported similar results. Musch and Ehrenberg (2002) reported that paranormal belief was associated with lower cognitive ability as assessed by final examination grades. Smith, Foster, and Stovin (1998) reported that IQ correlated negatively with global paranormal belief as well as specifically with belief in precognition, psi, and spiritualism. There have been a couple of studies that have not found a negative correlation between intelligence and paranormal belief. Stuart-Hamilton, Nayak, and Priest (2006) reported no significant relationship between intelligence and paranormal belief and Jones, Russell, and Nickel (1977) actually reported a significant positive correlation between the two. Although the general trend within the limited literature available is that paranormal belief is significantly associated with lower intelligence, at least as assessed by standard IQ tests, the relationships reported are fairly weak. This issue is discussed further in Chapter 6.

Thus it can be seen that there is a grain of truth in both of first two possibilities listed previously. There are numerous examples of deliberate fraud and hoaxes that have led to paranormal claims – but despite that the vast majority of such claimants are sincere. There are several studies that show that believers in the paranormal and superstitions tend to score somewhat lower than non-believers on IQ tests and other measures of general intelligence – but the correlations are fairly weak and inconsistent. Neither of these hypotheses taken alone comes close to explaining why some people believe in the paranormal and others do not. The main focus of this chapter is the third possibility put forward. What is the relationship between paranormal belief and experience and psychological health?

It is certainly not unreasonable to maintain that at least some reports of ostensibly paranormal experiences may reflect underlying psychopathology.

If paranormal forces really do not exist, then we might expect that a person who, as a result of a serious mental illness, has lost touch with reality would be more likely to believe they have had a personal paranormal experience than someone who is not so afflicted.

It is recognized that some mental problems are more serious than others. Although the term **neurosis** is not used as widely as it once was, it used to refer to a group of mental problems (such as phobias and **obsessive-compulsive disorder**) that would cause the sufferer considerable stress and anxiety and often have a serious impact on their functioning in everyday life. For all that, the sufferers still have good contact with reality, even to the extent that they recognize that their problems have no rational basis. **Psychosis**, on the other hand, is a term used to refer to a group of much more serious mental problems, such as **schizophrenia** and bipolar disorder, in which the sufferer may completely lose contact with reality. It used to be said that whereas neurotics build castles in the sky, psychotics live in them – to which was sometimes added, 'and psychiatrists collect the rent!'

In recent years there has been something of a move within clinical psychology away from a diagnostic category approach, in which patients are assessed in terms of whether they manifest this or that collection of symptoms in order to categorize them with a particular diagnostic label, towards an approach which considers the symptoms individually in terms of possible causes and treatment. Hand in hand with this, there has also been an increasing recognition that there is no clear cut-off point at which a personality trait moves from being within the 'normal' range to becoming 'clinical'. Instead, it is accepted that we all have our own particular profile when it comes to states and traits reflecting psychological maladjustment and the most important factor from a clinical point of view is whether or not an individual suffers an unacceptable level of distress and impairment as a result. Indeed, many symptoms which are often mistakenly viewed as being sure-fire indications of serious psychopathology, such as hallucinations, are in fact much more prevalent in the 'normal' population than is generally realized. This recognition of the fact that the strength of symptoms of psychopathology can vary along a continuum from non-existent through mild up to disabling is sometimes referred to as the 'dimensional' approach. The next section of this chapter will deal with the relationship between paranormal belief and experience and various personality measures that are, to a greater or lesser extent, associated with psychological dysfunction.

Personality measures associated with psychological well-being

Chapter 2 discussed a number of personality variables and other individual difference measures and the degree to which they were associated with paranormal beliefs and the tendency to report paranormal experiences. The variables discussed in this section also relate to personality but, because they are also measures of psychological well-being, it was decided to cover them in this chapter dealing with clinical perspectives, in line with the idea that there is no clear dividing line between 'normal' and 'abnormal'. The traits to be considered in this section are neuroticism, **psychoticism**, **narcissism**, negative and positive affect, obsessive-compulsive tendencies, bipolar tendencies, dissociativity, schizotypy, and transliminality.

Neuroticism

Neuroticism is regarded by psychologists as a fundamental personality trait. It refers to the enduring tendency that some people have to experience negative emotions such as anxiety, anger, guilt, depression, hostility, self-consciousness, and impulsivity. People scoring high on measures of neuroticism, such as the Eysenck Personality Questionnaire (EPQ; Eysenck & Eysenck, 1975) or the Revised NEO Personality Inventory (Costa & McCrae, 1992), tend to be emotionally unstable, cope poorly with the stresses of everyday life, and have poor interpersonal skills. High neuroticism is associated with phobias, panic attacks, and other anxiety disorders.

There are inconsistent observations of the relationship between *global paranormal belief* and neuroticism. Some researchers have found a positive relationship (Gallagher, Kumar, & Pekala, 1994; Lindeman & Aarnio, 2007; Thalbourne, Dunbar, & Delin, 1995; Williams, Francis, & Robbins, 2007) while others have found no relationship (Francis, Williams, & Robbins, 2010; Haraldsson, 1985b; Lester, Thinschmidt, & Trautman, 1987; Peltzer, 2002; Sjöberg & Wählberg, 2002; Svensen, White, & Caird, 1992; Willging & Lester, 1997).

Regarding individual aspects of paranormal belief, there is a reasonably consistent suggestion that neuroticism is related to those beliefs that suppose powerful external forces acting on the individual. Neuroticism has been related to belief in astrology (Fichten & Sunerton, 1983), precognition (Schredl, 2009), spiritualism (Peltzer, 2002), and superstitions (Dagnall, Parker, & Munley, 2007; Wiseman & Watt, 2004), though there was no relationship with belief in UFOs or ghosts (Lester, 1993).

Psychoticism

Psychoticism is another trait measured by the EPQ (Eysenck & Eysenck, 1975) and refers to the tendency a person has to exhibit certain traits often associated with psychosis. Psychopaths and criminals, as well as some actual psychotics, score highly on this measure. Eysenck (1964, p. 58) describes a person who scores high on psychoticism (but without actually being psychotic) as having the following traits:

(1) Solitary, not caring for other people; (2) troublesome, not fitting in; (3) cruel, inhumane; (4) lack of feeling, insensitive; (5) lacking in empathy; (6) sensation-seeking, avid for strong sensory stimuli; (7) hostile to

others; aggressive; (8) liking for odd and unusual things; (9) disregard for dangers, foolhardy; (10) likes to make fools of other people, and to upset them.

Considering that the recent surge of interest in all matters paranormal began with the counterculture movement of the 1960s, it seems reasonable that some aspect of nonconformity and rejection of social convention might be related to belief in the paranormal. However, the evidence is really not consistent.

A positive relationship between global paranormal belief and psychoticism has been observed (Francis, Williams, & Robbins, 2010) but non-significant findings have also been reported (Haraldsson, 1985b; Willging & Lester, 1997; Williams, Francis, & Robbins, 2007). Regarding individual aspects of paranormal belief, a positive relationship has been observed between psychoticism and belief in psi (Peltzer, 2002) and a negative relationship has been reported between psychoticism and belief in extraterrestrial life (Lester, 1993).

Narcissism

This personality trait is defined as being high in self-importance, tending to value the self above others, and believing in one's superior abilities or worth. The narcissistic personality likes to indulge in fantasies of power and success. Consistent with this description, studies have found that narcissism is related to belief in phenomena that offer personal control over other people or over the environment, for example, psi and precognition (Tobacyk & Mitchell, 1987) or ESP and psychokinesis (e.g. Roe & Morgan, 2002).

Negative and positive affect

Similar to the position regarding neuroticism, there is a reasonably consistent suggestion that negative affect as a personality trait is related to those beliefs that suppose powerful external forces acting on the individual. Negative affect or persistent anxiety has been associated with belief in astrology (Wuthnow, 1976), the supernatural (Beck & Miller, 2001), magical thinking (Keinan, 1994), and superstitions (Dagnall, Parker, & Munley, 2007; Maller & Lundeen, 1934; Wolfradt, 1997), and with global paranormal belief (Dudley, 2000, 2002; Dudley & Whisnand, 2000; Tobacyk & Milford, 1983). It has been suggested that paranormal beliefs and superstitions may develop as a result of childhood trauma that results in long-lasting anxiety. Superstitions may provide a coping mechanism and help the individual to foster a sense of control.

A particularly interesting study into the relationship between negative affect and paranormal belief was reported by Dudley (2000). Negative affect was manipulated experimentally to investigate its relationship with level of paranormal belief. In Experiment 1, participants completed the Positive and Negative Affect Scale (PANAS; Watson, Clark, & Tellegen, 1988) printed on coloured paper to induce mood: red for positive mood, white for neutral, and blue for negative mood. After this they completed the Revised Paranormal Belief Scale (RPBS; Tobacyk, 1988, 2004) on the same coloured paper. Paper colour did influence mood as expected, and also influenced the level of paranormal belief so that more belief was reported by participants who completed the questionnaires on blue paper. In Experiment 2, the opposite direction of effect was demonstrated. Participants who completed the PANAS after completing the RPBS (both questionnaires on white paper) reported more negative mood than those who completed the PANAS after completing a measure of locus of control (to control for the effects of self-reflection as a possible confound) or with no previous questionnaire. It was concluded that completion of the RPBS had induced a degree of negative mood. Thus, both experiments suggest a relationship between negative affect and paranormal belief. The explanation offered was mood-congruent memory, according to which positive and negative mood act as retrieval cues for memories associated with the corresponding emotion. When in a negative mood, induced in Experiment 1 by blue-coloured paper, participants were more likely to endorse paranormal beliefs, presumably because examples of belief could be readily recalled. In Experiment 2 participants presumably recalled instances of paranormal belief in order to complete the RPBS, and so recalled the associated negative mood. Dudley (2002) also found that participants who completed the RPBS before a measure of emotional intelligence scored lower on the latter than participants who completed this questionnaire first. This leads to the inference that completing the RPBS appears to depress emotional intelligence, a somewhat similar result to the induction of negative mood.

Beck and Miller (2001) reported that higher levels of negative affect over the preceding year were associated with increased levels of belief in paranormal phenomena and the supernatural in non-religious students, who had a relatively low level of initial belief. The interpretation was that prolonged negative affect would result in a change in previous patterns of beliefs and perhaps a motivation to explore avenues that might help to alleviate the negative affect.

A similar line of argument was proposed by Keinan (1994) to explain the observation of higher levels of magical thinking in people living under more stressful circumstances. During the Gulf War, residents who were living in areas likely to be hit by missiles, defined as high-stress areas, reported more magical thinking than residents living in lower-stress areas less likely to be hit by missiles. The theory is that magical thinking offers the illusion of control and this is comforting to people living in a hazardous situation with no real control over events. Magical thinking offers both the illusion that hazards can be predicted and therefore avoided and that, by following certain rituals, adverse events can be prevented. The relationship between magical thinking and stress was moderated by tolerance of ambiguity, interpreted as meaning that people with low tolerance of ambiguity have a greater need to find explanations for their circumstances and to obtain at least an illusion of control.

Keinan (1994) also proposed, as another possible explanation, that the existence of a high level of stress requires cognitive resources to deal with the source of stress and so leaves insufficient resources to rationally appraise an event. This leads to the conclusion that a paranormal explanation may be accepted more readily under conditions of stress.

Interestingly, there also seems to be a relationship between positive affect and paranormal belief. King *et al.* (2007) reported that positive affect increased participants' belief in UFOs after seeing a video claiming to show evidence of UFOs, but only in those participants who were high in experientiality – that is, people who said they tended to trust their hunches, to follow stereotypical lines of thinking, and to avoid thoughtful analyses and logical thinking were more likely to endorse UFOs if they were in a positive mood. This was interpreted as indicating that the combination of experientiality and positive mood interacted to produce an uncritical acceptance of the video 'evidence' for UFOs. Perhaps the presence of positive affect signals that the individual is in a safe situation in which there is no threat, and this indicates that rational, effortful thinking is not required. A hunch may suggest to the participant that the material in the video is correct and the positive affect may lead to uncritical acceptance of the hunch. Göritz and Schumacher (2000) also reported a positive correlation between emotional well-being and belief in the paranormal.

It is interesting to see that positive affect and stress have both been claimed to have similar effects in increasing levels of paranormal belief. This is consistent with Dagnall, Parker, and Munley's (2007) finding that participants who were high in positive or negative affect were more likely to endorse positive and negative superstitions.

Ideas to think about

What is the relationship between negative affect, positive affect, stress, and analytical versus intuitive thinking styles? What is their influence on paranormal belief?

Dudley (1999) had participants solve anagrams after being given either solvable or unsolvable problems. Following the unsolvable problems, the number of anagrams solved was positively related to level of paranormal belief, especially superstition. The conclusion was that superstition gave some protection against the resignation that accompanies failure to solve a problem. This interesting result could be interpreted as meaning that paranormal belief, and especially superstition, is an alternative to **learned helplessness**. Learned helplessness can occur when a human being is put into an aversive situation over which no control is possible. Eventually the individual simply gives up trying to escape from or improve the situation. Even if the situation is then altered in such a way that escape becomes feasible or the situation could be improved in some way, the individual will often simply make no effort to do so (Seligman, 1975).

This issue was also investigated by Matute (1994, 1995). She demonstrated that when people are faced with uncontrollable negative events they may react by generating a superstitious ritual and an accompanying belief that the ritual behaviour is effective in controlling the negative event. Participants were arranged in yoked pairs so that one had some control over an aversive loud auditory tone, while the other member of the pair had no control. The member of the pair with no control developed superstitious behaviour and a belief that the behaviour was effective, but the participant with control over the tone did not. Of particular interest, there was no evidence of learned helplessness in the sense that participants without control showed no sign of realizing that their efforts were pointless. It was concluded that the superstitious behaviour offered the illusion of control and protected against learned helplessness. This clearly places learned helplessness and superstition as opposing solutions to a problem and thus it seems that superstitions may have a function of protecting against learned helplessness.

Ideas to think about

Does this sound similar to the social marginality hypothesis? Do you think that researchers should look at the participant's sense of social marginality, and their long-term level of negative affect?

Obsessive-compulsive tendencies

People suffering from obsessive-compulsive disorder (OCD) are plagued by intrusive thoughts that cause anxiety and worry. They attempt to control their anxiety by engaging in repetitive behaviour, such as obsessive checking, washing, or idiosyncratic rituals, such as having to touch a door handle a specific number of times before entering a room. Although they usually readily acknowledge that their fears and the resultant behaviour are irrational, in severe clinical cases they find it impossible to overcome their obsessive-compulsive tendencies without clinical intervention (such as cognitive behavioural therapy) and even successful treatment is unlikely to completely eliminate the tendencies. As with many other psychological disorders, milder versions of the symptoms of OCD are common in the non-clinical population.

Many commentators have drawn attention to the similarity between aspects of obsessive-compulsive behaviour and superstitious behaviour. Both appear to be based upon magical thinking, insofar as there is often no rational justification for the behaviours involved, and both appear to be primarily directed at warding off misfortune or, in the case of superstitions, attracting good fortune. Both appear to be exacerbated by stress and the belief that perceived threats are beyond the control of the individual.

Einstein and Menzies (2006) reported that scores on the Magical Ideation Scale (Eckblad & Chapman, 1983) were higher in patients suffering from OCD than in normal controls or in patients suffering from panic disorder. Zebb and Moore (2003) replicated and extended a study of the connection between obsessive-compulsive characteristics and magical thinking in non-clinical participants by Frost *et al.* (1993). Frost *et al.* had reported significant correlations between OCD symptomatology and superstitiousness in a sample of females. Zebb and Moore investigated not only the association between OCD tendencies and superstitiousness, but also included measures of symptoms of anxiety disorders other than OCD, as well as measures of general psychological distress and perception of anxiety control. Furthermore, they collected data from both male and female students. Their results for the female students replicated Frost *et al.*'s findings closely, but they also found that superstitiousness was not solely related to OCD symptomatology but was also associated with other types of anxiety and general psychological distress. They suggested that 'superstitiousness is nonspecific and related more to perception of control than any specific form of psychological distress' (Zebb & Moore, 2003, p. 115). Interestingly, this pattern was only found for female respondents, who also scored significantly higher on superstitiousness than males. In the latter group, there was little relationship between superstitiousness and the other variables.

There is further discussion of the possible link between obsessive-compulsive tendencies and paranormal belief in the next chapter, focusing specifically upon the question of whether there is a link between magical thinking in childhood and the development of OCD in adolescents and adults.

Bipolar tendencies

Bipolar disorder, formerly referred to as **manic depression**, refers to a clinical condition characterized by intense mood swings from extreme elation (i.e. mania) to the very depths of misery and despair (i.e. depression). During manic phases, sufferers will appear to be euphoric, full of energy, and unable to sleep or concentrate. They will often devise grandiose and unrealistic plans, engage in risky behaviour such as gambling and substance abuse, or believe themselves to be on a special mission, for example, to save the world. During depressed phases, they will be so apathetic that they barely move or speak. They have no appetite or interest in anyone or anything. Life holds no joys and they have a totally negative view of the world, themselves, and the future. Extreme mania or depression may be associated with psychotic symptoms such as hallucinations and delusions.

In line with the dimensional approach, it is now widely recognized that bipolar tendencies can also be found in milder forms in the non-clinical population. A number of studies by Michael Thalbourne and colleagues have demonstrated a small but significant correlation between bipolar tendencies, both manic and depressive, and paranormal belief (e.g. Thalbourne & Delin, 1994; Thalbourne & French, 1995; Thalbourne, Keogh, & Crawley, 1999).

Dissociativity

The *Diagnostic and Statistical Manual of Mental Disorders*, published by the American Psychiatric Association, is intended to provide standard definitions of mental disorders. The fourth version of the manual, commonly referred to as 'DSM-IV', defined dissociation as follows: 'A disruption in the usually integrated functions of consciousness, memory, identity, or perception of the environment. The disturbance may be sudden or gradual, transient or chronic' (American Psychiatric Association, 1994, p. 766). However, in practice it has not proved possible to produce a definition of this rather amorphous concept that has been universally accepted and it has been applied to a range of different phenomena (McNally, 2003a; Mair, 2013).

As pointed out by McNally (2003a, p. 172, original emphasis), dissociation

> has come to denote a diverse range of experiences that may have little in common. Dissociative symptoms include *derealization*, a strange dream-like sense that one's surroundings are unreal; *depersonalization,* a sense of being disconnected from one's body; a sense that time is either slowing down or speeding up; and *amnesia*, an inability to recall important aspects of what happened.

Similarly, there is also controversy regarding the status of many of the clinical diagnoses that are labelled as dissociative disorders, such as the so-called *fugue states*, rare cases in which someone appears to completely, albeit temporarily, lose their memory of their own identity. Often precipitated by stressful life events, many cases have been shown to be desperate acts of malingering. Perhaps the most controversial diagnosis of all the dissociative disorders is **dissociative identity disorder**, formerly known as **multiple personality disorder**. A strong case can be made that this is what is known as an **iatrogenic** disorder; that is, it is an apparent disorder unintentionally produced by therapeutic intervention itself rather than being a true psychiatric disorder (see, for example, Mair, 2013; Spanos, 1996).

Regardless of the controversies surrounding the psychiatric diagnosis of dissociative disorders, many experiences that have been labelled as dissociative occur commonly in everyday life. Standard examples would include those occasions upon which you have realized that your mind had wandered during a conversation (or, perhaps more commonly, a lecture) and that you had not taken in what had been said. Or else you may sometimes have had the experience of suddenly 'coming to' at the end of a long boring drive and not really remembering how you got to your destination. Not surprisingly, some people are more prone to such experiences than others and a number of standardized measures of dissociativity have been developed for use with both clinical and non-clinical samples. People scoring high on such measures generally give the impression of often being a bit 'spaced out' or, to put it even more colloquially, 'away with the fairies'.

Several studies have demonstrated an association between dissociativity and paranormal belief (e.g. Irwin, 1994b; Pekala, Kumar, & Marcano, 1995; Wolfradt, 1997), but not all (e.g. Groth-Marnat, Roberts, & Ollier, 1998–9). Some studies have taken a more fine-grained approach. For example, Makasovski and Irwin (1999) reported that non-pathological dissociativity (essentially measuring the degree to which one becomes absorbed in the task at the focus of one's attention to the exclusion of other stimuli) did not correlate with paranormal belief but that tendencies towards pathological dissociation predicted belief in parapsychological and spiritual concepts. Rattet and Bursik (2001) found that dissociative tendencies were not related to self-reported precognitive experiences but were related to general paranormal belief.

A wide range of anomalous experiences appears to be associated with elevated levels of dissociativity (Pekala, Kumar, & Marcano, 1995; Richards, 1991; Ross & Joshi, 1992; Ross et al., 1991). For example, both Powers (1994) and French et al. (2008) found that individuals alleging alien contact showed higher levels of dissociativity than matched control groups. Studies have shown that elevated levels of dissociativity are found in children reporting past-life memories compared to those who do not in both Sri Lanka (Haraldsson, Fowler, & Periyannanpillai, 2000) and Lebanon (Haraldsson, 2002). Higher levels of non-pathological signs of dissociation have also been reported in people who have had an NDE compared to those who have not (e.g. Greyson, 2000a).

Schizotypy

Schizophrenia typically involves a range of distressing symptoms including hallucinations, paranoid and other delusions, disorganized speech and thinking, and extreme social withdrawal. Many modern commentators (e.g. Claridge, 1997, 2010) view the clinical manifestation of schizophrenia as simply being the extreme end of a continuum of an underlying psychological variable referred to as *schizotypy*. Some people may never experience any schizotypal symptoms throughout their entire lives but many people with moderate levels of schizotypy will experience some of them in a mild form but may still lead generally happy and productive lives without any need for treatment.

Schizotypy is the measure of psychopathological tendencies that has received the most attention with respect to its association with paranormal belief and experience. Milder forms of symptoms of schizophrenia, such as magical thinking and unusual experiences, are reported by schizotypal personalities and high scores on schizotypy scales are often seen as indicative of increased risk of developing full-blown schizophrenic psychosis. Schizophrenia itself, of course, often involves unusual beliefs of a paranormal nature, such as the belief that one's thoughts are being broadcast or that one can read others' minds. A large number of studies have demonstrated an association between schizotypy and general measures of paranormal belief and experience as well as various specific types of paranormal belief (e.g. Chequers, Joseph, & Diduca, 1997; Gallagher,

Kumar, & Pekala, 1994; Goulding, 2004, 2005a; Hergovich, Schott, & Arendasy, 2008; Houran, Irwin, & Lange, 2001; Irwin & Green, 1998–9; McCreery & Claridge, 1995, 1996, 2002; Peltzer, 2003; Pizzagalli *et al.*, 2000; Thalbourne, 1994b, 1998, 1999; Thalbourne *et al.*, 1997; Thalbourne, Dunbar, & Delin, 1995; Thalbourne & French, 1995; Tobacyk & Wilkinson, 1990; Williams & Irwin, 1991; Windholz & Diamant, 1974; Wolfradt, 1997; Wolfradt *et al.*, 1999; Wolfradt & Watzke, 1999).

It should be noted that schizotypy is, in fact, multidimensional, as is paranormal belief itself, as noted previously. There is some evidence to suggest that different factors of schizotypy may relate to different aspects of paranormal belief and experience in complex ways (e.g. Irwin & Green, 1998–9) but a full discussion of this issue is beyond the scope of this chapter. There is some debate regarding the factor structure of schizotypy but the factor that seems to most consistently correlate with paranormal beliefs and experiences is the one which concerns aberrant perceptions and beliefs, sometimes labelled the Unusual Experiences factor (Goulding, 2005a). This factor relates to sub-clinical tendencies towards hallucination and delusional thinking, that is, the positive symptoms of schizophrenic psychosis.

It should be noted that many of the studies listed measured schizotypy using Eckblad and Chapman's (1983) Magical Ideation Scale (MIS) which actually includes several items which relate directly to paranormal beliefs and experiences, such as 'If reincarnation were true, it would explain some unusual experiences I have had' and 'Horoscopes are right too often for it to be a coincidence'. Clearly, this raises the possibility of circular reasoning – that is, the correlations found may simply reflect the overlap between the MIS and scales used to measure paranormal belief/experience. However, several studies (e.g. Thalbourne, 1999; Thalbourne & French, 1995) have shown that the correlations between the measures remain highly statistically significant, if somewhat reduced, even if the paranormal items on the MIS are not included in the scoring.

It may be tempting to those who are sceptical of the paranormal to conclude on the basis of such evidence that those who believe in the paranormal are suffering from some form of psychopathology but this would be to grossly oversimplify the situation. For one thing, the high prevalence of paranormal beliefs and ostensibly paranormal experiences mean that such an assumption would imply that the majority of the population is suffering from mental illness. Secondly, the correlations found, although highly statistically significant, are typically no higher than about 0.6. This means that most of the variance in scores on paranormal belief scales cannot be accounted for in terms of schizotypy. Thirdly, the scores obtained by believers in the paranormal on measures of schizotypy, although typically higher than the scores of disbelievers, are by no means usually at the level of those suffering from schizophrenia. Finally, some atypical groups of paranormal believers, such as members of psychical research groups, appear to have schizotypy levels that are almost as low as the general population. It seems likely that many members of such groups believe in the paranormal for reasons other than personal experience.

Gordon Claridge (1997, 2010) has distinguished between two models of schizotypy. The first is the quasi-dimensional (or disease) model which views schizotypy as a milder form of schizophrenia and as an indication of vulnerability with respect to the risk of developing psychosis. The second model is referred to as the fully dimensional model, described by Anneli Goulding (2005a, p. 1070) as follows:

> Within this model, schizotypy is described as a personality continuum. The traits of this continuum are sources of healthy variation and also predisposition to psychosis. Thus, the fully dimensional model views schizotypy as something neutral, which sometimes is associated with good psychological health and sometimes with psychological ill-health (Claridge, 1997). The quasi-dimensional model on the other hand views schizotypy as something negative, related to psychological ill-health only.

This notion of the 'healthy schizotype' is supported by findings from a number of studies (e.g. McCreery & Claridge, 1995, 1996, 2002; Goulding, 2004, 2005a) thus also supporting the fully dimensional model of schizophrenia. It appears that although there is a definite link between schizotypy and paranormal belief/experience, this should not always be viewed as psychologically unhealthy. Indeed, both schizotypy and paranormal belief/experience appear to be correlated with such positive attributes as creativity, in line with the popular notion that creative genius is often linked to madness.

Transliminality

Thalbourne and Delin (1994), while recognizing that paranormal belief and experience correlate consistently with various measures of psychopathological tendencies, also presented evidence to show that they correlate with more positive traits such as creativity and mystical experience. They argued that a single common factor might underlie the inter-correlations between all of these factors and they tentatively labelled this common thread as *transliminality*. They initially defined transliminality as follows (p. 3): 'the extent to which the contents of some preconscious (or "unconscious" or "subliminal") region of the mind are able to cross the threshold into consciousness (in its sense of "awareness").' More recently (e.g. Thalbourne & Maltby, 2008, p. 1618) transliminality has been defined as 'a hypersensitivity to psychological material originating in (a) the unconscious, and/or (b) the external environment. "Psychological material" is taken to cover ideation, imagery, affect and perception, and thus is a rather broad concept.'

Thalbourne (1998) produced and subsequently refined a scale to measure transliminality (Houran, Thalbourne, & Lange, 2003; Lange *et al.*, 2000) and Thalbourne and colleagues have published many papers exploring the psychological factors associated with transliminality (for a review, see Thalbourne, 2010b). This concept and the empirical evidence supporting it are discussed more fully in Chapter 6 on cognitive perspectives. For now, it is enough to note that it is a concept that fits in well with such notions as the 'happy schizotype' described earlier. The concept of transliminality is essentially neutral with respect to the reality or otherwise of psi but provides a potentially useful framework for considering possible links between various measures of psychopathology and anomalous experiences in both clinical and non-clinical populations.

Reality monitoring

Another useful framework that can be applied to these issues is that of reality monitoring (Johnson & Raye, 1981; Johnson, Hashtroudi, & Lindsay, 1993). Reality monitoring refers to our ability to distinguish between mental events that are internally generated and those that reflect external reality. It is assumed that people differ along a continuum in terms of their ability to make such distinctions. In the perceptual domain, problems with reality monitoring would result in a tendency to hallucinate, as indicated by high scores on measures of the schizotypy factor Unusual Experiences. In the memory domain, they would result in a susceptibility to false memories. French (2003; see also French & Wilson, 2006) pointed out that a range of psychological variables that have been shown to correlate with susceptibility to false memories, such as dissociativity, fantasy-proneness, absorption, and hypnotic susceptibility, also correlate with paranormal belief and the tendency to report paranormal experiences. This raises the possibility that at least some reports of paranormal experiences are based upon false memories (see Chapter 6).

Psychosis, spirituality, and anomalous experiences

A number of studies have investigated the incidence of hallucinatory experiences in the general population (e.g. Tien, 1991; Poulton et al., 2000), suggesting that 10–15% of the non-clinical population experience hallucinations. Furthermore, approximately 20% of the general population report delusions (Poulton et al., 2000). In a similar vein, van Os et al. (2000) reported that 17.5% of their Dutch sample of over 7000 people was rated as having at least one symptom of psychosis based upon the Composite International Diagnostic Interview (CIDI; World Health Organisation, 1990) although only 0.4% were formally diagnosed as suffering from psychosis. In other words, as argued throughout this chapter, symptoms associated with psychosis are found within the non-clinical population much more frequently than is generally assumed. Furthermore, most of the people who experience such symptoms never receive a formal diagnosis of psychosis and often lead happy and productive lives. What are the factors that determine whether such symptoms will be labelled as psychotic as opposed to paranormal or even spiritual (Clarke, 2010)?

Heriot-Maitland, Knight, and Peters (2012) collected qualitative data via semi-structured interviews from six clinical and six non-clinical participants all of whom reported hearing voices. Voice-hearing is one of the most commonly studied anomalous experiences in non-clinical populations (e.g. Tien, 1991). Heriot-Maitland, Knight, and Peters were interested in determining whether factors associated with triggering such anomalous experiences could be distinguished from those determining the clinical consequences of such experiences. Much previous research (e.g. Brett *et al.*, 2007; Lovatt *et al.*, 2010) supports the idea that what determines whether or not an individual experiencing anomalous phenomena ultimately requires clinical treatment is the way that the experience is appraised.

Although Heriot-Maitland, Knight, and Peters's (2012) samples were small, their qualitative approach suggested a number of interesting lines of investigation for future larger-scale quantitative studies. It is striking that the out-of-ordinary experiences of the clinical and non-clinical samples are very similar, including both ostensibly paranormal experiences (e.g. telepathy, communication with the dead) and ostensibly spiritual experiences (e.g. communicating with God). The experiences in both groups typically had their onset during periods of stress but the non-clinical participants were better able to incorporate the experiences into their lives. The main factor that seemed to underlie this difference was the attitude of those around the experient. If significant others expressed validation and acceptance of the experience as opposed pathologization, the experiences were accepted and assimilated more readily.

Conclusion

The idea that certain types of paranormal belief may serve a protective function in psychological terms in some situations is supported by various forms of evidence. One obvious example of this is the fact that, perhaps not surprisingly, those who believe in life after death report having lower levels of death anxiety (e.g. Thalbourne, 1996). Indeed, there is a considerable amount of evidence to support the claim that those holding religious beliefs appear to be psychologically healthier than those who do not although there is some debate regarding the best explanation of such findings. It is unclear whether this reflects something intrinsic about the nature of religious beliefs or simply greater social support that typically accompanies active involvement in religious groups.

Both paranormal and religious beliefs appear to provide a framework for the believer that helps individuals to find meaning and to gain some sense of control. Even basic traditional superstitions appear to serve this function. Research suggests that levels of superstitious thinking increase when people are in a stressful situation that they perceive to be beyond their control (Dudley, 1999; Keinan, 2002). Even though the sense of control provided by such beliefs may be illusory, some evidence (Dudley, 1999) suggests that the adoption of such beliefs may protect against learned helplessness, meaning that once some degree of control is again possible, the superstitious person may well be able to cope better than her more rational non-superstitious counterpart.

Scientists tend to value truth above happiness. If the evidence suggests that paranormal and religious beliefs do not reflect the way the universe really is, then the scientist will always opt for rejecting such notions. In doing so, however, they must not make the mistake of assuming that all such beliefs have no value. As we have seen, in certain circumstances magical thinking appears to offer some protection against learned helplessness. But we must also avoid the risk of painting too rosy a picture of the possible benefits in terms of psychological well-being of adopting a paranormal or religious view of the universe. As the literature shows, for many individuals, such experiences and beliefs are often associated with distressing symptoms of psychopathology.

As practitioners, clinical psychologists must treat clients who are distressed by symptoms which they interpret as involving paranormal forces with great sensitivity and care. In many cases, the symptoms may be an indication of the first stages of a serious psychotic episode. Early intervention may be crucial to a good prognosis. However, there is always the danger that the client may withdraw from the therapeutic situation if their interpretation is challenged. On the other hand, there are obvious dangers of appearing, even implicitly, to endorse a paranormal interpretation. The ideal approach is to remain neutral with respect to the paranormality or otherwise of the client's experience but to concentrate on exploring all possible interpretations in a neutral manner, with the main emphasis on helping the client to come to terms with any distress they may experience as a result.

Suggested further reading

For interesting perspectives on psychosis, spirituality and anomalous experiences:

Clarke, I. (ed.). (2010). *Psychosis and spirituality: Consolidating the new paradigm.* 2nd edn. Chichester: John Wiley and Sons.
Vyse, S. A. (1997). *Believing in magic: The psychology of superstition.* Oxford: Oxford University Press. Chapter 6, pp. 169–95.

Developmental
Perspectives

4

Introduction

This chapter aims to consider the developmental antecedents of our paranormal beliefs. To what extent do the experiences and beliefs of childhood develop into the paranormal beliefs we hold as adults? We will address four main topics under this general theme. The first concerns magical thinking in children: where it comes from, how it changes with age, and whether it can be considered to be the forerunner of adult paranormal belief or something quite distinct. Are adult beliefs the same as childhood beliefs, a more mature version of childhood beliefs, or perhaps different to childhood beliefs but still related to them in some consistent way? Alternatively, there may be little relationship between childhood and adult beliefs concerning magic and the paranormal and the factors motivating earlier and later beliefs may be quite different. Investigation of this question is hampered by a lack of longitudinal research following the same individuals from childhood through to adulthood, but a representative literature investigating childhood beliefs and addressing a direct comparison of childhood, adolescent, and adult beliefs will be reviewed. The second topic is related to the first and asks the question: is there a connection between magical thinking in childhood and OCD in adolescents and in adults? The third topic addresses the possible continuity of superstitious belief between childhood and adulthood.

The fourth question concerns other aspects of childhood that might promote adult beliefs in paranormal phenomena. The major theme in this topic is the **psychodynamic functions hypothesis** (PFH) proposed and developed by Irwin (1992, 1993a, 2009). The PFH states that adult paranormal belief is an attempt to achieve a sense of control over one's own life in response to feelings of helplessness that arise as a result of a perceived lack of personal control in childhood. This situation can arise as a result of childhood trauma – for example, physical or sexual abuse – or from having authoritarian or overly intrusive parents, or perhaps a chaotic home environment. Fantasy-proneness is an important element of the PFH that is proposed to mediate between childhood trauma and adult paranormal belief and so the evidence of a relationship between fantasy-proneness (in children and adults) and paranormal belief that was reviewed in Chapter 2 will be further considered in this context.

First, let us look at some definitions of magic and magical thinking and the difference between belief in magic and superstition. Vyse (1997) explains that magical thinking takes two main forms. The first is that our actions or thoughts can cause events to occur without any logical connection; for example, the belief that a wish can come true, or that saying a magic word can cause an object to appear or disappear. The second is animism: the belief that inanimate objects are alive and can act and think, or animals can talk and have other human attributes. Similar to the first of these definitions, Bolton *et al.* (2002) offer a definition of magical thinking as thinking that involves causal influences not supported by cultural knowledge of real physical effects. This definition refers to cultural knowledge so as to allow, for example, that television might be regarded as magical in the absence of knowledge about electromagnetic radiation. As Harris (1997) points out, science is a recent phenomenon and magical thinking was pervasive worldwide before the explosion in scientific thinking that began three or four centuries ago.

Bolton *et al.* (2002) try to explain the widespread belief in magic by observing that people have a tendency to invoke a hidden causal structure behind the world that we observe with our senses. We tend to assume that objects in the world have **agency** and intent and that events occur for a reason. This may be related to survival in the sense that it is safer to assume that an entity or object is acting with intent and to take action accordingly than to ignore the possibility and neglect to take safety precautions. This idea is explored further in Chapter 8. Indeed, the theory that it is safer to assume deliberate causation than to assume blind randomness might explain how people are able to survive with an invalid understanding of the world. A couple of examples will explain this principle: the rain dance and food rituals. Although we now understand that a ritual dance will not make the rains come, there is probably little to be lost in a community social event, so this is a harmless (if inaccurate) piece of magical thinking. On the other hand, some cultural rituals around food preparation (washing hands before cooking, for example, and avoiding certain foods) may serve the purpose of protecting against food poisoning or parasitical infestation. So some examples of magical thinking have served a purpose in the past even without modern scientific understanding. Even the most rational of us may lapse into magical thinking occasionally: have you ever cursed a photocopier or a computer when it malfunctioned?

There is an overlap and a grey area between magical thinking and superstition, but there are some general differences. One is that magic requires some deliberate action – for example, casting a spell or making a wish – whereas superstition can invoke an event that occurs without personal intent – for example, a black cat crossing one's path, finding a four-leaf clover, or accidentally breaking a mirror. Another difference is that the performance of a superstitious ritual might actually work to bring about success by calming the nerves or boosting the confidence of the person carrying out the ritual, so enabling them to do the best of which they are capable. In contrast there is no realistic means whereby magic can work. This difference may not seem altogether clear-cut and indeed the overlap between magic and superstition could include personal idiosyncratic superstitions: for example, carrying a lucky pen into an exam might feel partly like a magic spell and partly like a superstition.

Childhood beliefs: Magical thinking and wishes

There are several sources of children's belief in magic, of which the most important are the peer group, parents, and culture in general: for example, children's television programmes (please see Chapter 7 for a fuller discussion of peer-to-peer, parent-to-child, and media transmission of belief). As explained by Vyse (1997), children have their own culture, with their own songs, customs, and systems of belief. These are all learnt from the peer group by processes of social learning and so passed down through generations of children. The peer group can be a powerful influence as acceptance by the group can be dependent on conforming to its rules and customs, creating a strong pressure to conform. Some magical thinking is also learnt from parents and other adults, often in the form of reading stories with a magical theme. Parents actively encourage belief in younger children by presenting stories in which magic and fairies and other supernatural figures feature strongly or by actively encouraging their children to believe in supernatural beings like Father Christmas, the Easter Bunny, and the Tooth Fairy (e.g. Rosengren & Hickling, 1994; Vyse, 1997). Parents and teachers may use the word 'magic' as a semi-explanation or answer to a question. So there is some adult encouragement of magical thinking in young children. Perhaps when the children start school this direct encouragement by parents becomes less common and this could contribute to the decline in children's belief, but there appears to be little direct research into this possibility.

Vyse (1997) makes the point that it is not entirely accurate to call children superstitious in the adult sense of the word. Children have pre-scientific intellects and do not reason according to the same rules as adults. Their reasoning and their causal attributions (the explanations they give for events) are different to those an adult might make but are common for their age. For example, a young child might believe in genuine magic when a rabbit is produced from a hat when an older child or an adult would suspect a conjuring trick. As we will see, children move away from magical thinking as they grow older but do not entirely abandon it, and some adults still indulge in magical thinking and personal superstitious rituals.

Several studies have investigated the presence of magical thinking in children and in particular the ages at which it is strongest. It appears that there is a peak age for believing in magic, which is around five–six years old, and that belief declines thereafter (e.g. Woolley, 1997a, 1997b). The proportion of children with imaginary companions may be as high as 65% and the peak age for children to believe in imaginary companions, as well as fantastical creatures like Father Christmas, monsters, witches, and other supernatural beings, is between three and eight years (Woolley, 1997a). Children engage in the highest levels of pretend play between three and eight years old (e.g. Evans *et al.*, 2002). Young children also believe in the efficacy of wishing up to about six years of age and then this belief declines (e.g. Vikan & Clausen, 1993; Woolley *et al.*, 1999).

Looking directly at magical beliefs, Phelps and Woolley (1994) conducted a study with 48 children aged four, six, and eight years. All of the children were shown a series of separate events that appeared to defy the laws of nature – for example, objects changing in size or moving without being touched. The events were divided according to their actual causes into those whose cause was learnt by younger children (e.g. a magnifying glass making an object look bigger), causes understood by somewhat older children (e.g. magnetic attraction making an object move towards another object without being touched), or causes that only older children would be expected to reliably understand (e.g. conjuring tricks). The participants in the study were asked to explain how each of the seemingly impossible events had occurred. Magic was invoked to explain the events more often by the younger children than the older children, and more often to explain events for which the cause was learnt later. This pattern of results suggests that magic tends to be invoked to explain events for which a child does not understand the real physical cause. Indeed, 92% of all the claims of magic were made when a child had no physical explanation for what caused an event. Another study by Johnson and Harris (1994) found that children between three and five years old call an event magical if it violates familiar physical constraints. Along similar lines, children with strong magical beliefs were less likely to use concrete physical explanations for two magic tricks in the study by Evans *et al.* (2002).

Rosengren and Hickling (1994) reported a similar set of results. They presented children aged four and five with a set of object transformations, some natural (e.g. cutting a piece of string to make it smaller) and some impossible (e.g. an object changing colour when touched). Before the demonstrations, children offered physical explanations for the natural events and said the others were impossible. After the demonstrations, the four-year-olds said the impossible transformations were magic while the five-year-olds were more likely than the four-year-olds to say that they were tricks. As in the Phelps and Woolley (1994) study, it seems that four-year-olds believe in magic as an explanation for events they do not know how to explain in natural physical terms but this tendency declines with age. According to Rosengren and Hickling (1994), this is replaced with a belief in the abilities of others to perform conjuring tricks.

Both the Phelps and Woolley (1994) and the Rosengren and Hickling (1994) studies involved interviews with the children to discover their understanding of magic. Both studies found that belief in magic as a power that can violate physical laws declines with age. Interestingly, belief that magic could only be performed by a person with special powers declined with age, and belief that the children themselves could do magic, or that magic could be learnt by anyone, increased with age. The latter pattern suggests that children were becoming aware that magic as performed by magicians is likely to be trickery. It appears that children come to believe that 'real' magic – for example, as performed by fairies – exists only in an imaginary world of stories. It should be noted that there was variation among the children in each study and differences in the beliefs of children at the same age. Some children at the youngest ages did not believe in magic, and some at the older ages retained their beliefs.

Subbotsky (2004a) investigated the ages at which children verbally express belief in magic and at what ages they accept magical explanations for anomalous events. Children of four and five said they believed in magic but by the age of six most children verbally denied that magic could occur in the real world. However, when they were presented with an anomalous event that could not occur in the real world (e.g. the transformation of an object inside a box without any visible intervention), children up to six years old were likely to accept a magical explanation for the event. When the trick was explained to the children, those aged five or below still expressed a belief that magic had occurred but the six-year-old children accepted that the apparent transformation was a trick. It was concluded that non-magical explanations are usually preferred over magical explanations by six-year-olds, but their scepticism towards magic (in the supernatural sense) is not firmly entrenched. Children of this age are prepared to believe in magic in the absence of another explanation. Things had changed by the age of nine; most of the nine-year-old children were sure the transformation was a trick from the start and did not accept the magical explanation, that is, their disbelief in magic in the supernatural sense was entrenched. There were, however, a few nine-year-olds who did retain some belief in magic though this was abandoned as an explanation when they were shown how the trick was done. It appears from this study that belief in physical causality, and scepticism towards supernatural magic, becomes more firmly entrenched between the ages of five and nine. This explains why young children may sometimes show their good understanding of physical causation and at other times may accept or invoke magical explanations for anomalous events.

So we can offer two main reasons for the age-related decline in the belief in magic. One is the increasing understanding of the real world and of natural physical explanations for events: for example, magnets can make objects move towards or away from each other without being touched and magnifying glasses can make objects look bigger. The other main reason for the decline in belief in magic is the awareness of conjuring tricks that can be learnt and practiced by anyone. Interestingly, there is little suggestion that parents attempt to intervene to deliberately suppress their children's beliefs in magic.

Wishing is another aspect of magical thinking that is commonly observed in children. The idea that wishing for something can make it come true is actively encouraged by parents, as in the tradition of wishing when blowing out the candles on a birthday cake. Woolley et al. (1999) interviewed 50 children aged around four and six, and found that 95% of the older children said that wishes sometimes come true, while 74% of the younger children said that wishes sometimes come true and 22% said that wishes always come true. The mean number of wishes expected to come true, out of five, was 3.59 in the younger group and 2.78 in the older group. The older group of children had more familiarity and experience with wishing than the younger group; perhaps this suggests that familiarity with wishing erodes belief, although strong levels of belief were still apparent in the six-year-olds. The parents of the older and younger children encouraged wishing about equally and none of the parents said they discouraged wishing, so it does not seem that parental discouragement could explain the decline in belief in the efficacy of wishing. It is interesting to note that the children were clear that wishing was a magical process and not a normal kind of thinking, so that their 'normal' non-magical thoughts could not affect events in the real world.

It is perhaps relevant to note another aspect of parental involvement in their children's wishing: 36% of parents encouraged their children's wishing in all circumstances, and the other 64% encouraged wishing if the object of the wish was likely to happen anyway. The observation that over half of the parents selectively encouraged wishing for things that were likely to occur does offer a potential reason for children's belief in wishing: their parents' actions created a false association between wishing and success. By selectively encouraging their children to wish for likely outcomes, parents raised the likelihood that any wish would be followed by the desired outcome. This does seem to have been at least partly overcome by experience, however, as the six-year-olds had lower levels of belief in the efficacy of wishing than the four-year-olds.

It is interesting to note the finding by Woolley, Browne, and Boerger (2006) that children aged three–six expected wishing to follow the same rules as ordinary physical causes. For example, a wish had to precede the event that it caused, not follow it (causes must precede effects). Also, the wish had to be the only cause of the event; if there was a normal physical cause then wishing was not invoked as an explanation. This suggests that children are applying rules of logic to the arena of wishing, acting like young scientists in trying to understand causal factors. Also, the discounting of the efficacy of a wish in the presence of a normal explanation reinforces the observations (discussed before) that belief in magic as an explanation of an anomalous event only arises when the child lacks a normal physical explanation.

Vikan and Clausen (1993) investigated whether children aged four–six believe that they can control another person by mental effort, either wishful thinking or magical thinking. The targets of wishful and magical thinking were obtaining something desired or avoiding a punishment. Most of the 48 participants (94%) indicated some belief that they could control others by their thoughts. There was no difference between the four- and six-year-olds in belief that they could control other people by thought. The interesting aspect is that the children also knew about their realistic means of exerting influences on other people: for example, through asking or persuasion – that is, children who thought they could control others by thought were also well aware of the ways in which they could influence other people by normal non-magical means. So it does not appear that belief in the power of control by thought was a substitute for other means of influencing or persuading people. There was no relationship between children's belief in control by thought and a measure of their ability to distinguish between fantasy and reality, so it does not seem the belief was the result of a failure to understand physical realities. The authors concluded that children believe their thoughts have causal efficacy, and this belief may be based on a lack of experience in the world. Some thoughts and wishes will occasionally be followed by the desired outcomes and children without a concept of chance or randomness may not appreciate that the link between their thoughts and the outcomes was only coincidence. With time and experience, one would expect children's belief in the power of wishing to diminish, but in this study there was no evidence of this occurring by the age of six.

Interestingly, Vikan and Clausen (1993) discuss the possibility that children may not routinely engage in wishful or magical thinking because they already have a sufficient repertoire of behaviours for influencing and persuading others – for example, by helping, asking, or teasing. Magical thinking may then be a feature of those who are less successful at influencing others by normal social interactive means.

To explore the factors that could lead children to believe in a supernatural being, Woolley, Boerger, and Markman (2004) introduced a group of three to four-year-olds and a group of four to five-year-olds to a new being they called the Candy Witch. This being eats the candy left out on Halloween and replaces it with a new toy. The researchers involved the children's teachers and parents in fostering belief in the Candy Witch by making puppets at school and by asking the parents to telephone the Candy Witch at home. The findings were that children came to believe quite strongly in the Candy Witch, as strongly as they believed in Father Christmas and the Easter Bunny. Strength of belief was not related to age overall and there was no tendency for children to become less inclined to believe in a fantastical being between the ages of three and five. There was some effect of age, however; the older children who were visited believed more strongly than the older children who were not visited. For younger children, their strength of belief did not depend on whether they were visited by the Candy Witch. So it seems that the older children, but not the younger children, were more convinced if they saw 'evidence'. This suggests that perhaps the older children were starting to think more like scientists and asking to see the evidence. Other researchers (e.g. Vyse, 1997) have noted a general trend for parents to withdraw their encouragement for belief in supernatural beings – for example, fairies.

It is important to note that belief in the power of magic and wishing coincides with adequate knowledge of the real world, and that those children who believe in magic and wishes can distinguish between real and imaginary objects and events. Wellman and Estes (1986) showed the ability of children aged three to six to distinguish between a mental event – for example, an image or a thought – and the real object to which it refers. For example, you cannot eat an imaginary cookie and you cannot see an imaginary kitten with your eyes. Children of these ages appeared to understand that mental objects and entities, but not those in the real world, can do impossible things: for example, an imaginary dog can fly or an imaginary apple can dance. In other words, children can make the ontological distinction between mental and real objects. Abilities did improve with age in this study but were present even in the three-year-olds. Other experiments have clearly demonstrated that children aged three to seven are able to understand that pretend objects or entities – for example, animals and monsters – do not really exist (e.g. Flavell, Green, & Flavell, 1986; Golomb & Galasso, 1995; Harris et al., 1991; Woolley & Phelps, 1994). According to Taylor, Cartwright, and Carlson (1993), children who had imaginary companions were as likely to be able to distinguish between fantasy and reality as those who did not have an imaginary companion.

Woolley and Wellman (1990) observed that by the age of three, children can generally distinguish between reality and pretence, between real objects and toys, and between reality and pictures. Also, Subbotsky (2004a) observed that children as young as four could distinguish between ordinary, lawful events, and anomalous events that should not occur in the real world. In this particular study, 45% of five-year-olds, 59% of six-year-olds, and 80% of nine-year-olds were able to distinguish between anomalous events needing a supernatural explanation and conjuring tricks. Woolley (1997b) and Taylor (1997) review evidence that young children are able to distinguish between fantasy and reality, although there are also some instances where very young children, around three years, show some confusion between reality and imagination (e.g. Woolley & Wellman, 1993; Woolley, 1997b).

So when children express belief in magic, it is not because they cannot tell the difference between the real world and worlds of the imagination. Rather, they are well aware that impossible events cannot happen to real objects and this is why they invoke a special process – magic – that transcends the laws of nature. Boyer (1997) points out that we need to think about two independent aspects of events: whether they are real or imaginary and whether they conform to intuitive expectations or are counter-intuitive. Children can quite happily regard an event as counter-intuitive but real. Indeed, this is the situation in which they are likely to reach for a magical explanation. Regarding wishing, Woolley (1997b) explains that children know that thinking about something will not make it happen, but wishing can make it happen; the difference being that wishing invokes magic. Again, magic is invoked to explain how natural laws of physics can be violated. Children's belief in magic illustrates a curious mixture of scientific thinking and unscientific thinking (by adult standards). Children around five–six years are aware that some special process must be invoked to explain events that violate the laws of nature but still believe in magic as an explanation.

It is also interesting to consider the observation made by Woolley, Boerger, and Markman (2004) that four to five-year-olds were more readily persuaded to believe in a new fantastical being, the Candy Witch, than the younger three to four-year-olds. This concurs with the concept proposed by Rosengren and Hickling (2000) that magical thinking requires a certain cognitive sophistication. Very young children may not have the capacity to believe in creatures for which they must use their imagination and suspend disbelief. Rosengren and Hickling (2000) also propose that the development of magical thinking is driven by a search for causal understanding of anomalies, in an early form of intellectual pursuit. Along these lines, it is also worth noting that an absence of pretend play is symptomatic of developmental disorders involving cognitive deficits (e.g. autism). From these various sources it seems that very young children, below about four years, are too young to be able to understand or invoke magical explanations for events.

It seems that there are peak ages for magical thinking, belief in the power of wishes, and belief in fantastical creatures: between three and eight and more precisely around five–six. These forms of belief are learnt from peers, parents, and cultural influences. Belief declines as the child becomes more aware of natural physical explanations for events and as the developing mind starts to demand more in the way of evidence and scientific reasoning. The next sections will consider whether any forms of magical thinking persist into adulthood.

Magical thinking from childhood to adolescence and adulthood

Piaget (e.g. 2008/1972) thought that magical thinking would exist in children up to approximately 11 or 12 years of age (what he termed the 'concrete operational period') but would decline with the development of formal operational thought, that is, scientific thinking and attention to evidence. As children learn about real physical causal relations in the world, they must forego their belief in magic. However, it appears that the situation is not that simple, and Piaget both over- and underestimated the age at which children turn away from magical explanation towards realistic ones. For example, younger children can distinguish a magical explanation from a real explanation (e.g. Flavell, Green, & Flavell, 1986; Wellman & Estes, 1986) although young children and preschoolers may be less adept at making the distinction than older children or adults (e.g. Woolley, 1997b).

On the other hand, magical thinking and superstitious beliefs are common among adults. For example, some common superstitions are endorsed by over 40% of the adult population (e.g. Woolley, 1997b). Adults also obey the magical law of contagion, including a reluctance to use a hairbrush belonging to someone they disliked even when it has been thoroughly disinfected and unwillingness to drink water from a container labelled cyanide even though they placed the label on the container themselves (Rozin, Millman, & Nemeroff, 1986). Adults have been shown to accept magical (psychic or telekinetic) explanations for transformations of objects that they were unable to explain using non-magical means (Subbotsky, 1993). Adults have also been shown to concede some possibility that their future lives could be influenced by magic (Subbotsky, 2005); perhaps in this study it was possible for magic to affect the future life because this is not yet fixed. There is considerable evidence of widespread adult beliefs in fantastical creatures, including ghosts, aliens, and the Loch Ness monster. Indeed, some people might argue that UFOs and aliens are the adult, modern equivalent of goblins and witches. Altogether, there is considerable evidence that adults, like children, use various forms of magical thinking.

Looking specifically at formal operational thinking, Lesser and Paisner (1985) compared adult members of a spiritual community with adult controls from the general population. They observed that both groups had similar levels of formal operational thinking but the former had more belief in a combined measure of supernatural concepts (astrology, faith healing, ESP, plant consciousness, UFOs, magic, and witchcraft). So it seems that magical thinking is not due to a failure to develop Piaget's last stage of formal operational thinking but can coexist with it. The authors concluded that the ability to apply logical forms of thinking can develop independently from concepts of cause and effect. In this study the members of the spiritual community had causal concepts that were similar to the egocentrism of young children: the belief that all things happen for a purpose, that there is little or no chance in the world, and that seemingly random events are in fact preordained in order to help the individual to learn a particular lesson. This coexisted with formal operational thinking and thus cannot be attributed to a lack of ability to think logically. Like children, the adults in this spiritual community could entertain both physical and magical concepts of causality. Similarly, in the study by Evans *et al.* (2002), there was clear evidence that children who were capable of logical thinking still believed in magic and the power of wishes. This has some similarity with the concept of two independent thinking styles, rational and intuitive, that was discussed in Chapter 2.

Woolley (1997b) observed that adults use magical thinking in situations of uncertainty where they lack information and explanations for events. In particular, adults use superstitious rituals particularly where they perceive they lack control over events and where important outcomes are at stake (e.g. Vyse, 1997; Rudski & Edwards, 2007). For example, as noted in Chapter 3, adults living under a highly stressful situation with some small threat of death had elevated levels of superstitious beliefs (Keinan, 1994) and superstitious rituals are particularly prevalent among sportsmen and -women (e.g. Vyse, 1997). Rudski and Edwards (2007) observed that college students were more likely to use lucky charms and rituals in situations where the outcome was important, the task was difficult, or the individual was underprepared, and there was an element of competition (see also Chapter 7). Piaget pointed out that adults might regress to magical thinking in times of fear and anxiety. He proposed that magical thinking fosters the illusion of control where there is no real control and so helps to protect against learned helplessness. Others – for example, Vyse (1997) – have also observed that adult magical thinking (in the forms of personal rituals and superstitions) occurs in situations where there is a lower-than-desired level of real control and where the stakes are high.

Woolley (1997b) makes the important point that if adult magical thinking is to be seen as a continuation of childhood magical thinking then it should be triggered by the same circumstances, that is, children should indulge in super-stitious beliefs particularly where they feel a lack of control and where impor-tant outcomes are at stake. This cannot be evaluated at present as there is no direct evidence pertaining to this issue. However, it must be noted that children generally lack control over their own lives and events that surround them to a greater extent than do adults so, in this sense, children would be expected to be chronically more prone to magical thinking than adults.

Woolley (1997a, 1997b) proposed that adult and child types of magical thinking have some similarity. They differ in the context under which they are invoked, or in details of their content, rather than in their fundamental type of thinking. It is a mistake to view the pattern of development as one in which children's magical thinking is replaced by adults' rational thinking; rather, both children and adults can think and believe rationally or magically. She discussed several ways in which the magical thinking of children and adults may differ in context and in content rather than in fundamental form. One is the cul-tural context in which magical belief is expressed: children are allowed and encouraged to do magical thinking more than adults and have their own sub-culture which contains magical ideas. In contrast, adults show magical think-ing mainly when under stress. The second difference refers to adults' superior levels of knowledge: for example, children have to learn that each fantastical entity (fairies, Father Christmas, etc.) is unreal. Also, as has previously been noted, the more children know about real causal effects of physics and science, the less they attribute events to magical causes. Related to this is the possibility that superior cognitive abilities and working memory would help adults more than children to construct natural (non-magical) causes for seemingly anoma-lous events.

The other differences are more subtle. It is possible that apparently large differences in adult versus child levels of magical thinking may be caused by posing simple yes/no questions demanding an absolute answer. In reality there may be more of a gradual shift in certainty. Perhaps children do not really believe very much more in magic than adults, but have more difficulty in dis-counting the possibility of magic and ruling it out completely. Thus, children may answer 'yes' to a question about magic even though they have a low level of belief. It should be noted that other researchers – for example, Chandler (1997) – disagree that children and adults' thinking is similar and propose that thinking follows different processes rather than merely having different content.

Several studies have directly compared magical or paranormal thinking in groups of people of different ages. Willging and Lester (1997) measured lev-els of paranormal belief in a sample of 94 adolescents with an average age of nearly 16. The most interesting finding was that scores on a measure of childhood paranormal experience were weakly correlated with present belief in life after death, but not with other aspects of present paranormal belief including extraterrestrial life and psychic phenomena. So it appears that the earlier paranormal experience had not left a strong mark on present belief. Maybe the participants reasoned that events occurring to them in early years had been outgrown and there was no reason to be swayed by them today?

Preece and Baxter (2000) surveyed over 2000 secondary school pupils aged 11 to 18 about their paranormal beliefs. For both boys and girls the level of belief declined with age and the steady decline in belief continued to postgraduate teacher trainees although there was still considerable paranormal belief in this group. The most popular forms of paranormal belief were ghosts and haunted houses, ranging from 77% in girls aged 11–14 to 31% in the teacher trainees. Peltzer (2003) also reported a decline in levels of magical belief between secondary school and university students in South Africa.

Going back many years, but still relevant, Conklin (1919) studied superstitious beliefs in college men and women aged 16–25. There were no differences by age in the number of superstitious beliefs within this age range, but 61% of those who said they currently did not believe in superstitions said they had believed in the past, suggesting that superstitious belief might decline from childhood to age 16. Maller and Lundeen (1933) observed that superstitious belief declined with age in a sample of school pupils aged 13–16.

In contrast, Glicksohn (1990) gave a sample of 72 adults aged 20–47 and a sample of 20 children all approximately 12 years old questionnaires measuring paranormal belief and subjective paranormal experience (i.e. experiences interpreted as paranormal by the individual). Adults and children gave similar answers to questionnaires, suggesting that patterns of experience and belief in the paranormal may not change appreciably between these ages.

There seems to be a broad consensus (though not always observed) that superstition and magical thinking declines with age from childhood through adolescence and into adulthood. This would be consistent with a gradual increase in scientific and logical thinking. It would also be consistent with an increasing number of negative observations of the power of magic and superstition that would rationally cause a decline in belief. There is, however, still belief in superstition and magic in adults, evident in behaviour although it may be verbally denied. It seems that scientific and logical thinking can coexist with a level of superstitious and magical thinking. The latter forms are more likely to be exhibited under stressful situations, where outcomes are uncertain, and where the stakes are high.

Legare *et al.* (2012) reviewed evidence from a number of areas that supported a radically different position to the broad consensus described previously. They argued instead that supernatural explanations often increase with age from childhood to adolescence and adulthood. Furthermore, they argued not only that natural and supernatural explanations frequently coexist in both children and adults across different cultures but that they coexist even within the same individual and are applied to explain the very same phenomenon.

They illustrate their claim with reference to explanations of the origins of life, illness, and death. To give but one example, in some South African communities contracting AIDS was simultaneously explained in terms of biology (e.g. the disease is caused by a virus) and witchcraft (e.g. witches can affect your judgement so that you make poor choices concerning sexual partners).

Superstition from childhood to adulthood

One clear point of continuity between child and adult thinking is the belief in personal and cultural superstitions that starts in childhood and persists seemingly without interruption into adulthood. This is often studied in high school, college, and university students, probably because of ease of access to large participant samples, and less often in community samples of adults.

Superstitions are ritualistic behaviours and beliefs that may be cultural (e.g. finding a four-leafed clover brings good luck), or shared (e.g. sporting teams may have their own particular rituals or songs), or they may be idiosyncratic (e.g. a lucky item of clothing or a lucky pen for taking exams). The extremely successful tennis player Bjorn Borg would not shave during a major tennis tournament because he feared it would bring bad luck. Many students bring lucky mascots and place them on the desk when sitting an exam. It is important to note the difference between a superstitious behaviour and a performance-enabling ritual. The latter serves the purpose of preparing the individual for the task ahead, perhaps by calming the nerves and allowing the individual to focus on the task in hand. In contrast, a superstition is performed to bring luck, and there is no real way for it to influence events. Thus, the meaning and origin is quite different (e.g. Bleak & Frederick, 1998).

Several studies have looked at the sources of superstitions. Conklin (1919) investigated this question in a sample of college men and women aged 16–25. Of the whole sample, 19% said their belief depended on a small number (often only one) of confirming experience; 22% said they learnt their superstitions from parents or elders; 47% acquired them through social suggestion (because associates do or for fun); 15% through social inheritance (childish credulity, never really thought about it); and 3% from books and newspapers. Altogether, social factors appeared to account for belief in superstitions in 84% of the sample. Maller and Lundeen (1933) observed that the most common sources of superstitions in school pupils aged 13–16 were – in descending order – first friends, then home, then educational establishments, and lastly personal observation. This concurs with Conklin's (1919) study in that it places forms of social learning ahead of personal experience in the acquisition of superstitions. Another consistent finding was reported by Emme (1940) who reported that parents were the largest source of superstitious beliefs, with friends and education also important.

Turning to children's superstitions, Vyse (1997) listed a similar set of sources for their acquisition: direct instruction from parents, social learning and imitation, and pressure to conform to the beliefs and behaviours of peer groups. In a rare example of a study offering direct experimental evidence, Higgins, Morris, and Johnson (1989) observed social learning of what they termed superstitious behaviour in preschool children aged three–five years. These children were shown video clips of other children performing a mean-ingless ritual with a doll and receiving marbles in exchange. The marbles were actually dispensed to a schedule unconnected with the ritual behaviour. Children in this experiment did learn to perform the same ritual as they had observed on the video, confirming the possibility of social learning of supersti-tious rituals.

Maller and Lundeen (1933) looked not only at sources for learning supersti-tions but also at sources for disconfirming superstitions. These were in direct reversal of the sources for the acquisition of superstitions: first personal obser-vation, then educational establishments, then home, and lastly friends. These researchers also calculated a 'corrective index' for each source of superstitions, as the ratio of the number of items said to be false to the number of items said to be true. A ratio of more than one suggests that the particular source tends to disconfirm rather than to confirm superstitions. The younger pupils (aver-age 13 years) had a lower corrective index than the older pupils (average 16 years), suggesting that less effort is put into correcting the superstitious beliefs of younger children. This seems broadly as one might have expected, given that parents so often actively encourage children to indulge in imagination and enter realms of fantasy. The exception was educational establishments in which the corrective index did not differ by age. Similarly, Emme (1940) reported that specific instruction reduced levels of superstitious belief.

What is of particular interest in the Maller and Lundeen (1933) study is that the corrective index for boys was higher than that for girls. This was most strongly the case for educational establishments, then for the home, and was barely apparent for friends, who were a strong source of belief for boys and girls. In other words, parents and schools put more effort into correcting the false superstitious beliefs of boys than of girls. This may be part of the tradition of expecting boys to show more interest and aptitude in science than girls. It would be natural for teachers and parents to correct the false beliefs of boys if they were expected to engage more strongly with scientific education and with potential careers. One does wonder to what degree the stronger levels of belief in most paranormal phenomena observed in women compared to men may result from early encouragement versus discouragement of superstitious belief. The answer to this question may depend on the degree to which childhood and adolescent superstition predicts adult paranormal belief, which is not clearly understood.

Vyse (1997) expressed the opinion that superstitious behaviour in children should not truly be regarded as the same as adult superstition because children lack the same critical faculties to distinguish sensible from non-sensible beliefs. It is during childhood, however, that children will learn many cultural super-stitions which they may carry forward into adulthood. Perhaps children may also acquire a general attitude towards the possibility of influencing outcomes by seemingly unconnected rituals and this may make them prone to acquiring superstitions later in life. This kind of process could explain the connection between failure of adults to disconfirm superstitious beliefs in girls (relative to boys) and higher levels of paranormal belief in women (compared to men). There is more on this topic in Chapter 2 which deals generally with individual differences.

There are several reasons why children might have more superstitions than adults. They have necessarily had less experience and opportunity to learn that their superstitions are not realistic; Emme (1940), for example, documents the disconfirming effect of experience. There is also an effect of specific instruction from parents and from educational establishments that will tend to be stronger in older children and adults than in younger children. Perhaps also children have less control over their own lives than adults and so seek to compensate by indulging in illusory means of achieving some degree of control.

The illusion of control seems to be the key to understanding superstition; in particular, the desire to achieve more control over an event that contains a large element of uncontrollability or unpredictability (e.g. Bleak & Frederick, 1998; Vyse, 1997). This could explain observations that soldiers are particularly prone to superstition (e.g. Vyse, 1997). It could also explain the high level of superstition among sportsmen and -women (e.g. Bleak & Frederick, 1998; Burger & Lynn, 2005; Vyse, 1997). In all these cases, there is an opposing force with conflicting objectives that imposes a large degree of uncertainty and uncontrollability over the outcome of a contest. Sica, Novara, and Sanavio (2002) found that superstitious students tended to estimate the level of threats more highly than non-superstitious students, confirming the role of perceived threat in the maintenance of superstitious beliefs.

It seems that superstitiousness is quite common in children and in adults. Belief is acquired mostly through social processes from peers and families. In contrast, belief is disconfirmed through direct experience and by educational establishments. The observation made by Maller and Lundeen (1933) that boys were discouraged from believing in superstition to a greater extent than girls could link with the higher levels of paranormal belief that have been observed in women than in men (see Chapter 2) but this would need to be confirmed with a modern study.

The relationship between childhood magical thinking and obsessive-compulsive disorder

It has been proposed that there might be a connection between the kind of magical thinking that occurs in childhood and OCD, a condition that may arise in late childhood, adolescence, or adulthood. OCD is characterized by intrusive thoughts of terrible events – for example, illness or harm to a loved one – which bring great distress to the individual. As described in Chapter 3, people who experience these intrusive thoughts may then engage in compulsive rituals in the belief that they will prevent the adverse events from occurring.

OCD includes the belief that thoughts can cause events to occur and this forms an obvious connection with magical thinking. The belief is sometimes known as thought–action fusion (see, for example, Evans *et al.*, 2002). The use of compulsive rituals to ward off disaster in OCD is also reminiscent of the use of superstitious rituals to ward off bad luck or to bring good luck. The major difference is the obsessive nature of the thoughts and the compulsive nature of the rituals in OCD which can interfere severely with daily life. The desire to perform magical and superstitious rituals is less frequent, less intense, and more easily dismissed than in OCD, while the rituals themselves interfere less with daily life (e.g. Evans *et al.*, 2002). Regardless of this difference, the similarity in concept between superstition and OCD raises the possibility that OCD may be the adult or extreme expression of developmentally normal magical thinking. There are estimates that some degree of rituals, compulsions and intrusive thoughts are present in over 80% of the adult population (e.g. Rachman & de Silva, 1978).

Children first acquire rituals around two years and can be very upset – for example, throwing a temper tantrum – if they are prevented from performing them, suggesting a high level of subjective distress. Rituals decline once the child starts school. Perhaps children learn more normative behaviours from their peers and hence the use of rituals diminishes, or perhaps there are so many more exciting things to do than carry out their rituals. However, the insistence on rituals still persists in children with fears and phobias (e.g. Evans *et al.*, 2002) and so may be a response to higher levels of anxiety.

A number of studies have specifically investigated links between magical thinking and OCD in children. The Bolton *et al.* (2002) study of 127 schoolchildren aged from five up to 16 found that magical thinking was related to obsessive-compulsive thinking more than to other forms of anxiety. In boys, there were weaker relationships with other forms of anxiety and in girls there were no other relationships and magical thinking was associated only with obsessive-compulsive thinking. However, sample sizes in each gender and age range were small, so perhaps weak relationships with other forms of anxiety might exist. As noted in Chapter 3, Zebb and Moore (2003) found superstitiousness to correlate with both OCD tendencies and other measures of psychological distress in a sample of female students although no such correlations were found for male students.

In contrast, Leonard *et al.* (1990) found that children with OCD were no more superstitious than non-clinically referred children. They also concluded that differences in timings and context of the OCD symptoms and superstitious behaviour argued against the view that OCD is on a continuum with superstition. Similarly, Simonds, Demetre, and Read (2009) interviewed 102 non-clinical children aged between five and ten. General belief in magical causation was associated with various forms of anxiety but not specifically OCD, and the association was only for boys, not for girls. So the level of magical thinking did not distinguish between OCD and other forms of anxiety.

Evans *et al.* (2002) interviewed 31 children about their beliefs concerning magic and wishes. Children's magical beliefs, particularly their beliefs about the efficacy of wishing, were related to their parents' assessment of their use of rituals and compulsions. Thus, normal compulsive behaviours had some relation to magical beliefs and wishing. These compulsive behaviours included rituals for mealtimes and bedtime, likes and dislikes, and arranging objects precisely. These behaviours also occur in pervasive developmental disorders and in OCD but at a higher and more problematic level.

Taking all this evidence into account, it seems possible, but not confirmed, that magical thinking in childhood may be linked to the later incidence of OCD. The conceptual similarity between beliefs about the power of magical thought and wishing, and the thought–action fusion that is found in OCD, lead to the expectation that a link might exist. More research would be needed before a definite conclusion could be reached. It is to be hoped that the research will be carried out if only because of the possibility that encouragement of magical thinking in children, or the failure to discourage such behaviour, might help to foster problematic behaviours in adults.

The psychodynamic functions hypothesis

This was first proposed by Irwin (1992) and has been developed further by Irwin and others. The original PFH proposed that paranormal belief is an attempt to impose a sense of control over life events by people who have feelings of helplessness, insecurity, and lack of control resulting from some childhood trauma. The need for a sense of control can, in an individual who is highly fantasy-prone, lead to belief in the paranormal and to subjective paranormal experiences. For example, astrology, precognitive dreams, and other methods of predicting the future, as well as concepts of fate in general and superstition, provide some assurance of future events which helps to stem the fear of unpredictability and lack of control. Kennedy (2007) discusses how the need for control in an uncertain world can predispose towards belief in aspects of paranormal phenomena, especially those that offer some promise of control, or at least understanding, of the seemingly random forces that influence the events in our lives.

There are clearly several lines of evidence that could support this PFH. One: that people who have suffered childhood abuse have an elevated need for a sense of control over life events, and that belief in the paranormal provides that sense of control. Two: that childhood abuse is linked to fantasy-proneness in adulthood. Three: that fantasy-proneness in adulthood is linked to paranormal belief. These connections will be examined separately.

Several studies offer evidence supporting the proposition that people who had abusive or traumatic childhoods have a need to acquire a sense of control over life events and that paranormal belief can provide that sense of control. People who believe more strongly in the paranormal have a greater need for control (e.g. Irwin, 1992; Keinan, 1994) and this may be especially true for women (e.g. Irwin, 2000b). Believers may also have a stronger, though illusory, feeling that they are in control of events in the context of games of chance (e.g. Blackmore & Trościanko, 1985; Joukhador, Blaszczynski, & MacCallum, 2004; Rudski, 2003; Tobacyk & Wilkinson, 1991). Other studies offer wider evidence that belief in the paranormal may confer a sense of general control. For example, Kennedy (2007) proposed that belief in psi may give the believer a sense of control and efficacy, especially in social situations, and it may help to foster a sense of meaning or purpose in life. Perkins and Allen (2006) suggested that certain paranormal beliefs, including psi, precognition, and spiritualism, may offer emotional comfort to adult survivors of childhood abuse by giving a sense of control. In addition, several studies have observed higher levels of paranormal belief in adults who report that, as children, they experienced physical or sexual abuse (e.g. Irwin, 1992; Lawrence *et al.*, 1995; Perkins & Allen, 2006; Ross & Joshi, 1992) or alcoholic parents (Irwin, 1994a).

Turning to the link between reports of abuse in childhood and fantasy-proneness in adulthood, several studies have found a connection (e.g. Irwin, 1994c; Lynn & Rhue, 1988; Sanders, McRoberts, & Tollefson, 1989, regarding the related concept of dissociation; Wilson & Barber, 1983). Indirectly, Irwin (1991a) reported that people with a higher level of fantasy-proneness also reported poorer psychological functioning as would be a common consequence of suffering abuse in childhood.

The third claim, that fantasy-proneness is associated with paranormal belief and experience, is well supported, as shown by the evidence reviewed in Chapter 2. To summarize briefly, there is a cluster of personality facets including fantasy-proneness, absorption, hypnotic susceptibility (Chapter 2), and dissociation (Chapter 3), which all have in common that they include the ability to enter a world of imagination and to sense it strongly and without distraction. All of these personality facets have been related to belief in paranormal phenomena and belief that the individual has had a personal paranormal experience, especially out-of-body and near-death experiences (see Chapter 5), and UFO and alien contact experiences (see Chapter 9). However, fantasy-proneness is not related only to these specific types of paranormal experience but to the whole range of paranormal experiences and paranormal beliefs. For example, Irwin (1990) found a link between fantasy-proneness and belief in psi, witchcraft, spiritualism, extraordinary life forms, and precognition, and this was verified by Irwin (1991a).

It is rare to find a study offering direct experimental evidence of a connection between fantasy-proneness and susceptibility to a novel paranormal belief; one such study was that reported by Woolley *et al.* (2004), described earlier in this chapter. As noted, children aged three–five were introduced to a new fantastical entity known as the Candy Witch (designed to be non-frightening, along the lines of the Tooth Fairy, the Easter Bunny, and Father Christmas). Those children with higher fantasy orientation, who indulged in more pretend play, and had more belief in fantastical creatures and more imaginary companions, came to believe more strongly in the Candy Witch. This relationship between fantasy orientation and belief in the Candy Witch was maintained for a year and was apparent in a follow-up interview. Other studies reporting a relationship between fantasy-proneness and paranormal experience or paranormal belief were discussed in Chapter 2.

An extensive study by Lawrence *et al.* (1995) sought to investigate all of the steps of the PFH. This study gave questionnaires to 80 participants on paranormal belief and experience, childhood fantasy, and childhood trauma. A statistical technique known as Structural Equation Modelling suggested a model of causal influence from childhood trauma to childhood fantasy to paranormal experience to paranormal belief, and a direct link from childhood trauma to paranormal experience (please refer to Figure 4.1). Contrary to Irwin's model, there was only a small direct link from childhood fantasy to paranormal belief and the model provided a better fit to the data when this direct link was dropped. Thus, it is possible that fantasy-proneness exerts its influence on paranormal belief only through paranormal experience. It is also worth noting that in this model paranormal belief resulted from, rather than causing, paranormal experience. So these participants tended to believe in the paranormal because they had experienced some phenomena rather than the belief arising first and allowing the experience to be interpreted as paranormal.

So far, there seems to be a good body of support for the PFH. So let us consider ways in which the hypothesis might be extended. One way relates to the observation that people who have suffered childhood abuse may be socially lonely with few family and friends and this might also dispose them towards paranormal belief. For example, ESP might offer a sense of connection with other people and other places and that helps to alleviate feelings of loneliness. The belief that one has experienced some paranormal phenomenon might foster a sense of kinship and common purpose with other people having had the same experiences. Membership of a group dedicated to exploring paranormal phenomena, whether formal or informal, would lessen the sense of social isolation: for example, a group of **UFOlogists** might meet up regularly or there might be an astrology course with regular weekly classes. Consultation with a psychic or medium could provide comfort and consolation to a person in distress.

There is some evidence to support this extension to the PFH. Several studies have suggested that feelings of loneliness can result from childhood trauma

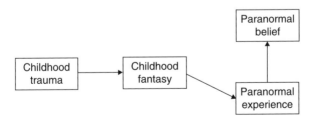

Figure 4.1 A simplified version of the psychodynamic functions hypothesis (e.g. Irwin, 2009) showing the relationships found to be significant in Lawrence *et al.* (1995)

(e.g. Gibson & Hartshorne, 1996; Rew, 2002; Tyler, 2002). A number of studies have found that people with a stronger sense of social alienation also tend to have stronger paranormal belief (Emmons & Sobal, 1981; Tobacyk, 1985; Tobacyk & Pirttila-Backman, 1992; Wuthnow, 1976). This extension of the PFH also fits with the observation that women tend to believe in most paranormal phenomena more strongly than men (explored in Chapter 2). Women generally have a greater desire for a sense of social connectedness and seek to have many sources of social support (e.g. Kennedy, 2007).

A comprehensive study examined the whole model that links childhood trauma with paranormal belief. Rogers, Qualter, and Phelps (2007) found that participants who had experienced more childhood trauma had higher levels of fantasy-proneness and were more socially lonely, that is, had fewer friends. Both of these factors – fantasy-proneness and social loneliness – led to higher levels of global paranormal belief. It is worth noting that survivors of childhood trauma were particularly likely to endorse paranormal beliefs if they were also highly fantasy-prone. The combination of these two factors, childhood trauma and fantasy-proneness, was associated with the highest levels of paranormal belief. This provides clear support for the PFH.

Irwin (2009) expanded the PFH to include adults who have experienced any perceived lack of control in childhood, not necessarily a specific trauma. Other factors contributing to a perceived lack of control in childhood might be having older siblings or authoritarian parents who tried to exercise a great deal of control over the child's life and allowed the child little voice in decision-making. Parents who were overprotective or intrusive could also make a child feel a lack of personal control. Also, parents who behave inconsistently, or who are emotionally cold and rejecting, could prevent a child from learning a sense of mastery (Irwin, 2009). People with these experiences are theorized to feel the need for a sense of control or mastery over their adult lives which leads them to develop a set of beliefs – that is, paranormal beliefs – to offer that sense of control.

To investigate this extension to the PFH, Watt, Watson, and Wilson (2007) gave questionnaires measuring perceived childhood control and paranormal belief to 127 adults. They found that higher levels of paranormal belief were associated with lower levels of perceived childhood control – that is, there was a negative association. This offers direct support for the expanded PFH and strengthens the proposition that experiences of reduced control in childhood require a psychological coping mechanism which, for some, may be paranormal belief. Irwin (2009) also noted that paranormal belief might result not from parental abuse as such, but from the fact that abuse is more likely to occur in a family environment which is chaotic or unpredictable. It might be this chaos and unpredictability which prevents a child from developing an appropriate sense of personal control. Further evidence was offered by Granqvist and Hagekull (2001) who found that New Age belief was higher in their (Swedish) participants who reported that they were insecurely attached to their parents.

Ideas to think about

What is the connection between the theory that an abusive or overly controlling childhood may lead to subsequent belief in the paranormal, and the concept of an external locus of control?

A word of warning should be given. Even though there is evidence that an aversive or overly controlled childhood is associated with stronger paranormal belief in adulthood, this does not establish the precise means by which the former causes the latter. All of the research is necessarily correlational – meaning that it examines differences that already exist between individuals, and relationships that already exist between different aspects of personality and beliefs. There is no direct empirical evidence that manipulating experience of childhood abuse or sense of personal control causes the individual to develop a fantasy-prone personality. Neither is there any direct evidence that a fantasy-prone personality results in higher levels of paranormal belief. Such direct evidence is necessarily lacking for the very good reason that it would be unethical to cause trauma or a perceived lack of personal control in a child (or an adult, come to that). Because of the nature of the research and the resulting evidence, we must always bear in mind that some other factor could be responsible for the relationships that we have observed.

For example, given the likelihood that an abusive or overly controlling childhood would lead to elevated levels of depression or anxiety, it is possible that these factors mediate the relationship between childhood circumstances and paranormal belief, rather than fantasy-proneness. Evidence was examined in Chapter 3 that paranormal beliefs are more common in people who suffer from neuroticism and negative mood so this model is plausible. Chorpita and Barlow (1998) explain that early experience of diminished control could lead to a general tendency to perceive events as outside one's control. This would be likely to lead to greater anxiety, which could generate a pervasive tendency to seek a sense of control wherever this may be found. In a controlled experiment, Presson and Benassi (2003) showed that students who were higher in depressive symptoms were more likely to perceive illusory control over a series of events that was actually random. It was especially interesting that this occurred only when the aspect of illusory control was presented in the form of psychokinesis or precognition and did not occur in the absence of a paranormal explanation.

It is not possible to rule out the alternative explanation based on anxiety and depression for the connection between aversive childhood circumstances and adult paranormal belief. The inability to perform direct experimental studies means that the door must remain open to alternative accounts. This applies to any hypothesis for which the evidence is almost entirely correlational.

Having said this, it should be noted that the possibility of a connection based on neuroticism and negative affect does not offer an alternative to the PFH so much as a way of extending the hypothesis. If paranormal belief in adulthood is a means of coping with the depression and anxiety that may be the long-lasting effects of an abusive or overly controlling childhood, then this would certainly fit within the outline of the PFH. The adult is using paranormal belief to fulfil a psychodynamic need arising from adverse childhood circumstances.

Ideas to think about

The evidence reviewed in Chapter 2 suggests that belief in external forces or fate controlling one's outcomes (e.g. astrology, superstition, precognition, ghosts, and spiritualism) is sometimes higher in socially excluded groups, including the unemployed and those unable to work; the divorced, separated, and widowed; black rather than white US Americans; and the young rather than the old. Perhaps groups who experience uncertainly about their future and their place in society are more vulnerable to types of belief that may suggest to them that outcomes are already decided and that the individual has little power over events (e.g. Torgler, 2007). How does this relate to the PFH?

Given this body of evidence that people whose childhoods were traumatic or lacking in a sense of personal control are more likely to believe in the paranormal, it is relevant to ask whether paranormal belief does, in fact, offer any sense of control. This point is not at all clear-cut. Kennedy (2003) noted that the most common aftermath of a paranormal experience is an increase in feelings of spirituality, rather than a feeling of control over life events and circumstances. Indeed, a strong characteristic of research into psi phenomena is the apparent difficulty of controlling these phenomena, and this is often taken to imply that psi powers are inherently hard to control. This reasoning challenges the idea that belief in psi offers the individual a sense of control. This argument could easily be extended to paranormal phenomena in general and not only to psi, since spiritualism, witchcraft, precognition, and extraordinary life forms would seem to be as hard to control as psi powers. Further, if women more than men desire connectedness, and men more than women desire control, then both of these are consistent with the higher levels of psi and other paranormal beliefs in women. The lack of controllability of paranormal phenomena would explain their relative lack of appeal to men and the reported spiritual effects of psi experiences would explain their appeal to women.

Better support for the PFH comes from studies into superstition as a protection against learned helplessness. As described in Chapter 3, Dudley (1999) and Matute (1994, 1995) offered direct experimental evidence that people faced with an impossible task, or those in an aversive situation with no means of control, were less likely to succumb to learned helplessness if they believed in superstitions. This clearly places superstition as a form of paranormal belief that can protect against feelings of helplessness in the face of aversive circumstances that offer no way out. It seems plausible that this would link childhood trauma or perceived lack of personal control with adult belief in superstition. Irwin (2009) noted that even if people realize that they actually have little control over events, the vaguest hope that some supernatural means of control does exist could provide some comfort. In addition, Fitzpatrick and Shook (1994) showed that self-esteem in college students was associated with higher levels of belief in superstition, which might suggest that superstitious beliefs help to maintain positive self-esteem. Further evidence along these lines comes from a study by Lillqvist and Lindeman (1998) in which interest in astrology, as measured by enrolment in a college course, was associated with a higher belief in personal control over life events. It is also relevant that participants in this study (whether enrolled on the astrology course or a different course) had a higher level of interest in astrology if they had experienced a greater number of recent crises. So this study supports both the link between aversive events and paranormal belief, and the link between paranormal belief and fostering a sense of control. What these studies do not help to explain is why an aversive or controlling childhood would be associated with the wide range of paranormal beliefs and not only with superstition or astrology. Thus, this can only be a partial explanation for some forms of paranormal belief.

Perhaps paranormal belief can be seen as a coping strategy to deal with life's problems. When challenges are too difficult to tackle, rather than dwelling on the stress and anxiety they cause, an alternative is to use a strategy of avoidance. Faced with a problem, one option is to turn away and use distracting techniques to avoid feelings of stress. By turning attention to other ideas, people can distract themselves from their current problems and concerns and so avoid feelings of anxiety and inadequacy. Investigating this possibility, Callaghan and Irwin (2003) found a weak relationship between belief in the paranormal and use of the avoidant coping strategy. Paranormal belief was also linked with non-use of the task-oriented strategy that involves actively trying to overcome problems. They concluded that paranormal believers try to deny their distress or distract themselves from facing up to it. This would suggest that paranormal belief helps the individual mainly by distracting them from their problems. Rogers et al. (2006) also investigated the idea that belief in the paranormal may be akin to an avoidant coping strategy for dealing with stress, that is, using fantasy-based distraction as a technique. They found that active-behavioural coping predicted lower levels of paranormal belief and avoidant coping was weakly related to higher levels of paranormal belief. Both of these effects interacted with emotional intelligence in a complex pattern and the relationships were all weak.

So it does appear that paranormal belief may help people to cope with the negative emotion caused by life's difficulties and challenges by a strategy of avoidance. There is one problem, though, for the PFH: Rogers et al. (2006) noted that this doesn't fit very well with Irwin's (1992) idea that paranormal belief is used to give the individual an illusory feeling of control. The avoidance strategy seems unlikely to lead to a heightened sense of control over events and outcomes.

Perhaps the individual who entertains belief in the paranormal is seeking for understanding and acceptance of life rather than control. As suggested by Rogers *et al.* (2006), paranormal believers may use their beliefs to reinterpret the experiences they find distressing in an attempt to make them more meaningful and less threatening. This could be considered as more of an active coping strategy than an avoidant one. For example, the belief that events and outcomes are predestined and so cannot be altered might help an individual to accept the adversities they faced in childhood. A belief in reincarnation could help an individual to accept an abusive childhood through the idea that their experiences are part of what they need to learn in the present incarnation. Accepting that powerful forces or entities have control over one's life is a means of denying blame and responsibility for failures and mistakes. This could serve to protect the fragile ego of a person who suffered abuse in childhood. Evidence consistent with this possibility was offered by Fitzpatrick and Shook (1994) who observed that superstitiousness and belief in precognition (both potential ways of placing blame for failures outside the individual) were related to higher levels of self-esteem.

Many researchers and theorists (e.g. Irwin, 1991a, 2003, 2009; Lindeman, 1998; Presson & Benassi, 1996) have noted that humans have a need to understand themselves and the world around them and to have a belief that the world is meaningful (see also Hutson, 2012). An assurance that there is order and meaning in the world helps to foster good psychological functioning, as opposed to a belief that all is random and meaningless that can foster hopelessness and helplessness. Thus a system of paranormal belief may help the individual by offering to make sense of their life. Irwin (1991a) also points out that it is not necessary for the paranormal belief system to be correct or verifiable, merely that it is perceived as plausible is enough to fulfil its function of providing psychological security. Irwin (2003) offered evidence from a questionnaire study that level of belief in the paranormal was related to the view that the world is a meaningful place. This was interpreted as meaning that paranormal beliefs can function as a defence mechanism against the fear of a random and unpredictable world.

So perhaps the control that paranormal believers are seeking is not a literal form of control, but rather an intellectual mastery and an understanding of life's major events (Irwin, 2009). This raises an analogy with the magical thinking of children that is used to account for physical anomalies inexplicable by current scientific knowledge or knowledge of conjuring tricks. If this is the case, then it provides something of a link between childhood beliefs in magic and adult belief in paranormal phenomena; both serve the function of helping to understand an otherwise mysterious world.

To summarize: although there is good evidence to link an aversive or overly controlled childhood with fantasy-proneness and paranormal belief, there is no compelling case for a particular causal connection. Also, it is not at all clear that paranormal belief provides the sense of control that is central to the PFH and, with the exception of superstition, it seems unlikely that paranormal belief actually provides much sense of control. In addition, paranormal belief is associated with avoidant rather than active coping strategies. It is possible that paranormal belief may provide a means of understanding and accepting life rather than trying to control it, though confirmation of this idea must await the results of further research. This would provide a link with children's magical thinking.

Suggested further reading

For more on the psychodynamic functions hypothesis:

Irwin, H. J. (2009). *The psychology of paranormal belief: A researcher's handbook.* Hatfield, UK: University of Hertfordshire Press. Chapter 7, pp. 91–106.

For information about magic and superstitions in general:

Vyse, S. A. (1997). *Magical thinking: The psychology of superstition.* Oxford: Oxford University Press.

For a discussion of magical thinking among children:

Subbotsky, E. (2004b). 'Magical thinking – Reality or illusion?' *The Psychologist*, 17, 336–9.
Woolley, J. D. (1997b). 'Thinking about fantasy: Are children fundamentally different thinkers and believers from adults?' *Child Development*, 68, 991–1011.

Psychobiological
Perspectives

5

Introduction

There are several types of anomalous experiences for which causal explanations involving psychobiological processes have been proposed. What is common to these explanations is the idea that some individuals have particularly active, or variable, neural (brain) systems that produce anomalous physical and psychological sensations. The individual seeks an explanation for these sensations and may combine them with culturally appropriate accounts to produce a subjective anomalous experience. The individual may believe that they have experienced a genuinely paranormal event, not knowing that there may be a conventional neurological explanation.

The anomalous experiences considered in this chapter include: hallucination, a perceptual experience in the absence of appropriate external stimulation; a sense of presence when there is no other person actually present; OBE, in which the individual feels that their sense of self is located outside their body and sees the world from a different perspective; NDE, in which an individual close to physical death experiences sensations and perceptions sometimes associated with an afterlife; and sleep paralysis, which is discussed more fully as a contributing factor to the alien abduction experience in Chapter 9. These experiences may all be termed *subjective paranormal experiences* to indicate that they often seem to have a paranormal quality to the individual having the experience, but we are not sure that they necessarily have a paranormal cause. There are frequently several competing explanations for the same anomalous phenomenon and it is entirely possible that several neural processes may combine in order to produce a particular experience. There are usually nonpsychobiological explanations for the same anomalous experiences and some of these will also be described and considered in this chapter.

Subjective paranormal experiences appear to be quite common in the general population. For example, around 10% of the population claim to have had an OBE (Alvarado, 2000) and 10–15% claim to have had a hallucinatory experience (e.g. Bentall & Slade, 1985; Poulton *et al.*, 2000; Tien, 1991; see

Chapter 3). Some studies estimate that up to 20% of people who experience cardiac arrest and are resuscitated may have an NDE (Greyson, 2003). Sleep paralysis may be experienced by up to 50% of the population at some time (French & Santomauro, 2007; Santomauro & French, 2009). So the experiences discussed in this chapter are likely to be familiar to many of our readers.

The first sections of this chapter are organized around the psychobiological processes that are offered as potential causal explanations of anomalous experiences. These are **REM (rapid eye movement) sleep** intrusions into the waking state, general background level of cortical arousal, temporal lobe hyperactivity and lability, neural interconnectedness and transliminality, and hemispheric dominance. The OBE and NDE are discussed as separate sections because of their complexity and their relationship to multiple causal explanations.

Many of the psychobiological theories about what causes these anomalous experiences are rather new and much of the research is also very recent. Although these experiences have been around for all of recorded history, it is only very recently that we have been able to offer scientific rather than mystical or supernatural explanations. Let us hope that we will continue to deepen and consolidate our understanding of these strange and interesting experiences.

REM sleep intrusions into the waking state

Sleep paralysis occurs when a person is falling asleep (the **hypnagogic** state) or waking up (the **hypnopompic** state). It seems to be an intrusion of some of the aspects of REM sleep (or Stage 1 sleep, according to McCreery, 2008) into the waking state. It is a surprisingly common experience and is often quite frightening, being characterized by the inability to move which may be accompanied by difficulty in breathing and by a sense of presence which may be combined with visual and auditory hallucinations (e.g. Adler, 2011; French & Santomauro, 2007; Santomauro & French, 2009). The individual is wide awake and can open their eyes but cannot move any other part of their body. It is believed that the paralysis that exists during sleep, to stop us from acting out our dreams, persists for a few minutes when we awake (the hypnopompic state) or starts a little while before we enter the dreaming state of consciousness (the hypnagogic state) in episodes of sleep paralysis. Given that the sleeping state comprises several changes in the body and the brain, it seems plausible that sometimes these aspects may get out of step with each other.

Hallucinations seem to be a very frequent part of the experience, occurring in around 75% of participants who suffered from sleep paralysis (Cheyne, Newby-Clark, & Rueffer, 1999). These can be visual, perhaps seeing a person or other being; auditory, hearing breathing, talking, or humming sounds; tactile, perhaps a sense of pressure or touching; or proprioceptive – for example, a sense of floating, being lifted up, or an OBE. An episode of sleep paralysis is often interpreted as a malevolent entity trying to suffocate the individual (e.g. Adler, 2011; French, 2011a; French & Santomauro, 2007; Santomauro & French, 2009), such as a ghost or a demon.

Sleep paralysis, as discussed in detail in Chapter 9, is also a contributory factor in explaining claims of alien abduction. Although explicit hallucinations of aliens are quite rare during a sleep paralysis episode, many UFOlogists claim that if you have experienced the symptoms described, you have probably been abducted by aliens but that they have then 'wiped' your memory about the details of the abduction. If the individual believes this explanation of their anomalous experience, they may decide to undergo **hypnotic regression** in a misguided attempt to 'recover' the memory. Then they may well end up with a detailed memory of having been abducted by aliens which they wrongly take to be an accurate memory of a real event whereas in fact it is a false memory.

Indeed, individuals who believe they have experienced an encounter with an alien or have been abducted and taken aboard a spaceship are more likely to suffer from sleep paralysis than those who have no such beliefs (French et al., 2008; Holden & French, 2002; McNally & Clancy, 2005). Thus, sleep paralysis may be a contributory factor in many alien abduction experiences. While it might seem fanciful to suppose that one has been abducted by aliens, this does at least provide some explanation for the sleep paralysis which can be a very frightening experience. In the absence of any knowledge of a scientific explanation, and in a culture which indulges in fictional accounts of alien encounters, this might seem like the best available explanation. This observation points to a need for greater awareness of sleep paralysis among the general population and more knowledge of its underlying causes (Santomauro & French, 2009).

McCreery (2008) makes a connection between dreaming and psychotic episodes, noting the similar phenomenology. He proposes that some individuals may experience 'micro-sleeps' which are brief intrusions of sleep into the waking state. These intrusions may result in the experience of seemingly realistic hallucinations which are hard to distinguish from reality. This might be particularly likely in individuals who are highly fantasy-prone or who are likely to dissociate (see Chapters 2, 3, and 4 for discussion of these traits).

There is not yet conclusive evidence for the idea that sleep intrusions into the waking state are responsible for sleep paralysis or hallucinations (Appelle, Lynn, & Newman, 2000) but this is a plausible and interesting theory. The power to potentially explain some relatively common anomalous experiences makes this a possibility worthy of investigation.

Cortical arousal

Anomalous experiences, including precognition, psychic experiences, and OBEs, have been linked with the personality trait of extraversion (e.g. Gallagher, Kumar, & Pekala, 1994; MacDonald, 2000; Maltby & Day, 2001a, 2001b). As described in Chapter 2, extraversion has several components including: sociability, the desire to enjoy the company of others; sensation seeking, the desire to have new and stimulating experiences; and impulsivity, being spontaneous and likely to act on an urge (e.g. Costa & McCrae, 1995). Eysenck (1967) originally proposed that extraverts tend to be cortically under-aroused and so they seek out stimulating experiences to raise their level of cortical arousal to a more subjectively optimal level. The search for cortical stimulation could lead extraverts to seek out certain practices and situations in which subjective paranormal experiences may be more common. For example, extraverts might be more likely to take psychedelic drugs (Gallagher, Kumar, & Pekala, 1994; Maltby & Day, 2001a, 2001b), or visit a professional psychic or medium, or attempt to learn how to perform feats including astral travel (OBE). So having low cortical arousal might make extraverts more likely to have subjective paranormal experiences.

As an alternative explanation, Eysenck (1967) proposed that low cortical arousal might make it easier for extraverts to detect a weak signal of telepathy or precognition. A weak stimulus is more easily detected against a less noisy background and there is some support for the idea that extraverts may perform better in tasks involving psi (e.g. Honorton, Ferrari, & Bem, 1992).

Lots of studies have looked at the personality trait of sensation seeking. As defined by Zuckerman (1994), this includes the tendency to be interested in ideas that are not part of the mainstream and to be motivated to explore strange forces, which could clearly predispose an individual towards paranormal belief and anomalous experience (see Chapter 2). Gallagher, Kumar, and Pekala (1994) reported that certain aspects or types of sensation seeking were correlated with the tendency to have anomalous experiences. This tended to be the internal side of sensation seeking which consists of seeking novel experiences, unusual daydreams and fantasies, and internally generated feelings, rather than drug-taking or general thrill-seeking. So, perhaps anomalous experiences are more likely to occur to someone who enjoys a rich internal fantasy life. Irwin (2009) theorized that people who have repeated anomalous experiences are sociable but also like to engage in rich and vivid internal fantasy rather than seek out external stimulation. This is consistent with the idea that people with higher levels of paranormal beliefs and experiences are more fantasy-prone (see Chapter 2).

It is tempting to speculate whether this inclination to engage in internal fantasy might be associated with the tendency to accept an imaginary event as a real event. For example, Bentall and Slade (1985) reported that people who scored high on a scale measuring predisposition to have hallucinations, compared to those who scored low, were more likely to falsely report a weak auditory signal. The authors concluded that people who tend to have hallucinations do not perform reality testing well and are more likely to accept an imaginary event as a real event.

These studies linking the personality traits of extraversion and sensation seeking to anomalous and paranormal experience are all correlational and retrospective, so other factors could be responsible for the observed associations. Perhaps the association is due to a tendency to pay more attention to unusual experiences and to interpret mildly anomalous experiences in unusual ways rather than to actually have such experiences more frequently than others. It is also interesting to note that although the association seems to be reasonably consistent (e.g. Irwin, 2009), the correlations are also typically quite weak so that only a small proportion of variation in anomalous experience can be explained by these personality traits.

Temporal lobe hyperactivity

It has been consistently reported that a relatively high level of activity in the temporal lobes of the brain is associated with reports of paranormal and mystical experiences. These include a sense of presence when no one is in the room, apparitions, OBEs, or a sense that one is the focus of some special significance, perhaps being given a special revelation or a mission to accomplish (e.g. Booth, Koren, & Persinger, 2005; Cook & Persinger, 1997, 2001; Fenwick, 2001; Meli & Persinger, 2009). A relatively high level of activity in the temporal lobes could be due to a number of different causes: temporal lobe epilepsy; stimulation of the temporal lobe in a normal brain – for example, through transcranial magnetic stimulation (TMS); acquired injury in the temporal lobe; or simply naturally occurring variability within the population. Patients with temporal lobe epilepsy are particularly likely to report frequent mystical experiences (e.g. Persinger, 2001).

In an attempt to account for spontaneous reports of mystical experiences in the general population, Persinger and Makarec (1987) proposed that major complex partial epileptic signs (CPES), somewhat similar to temporal lobe epilepsy but on a weaker scale, may be distributed widely in the general population. They proposed that many people have non-convulsive experiences similar to, but less intense than, those of patients with temporal lobe epilepsy. To investigate this idea, over 400 participants completed the extensive 140-item Personal Philosophy Inventory which measures, among other things, indications of temporal lobe hyperactivity, for example: 'Sometimes an event will occur that has special significance for me only' and 'I have had a vision'. The results showed that many people not diagnosed with epilepsy seem to have a level of hyperactivity in their temporal lobe which could generate the occasional 'micro-seizure' lying on a continuum with clinical epileptic seizures. Particularly interesting was the observation of a clear relationship between the frequency of mystical experiences (e.g., a sense of oneness and connectedness, or a sense of presence when there is no on in the room) and indications of temporal lobe hyperactivity derived from responses to the Personal Philosophy Inventory (PPI).

This theory suggests that hyperactivity in the temporal lobe, of a subclinical level, may be responsible for some spontaneous anomalous experiences in the general population. Interestingly, some events that are believed to be associated with apparitions, including meditation, fasting and hypoglycaemia, fatigue, lack of oxygen, use of mind-altering drugs, and the neurochemical changes associated with bereavement are also known to affect temporal lobe activity (Persinger & Makarec, 1987). The appearance of apparitions of the deceased person to a recently bereaved individual is relatively common (e.g. 14% of the people sampled by Rees, 1971).

Why would temporal lobe hyperactivity be associated with mystical experiences? Persinger (2001) proposed that these experiences stem from a tendency to associate unusual sensory experiences with enhanced meaning for the individual. This could arise from a more active functioning of the amygdala which associates emotion with external objects and events, resulting in more frequent experiences in which an event appears to have deep personal significance. Common themes are the perception that one has been selected by a powerful entity or has been given a special purpose in life. Persinger (2001, pp. 515–16) proposed that 'the deep personal or emotional significance of a paranormal experience is a predictable property of a labile amygdala processing unusual perceptual events'. It is likely that a weakness in reality monitoring would also play a part.

The association of temporal lobe hyperactivity and lability with mystical and anomalous experiences seems well attested. But Persinger has gone further to try to offer an explanation for the appearance of various phenomena associated with ghosts and hauntings – for example, the appearance of apparitions and the sense of presence. This explanation is supported by the results of experimental work conducted by Persinger and colleagues (e.g. Persinger, 2003). The proposal is that fluctuations in the earth's background magnetic field can interact with the temporal lobe, especially in individuals with a particularly sensitive temporal lobe, to produce a sense of a presence and visual hallucinations. Persinger's experiments with colleagues have documented that a sense of presence can be reliably evoked by applying weak magnetic fields (less than one micro-Tesla) in a complex temporal pattern to the temporal lobe in the right hemisphere and then to both hemispheres. According to Persinger, this encourages the left hemisphere to incorporate and interpret the representation created by the right hemisphere (e.g. Booth, Koren, & Persinger, 2005; Cook & Persinger, 2001; Meli & Persinger, 2009). These laboratory-based, experimental studies are especially relevant in that they typically compare periods of time in which the temporal lobes were stimulated with periods in which they were not stimulated to try to rule out the effects of expectation on the occurrence of subjective paranormal and mystical experiences.

This explanation offers the intriguing possibility that such transcerebral magnetic stimulation may lie behind many reports of ghosts and hauntings. The proposition is that specific places at which many people claim to have experiences of hauntings may have weak, temporally complex, magnetic fields that can influence brain activity (Persinger, 2001). This could lead to the appearance of apparitions in certain sensitive individuals. Some support comes from the report by Braithwaite and Townsend (2008) that a person moving around at night, in a bed containing ferrous material, could potentially distort the background magnetic field. This could perhaps create the kind of complex changes in the magnetic field that could interact with the temporal lobes to generate subjective experiences of apparitions although this conclusion is highly speculative at the present time.

Unfortunately, other laboratories have not been able to replicate the effects of transcranial magnetic stimulation on producing a sense of presence. Granqvist *et al.* (2005) and French *et al.* (2009) failed to replicate the influence of weak and temporally complex magnetic fields on subjective paranormal experience. St-Pierre and Persinger (2006) argue that Granqvist *et al.* did not use the correct methodology, and although this is rejected by those authors the debate cannot easily be resolved without further replication studies. Braithwaite (2011) also points out that there is no convincing evidence, as yet, relating reports of hauntings and apparitions to known variations in geomagnetic fields. Only two locations so far, out of nearly 50 investigated, have been shown to have temporally complex magnetic fields (Braithwaite, 2008a).

An alternative hypothesis was suggested by Braithwaite (2011). He acknowledged that it is possible that a weak and temporally complex magnetic field can increase the intensity of an anomalous experience rather than creating the entire experience. An anomalous experience may be generated by a combination of other factors in the environment – for example, a low level of lighting, shadowy corners, unexplained noises – or factors associated with the individual – for example, prior belief, suggestibility, social contagion, and expectation. The role of the weak magnetic field is then to produce arousal which biases the interpretation of unusual sensory experiences (Beyerstein, 1999). Several studies have found evidence that prior expectation and belief has an influence on the likelihood and intensity of a subjective anomalous experience (e.g. French *et al.*, 2009; Granqvist *et al.*, 2005; Houran, Wiseman, & Thalbourne, 2002) and Houran, Wiseman, and Thalbourne (2002) also explored the influence of low lighting and shadowy corners.

French *et al.* (2009) tried to use complex electromagnetic fields (EMFs) to create anomalous sensations associated with haunting. They also used infrasound, following suggestions that the presence of infrasound may be associated with the tendency to report anomalous sensations, in susceptible individuals (Tandy, 2000; Tandy & Lawrence, 1998; but see Braithwaite and Townsend, 2006, for a critique of this claim). Participants were asked to wander freely around a specially constructed room for 50 minutes while they were exposed to either infrasound or complex EMFs, or both, or neither. Participants were informed in advance they might experience anomalous sensations and they were asked to record on a floor plan their location, the time, and a description of the sensations. This enabled the researchers afterwards to examine whether anomalous sensations were more likely to be reported when the participants were exposed to complex EMFs, to infrasound, or to both in combination. Participants also completed a questionnaire measure of temporal lobe lability (psychological experiences typically associated with temporal lobe epilepsy but distributed throughout the general population at a weaker and subclinical level). Many participants reported anomalous sensations but the sensations were not related to experimental condition, offering no support for the proposition that complex EMFs or infrasound might be responsible for some haunting experience. However, the reports of anomalous experiences were related to participants' temporal lobe scores (assessed using the PPI) so that participants with the highest temporal lobe lability scores also reported the greatest number of anomalous experiences. There is a strong possibility that participants who reported anomalous sensations might have been responding to suggestion as scores on Persinger's PPI are known to correlate with suggestibility. The round, featureless white room in which the experiment was carried out may have constituted an environment of mild sensory deprivation and in these circumstances it is more likely that people will feel some anomalous experiences.

In summary, the proposition that mystical experiences and the sense of presence are generated by activity in the temporal lobe has considerable support. The additional hypothesis of Persinger and colleagues that the types of anomalous experiences associated with hauntings may depend on some characteristics of the local geomagnetic field is somewhat less well supported and in particular there have been failed replications outside of Persinger's laboratory. A cautious conclusion might be to wait for the results of replications in other laboratories using double-blind procedures. It would also be desirable to have a clearer explanation of how weak, temporally complex magnetic fields could interact with the human brain (Braithwaite, 2011). Although the principle that magnetic stimulation can affect the workings of the human brain is well accepted, the low amplitudes used by Persinger in his research are below the level at which magnetic stimulation is known to induce neurons to fire in the human brain.

Neural interconnectedness and transliminality

Transliminality was introduced in Chapter 2 and will be discussed more fully in Chapter 6, where it was defined as 'a hypothesised tendency for psychological material to cross (*trans*) the threshold (*limen*) into or out of consciousness' (Thalbourne & Delin, 1994, p. 31). It is proposed that individuals differ in terms of the permeability of the threshold between that which is typically conscious and that which typically is not. A person who is high in transliminality would often become aware of thoughts, images, perceptions, and emotions that would normally remain buried in the unconscious. Some of these may be internally generated and some of these may be due to external stimulation too weak to be noticed by most people under most circumstances. Chapter 6 will explain how this property of transliminality might be associated with creativity and also with subjective paranormal experiences and belief in the paranormal (e.g. Thalbourne & Delin, 1994). Transliminality is measured by the Revised Transliminality Scale (Thalbourne, 1998), subsequently further revised by Lange *et al.* (2000), which contains questions relating to mystical experiences, altered states of consciousness, a sense of presence, heightened awareness of the senses, and vivid imagination.

Thalbourne and Maltby (2008, p. 1618) developed the notion of transliminality to suggest that it represents a hypersensitivity to material from either the unconscious mind or from the external world. It is interesting to note the relationship between transliminality and temporal lobe activity (e.g. Thalbourne, Crawley, & Houran, 2003; Thalbourne & Maltby, 2008) and the suggestion that transliminality may be caused by hyperconnectivity between the temporal lobe and sensory areas of the brain. Such hyperconnectivity might easily result in oversensitivity to sensations from the external world. Also, given that the neural substrate of imagination lies in the same cortical structures that serve to deliver externally derived sensations, the same hyperconnectivity could also result in oversensitivity to internally generated material. The observed association between transliminality and temporal lobe activity might also explain why transliminality is often associated with mystical experiences that seem to depend on activity of the temporal lobe.

Some support for this notion comes from the study by Cohn (1999) of Scottish families in whom there is a tradition of 'second sight'. This refers to spontaneous and vivid imagery, in multiple senses including visual, auditory, and kinaesthetic, which is interpreted as information about an event taking place at a distance (similar phenomena happen in other cultures, of course, but may not be termed 'second sight'). Cohn noted that the tendency to experience second sight seems to be inherited within families which points to the possibility of psychobiological causation. This could be furthered by the tendency to assortative mating, so that people with second-sight experiences are more likely to marry other people who also have these experiences. Possibly, the sensitivity of the sensory systems, or their connectivity with the temporal lobe, is a partially heritable factor.

Thus, there may be a psychobiological origin of some subjective paranormal experiences, including perceptions that do not appear to have a conventional external origin and mystical experiences. The origin may be hyperconnectivity between the temporal lobe and sensory areas of the brain. As yet this line of investigation awaits further investigation before any firm conclusions can be drawn.

Hemispheric dominance

There have been numerous observations of a relationship between the side of the brain that is generally dominant, or more active, and paranormal beliefs and experiences. These observations are less well supported by comprehensive theories although some attempts have been made to link paranormal beliefs and experiences to the known properties of the right cerebral hemisphere.

Compared to the majority of people in whom the left cerebral hemisphere is dominant, Pizzagalli et al. (2000) noted that there have been many reports of increased right hemispheric performance on various tasks (e.g. verbal, visual, and spatial) in people who have higher levels of paranormal belief. Their own EEG (electroencephalography) investigation revealed that paranormal believers had higher levels of right hemispheric activity than non-believers during resting task-free periods. Similarly, Brugger and Graves (1997a) reported a correlation between the level of paranormal thinking and hemispheric asymmetry in healthy individuals such that believers had more right hemisphere activity. In an EEG study, Gianotti, Faber, and Lehmann (2002) reported more activity in the right hemisphere (in the beta wave band) in believers than in sceptics. Finally, Kurup and Kurup (2003) observed that people with a greater degree of right hemispheric dominance were more likely to be highly spiritual.

Pizzagalli *et al.* (2000) noted that the left hemisphere is strongly associated with the processing of close semantic relations, while the right hemisphere is more associated with the processing of weaker or more remote meanings and connections. A higher activation of the right hemisphere may lead to the making of more connections between loosely associated or unassociated objects and events, which may result in an overestimation of the meaningfulness of naturally occurring coincidences. This could lead to a higher level of paranormal belief (Brugger & Graves, 1997b; Houran & Lange, 1998). Interestingly, this could also lead to a creative style of thinking (Leonhard & Brugger, 1998). It is interesting to consider the association of the left hemisphere with rational, analytical thought which suggests that possibly a relative lessening of input from the left hemisphere, compared to the right, could result in a lower degree of logical thinking. This would be consistent with observations that paranormal belief is negatively correlated with rational thinking (Aarnio & Lindeman, 2005) and positively correlated with intuitive thinking (Aarnio & Lindeman, 2005; Genovese, 2005; Hollinger & Smith, 2002). Right hemisphere activation has also been associated with OBE (McCreery & Claridge, 1996; Munro & Persinger, 1992).

Persinger (2001) noted that the sense of presence was particularly likely to be invoked following stimulation of the right temporal lobe. One possible explanation is that the sense of self is strongly associated with linguistic processes in the left hemisphere. Persinger and Richards (1991) theorized that intrusions from equivalent processes in the right temporal lobe, made hyperactive by deliberate stimulation, may create the sense of another sentient presence (Persinger, 2001). This could even explain why a sense of presence is particularly likely to be experienced during certain types of religious ceremonies. Singing and chanting in large groups promotes right hemisphere activity, which invokes a sense of presence, which is then labelled according to the context of the activity. More speculatively, Persinger (2001) proposes that the sense of presence may be responsible for the phenomena of the Greek Muses. These were goddesses who inspired literature, music, poetry, and dance by imparting knowledge and ideas to a receptive individual. The possible attribution of the Greek Muses to the sense of presence is also supported by the observation that creative individuals are more likely to have highly labile temporal lobes and that creative processes are often associated with the right hemisphere. Other researchers, however, have not replicated the relationship between right hemisphere activation and apparitions (e.g. Houran, Ashe, & Thalbourne, 2003). So the association of right temporal lobe activation with the sense of presence has not been clearly demonstrated.

Another interesting aspect of the sense of presence is its association with the use of psychoactive drugs. Strassman (2001) gave participants DMT (N, N-Dimethyltryptamine, the active ingredient in ayhuasca, which is used in shamanic rituals) and found that they reported sensed presences. In fact, the experiences of these participants were very similar, including the sensed presences and OBEs, to the sensations created by transcranial magnetic stimulation of the temporal lobes. Luke and Kittenis (2005) also reported that participants who had ingested DMT were more likely to have had previous experiences in which they seemed to encounter an anomalous entity. The association of the sense of presence with use of DMT was enhanced by the suggestion that DMT may be created in the pineal gland (Strassman, 2001) which is affected by naturally occurring electromagnetism. This is consistent with previous observations that a sense of presence can be artificially provoked by magnetic stimulation of the temporal lobes. Thus, the manufacture of DMT in the pineal gland may conceivably provide a pathway for the influence of electromagnetism on the sense of presence.

Another association of the pineal gland with a sensed presence was proposed by Persinger (1993) in his observation that reduced levels of melatonin, which is also produced in the pineal gland, are associated with bereavement apparitions (appearances of a recently deceased person). Persinger proposed that geomagnetism affects the pineal gland to produce less melatonin, which affects the sleep–wake cycle leading to disturbed sleep, and that night-time awakenings may be associated with a bereavement apparition in those who have recently lost a loved one.

Overall, it seems there are some interesting theories and empirical data associating the right hemisphere with paranormal beliefs and with the sense of presence. The former can be tentatively related to the known differences in processing styles between the two hemispheres and the latter to the functions of particular neural structures within the right hemisphere.

Out-of-body experiences

An OBE occurs when the sense of self, which is normally perceived as residing behind the eyes, is experienced as floating outside the body. Both the visual perspective and the sense of self seem to have moved to a location above the body and looking down: phenomena known as illusory perspective and illusory self-location, respectively (Blanke & Arzy, 2005). The individual having the OBE typically feels quite awake and the perceived world seems to be odd and distorted but is more real than a dream. Around 10% of the population may experience the OBE (Blackmore, 1982; Irwin, 1985b) and the experience has been reported in cultures all round the world (Greyson, 2000b). Some OBE experiencers have reported seeing their own body, known as autoscopy, though this is not the case for all OBE experiencers (Braithwaite et al., 2013; De Ridder et al., 2007). Alvarado (2000) reported that around 7% of OBE experiences also involve the sense of a cord connecting the disembodied self to the body.

There are two main types of explanation of the OBE. One is known as the 'projection model' (Alvarado, 2000) in which something capable of sustaining consciousness, perception, volition, and a sense of self actually leaves the body and travels to a location separated from the body. The other type of explanation is that the experience is subjective rather than objective and that nothing really leaves the body, although the experience feels very real and convincing to the individual. The idea of a volitional OBE is sometimes known as 'astral travel' and is a feature of shamanic rituals and beliefs.

It has been proposed that the OBE phenomenon results from a failure to integrate information received from different senses: being aware of one's spatial position (proprioception); being aware of one's balance and posture (vestibular sensation); the sense of touch (tactile information); information about the body's movement (motoric); and visual information (e.g. Blackmore, 1982; Blanke et al., 2003; Braithwaite et al., 2013; Cheyne & Girard, 2009). This integration would normally take place at the temporo-parietal junction and particularly on the right side of the brain (Blanke & Arzy, 2005; De Ridder et al., 2007). It is the integration of this information into a coherent whole that generates the sense of the self as being resident in the body, or the 'embodied self', with a true perception of location and position. Sometimes it may happen that some discrepant information is received and so the brain must decide how to impose coherence on information from the different senses and how to ignore the discrepant information, perhaps by regarding it as 'noise' rather than 'signal'. If the discrepant information is particularly strong, or perhaps if it is received from more than one sense, then it may not be possible to either ignore it or to integrate it with other, veridical information. One solution to this dilemma might be a subjective OBE (Blanke & Arzy, 2005). In this sense, an OBE can be thought of as an alternative model of reality which places the experienced sense of self in an unusual location outside the body.

Braithwaite et al. (2013) presented evidence that participants with cortical hyperexcitability (measured by a pattern-glare task) were more likely to have previously experienced multiple OBEs than participants with a lower level of cortical excitability. They speculated that hyperexcitability in the sensory and association areas of the cortex may lead to a disruption in incoming sensory signals and in turn this could lead to a breakdown in the stable integration of multiple signals and thus to an OBE. The cortical hyperexcitability may also explain the realistic sensory qualities of the OBE and why they are often reported as feeling vivid and very real (Blackmore, 1982). The position within the temporal lobe of the secondary visual cortex, the auditory cortex, and the association cortices strengthens the association of OBEs with processes in the temporal lobe. This is an intriguing possibility, although very recently presented, and more evidence will shed light on this idea.

Direct support for the hypothesis that the OBE is produced by a failure to integrate information in the right temporo-parietal junction comes from cases in which deliberate neural stimulation of the right temporo-parietal junction has produced an OBE such as the 43-year-old woman reported by Blanke *et al.* (2002) and the 63-year-old man reported by De Ridder *et al.* (2007). These cases of deliberate neural stimulation agree with other studies of neurological patients that the right temporo-parietal junction is implicated in the OBE. The general association of the OBE with neural processing in the right temporal lobe is supported by observations that OBE experiencers have a relatively high level of activation of their right hemisphere (McCreery & Claridge, 1996; Munro & Persinger, 1992) and a relatively high level of temporal lobe signs (Braithwaite *et al.*, 2013).

There are differing views on the relationship of the OBE to autoscopy in which the experiencer sees their own body at some distance. Comparing the location of neural activation in the patient observed by Blanke *et al.* (2002), who had an autoscopic experience, with that of the patient observed by De Ridder *et al.* (2007), who did not, it may be the case that an autoscopic experience occurs when there is also activation of the more posterior visual pathways. This could explain why OBE experiencers frequently, but not always, see their own body: for example, only 53% of the participants in Braithwaite *et al.*'s (2012) study reported seeing their own body during their OBE. An alternative proposition is that an OBE occurs in a patient lying in a supine position while an autoscopic experience occurs only if the individual is sitting or standing (Blanke & Arzy, 2005). This would suggest that proprioceptive and tactile sensations influence the form of the experience.

The prefrontal cortex also has a role in the representation of the sense of self (Easton, Blanke, & Mohr, 2009), and so if the neural pathway from the prefrontal cortex to the temporo-parietal junction is disrupted, then the sense of the embodied self may be disrupted as a consequence. Easton, Blanke, and Mohr (2009) found that their participants who had previously experienced OBEs performed worse in a task of perspective switching, designed to measure fronto-parietal connectivity, than the non-OBE experiencers. This suggests that poorer fronto-parietal connectivity may be a factor in the OBE, perhaps because there is a failure to integrate the sense of self with other body senses, and so a failure to experience the self as located within the body.

More generally, the task of perspective switching relative to the participant's own body is proposed to involve the same brain processes as are implicated in the OBE (e.g. Blanke *et al.*, 2005). In a typical task, the participant is shown a figure either facing towards them or away and is asked to decide whether the figure is wearing a glove on their right or left hand. Most participants find it harder when the figure is facing them and they have to switch perspective. In a sample of normal undergraduates, who had no clinical signs of temporal lobe disturbance, Braithwaite *et al.* (2011) found that people who had previously experienced at least one OBE were worse at switching perspective in the task. This might seem counter-intuitive when we consider that an OBE consists of taking an alternative perspective – surely the OBE experiencers should be better at switching perspectives? Perhaps the explanation is that for someone who has OBEs, their perspective is less stable and not always entirely under their own control.

So far these explanations for the OBE have concentrated on the neural processing that may be disrupted in an OBE. A different type of explanation focuses on the cognitive processes involved in constructing the sense of the embodied self. Blackmore (1982, 1996) explains that our sense of self, and our visual perspective, are both constructed by the brain based on data received from the senses (via 'bottom-up' processing) and our expectations (via 'top-down' processing). Normally our visual perspective is presented from a position just behind our eyes and our sense of self is similarly situated. Probably the close relation between our visual perspective and our sense of self is due to the importance of vision in our lives. However, under conditions of tiredness or stress, our sense of self and our visual perspective may both be presented from a 'bird's eye' perspective slightly above and usually behind our bodies, rather than the veridical perspective. This alterative perspective seems to be favoured in memory and imagination; we often see ourselves from this bird's eye perspective. It is worth noting that we never experience the world from both perspectives simultaneously but only from one perspective at a time. Evidence in support of this theory is that OBE experiencers are typically better at taking the bird's eye perspective than non-experiencers. Thus, the OBE may result from some confusion about which of the alternative models of reality is the most appropriate. The OBE typically arises under conditions of sleep, anoxia, and drug-induced states when sensory input is likely to be reduced and when integration of information from different senses is likely to be less effective (although OBEs can occur at other times). This explanation can also account for why the OBE seems so real – the OBE is the currently constructed model of reality and it is based on current visual input.

Wilde and Murray (2009) reported their interviews with two women who had OBEs while meditating. They noted that a substantial minority of OBEs occur while meditating and propose that the OBE is linked to the states of relaxation and low arousal which occur during meditation. They suggested a key role for the trait of absorption, which facilitates entry into the state of relaxation and external direction of attention that is conceptually similar to the meditative state and the state that often precedes an OBE. Similarly, Irwin (2000c) theorized that an OBE may occur when the individual enters a state of absorption, becoming engrossed in experience, and is dissociated from their somatic input. Wilde and Murray noted several previous studies which found an association between the tendency to have OBEs and the traits of absorption and dissociativity (e.g. Irwin, 2000c; Murray & Fox, 2005; please refer to Chapter 3 for information about these traits). It was interesting to note that the two female participants of Wilde and Murray (2009) found the OBE a useful tool in resolving their psychological conflicts and one which had personal and transformational value.

There are some people who assert that the OBE is exactly what it seems to be, that is, consciousness leaving the body and existing independently of its neural substrate. French (2005b) noted that sometimes studies have presented information in a hospital ward such that it would only be visible from someone close to the ceiling and looking down, which is the typical OBE vantage point, in an attempt to investigate whether the OBE is real. So far no conclusive evidence has been found from these studies that any person's consciousness has occupied such a vantage point, and no OBE experiencer have been able to accurately report the contents of information presented in this way (see Chapter 11 for further discussion).

Another type of investigation into the possibility that the OBE is an objective (rather than a subjective) phenomenon concerns the possibility that the presence of the self might be detected at an alternative location away from the body. This type of study involves participants who claim to be able to produce an OBE under their own volition, so that information received from detectors at the remote location can be compared between different periods of time during which the individual was or was not in an out-of-body state. Alvarado (2000) noted that studies of this type have produced inconsistent results and Irwin and Watt (2007) also concluded that there is very little reliable evidence of a presence being detected at the OBE location.

It would appear that considerable progress has been made in understanding the neurological origins of the OBE. The convergence of evidence from studies of neurological patients and from studies of direct cortical stimulation strengthens the case that the OBE depends on a failure to integrate information from various senses that normally takes place in the right temporo-parietal junction. Future studies could usefully explore the ways in which the cognitive system constructs the OBE and its dependence on the particular sensory information available at the time of the experience.

Near-death experiences

An individual who comes close to death, or thinks they are close to death, may have an NDE. NDEs seem to occur quite frequently among people who have survived cardiac arrests and some researchers estimate that between 10% and 20% of survivors may have an NDE (e.g. French, 2005b; Greyson, 2003; Schwaninger et al., 2002; van Lommel et al., 2001). For this reason, much of the research into the NDE takes place in hospitals by interviewing people who are recovering from cardiac arrests to ask them whether they have had an NDE. The advantage of conducting research in this way is that the interview can take place soon after the experience while the memory is still fresh in the mind of the patient. An alternative approach is to do a general survey of the whole population, but this will yield accounts that may be several years old.

NDEs tend to have common elements that were first documented by Moody (1975) and Ring (1980). These are peace and well-being (60% of NDEs); a floating OBE looking down on one's body (37%); passing though a tunnel or a spiral chamber (25%); being drawn towards a brilliant light, which may be interpreted as a God-like figure, sometimes with a non-judgemental review of one's life (16%); entering a beautiful place, perhaps seen as a garden, and encountering departed loved ones or a spiritual guide (10%). Figures in brackets refer to Ring (1980). Although it is not particularly emphasized by either Moody (1975) or Ring (1980), another common feature of the NDE is the belief that one is dead; this occurred to 50% of the patients in van Lommel *et al.*'s (2001) study who experienced NDEs. An interesting feature of the NDE is that the variety of elements means that two people can have quite different experiences with little in common, though they are still classed as NDEs. Although it was initially thought that all NDEs were positive, it is now known that some NDEs are unpleasant, even terrifying. Some people find themselves visiting a hellish region and meeting demons, or perhaps finding themselves inhabiting an isolated, featureless void.

Similar to the experience itself, the after-effects of the NDE can be positive or negative. Positive after-effects include no longer being afraid of dying, the sense of being given a second chance, and wanting to do something worthwhile in life. People may become more spiritual, less **materialistic**, more religious, and less competitive (Ring, 1980). Some people feel a sense of being connected to the universe and feeling that the world is a benevolent place. On the down side, there may be frustration at being unable to communicate adequately the experience or a fear of ridicule. Many people are unable to return to their previous life and relationships and some subsequently become divorced. After a particularly negative NDE there may be an enhanced fear of dying and symptoms of post-traumatic stress disorder with flashbacks to the experience (Greyson & Bush, 1992).

French (2005b) describes and evaluates many different explanations for the NDE. Each seems to be capable of accounting for some of the common elements of the NDE though none can account for all of the elements. It seems likely that some combination of these explanations applies to all (or virtually all) cases of the NDE so we can consider that we have non-paranormal explanations for the NDE although some of the explanations are somewhat speculative at this point. It seems plausible that many of the causal factors could co-occur which brings us even closer to a scientific and non-supernatural explanation.

One type of explanation is that the individual's consciousness becomes detached from their unconscious brain and travels to another place, or remains in the room with the patient but detached from their body. This is supported by reports from patients that they could see and hear events occurring while their brain was unconscious and their EEG recording showed little or no cortical activity. Patients often describe quite accurately the attempts to resuscitate them. Patients also report that their memories were clear and lucid which suggests that considerable cognitive activity was taking place while the brain was essentially unable to sustain this activity. However, this type of explanation is severely criticized by Crislip (2008; see also French, 2009b) who argues that there is insufficient evidence that the remembered events actually took place during a period when the brain was unconscious and showed no cortical activity. It is quite possible that the remembered events occurred before or after the period of unconsciousness or that the patient was minimally conscious and able to see or hear. The lack of apparent activity in an EEG recording is not a strong indication that no brain activity was taking place because the EEG is known to be unable to detect all brain activity. This line of argument was deemed unlikely by Parnia and Fenwick (2002) who noted that unconsciousness occurs too quickly for the entire NDE to have occurred while the patient was lapsing into unconsciousness, and that when the patient is recovering from unconsciousness their thinking is confused and not at all clear and lucid. To counter this, French (2005b) explained that altered states of consciousness have a large impact on time perception so that a great deal of time can appear to pass during a short interval. Further, although the patient may feel that their thinking during their NDE was clear and lucid, this may be a false perception. People experiencing oxygen starvation often feel that their thinking is clear but their actions may portray a state of confusion.

The other major problem with this type of explanation is that there is very good evidence that consciousness depends on the brain and cannot therefore be detached from the brain. There is a dependency of the mind and consciousness on its neural substrate so that it would not be possible for consciousness to become detached from the brain and exist in a different location (e.g. Velmans, 2000). Although life after death forms a major part of many (though not all) religions, and the NDE is sometimes interpreted as a glimpse of the afterlife, there is no means of verifying this interpretation.

A second type of explanation is the biochemical explanation, under which many aspects of the NDE are due to the actions of neurotransmitters released by the brain under stress. Consider that atropine produces a sense of flying through the air; ketamine (an anaesthetic) can produce an OBE and a sense of moving through tunnels and seeing lights; and LSD can produce feelings of oneness with the universe and hallucinations. The existence of receptors for these chemicals suggests that there must be naturally produced brain chemicals which also activate these receptors and perhaps these natural brain chemicals are released under stress. This could certainly explain many aspects of the NDE but other aspects, including the life review and meeting departed loved ones, seem to rely on activation of autobiographical memories, and there is no proposal for how neurotransmitters might be responsible for these features (French, 2005b).

Carr (1982) proposed that endorphins are responsible for NDEs. Endorphins are known to be released at moments of great stress and they are responsible for creating feelings of bliss and well-being and for combating pain. Some circumstantial evidence in support of the role of endorphins was offered by

Judson and Wiltshaw (1983) who observed that a pleasant NDE turned into an unpleasant experience when naloxone, which blocks the action of endorphins, was administered. However, endorphins are not known to produce hallucinatory experiences.

One specific explanation centres on the drug ketamine (Jansen, 1997). The state of consciousness that can be induced by ketamine resembles the NDE in some respects, including the dark tunnel, the bright light, the sense of being dead, the OBE, and the mystical experiences. The idea is that stress can create an excess of the neurotransmitter glutamate, which overactivates receptors for the neurotransmitter NMDA in the temporal and frontal lobes so that these receptors may begin to die off. Ketamine can block these receptors and so protect them. The ketamine hypothesis of the NDE is that there is a naturally occurring brain chemical which acts in the same way and so produces the similar set of subjective experiences. The problem with this hypothesis is that no such naturally occurring chemical has been located so far.

A third type of explanation is the lack of oxygen that occurs commonly in a patient who is experiencing cardiac arrest. Anoxia (no oxygen) and hypoxia (low level of oxygen) can cause altered firing of the neurons in the occipital cortex that can produce the visual experience of passing down a tunnel. Anoxia first produces feelings of power and well-being, and then later may turn to hallucinations, which mimics the common sequence of events in an NDE (Ring, 1980). A particularly interesting study was reported by Whinnery (1997) who looked at the experiences of fighter pilots who had blacked out under gravity-induced loss of consciousness (G-LOC). Whinnery examined almost 1000 instances of G-LOC syndrome which described experiences of tunnel vision, bright lights, floating sensations, OBEs, and vivid dreamlets of beautiful places. The individuals also experienced euphoria and dissociation and the intrusion of thoughts of family and friends and memories of their life. These experiences are very similar to the common elements of the NDE which makes lack of oxygen seem like a plausible candidate for many aspects of the NDE. However, some aspects of the NDE were not experienced by these fighter pilots: the mystical insights and long-lasting transformational aftereffects were not generally apparent. Possibly this is because the individuals in this study were not expecting to die (French, 2005b). Alongside anoxia or hypoxia, it is common to observe hypercarbia (elevated level of carbon monoxide) which produces similar symptoms.

A fourth explanation centres on the temporal lobe. It is noted that damage to the temporal lobe, or direct cortical stimulation, can produce experiences similar to the NDE, including OBEs, hallucinations, and memory flashbacks (e.g. Blanke et al., 2002). It is also noted that the temporal lobes are particularly sensitive to anoxia. Finally, NDE experiencers in the study by Britton and Bootzin (2004) had more epileptiform temporal lobe EEG activity than non-experiencers (although a drawback of this study is that the non-experiencers had not come close to death, so perhaps were not an ideal control group).

There are also psychological explanations, for example, that the NDE is a defence against the fear of dying. Perhaps the individual dissociates from the reality of their physical predicament and enters into a fantasy (Irwin, 1993b) or perhaps they use depersonalization to detach from their predicament and indulge in pleasant fantasy (Noyes & Klett, 1976). These explanations are supported by evidence of higher absorption and fantasy-proneness (see Chapter 2) among people who have had an NDE than those who have not (Irwin, 1985b) and higher levels of dissociative symptoms (Greyson, 2000a). However, it cannot explain some elements like the tunnel, the bright light, and the intrusion of autobiographical memories.

Nelson *et al.* (2006) proposed that the NDE may stem from an intrusion of a brief period of REM sleep into a non-sleep state. They noted that REM sleep contains vivid and story-like dreams and that this could explain this type of content in an NDE. They also noted that many people experience REM intrusions into the waking state, typically when falling asleep or waking up, and that this might predispose them to experience an REM intrusion under conditions of extreme stress. Their survey suggested that people who tended to experience REM intrusions in their everyday life were also more likely to have an NDE under appropriate circumstances. This is an interesting proposition worthy of further study. However, as Long and Holden (2007) point out, the evidence so far is very preliminary and was obtained from retrospective studies. Ideally the evidence would be confirmed in other studies so that the incidence of REM intrusions prior to the NDE can be confirmed.

Putting this all together, a comprehensive account of the NDE is likely to involve a lack of oxygen, elevated levels of some neurotransmitters produced under stress, hyperactivity of the temporal lobe, and psychological defence mechanisms. Different causes can explain different components of the NDE and this seems reasonable given the variation in individual NDE experiences (Blackmore, 1996). But – and there is always a caveat – some people have had an NDE without any of these possible causes known to have been present. So perhaps all of these explanations should be regarded as somewhat speculative for the moment.

Conclusion

There are many different kinds of psychobiological explanation for anomalous, paranormal and mystical experiences, each accounting for different types of experiences. Some of the explanations are well supported by empirical evidence – for example, temporal lobe involvement in mystical experiences – and others are more speculative, including the association of hauntings and apparitions with variations in the local geomagnetic field. Many of the hypotheses are quite new, and given limited research funding for the field of anomalistic psychology, the body of empirical data is sometimes lacking.

Box 5.1 Difficulties in investigating anomalous experiences

A common feature of anomalous experiences is their subjective nature; no one except the person having the experience knows what it feels like. The only way to find out about the experience is to listen to the individual's account, but this introduces a particular difficulty in that their account of their experience relies on **introspection**, defined as the examination of one's own internal mental processes. Introspection has not always been regarded as a valid method of study and it is recognized that there are various sources of error and bias in an introspective account (Pekala & Cardeña, 2000). There is the potential for reconstruction, in which the memory of an experience is mixed with the memories of other experiences and with general knowledge and expectation. Or perhaps there might be confabulation, in which people share their stories and introduce elements from other stories into their own. Or maybe the story might be reconstructed to fit a cultural stereotype. It is even possible that the individual might exaggerate some elements of their story in order to make it sound more interesting.

Even if the individual is trying hard to be scrupulously honest, the problem remains that some experiences are simply difficult to put into words. What the listener imagines when they hear the account may be quite different from what the narrator intended. William James (1902/1958) commented on the ineffability of mystical experiences, that is, the impossibility of capturing them adequately in words. Another problem lies in asking people to give retrospective accounts of events that occurred some time ago. These are more prone to inaccuracy and various forms of reconstruction than concurrent accounts but the latter are difficult to collect. Anomalous experiences cannot typically be produced on demand and so the researcher has no choice but to gather accounts of past experiences (Pekala & Cardeña, 2000).

In some cases it may be possible to create the anomalous experience, for example, by creating a sense of presence by transcranial magnetic stimulation of the temporal lobe, but this is not generally the case. In other cases, the likelihood of an individual having a certain type of experience is sufficiently high to make it worthwhile interviewing everyone in a particular situation. For example, between 10% and 20% of individuals who survive a major cardiac arrest may have an NDE (French, 2005b), so a survivor may be interviewed a few days later. For most anomalous or mystical experiences, however, the researcher is reliant on retrospective accounts.

Pekala and Cardeña (2000) point out that experiences must be reliably described before they can be explained (i.e. the epistemology must precede the metaphysics). Our explanatory theories can only be as good as the data they are attempting to describe. Thinking back to the various types of anomalous experiences considered in this chapter, do you think that individual accounts can be believed as veridical subjective experiences? How much do you think the accounts may have been coloured by culturally available knowledge, confabulation, and imagination? What kinds of problems do you think this poses for investigations of the psychobiological underpinnings of anomalous experience?

More research would help us to understand the psychobiological origins of many anomalous experiences and thus come closer to an understanding of their proper significance in our lives. It is important that the research should be carried out in a properly controlled manner. Laboratory-based experiments in which the conditions are controlled, and in which both the participant and the researcher are blinded to the condition, would generate the strongest evidence. If an experiment could be devised that was replicable in many laboratories, offering a well-developed neurological explanation for a type of anomalous experience, this would generate considerable interest.

Looking back at the explanations in this chapter, they do not seem to be particularly well known in the general population. The lack of knowledge of these potential explanations seems likely to account for much paranormal belief. Someone who has a vivid or frightening experience, especially if the experience is repeated, will naturally seek an explanation. If scientific explanations are hard to access, being published only in academic journals, or hard for the layperson to understand, then it is quite understandable if the individual reaches for a culturally available explanation even though it may lack for rigorous scientific support. It is to be hoped that knowledge of these alternative explanations will become more generally available and thus people will be able to understand their experiences in ways that are solidly founded on scientific evidence.

Suggested further reading

For information on sleep paralysis:

French, C. C. & Santomauro, J. (2007). 'Something wicked this way comes: Causes and interpretations of sleep paralysis'. In S. Della Sala (ed.), *Tall tales about the mind and brain: Separating fact from fiction* (pp. 380–98). Oxford: Oxford University Press.

For the effects of temporal lobe hyperactivity:

Braithwaite, J. J. (2011). 'Magnetic fields, hallucinations and anomalous experiences: A sceptical critique of the current evidence'. *The Skeptic*, 22.4/23.1, 38–45.
Persinger, M. A. (2001). 'The neuropsychiatry of paranormal experiences'. *Neuropsychiatric Practice and Opinion*, 13, 515–24.

For a review of transliminality research:

Thalbourne, M. A. (2010b). 'Transliminality: A fundamental mechanism in psychology and parapsychology'. *Australian Journal of Parapsychology*, 10, 70–81.

For more on the OBE and NDE:

Blanke, O., Ortigue, S., Landis, T., & Seeck, M. (2002). 'Stimulating illusory own-body perceptions'. *Nature*, 419, 269–70.
French, C. C. (2005b). 'Near-death experiences in cardiac arrest survivors'. *Progress in Brain Research*, 150, 355–72.
French, C. C. (2009b). 'Near-death experiences and the brain'. In C. Murray (ed.), *Psychological scientific perspectives on out-of-body and near-death experiences* (pp. 187–203). New York: Nova Science Publishers.

Cognitive Perspectives

Introduction

Anomalistic psychologists, as described in Chapter 1, generally adopt the working hypothesis that paranormal forces do not exist. So we are faced with the challenge of explaining why and how people come to believe in the paranormal and to think that they have had paranormal experiences. A likely explanation for at least some instances or paranormal belief is a collection of features of our perception, our reasoning, and our memory, which can lead us to believe we have experienced events that did not really occur, or did not occur in quite the way in which we think we perceived them. For example, a visual illusion could lead someone to believe that they had seen a ghost, or a failure to appreciate the possibility of **hindsight bias** could lead to the belief that a dream resembled a later occurrence more closely than is truly the case. Generally, a failure to appreciate the true probability of a combination of circumstances could lead to a perception that some supernatural force was at work when random coincidence is quite a plausible explanation.

This chapter will explore some of the features of cognition that have been theoretically or empirically linked with subjective paranormal experience and belief. We shall see that there are distinct ways in which our thought and memory processes can contribute to belief in paranormal forces and entities. The term 'subjective paranormal experience' will be used to describe experiences that are genuinely believed to be paranormal by the individual, whether or not they really are. Of course, we must bear in mind that it is possible that paranormal forces do really exist and that some people are more perceptive and more able to recognize anomalous events than others. However, in this chapter we will explore evidence that distinct errors in reasoning are associated with paranormal belief, which argues that at least some subjective paranormal experiences are entirely normal – though still very interesting.

It should be noted that we are not trying to imply that there are major flaws in our psychology. For the most part, our thought processes and our memories are reliable and consistent and they deliver us an accurate account of the world around us. But there are circumstances under which our cognitive processes can deliver misleading impressions.

The major topics in this chapter will be errors in thinking and reasoning; misunderstanding of probability, common **heuristics** (availability and representativeness), illusions of correlation and control, selective processing of evidence, perceptual biases, errors in memory and false memory, non-conscious processing, and Thalbourne's model of transliminality. If sceptics are correct and the paranormal is not real then we should expect to find some differences in cognition or cognitive abilities between those who do and do not believe in the paranormal. We will examine the evidence for such individual differences and draw connections with the topics in Chapter 2.

Reasoning ability and critical thinking

The evidence is decidedly mixed for lower levels of reasoning ability in general, or critical thinking in particular, in believers compared to non-believers. Some researchers have found that believers in paranormal phenomena scored lower than non-believers on a measure of critical thinking ability (e.g. Alcock & Otis, 1980; Gray & Mill, 1990; Tobacyk & Milford, 1983, but only for the superstition scale of paranormal belief). Others have failed to replicate this relationship with critical thinking (e.g. Hergovich & Arendasy, 2005; Royalty, 1995) although there was an association of general reasoning ability with lower levels of belief in superstition and precognition (Hergovich & Arendasy, 2005).

Brugger and Graves (1997b) asked participants to play a simple computer game in which they were not told the rules for administering punishment or reward, but were asked to find out how the game worked by playing it. Believers in the paranormal tested fewer hypotheses during the task compared to non-believers, but ended up believing more strongly in those hypotheses which they did generate. This suggests perhaps too much readiness on the part of believers to accept an answer on too little evidence and too little inclination to test the answer carefully. This would certainly point to a relative lack of critical thinking in believers.

Aarnio and Lindeman (2007) proposed that belief in paranormal phenomena stems from what is termed an 'ontological confusion' between phenomena from different domains: *physical* (objects in the real world), *biological* (living creatures), and *psychological* (e.g. thoughts, beliefs, desires, memories, symbols). For example: 'building memory' confuses the physical building with the psychological attribute of memory; communication with spirits depends on the unlikely idea that a psychological process (speech) can be generated without a biological brain or body; and psychokinesis depends on the idea that a thought can directly interact with a physical object. Basil Fawlty committed an ontological error when he accused his car of breaking down deliberately (a physical object cannot have the biological property of intentionality).

Aarnio and Lindeman (2007) found that believers made more numerous ontological confusions between the physical, biological, and psychological domains than non-believers, though they were just as accurate in assessing the truth of purely literal statements and so were able to recognize an unfounded belief as long as it did not involve an ontological confusion. Believers also assigned more intentionality to random and natural events than did non-believers: for example, 'Your car crashed and as a result you met someone whom you later marry; did your car crash for a purpose?' The believers were more likely to answer 'yes'. Similar results were reported by Lindeman *et al.* (1998) and by Lindeman and Saher (2007).

This is an interesting way of thinking about paranormal belief with some potential for explaining a wide range of beliefs. It may connect the thinking of children, who have not yet learned to categorize objects and entities reliably between the physical, biological, and psychological domains, with the thinking of adults who know how to categorize but nonetheless still make some mistakes.

It also relates to the notion that we are instinctive *dualists* (see Chapter 11), which means that we tend to regard ourselves as comprising a physical body and a separate mind or spirit or soul. In a sense, of course, our mind is not the same thing as our body, but this does not mean that our mind can become detached from our body and exist independently. Nonetheless, the dualist view makes it relatively easy to believe in a range of paranormal phenomena including ghosts, OBEs, telepathy (where information travels from one brain to another without being carried by any known medium), psychokinesis, and others.

Irwin (2009) points out an important caveat regarding the research into critical thinking skills of believers and non-believers. It is possible that participants in these studies might have been aware of (or suspected) a sceptical stance in the experimenters and that those believers with stronger critical reasoning abilities might have adjusted their responses in the direction of lower paranormal belief to gain the approval of the experimenter. This could, in principle, be sufficient to produce the observed relationships between reasoning ability and paranormal belief. Irwin offers a study of his own (Irwin, 1991b) in support of this possibility, but others have failed to replicate his results (Smith, Foster, & Stovin, 1998; Watt & Wiseman, 2002). This remains as a possibility but there is not yet sufficient data to evaluate it.

On balance, it seems that there may be a deficit in some aspect of critical thinking or reasoning in those who believe in paranormal phenomena compared to non-believers and ontological confusion may be a part of this general deficit. More evidence would be necessary to reach a firm conclusion and to clarify which aspects of reasoning are related to which facets of paranormal belief. Future research will show whether the concept of ontological confusion will be replicable and useful in thinking about paranormal belief.

Syllogistic reasoning

This refers to a particular type of logical problem in which two propositions are given and then a conclusion. You are asked to judge whether the conclusion necessarily follows from the propositions, or whether it does not (it may contradict the propositions or there may be insufficient information to judge). For example, if the propositions are 'All swans are white' and 'Sammy is a swan', then the conclusion 'Sammy is white' is true and follows logically from the propositions. But if the propositions are 'All swans are white' and 'Sammy is white', then the conclusion 'Sammy is a swan' does not necessarily follow – other creatures are white as well as swans, so there is insufficient data to tell whether the conclusion is true or not. And if the propositions are 'All swans are white' and 'Sammy is brown', then the conclusion 'Sammy is a swan' must be false.

Let us consider some examples with a paranormal theme. *Proposition 1*: If telepathy exists, then one person can predict what another will say. *Proposition 2*: Sometimes one person does predict what another person will say. *Conclusion*: Telepathy exists. Or another one: *Proposition 1*: If the government is covering up the evidence for UFOs, then they will deny that any UFO landings have taken place. *Proposition 2*: The government does deny that any UFO landings have taken place. *Conclusion*: The government is covering up the evidence for UFOs. In both cases there are other explanations for Proposition 2 – two people who know each other well may be able to predict what the other will say, and the government may deny that there is any evidence of UFO landings for the simple reason that there is no such evidence. So in both cases, the conclusion does not necessarily follow from the two propositions. But some people would be inclined to say, wrongly, that the conclusion follows logically. This is an error known as 'affirming the antecedent'.

Sutherland (1992) proposed that people find it easier to reason from cause to effect than backwards from effect to cause. In each of the previous examples, Proposition 1 can be thought of as the cause and Proposition 2 as the effect. People incorrectly assume that the cause given is the *only possible cause* and so the conclusion must be true. Of course, in these examples, the cause given is not the only possible cause and the conclusion is not necessarily true.

This type of difficulty in **syllogistic reasoning** from effect to cause may be responsible for some instances of paranormal belief. If an observation is consistent with a paranormal cause and also with random coincidence, then nothing can be safely concluded from the observation. But a person with weak reasoning skills may infer that the observation supports a paranormal hypothesis, failing to consider the other possibility. Indeed, an important aspect of reasoning is to consider all possibilities, not just the preferred hypothesis but other hypotheses also (Gray & Mill, 1990; Sutherland, 1992).

If failure on this type of reasoning lies behind some instances of paranormal belief, then we should expect to find differences between believers and non-believers in syllogistic reasoning ability. Wierzbicki (1985) showed that believers were less able to do syllogistic reasoning than non-believers and this was replicated by Lawrence and Peters (2004) and Roberts and Seager (1999). Watt and Wiseman (2002) also replicated these results using syllogisms with a non-paranormal theme, which is important as it indicates that believers may have general deficits in syllogistic reasoning rather than only deficits that touch on prior belief. Then it is possible that these deficits might be a part of the process by which some instances of paranormal belief are formed. In contrast, Irwin (1991b) did not find any relationship between reasoning ability and paranormal belief, although his choice of reasoning task was criticized (e.g. Roberts & Seager, 1999).

Altogether, it seems plausible that a failure of syllogistic reasoning, and in particular reasoning from effect to cause, may underlie some examples of paranormal belief. A failure to appreciate that other, non-paranormal, explanations are possible could be implicated.

Shermer (1997) points out that just because an event is not explained does not mean it is inexplicable. Sometimes there may be a variety of possible explanations and we do not have enough information to choose between them. Sometimes there may be an explanation that we do not yet understand. To conclude that an event is paranormal is to decide that there is no rational explanation and this should not be done without very thorough searching through all the possibilities. There are those who would argue that there is never a case for saying that a particular event had a paranormal cause because we can never go back to do a proper investigation to see which normal causes might have been operating. An event in the past, unless it occurred under tightly controlled laboratory conditions, will typically have been subject to too many random circumstances to safely draw any firm conclusion about the presence or absence of a paranormal cause.

The danger of groupthink

Sutherland (1992) discusses the problem of **groupthink,** a phenomenon described by Janis (1982) that can occur when a group of people with similar attitudes and beliefs get together. Simply by interacting together the members of the group can adopt more and more extreme attitudes in the direction of their common beliefs. There are several theories about why this can happen and McCauley (1989) describes a few of them. One is that people might adopt stronger beliefs in order to win the approval of the group. Since the group is gathered together because they all believe the same thing, by expressing a stronger version of that belief a person can become a more popular or dominant character within the group. A related factor is that a member who expresses a dissenting view may be ignored and ostracized (e.g. Janis, 1982, p. 5). Turner *et al.* (1992) confirmed the influence of group cohesion on groupthink and poor decision-making, although there have also been replication failures (see Park, 1990, for a review of research).

Another concern is that since the group all share a common belief it is unlikely that a contrary view will ever be expressed, so the unanimity of the group may create the illusion that there is no other view. Additionally, members of the group will validate each other's beliefs and so encourage each other to have increased confidence in those beliefs. Turner and Pratkanis (1998) describe how a cohesive group may fail to search for information outside the group or to give alternatives proper consideration.

It is easy to see how this can apply to belief in paranormal phenomena. If a small group of friends regularly discuss their beliefs, then the ingredients are all in place for groupthink: the absence of contrary views, validation of each other's beliefs, and a desire to win approval of the group by taking a strong view. The more attractive the group is to the individual, and the more highly the individual values inclusion in the group, the more influence the group can have on their thinking.

Misunderstanding of probabilities

Several researchers (e.g. Blackmore & Troscianko, 1985; Sutherland, 1992) have argued that paranormal belief arises because people lack the ability to calculate the probability of an event occurring by chance or the probability of two separate events coinciding. An occurrence might look so unlikely that there must be a paranormal cause – for example, thinking about an old friend you haven't seen for several years and then receiving a phone call from the friend soon after.

Here is an example of how a failure to calculate probabilities can lead to paranormal belief. Denman (2010; after Paulos, 1988) noted that one might define a 'matching' dream as one in which the events of the dream occurred soon after with sufficient similarity to have a probability of only one in 10,000. If one dream each night is remembered, then the probability of a matching dream each night is one in 10,000 or 0.0001. So the probability of no matching dream on any night is 0.9999. The probability of no match on two consecutive nights is 0.9999 x 0.9999 and the probability of no match in a year is 0.9999 multiplied by itself 365 times, which works out as 0.9642. So there is a 3.6% chance that any person will have an apparently precognitive dream in any given year. There is an even chance of a precognitive dream in 19 years, which means that in a psychology undergraduate class at least half of the students should have experienced at least one apparently precognitive dream over their lifetime. Failure to appreciate this possibility could lead to the perception that precognitive dreams are a real phenomenon when all that is really happening is the working of probability over a large number of dreams and large number of people. An apparently precognitive dream is likely to be exciting and dramatic and so it likely to be remembered, which makes this a plausible and realistic explanation. Indeed, Blackmore (1997) reported that 10% of a newspaper survey claimed to have dreamt of someone they had not seen for many years shortly before encountering that person.

As another example, consider the 'birthday problem' (e.g. Kahneman & Tversky, 1972), a well-known challenge of probability estimation. Look at the birthday problem and note down your answer before you read any further.

Ideas to think about: The birthday problem

How many randomly selected people would be needed to have an even chance (50% likelihood) that at least two of them have the same birthday? Try this now and make a note of your estimate before you read the answer.

The way to calculate this is to take any person at random. The probability that the second person has a different birthday is 364 divided by 365 (ignoring leap years) because there are 364 days of the year that are different to the first person's birthday. Similarly, the probability that a third person has a different birthday to both of the first two is 363 divided by 365, and so on, down to the 23rd person who had a probability of 343 divided by 365 of having a different birthday to everyone else. Multiply all these together and you get just under 50% probability that everyone has a different birthday. So the probability that any two people have the *same* birthday is just over 50%. The correct answer is lower than most people think, a popular guess being about 180 people, but unless we have some knowledge of probability we would not be able to work this out correctly and would have to make an intuitive guess.

Here are another two probability puzzles for you to try from the website www.braingle.com/brainteasers: note down your estimates before you read the correct answers.

Ideas to think about

Matching socks

Mismatched Joe is in a pitch dark room selecting socks from his drawer. He has only six socks in his drawer, a mixture of black and white. If he chooses two socks, the chance that he draws out a white pair is 2/3. What is the chance that he draws out a black pair?

Knights of the round table

King Arthur, Merlin, Sir Lancelot, Sir Gawain, and Guinevere go to their favourite restaurant. They sit down at a round table for five people, and as soon as they do, Lancelot notes, 'We sat down around the table in age order! What is the probability of that?' Merlin knows that this can be solved easily without using magic.

The answer to the matching socks puzzle is none at all. The only way to get a 2/3 likelihood of choosing a white pair is to have five white socks and one black sock. There are ten possible pairs of white socks (each white sock paired with each other so 4 + 3 + 2 + 1) and five possible mismatched pairs (the black sock with each of the white socks) so 2/3 chance of a white pair.

The answer to the knights of the round table puzzle is one in 12 – and this is how you can work it out. Take the youngest person first. The second youngest could have sat either to the left or the right of the youngest (because we can have either clockwise or counterclockwise seating) so could have chosen two out of four remaining seats, with a probability of one in two. The third youngest must sit in the seat that follows the sequence, out of three remaining, with probability of one in three. The fourth youngest must follow the sequence with two remaining chairs, with probability of one in two. The oldest has only one seat remaining. So the answer is 1/2 x 1/3 x 1/2 = 1/12. There are plenty more puzzles on the website for you to try.

A specific and tragic example of failure to understand probability is the case of Sally Clark, found guilty of killing her two small children, and then cleared in 2003 of any wrongdoing. Sally was convicted on the basis of expert testimony offered by a paediatrician who included in his testimony the statement that the odds of two sudden infant deaths (SIDs) in the same family are 73,000,000 to one. This probability was obtained by multiplying together the odds of a single SID. Now this would be an appropriate probability calculation if – and only if – two conditions are met. One is that the two events must be independent, that is, the second SID must be independent of the first. But when the cause of death may be some genetic factor that runs in the family (as was the later discovered to be the case), the two cases are not necessarily independent, and the odds of two SIDs in one family are much reduced. The second condition is that the prediction must be made in advance, so out of all the mothers in the UK Sally Clark in particular must be predicted to experience two SIDs. But this condition was not met either; Sally was identified after the fact, not in advance, making this an invalid calculation of probability. Consider that the odds of winning the lottery are millions to one. Using the same logic this must mean that any person who wins has cheated. But we know that someone wins (nearly) every week simply because there are millions of tickets sold. A very unlikely outcome will happen eventually if given sufficient chances to occur, as is the case with lottery tickets and, tragically, with SIDs. The difference is whether a person is identified before the fact, in which case the odds of an event happening to a particular person are indeed millions to one, or whether they are identified after the fact, in which case the calculation of probability is rhetorical and invalid. Sally died of alcohol poisoning three years after being released from prison. Neither the 'expert' witness nor the judge or jury know enough about statistics or probability theory to contradict the 'expert' testimony in this case. The Royal College of Statisticians did, and wrote to the Lord Chancellor's Office to point out the error, an action that was instrumental in getting the case reviewed.

This same kind of logic applies to any amazing coincidence. The odds against may be millions to one that you might think of a person you haven't seen for many years just minutes before they call you, but you need to think about all of the other possible coincidences that could have happened but didn't. Think of all the people you know, how often you think about them, and what kind of event would count as a coincidence: phone call, Facebook, bump into them on the street, meet them on holiday, see them on television, etc. Then think about all the other kinds of coincidence that didn't happen either: the holiday you went on and didn't meet an old school friend, the pub you popped into unexpectedly and didn't meet the person you later married – the list is endless. Picking on a single coincidence and holding it up as requiring explanation is misunderstanding the principles of randomness and large numbers. An amazing coincidence requires explanation only if you predicted it in advance.

One other point: the same external event that made you think about your old school friend could be the trigger that caused them to look you up on Facebook. Perhaps there was an item in the news that barely registered on your consciousness but was enough to provoke an old memory. Before being too impressed by a coincidence, perhaps you could try to think of all the external events that might have triggered the coincidence, or at least reduced the odds of its occurring.

Looking at the empirical evidence for a connection between understanding of probabilities and paranormal belief, Blackmore and Troscianko (1985) found that believers were less accurate in tasks of estimating probabilities. Specifically, the believers underestimated the likelihood of events occurring by chance (the 'chance baseline shift') so that they were more surprised and impressed by the outcome – although the outcome was compatible with random chance. Other researchers have also reported evidence that supports the argument that believers are less accurate in calculating probabilities than non-believers though they have not all supported the baseline shift (Blagrove, French, & Jones, 2006; Brugger, Landis, & Regard, 1990; Rogers, Davis, & Fisk, 2009; Sutherland, 1992). However, others have found that probabilistic reasoning skills in general and judgements of probability were not related to paranormal belief (e.g. Blackmore, 1997; Matthews & Blackmore, 1995; Roberts & Seager, 1999; Stuart-Hamilton, Nayak, & Priest, 2006; Dagnall, Parker, & Munley, 2007), although there was a relationship with the specific factor of misperceptions of randomness.

A somewhat contrasting view was offered by Musch and Ehrenberg (2002) who found that believers performed worse than non-believers on a variety of tasks of probabilistic reasoning, but were also generally lower in cognitive ability (as measured by examination grades). There was no relationship between paranormal belief and probabilistic reasoning that was not accounted for by general cognitive ability. This suggests that general cognitive ability, rather than specifically a deficit in understanding of probability, may be what leads to paranormal belief.

Bressan (2002) found that paranormal belief was related to the frequency of meaningful coincidences that people reported in their own lives. She argued that believers do not misunderstand probability in general but have a stronger tendency to find connections between separate events compared to non-believers. So believers are just as likely to understand the true likelihood of a coincidence, and the difference between them and non-believers is that the believers observe more coincidences occurring and so they are more likely to invoke a paranormal explanation on some occasions. Other people with a lower propensity to connect events or search for causes are less likely to require explanations (see also Brugger & Graves, 1997b; Brugger & Taylor, 2003).

Along the same lines, Wiseman and Smith (2002) reported that believers found horoscopes to be more personally accurate (and less generally applicable) than non-believers. Interestingly, this was true of the 'target' horoscopes supposedly for the participant's precise birth date and also for the control horoscopes that were presented as being randomly picked. This rules out an explanation based on prior belief, which would predict higher similarity ratings from believers for the target horoscopes but not the control horoscopes (the control horoscopes should have been rated as equally accurate by believers and non-believers). Instead, this finding supports Bressan's (2002) proposal that believers see more connections between separate events than non-believers.

Taking all this evidence into consideration, it does not seem that a simple failure to estimate probability accurately can explain much paranormal belief. The evidence for worse probability estimation skills in believers than non-believers is inconsistent. Alternative explanations, including general cognitive ability, or a tendency to see more connections between separate events, would be interesting lines for further research although too little evidence exists as yet to form a firm conclusion.

The specific example of regression to the mean

A specific element of probability theory that has particular relevance to certain types of unsubstantiated belief is the concept of **regression to the mean**. This says that when a particular attribute varies in a random or a cyclical pattern, a particularly high level is likely to be followed by a downturn and a particularly low value is likely to be followed by an increase. This can be illustrated very simply in Figure 6.1. Our health often varies in this type of cyclical pattern – for example, we may get a cold that gradually worsens for a few days and then gradually improves. Several medical conditions can run in this type of pattern, including back pain, morning sickness, fatigue, arthritis, migraine, toothache, and many others.

Most people would try a new form of treatment when they are feeling particularly low – in which circumstance it is likely that they are soon going to see an improvement as part of the underlying cycle of their condition even if they had not tried a new form of treatment. In the absence of this understanding, however, the natural tendency would be to credit the treatment with the improvement in the condition. In this way, a medically ineffective form of treatment – for example, Reiki or homeopathic medicine – can be credited with helping to

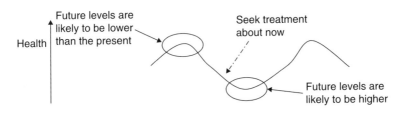

Figure 6.1 Illustration of the principle of regression to the mean

improve a medical condition (Singh & Ernst, 2008). The placebo effect is, of course, another explanation for why someone might perceive an improvement in her health after taking a medically ineffective treatment. It does seem plausible, though, that regression to the mean could be what inspires some belief.

Repetition avoidance

Many researchers (e.g. Blackmore & Troscianko, 1985) have reasoned that the tendency to see patterns and forms in random displays might encourage paranormal belief – for example, the belief that one has seen a ghost. So, people who underestimate the likelihood that random patterns might occasionally form clusters or meaningful shapes have a greater chance of being convinced that some paranormal force is at work.

In an early demonstration of errors in repetition avoidance, Wagenaar (1972) asked participants to generate a series of random numbers using the digits zero to nine. People generally avoid repetitions of the same digit believing that this is not random. Can you work out the true likelihood of a repetition? This example is related to the 'gambler's fallacy' or the belief that, for example, a run of black must be followed by a red. This is not true for the simple reason that each turn is independent of all previous turns so each turn has a 50/50 chance of being red or black regardless of what came before.

Several studies have found that believers avoid repetitions more than non-believers in various types of task. This suggests that believers have poorer understanding of the laws of probability and randomness (e.g. Bressan, 2002; Brugger & Baumann, 1994; Brugger, Landis, & Regard, 1990; Brugger et al., 1995; Brugger & Taylor, 2003; Musch & Ehrenberg, 2002). However, there have also been failures to find any difference in repetition avoidance between believers and non-believers (e.g. Blackmore & Troscianko, 1985; Lawrence, 1990–1).

It seems there is a consensus (though not unanimity) that believers show stronger repetition avoidance than non-believers. This could be related to a tendency to misunderstand the true probability of chance coincidences, which could lead to a perception that more anomalous events have occurred. It is easy to see how this could generate a higher level of belief in some kinds of paranormal phenomena.

The availability heuristic

A heuristic is a mental routine for generating an approximate solution to a problem quickly and with little effort. It will seldom come up with the very best answer but will usually produce an answer that is good enough. Life consists of a multitude of decisions and to ponder each carefully would leave us no time for living, so heuristics are vital. The downside is that occasionally a heuristic can generate a decision that is a long way short of being the best.

The **availability heuristic** is a tendency to rely strongly on those examples and instances that spring readily to mind. By and large this is a sensible approach as it means we will base our thinking on recent and common examples, which are likely to be relevant to the decision at hand. Further, we will incur minimal effort in trying to recall relevant information. But there are occasions when the availability heuristic can lead us into misleading conclusions. When someone is trying to think of an explanation for an anomalous event, a vivid explanation or one that has been recently encountered is likely to spring easily to mind (Sutherland, 1992). This could explain the power of the media to influence the explanations people accept for anomalous events. There is a wealth of books, TV series, and films about the paranormal and almost always these present paranormal phenomena as real. So when one perceives a strange coincidence, or sees a shadowy shape in an old building, an explanation in terms of telepathy or ghosts is readily available. Every time a paranormal explanation is accepted, of course, it increases the availability of this type of explanation for the next occurrence. In this way the availability heuristic could also explain the persistence of belief.

As an example, Singer and Benassi (1981) had a stage magician perform some tricks in front of an audience of undergraduate students. Some students were told that the performer was a magician and others that he was psychic. Despite being told the truth, around two-thirds of the students who were told the performer was a magician said they thought the performer was psychic, and 58% still thought he was psychic even when they explicitly acknowledged that a magician was capable of the same performance. It seems that the vividness of the visual demonstration captured the attention of the audience and presented the psychic explanation as much more readily available that the alternative explanation.

The representativeness heuristic

The **representativeness heuristic** (Kahneman & Tversky, 1972) says that causes should resemble their effects, and is often applied to topics like astrology and graphology. So, people are said to resemble the animals or symbols that characterize their astrological signs – for example, Leo (lion) is said to be arrogant and Libra (scales) is said to be fair-minded. In graphology, people with large, flowing handwriting are said to be generous and those with small lettering are

---

Box 6.1   The taxicab problem

A cab was involved in a hit and run accident at night. Two cab companies, the Green and the Blue, operate in the city. Of the cabs in the city, 85% are Green and 15% are Blue. A witness identified the cab as Blue. The court tested the reliability of the witness under the same circumstances that existed on the night of the accident and concluded that the witness correctly identified each one of the two colours 80% of the time and failed 20% of the time. What is the probability that the cab involved in the accident was Blue rather than Green knowing that this witness identified it as Blue?

---

said to be mean. There is no evidence that any of these alleged relationships are true (e.g. Gilovich, 1991).

Another example of the representativeness heuristic is the tendency to ignore the base rate when making decisions and to look only at the characteristics of a particular example. This is illustrated with the taxicab problem (see Box 6.1). Please try to answer the problem for yourself before you read on.

Most people give the answer as 80% because the witness said the cab was blue and the witness is 80% accurate in their colour judgement. But this is not correct because it ignores the base rate, which is the 85% probability that the cab was green in the first place. The correct calculation goes like this: the probability of a blue cab being identified as blue is *probability of a blue cab* × *probability of correct identification* = 15% × 80% = 12%. The probability of a green cab being identified as blue is *probability of a green cab* × *probability of incorrect identification* = 85% × 20% = 17%. So the probability that a cab identified as blue is actually blue is 12% divided by (12 + 17) = 41%. In other words, it is more likely that a cab identified as blue is actually green than blue. This is the true probability taking into account the base rate information.

Let's see if this might apply to paranormal belief. Suppose a friend gives you an account of a spooky coincidence for which there is no natural explanation and so she insists that some kind of precognition or telepathy was at work. You have two choices: either there was genuinely some telepathy or precognition, or your friend is mistaken in her account of the facts. Let us put this into the framework of the taxicab problem. If your friend is 90% accurate in her account of the incident but the prior probability of psi (in this example, telepathy or precognition) is only 1 in 100, then the calculation looks like this (the probabilities add up to 100%):

Probability of psi correctly identified as psi	= 1% × 90%	= 0.9%
Probability of non-psi wrongly identified as psi	= 99% × 10%	= 9.9%
Probability of non-psi correctly identified as non-psi	= 99% × 90%	= 89.1%
Probability of psi wrongly identified as non-psi	= 1% × 10%	= 0.1%

So even if your friend is 90% accurate in her description, the probability that psi (telepathy or precognition) has occurred is still only $0.9 / (0.9 + 9.9) = 8.3\%$. Of course, the prior probability of psi can be estimated differently by different individuals. If the prior probability of psi is sufficiently low then no description of a single anecdote can ever be convincing as evidence because there is always a possibility that people can be mistaken in their recollection of events. If the prior probability of psi is higher then less eyewitness accuracy is required to conclude that psi was at work. Both belief and disbelief can be self-maintaining.

Illusory correlation

A phenomenon that often depends on the availability heuristic is **illusory correlation** (e.g. Sutherland, 1992). This occurs when two events appear to occur together more often than would be expected by chance, although in fact there is no relationship between them. Examples include the belief that a lucky mascot brings good fortune or that someone with the astrological sign of Cancer will be intuitive. Believers may have a stronger tendency towards illusory correlation than non-believers (e.g. Tobacyk & Wilkinson, 1991).

Think of a 2×2 table like the one shown next. Cell A contains those occasions when the mascot was carried and good luck resulted, which are likely to be noticed and remembered because they are striking and fortunate. But knowing the number of cases in cell A does not tell us whether the two events are really related. We need to know also how many times we carried the mascot but had average or bad luck, in cell C. Then the likelihood of the mascot bringing good luck is $A / (A + C)$. But even this does not tell use whether the mascot is beneficial. To answer that question we need to compare the likelihood that carrying the mascot will bring good luck, $A / (A + C)$, with the likelihood that not carrying the mascot will bring good luck, $B / (B + D)$. If these likelihoods are the same then carrying the mascot does not bring good luck.

	Mascot	*No mascot*
Good luck	A	B
Average/bad luck	C	D
Total	A + C	B + D

People tend not to realize that it is necessary to know the number of cases in all of the cells in this table. It helps, of course, to draw the table, and it helps to have come across a similar question before. The problem here is a shortfall in *counterfactual thinking*. It is much easier to think about what is than what is not; it is easier to think of positive examples than negative examples. Incidents crop up only occasionally so it is natural to remember only the striking cases, those where both events occur (cell A). Selective memory for the striking cases gives a false impression of the true likelihood.

These concepts of the availability heuristic and illusory correlation can be applied to explain particular types of paranormal belief, for example, many superstitions could be created and maintained in this way. The occasions on which one saw a black cat and soon after received some unexpected good fortune would be striking and would be easily recalled. The occasions on which one did not see a black cat and nothing especially wonderful happened (which are probably most days) would not be memorable and so would not be taken into consideration.

Illusory control

Belief in psychokinesis may arise from the perception that one is able to exercise control over a physical event which is actually independent of one's actions. This belief would be encouraged by an overestimate of the proportion of occasions on which the outcome matched our desires or intentions.

We have a tendency to attribute outcomes to our own agency and to falsely perceive that random processes are under our control. Skinner (1948) found that even pigeons have the tendency to make spurious connections between their actions and a desired outcome. He placed hungry pigeons in a box that dispensed food at regular intervals. The pigeons acquired idiosyncratic behaviours or tics, so that whatever they were doing just before some food appeared, they did over and over again. Food was not dispensed every time the pigeon performed its ritualistic behaviour but sufficiently often to reinforce the behaviour. Skinner referred to this as 'conditioning by coincidence'.

Superstitions can arise in the same way. If one received an unexpectedly good outcome of an endeavour, then one might try to determine what it was that caused the outcome. Anything that was done on this occasion that had not been done before might be seized on as the lucky charm. Then one might be inclined to repeat the same action or carry the same lucky charm in the future. Failure to ever neglect the good luck charm would deny the possibility of observing that it actually did no good at all.

Several researchers have observed that believers estimate they had more control than they actually did compared to non-believers (e.g. Blackmore & Troscianko, 1985; Brugger, Regard & Landis, 1991; Schienle, Vaitl, & Stark, 1996). Interestingly, Langer (1975) found that the illusion of control was related to the perception that *skill* rather than mere chance was involved – for example, people believed that picking their own raffle ticket would increase the likelihood of winning. Ayeroff and Abelson (1976) reported a similar finding, that is, people in an ESP card-guessing task reported a higher estimate of success if they had a warm-up period and were allowed to choose their own deck of cards, both factors that would increase success in a game of skill but have no impact on a game of chance. This might suggest that perhaps people do not entirely appreciate the difference between a game of skill and a game of chance.

However, Irwin (2009) sounds a note of warning, pointing out that the illusion of control is specific to the particular situation. Paranormal believers do not think that they are in control in all areas of their life. Indeed, that would be inconsistent with the evidence of a relationship with external locus of control (see Chapter 2). Further, Irwin (2009) points out that there is some evidence that the illusion of control arises only in people who have a high need for control. He proposes that the illusion of control is the consequence and not the cause of paranormal belief in people with a high need for control and that the activation of the illusion of control may be psychologically reassuring by providing the impression that the individual can influence external events.

This seems like a plausible argument and, given that none of the studies reporting a relationship between paranormal belief and the illusion of control can say anything about the question of causality, it seems safer to assume that this illusion has little to say about the origins of paranormal belief apart from everyday superstitions.

Distorting the evidence

Several studies have offered evidence that our perception of events is coloured by our prior beliefs. For example, Russell and Jones (1980) conducted a study with undergraduate participants, divided into believers and non-believers, who were asked to read a short passage that either supported or challenged ESP. Believers recalled the passage more accurately if it supported ESP than if it challenged ESP; they remembered more of the supportive passage than the challenging passage, and they distorted the message of the latter. There was no difference in the accuracy of recall for non-believers, who remembered both passages equally well. This result is particularly interesting when you consider that sceptics are often accused of being closed-minded and not prepared to listen to new ideas or examine new evidence.

In a similar type of study, Jones and Russell (1980) asked undergraduates to watch two demonstrations of ESP arranged so that one was successful and the other was unsuccessful. The believers recalled both demonstrations as successful, whereas the sceptics recalled accurately that one demonstration was successful and one unsuccessful. The sceptics also reported some change of attitude in the successful condition but believers did not in the unsuccessful condition. This study might suggest that, under certain circumstances, non-believers are more open and prepared to change their minds according to observed data than the believers. In a similar study by French (1992b), the believers rated a demonstration as providing more evidence of ESP than the non-believers. To their credit, the believers as well as the non-believers reduced their ratings of evidence for ESP when it was explained that the demonstration was based upon trickery (although their ratings remained higher than the non-believers).

Wiseman, Smith, and Wiseman (1995) decided to test out the accuracy of people's observation and memory in a realistic séance setting. It is important to do this realistic type of research because the heightened sense of anticipation and excitement during a genuine séance compared to a laboratory experiment may alter the accuracy of eyewitness testimony. The key findings were: some participants said that objects had been handled which had not been touched at all; some participants said that objects moved which had not moved; and some participants failed to detect the movement of the table by four inches. Overall, believers were more likely to believe that something paranormal had occurred, and were less accurate in their descriptions of the events. This is particularly striking since the 'séance' lasted only ten minutes and participants gave their accounts immediately afterwards.

Thus, it appears that we may sometimes distort the evidence to suit our prior beliefs. There is a danger that we may become even more firmly entrenched in our beliefs by the processes we use to maintain them: we search for flaws in the evidence offered by the opposition and we try to find alternatives to their explanations, whereas we accept the argument we agree with uncritically. In other words, exposing people to a substantial set of objective evidence that contradicts their views on a complex social topic may not cause them to change or moderate their views but rather to become even more entrenched (e.g. Kuhn, 1989; Lord, Ross, & Lepper, 1979; Roe, 1999).

This attitude is often sensible when an objective truth is known, in which case it would be wise to look carefully at a study with a contrary conclusion. Any study which claims that 'black is white' has a flaw in it somewhere! But when the objective truth is not clear, as is usually the case for a complex social issue, it is wise to listen carefully to both sides of a debate (Sutherland, 1992). The **confirmation bias** means that only one side of the argument will be given proper consideration so this can limit the quality of debate. The danger that opposing evidence will be used to polarize individuals' views may even reduce the likelihood of reaching a social consensus.

Gilovich (1991) points out that the degree to which we should be open-minded about anomalous events depends on the quality of evidence that would be overturned if we accept the new events. If we would need to overturn a law of nature with huge supporting evidence then we should view the anomalous event with considerable scepticism. But when the new event has its own rigorous evidence, and would overturn nothing underpinned by scientific research of equivalent quality, then we should be quite open to the new possibility. Compare and contrast the existence of ghosts with the challenge faced by Galileo and his theory of the solar system.

Wiseman and Greening (2005) reported two experiments in which there was a pseudo-psychic demonstration of key bending. In these studies, participants who heard a verbal suggestion that a key continued to bend after it was put down were more likely to report that they perceived the key continuing to bend than another group of participants who heard no such suggestion. These last two studies reported no difference between believers and non-believers, but rather demonstrated that participants in general are capable of being influenced in their perception and memory by expectation regarding the 'psychic' nature of a performance.

Sutherland (1992; and also Lord, Ross, & Lepper, 1979) summarizes a series of steps that believers or non-believers could take to maintain their beliefs in the face of contrary evidence. First: avoid exposure to contrary beliefs in the first place by selective engagement with the media and careful choice of friends. Second: refuse to believe any evidence with which you do not agree. Third: interpret new evidence in the light of existing beliefs, by attending to the strengths of confirming evidence and the weaknesses of disconfirming evidence, and accepting the confirming evidence uncritically while scrutinizing disconfirming evidence. Fourth: selectively recall only the evidence with which you agree so that this is the only evidence to have a lasting effect.

In summary, it would seem plausible that distorted perception and consideration of the evidence can serve to maintain paranormal belief. It is less clear that this would help to create paranormal belief in the first place, so alternative explanations are still needed for how a belief might get started.

Confirmation bias

Confirmation bias is the tendency to seek out information that can confirm our beliefs and not to look for information that might challenge them. If we only look at information that conforms to our beliefs, then there is no reason to change those beliefs (e.g. Sutherland, 1992). As an example of confirmation bias, Snyder (1981) told participants that the person they were about to meet was either introverted or extraverted. Participants who were told that the person was extraverted asked more questions about stereotypically extraverted than introverted activities, and participants who were told that the person was introverted did the opposite. So participants asked questions to confirm their beliefs but not to challenge them.

One of the early examples of confirmation bias was the card puzzle of Wason (1960). In one version of the task, there are four cards, two showing letters – for example, A and B – and two showing numbers – for example, 4 and 7. You are asked to investigate the rule that 'If a card has a vowel on one side, then it must have an even number on the other side' and you are allowed to turn over two cards. Most adults – around 90% – get the answer partly wrong. They suggest turning over the A card to see if it has an even number on the other side, which is clearly correct, because if the A card does not have an even number on the other side then the rule has been broken. But then they suggest turning over the 4 card which is where the error lies. Turning over the 4 card can tell you nothing; if it has a consonant on the other side, this does not break the rule – the rule does not specify that *only* a vowel has an even number on the other side. This is where people make their mistake – they listen to the words 'If a card has a vowel on one side, then it must have an even number on the other side' but what they hear is 'If *and only if* ...' which makes all the difference.

If you want to test whether a rule has been broken, then you need to seek out information to challenge the rule. Look at another similar example: 'If a person is drinking beer, then they must be 18 or over' and the cards 17, 18, beer, and cola. Which two cards would you turn over? Most people get this one right by turning over the 17 card to check that the person is drinking cola and the beer card to see that the person is 18 or over. It is clear in this case that in order to test whether the rule is correctly followed we need to try to see if the rule has been broken.

Unfortunately, the idea of trying to disconfirm a rule is not commonly understood. Scientists know this concept under the term 'falsifiability' and understand that in order to test a scientific hypothesis we need to try to prove it wrong. If repeated tests fail to disconfirm a hypothesis, then we give the hypothesis our provisional acceptance. People without scientific training are probably not aware of this principle and hence the problem of confirmation bias. If people do not realize that confirmation does not prove a rule then they may be convinced by a pile of confirming examples that a rule is valid, failing to realize that the examples are equally compatible with other explanations.

The Barnum effect

The **Barnum effect** (also known as the Forer effect) is named after the circus owner P. T. Barnum whose shows were said to have 'something for everyone'. It refers to the tendency to rate a statement as personally accurate and specific even though it could relate to almost anyone. The Barnum effect is stronger under these circumstances: you are told the statement has been generated for you in particular; you believe in the authority of the person making the statement; and the statement describes mainly positive traits (without going over the top). The Barnum effect is an example of the more general phenomenon of so-called **subjective validation** which refers to any situation where two unrelated stimuli or events are perceived to correspond in various ways because the observer has the expectation that such correspondences must exist. Subjective validation, in its turn, is one example of confirmation bias.

Here are some examples of Barnum statements:

> You can be a very considerate person, very quick to provide for others, but there are times, if you are honest, when you recognize a selfish streak in yourself. I would say that on the whole you can be a rather quiet, self-effacing type, but when the circumstances are right, you can be quite the life of the party if the mood strikes you.

> Sometimes you are too honest about your feelings and you reveal too much of yourself. You are good at thinking things through and you like to see proof before you change your mind about anything. When you

find yourself in a new situation you are very cautious until you find out what's going on, and then you begin to act with confidence.

What I get here is that you are someone who can generally be trusted. Not a saint, not perfect, but let's just say that when it really matters, this is someone who does understand the importance of being trustworthy. You know how to be a good friend.

Read these statements carefully and try to imagine a person for whom these are *not* true. It isn't easy, is it? These statements apply to more or less everyone, but the trick is that they seem to be specific. If you are a practicing psychic consultant, you can expect your clients to be impressed by the use of Barnum statements (e.g. Shermer, 2008) and they will cost you nothing to prepare. Confirmation bias can help to explain the success of Barnum statements; we look for evidence, examples, and anecdotes to confirm a statement but not to prove it false.

There is evidence that the presentation of a Barnum statement can increase the level of belief. Students who gave their course tutors a sample of handwriting and received in return a Barnum-style 'personality description' reported an increased level of belief in graphology (the 'science' of reading personality from handwriting). The students decreased their level of belief again after debriefing (Boyce & Geller, 2002).

Seeing forms in randomness

It has been proposed that believers might be more likely to see meaningful objects or entities in random patterns (e.g. Shermer, 2011). This could potentially explain sightings of ghosts or aliens or other anomalous creatures. For example, Brugger *et al.* (1993) reported that believers were more likely than non-believers to think they had seen some meaningful form in a random pattern of pixels. Other researchers have observed that believers are more inclined to make connections between random drawings (Wiseman & Smith, 2002). Please take a look at Figure 6.2a without looking at the caption. Does anything strike you? Repeat for Figure 6.2b.

Blackmore and Moore (1994) wondered whether believers might have a different criterion for seeing forms under difficult perceptual conditions. They found that believers said they could see objects (e.g. leaves, bird, fish, axe) that were distorted and hard to identify at a greater level of distortion than non-believers, suggesting a greater tendency to see forms in randomness. However, the believers were not more likely to be correct in their identification of the objects. So it seems that believers are simply more likely to try to see something in a random pattern but do not have superior perceptual abilities. Interestingly, this was supported by the observation that believers also reported more frequent misidentifications of people they know in everyday life.

It seems that there is evidence that believers are more likely to see patterns in randomness than non-believers. As a visual bias, this might increase their

Figure 6.2a   Can you see the face?

Figure 6.2b   Can you see the phoenix?

chances of seeing ghosts, aliens, or any other anomalous creature. As a bias in perception of more abstract information, it might increase their chances of believing in horoscopes, handwriting analysis, or even possibly the work of a spirit medium or any kind of fortune-teller. Of course, it could be argued that believers are seeing genuine connections that non-believers are biased against perceiving, but this would contradict the findings of Blackmore and Moore (1994) that believers saw more patterns but were not more accurate (refer to Chapter 8 for more discussion of individual differences in the propensity to see patterns where none exist and the potential evolutionary role of this propensity).

Perceptual errors

One type of perceptual error that might underlie some instances of belief in UFOs is the autokinetic effect. When you stare at a point of light against a dark background, after a while it will appear to jump about. This is because the cells in the retina of the eye become exhausted staring at the point of light and so the eye automatically makes a small movement, known as a saccade, on order to focus the light onto different cells, which makes the point of light appear to move. An individual staring at a light in the sky at night could then perceive a stationary light to move erratically and very fast – like a UFO.

Another type of perceptual error is the phenomenon of ghost photography, in which a figure will appear in a photograph when it is developed, yet the person taking the photograph is certain there was no figure in the shot. How can this arise? Perhaps the figure in the photograph moved into the shot just before the photo was taken; but how could this happen and the photographer not notice? If you have not seen it already, then please search on the Internet for a short film clip using the search words 'basketball' and 'awareness'. Follow the instructions and count the number of times the people wearing white clothes pass the basketball to each other. Please do this before you read the next paragraph.

If you are anything like the authors of this book (and many others), then you failed to notice the moonwalking bear (alright, a person in a bear suit). The observation that many people do not see the moonwalking bear does perhaps suggest that it might be possible for someone to walk into a photograph without being seen by the photographer.

How faulty is our reasoning and perception?

Shermer (1997) explains that our brains have evolved to detect patterns and relationships so that we can make sense of the world around us and act in ways that ensure our survival and well-being (see also Chapter 8). For example, knowing that beans should be planted in early May when there is plenty of rain is an item of knowledge that promotes our well-being. There is, however, a problem with real world knowledge based on observation – it doesn't work 100% of the time, and although a relationship is generally true, there are often exceptions. Sometimes May is a very dry month. So the relationships we observe in the natural world are probabilistic rather than fully deterministic. By following our observations we can increase our chances of success but there is no guarantee of a good outcome.

This poses the problem of how to decide whether we should base our decisions on a particular observed relationship. We can err in two directions – we can fail to obey a rule that would be helpful, or we can obey a rule that does not help at all. Given only probabilistic and imperfect knowledge we have the choice to adjust our criterion in the direction of more belief or less belief but either way will cause some errors. If we shift our criteria in the direction of more belief, then we are less likely to miss out on helpful knowledge, but we are liable to the error of adopting arbitrary rules that add nothing to our benefit. If we shift in the direction of less belief, then we may miss opportunities to gain some advantage. Where is the sensible place to draw the line? Perhaps we should consider that many rules which are not actually reflected in reality do little or no harm. If we wear a lucky charm while planting our beans we won't get a better crop, but there is little cost in observing this practice. So we can see how harmless beliefs can survive. Especially if we are diligent in our observance and never test the reality of our belief by planting beans without carrying our lucky charm, we will never learn that this rule has no bearing on reality.

There is a case for thinking that some superstitions may actually benefit the individual. Chapter 2 reviewed evidence that superstitions may protect against learned helplessness and demoralization and may foster continued engagement with activities that could pay off in the long run. Superstitions may also help to boost one's confidence and help one to relax, which in certain situations could promote good performance of a task. Common shared superstitions can also be socially unifying which is generally a good thing.

Sutherland (1992) explains that the evolution of the modern technological world has outstripped the evolution of our brains so that we are sometimes ill equipped to make the complex decisions we are now required to make. Our ancestors probably had fewer decisions to make and were safer going along with the majority view and sticking to customary practice. This is not always a rational response for us today and can lead to erroneous beliefs, although, as we have mentioned, most paranormal beliefs do no harm and some may be of use in maintaining our psychological health.

Selective scientific research

Shermer (1997) points out that scientists and researchers, too, suffer from biases or limitations in perception, and that these colour all of the knowledge that becomes available to us. In simple terms, we can only find what we are looking for. If a researcher conceives the hypothesis that people who believe they have been abducted by aliens are suffering from some form of delusion, and investigates the presence of schizotypical symptoms, then these symptoms can either be found or not. If the symptoms exist in a group of alien abduction (AA) experiencers at a higher level than the general population, then there is a good chance the work will be published and become part of collective knowledge. But the key point is that this research cannot unearth evidence that AA experiencers are likely to suffer from sleep paralysis, because it is not looking for such evidence. It is not looking at sleep paralysis at all. We can only find what we are looking for, and if a hypothesis is not proposed, it will not be investigated. In this way, the perceptions of scientists and researchers about what is worth investigating determine the discoveries that can be made.

Biases in memory

As well as biases in thinking and in perception, it is possible that belief in the paranormal is related to biases in memory (French, 2003; French & Wilson,

138 ANOMALISTIC PSYCHOLOGY

2006). There has been a large body of research into the accuracy of eyewitness testimony in a forensic (legal) setting and the general conclusion of this research is that memory is subject to many biases and distortions and that eyewitness testimony can be extremely unreliable (Cohen, 1989; Loftus, 1979). As long ago as the 1880s, scientists were conducting systematic investigations of the accuracy of eyewitness testimony for events that occurred during séances in order to investigate whether the average person attending a séance would be able to detect if any fraud had occurred. When the people attending the séances described afterwards the events that had occurred, they omitted many important details and recalled other details in the wrong sequence. Overall, their testimony offered insufficient detail and accuracy to be able to tell whether the phenomena witnessed during the séance could have been faked (Hodgson & Davy, 1887).

Wiseman and Morris (1995a) showed a group of students a film of two 'pseudo-psychic' demonstrations, such as ostensibly psychokinetic metalbending (the effect actually being achieved by sleight of hand). Afterwards, the participants answered factual questions, half of which were important to the nature of the trick (e.g. 'Did the fork always remain in sight?') and the other half were about other aspects of the performance. The results showed that believers recalled less of the important information than the non-believers, but not less of the unimportant information. This suggests that the believers' memories, or their powers of observation, were not at fault in general, but that they were specifically less accurate in their observation of the key points of the demonstration that related to their belief that something paranormal had occurred. French (2003) proposed that the sceptics watched the demonstration with the intent of finding out how the 'trick' was done and so it is likely they paid more attention to such crucial details than the believers, who might have been more inclined to sit back and enjoy the show. Similarly, Smith (1993) showed two groups of participants a film of apparent psychic surgery and told one group that the film contained a demonstration of something paranormal but the other group that the film showed a trick. The group who thought they were watching a trick had better memory for the film than the group who thought they were watching a psychic performance. Other studies have found non-believers' memory to be more accurate than believers' (e.g. Jones & Russell, 1980; Wiseman, Smith, & Wiseman, 1995) described in more detail previously (see *Distorting the Evidence*). This is related to the earlier section on alternative explanations and syllogistic reasoning and also to confirmation bias.

In summary, it would appear that believers and non-believers are liable to be influenced by prior expectation in their reports of a demonstration of an ostensibly paranormal phenomenon. It is clear that our memory is driven not only by the actual data (known as 'bottom-up processing') but also by our expectations and prior beliefs (known as 'top-down processing'). There is a reasonable body of research to suggest that believers may be less accurate in their perception and recall than non-believers for ostensibly paranormal events. It would seem that all eyewitness accounts of supposedly paranormal events should be treated with some caution.

French (2003) suggests that we should always be careful before we accept any claim that an event has occurred which defies the laws of physics and of nature. He suggests that we should ask ourselves whether it is more likely that the person making a claim has been deceived or that a law of nature has been violated. After all, we are surrounded by evidence that people make mistakes and recall events incorrectly. As the philosopher David Hume pointed out in 1748:

> No testimony is sufficient to establish a miracle unless that testimony be of such a kind that its falsehood would be more miraculous than the fact which it endeavours to establish.

Hindsight bias and selective memory

Hindsight bias refers to the distortion of our memories by knowledge of later events. This can have the effect of making a particular outcome seem to fit a prediction much more closely than it really does, by distorting the memory of the prediction to fit the later events. It is clear that this bias has some potential for explaining the widespread belief in precognitive dreams and in the accuracy of astrological or other predictions. James Randi (1990) recommends, in his list of rules for making a living as a fortune-teller, the deliberate use of vagueness so that a prediction can be interpreted in several different ways. Metaphors are good for being vague so these are also recommended.

Selective memory refers to the tendency to remember only the most dramatic and interesting events and to forget those that seem less salient or those that are in some way ambiguous. Suppose that we dream many times every night but typically we forget our dreams on waking. If nothing occurs to remind us of a dream within the next few hours, it is likely to be forgotten forever. But suppose that something occurs during the day that resembles some aspect of a dream, this might trigger a recollection of the dream. But how accurate is our recollection of the dream? This is impossible to say. We only recall the dream when an event of the day triggers the recollection, so how can we possibly ascertain what the original memory might have contained until it was contaminated by later events? A similar thing might happen when we go to a 'psychic' (e.g. astrologer, tarot card reader, psychic consultant, etc.) for a consultation. The psychic might generate multiple predictions too fast for us to remember them all. But we will be inclined to remember the ones that later on seem to come true. James Randi (1990) includes the scattergun approach in his list of rules for making a living as a fortune-teller. He explains that people will not systematically record every prediction and check those that do not come true. Our memory is selective in this way; we recall the hits and forget the misses.

Gilovich (1991, p. 62) compares one-sided unfocused events with two-sided focused events. The latter are those that must occur and have one of two outcomes (you either pass your driving test or not) while the former are those that either happen at an unspecified time or do not happen. It is these events that will trigger a recollection of a prediction or a dream if they occur but will pass unnoticed if they do not. No one records all of their dreams in detail in order to accurately calculate the proportion that later come true.

False memory

This section will examine the possibility that many sincere accounts of alien abduction or past-life regression are in fact false memories, often created via a process of hypnotic induction.

Several studies have shown that false memories can be generated spontaneously by a substantial minority of the general population without any deliberate influence by any other person. For example, children provided sincere eyewitness accounts of a dramatic event (a sniper attack on a school playground) when they had definitely not been present (Pynoos & Nader, 1989). Four survivors of cardiac arrests who did not report NDEs at the time claimed two years later to have had such an experience (French, 2001d). Participants in an experiment reported that they remembered seeing footage of a bombing of a Bali nightclub for which there was no photographic record (Wilson & French, 2006). So the potential for false memories to arise naturally seems to be quite substantial and there are several more examples (e.g. Loftus, 1993).

There are also concerns that some therapists who are using hypnosis to try to recover 'repressed' memories may be responsible, instead, for creating false memories. Spanos, Burgess, and Burgess (1994) explain that the hypnotic procedure provides a situation in which people can easily mix fragments of memory with pre-existing beliefs, fantasy, and imagination to come up with a 'recovered memory' they sincerely believe but which never occurred. A person who believes they have been abducted by aliens, perhaps because of some strange dreams or sleep paralysis (see Holden & French, 2002) but who has no memory for the abduction may come to think that they might have a repressed memory. Indeed, aliens are credited by some with the ability to wipe clean one's memory for an abduction event. Then if the individual goes to a therapist known to specialize in helping people to recover repressed memories, who uses a hypnotic procedure, we have most of the conditions in place to create a false memory: a client convinced that there is a memory to recover; background knowledge of what the memory might contain (from the media and friends); willing cooperation with the hypnotic procedure; and perhaps a therapist with too little regard for the pitfalls and dangers of hypnosis for memory enhancement.

One factor which does seem to increase the likelihood of a false memory becoming established is the technique of 'imagination inflation' (Loftus, 2001). This relies on the principle that real memories have more perceptual information (e.g. what could you see?), more contextual information (e.g. what happened immediately before and after?), and more affective information (e.g. how did you feel at the time?) than imaginings. Therefore, concentrating on imagining an event with these details can make it seem more real. This was confirmed in a study by Garry *et al.* (1996) in which participants declared increased confidence that certain childhood events had happened to them (e.g. being lost in a shopping mall) after engaging in active imagination of these events.

This is an example of a 'source monitoring' error in which the individual cannot identify the source of information – was it something that actually happened or something they imagined? Spanos, Burgess, and Burgess (1994) explain how the questions asked by a hypnotist or interviewer can give clues to enable the individual to construct a more fully detailed and realistic fantasy account of an event that never occurred.

There is direct empirical evidence that false memories can be created during hypnosis. Spanos *et al.* (1991) used hypnosis to persuade volunteers to regress to past-lives. Thirty-five of the 110 participants produced a past-life identity and were able to supply some details of the person and their environment (although often not accurate). Of particular importance, the past-life memories showed the influence of the researcher, both in the content of the memories and the confidence with which the participants viewed the memories as real versus imaginary. Also, participants' prior belief in reincarnation was related to the degree of credibility attached to the past-life memories. It seems reasonable to assume that the same principle could easily apply to recovered memories of alien abduction (e.g. Spanos, Burgess, & Burgess, 1994).

The evidence so far suggests that false memories can be created in a substantial minority of the population and that hypnosis is frequently implicated. There is some evidence that false memories are more easily created in those who believe in the paranormal or who have reported paranormal experiences (e.g. Clancy *et al.*, 2002; Dagnall, Parker, & Munley, 2008; French, Wilson, & Davis, 2012; Wilson & French, 2006) but there have also been some failures to find a link between paranormal belief and experience and the susceptibility to false memories (e.g. Blackmore & Rose, 1997; French *et al.*, 2008; Rose & Blackmore, 2001).

Individual differences

These include: educational level, scientific education, intelligence, worldview and thinking style, creativity, and transliminality and non-conscious processing. Some of these topics were introduced in Chapter 2 and will be considered in more detail here.

Educational level

Many researchers have examined this question and there is substantial evidence that higher educational level is associated with lower global paranormal belief (Aarnio & Lindeman, 2005; Donovan, 1998; Orenstein, 2002;

Schulter & Papousek, 2008; Sjöberg & Wåhlberg, 2002) and with lower levels of belief in *astrology or fortune-telling* (Donahue, 1993; Newport & Strausberg, 2001; Otis & Alcock, 1982; Rice, 2003; Torgler, 2007; Wuthnow, 1976); *spiritualism or ghosts* (Newport & Strausberg, 2001; Otis & Alcock, 1982); *superstition and luck* (Otis & Alcock, 1982; Plug, 1976; Torgler, 2007), *UFOs* (Donahue, 1993), and *precognitive dreams* (Blagrove, French, & Jones, 2006). These observations allow one of two interpretations: perhaps people with a higher level of education became sceptical as a result of their prolonged interaction with other professional academics, or alternatively those with a sceptical attitude may be more attracted to an academic career. The data do not permit a choice between these alternatives.

The picture is not entirely one-sided and a higher level of education has been associated with stronger belief in ESP, psi, or mental healing (Emmons & Sobal, 1981; Haraldsson, 1985a, in USA and Germany; Newport & Strausberg, 2001; Rice, 2003) though sometimes with lower belief (Otis & Alcock, 1982). It seems that those with a more successful academic career may sometimes be more inclined to believe in mental powers.

A couple of interesting features of the research will be noted. Otis and Alcock (1982) pointed out that for the professors in their study, there was a relationship between belief and personal experience for the factors of spiritualism, psychic abilities, and fortune-telling, suggesting that this group would not have an appreciable level of belief without personal experience. Perhaps a higher educational level is accompanied by a higher level of reliance on observable data, but this does not protect against belief in the presence of subjective paranormal experience. In the students and members of the general public, belief did not appear to depend on experience.

Farha and Steward (2006) found that a sample of college students reported lower levels of belief than a large-scale Gallup Poll in the general population, consistent with the general consensus pattern. However, the older students had higher levels of paranormal belief than the younger students, which might suggest that at the college level of education the extra years of formal schooling had led to an increase in paranormal belief. The study had over 400 participants so the findings are unlikely to be due to some random idiosyncrasy of their sample. Perhaps the extra years of education had taught the students to be more open-minded and accepting of new ideas but failed to equip them with the critical thinking skills to be appropriately selective in the new ideas they were happy to entertain. Interestingly, they also reported lower levels of scepticism than the general population, which fits with the hypothesis than higher education equips students to be more open-minded. Tobacyk, Miller, and Jones (1984) reported a similar finding comparing paranormal beliefs of college and high school students.

Irwin (2009) raises a note of caution, pointing out that educational level is confounded with socio-economic status and age, and hence the relationships observed may have more to do with social factors than purely educational factors. The facets of paranormal belief associated with higher educational level seem to be those that emphasize the possession of superior mental powers, and Chapter 2 reviewed evidence that these facets of paranormal belief are those which are more strongly espoused by people of higher socio-economic status. More puzzling is the finding that higher educational level is associated with belief in alternative health remedies reported by Ni, Simile, and Hardy (2002) in a survey with over 30,000 respondents. It seems likely that once again this may reflect the fact that socio-economic status is correlated with educational level as it is only those with substantial amounts of disposable income who can afford to spend money on alternative medicine.

Scientific education

Several studies have found that science students, compared to students of arts or humanities, have lower levels of belief in the paranormal in general (Aarnio & Lindemann, 2005; Bhushan & Bhushan, 1987; Gray, 1990; Gray & Mill, 1990; Morier & Keeports, 1994; Tobacyk, Miller, & Jones, 1984), in parapsychological phenomena and spiritualism (Otis & Alcock, 1982; Tobacyk, Miller, & Jones, 1984), and fortune-telling and alternative medicine (Grimmer & White, 1992). There have been failures, though, to find any difference between science students and others in degree of paranormal belief (Walker, Hoekstra, & Vogl, 2002). In comparison, Otis and Alcock (1982) found that staff and students in the English department had higher levels of belief in spiritualism, psychic abilities, and fortune-telling than some other (but not all) departments. In the English department, it may be that objective data is less highly valued, and creativity and open-mindedness are more strongly encouraged.

It is tempting to assume that a scientific education can persuade people to place more reliance on observable data and to improve their reasoning and critical thinking skills. For example, Gilovich (1991) proposed that social scientists might be particularly able to reason with probabilities, because the subject matter of their learning (i.e. human behaviour) is irregular and uncertain. In support of this supposition, there is evidence that scientific education is associated with improved reasoning and critical thinking skills (e.g. Lehman, Lempert, & Nisbett, 1988, conditional reasoning and probability; Gray & Mill, 1990, assessing the quality of evidence for a particular claim; Fong & Nisbett, 1991 and Nisbett et al., 1987, formal statistical reasoning). Of particular interest, Morier and Keeports (1994) found that teaching on the scientific method and the characteristics of pseudosciences led to reduced levels of belief in the paranormal.

It seems there is a general consensus that a scientific education results in improved critical thinking and reasoning skills and is associated with a reduction in paranormal belief. Perhaps the emphasis on observation and data, on statistical models and hypothesis testing, and on alternative explanations and counterfactual thinking fosters a critical frame of mind, and this weakens belief. However, we must remember that correlation does not imply causation and we should not conclude that it is scientific education in itself that fosters disbelief. The alternative possibility must be considered, that individuals with a critical frame of mind are attracted to scientific subjects and that this difference precedes their experiences in higher education. Most of the evidence cited before is correlational, that is, we observe a relationship that already exists, so we cannot tell whether greater scepticism precedes or is the product of a scientific education.

Intelligence

IQ has been found to be negatively related to paranormal belief. As IQ goes up, there is a lower level of belief in *superstitions* (e.g. Killen, Wildman, & Wildman, 1974; Thalbourne & Nofi, 1997), and in *psi, precognition,* and *spiritualism* (Smith, Foster, & Stovin, 1998). However, there have also been failures to find any relationship between intelligence and *global paranormal belief* (Royalty, 1995; Stuart-Hamilton, Nayak, & Priest, 2006; Thalbourne & Nofi, 1997; Watt & Wiseman, 2002) and even a finding of higher intelligence associated with more belief (Jones, Russell, & Nickel, 1977).

Indirect estimates of intelligence can be found by comparing college grades, and several studies have found that college students with higher grades have lower levels of paranormal belief compared to students with lower grades (e.g. Messer & Griggs, 1989; Musch & Ehrenberg, 2002; Otis & Alcock, 1982; Tobacyk, Miller, & Jones, 1984). There have also been failures to replicate this effect (e.g. Thalbourne & Nofi, 1997) or contrary findings of higher grades with increased belief in psi and psychic healing (e.g. Haraldsson, 1985a; Tobacyk, Miller, & Jones, 1984). It is interesting that these contrary findings relate to a mental power, as one might expect that people who achieve strong academic results would be ready to believe in the power of the mind in general.

It should be noted that the observations of a relationship between higher academic grades and lower paranormal belief does not necessarily imply that intelligence or academic ability causes increased scepticism. It may be that students who engage more strongly with their studies are likely to achieve better grades and also to absorb the general culture of their academic school which is likely to include a critical sceptical tone (e.g. Irwin, 2009; Messer & Griggs, 1989). So the underlying reason would be engagement, rather than intelligence as such, although the two are likely to be related.

In view of the inconclusive evidence linking intelligence or college grades to paranormal belief, it seems likely that intelligence or academic aptitude in itself is responsible for only a small proportion of the general belief in paranormal phenomena. It seems likely that critical thinking and reasoning skills, or specific cognitive and perceptual biases and distortions, are also responsible.

Worldview and thinking style

Irwin (2009) discusses the concept of a *worldview* as a systematic approach to perceiving and reasoning about the world and distinguishes two main worldviews, the subjective and the objective. The **subjective worldview** is characterized by the belief that knowledge is gained through introspection and reflection whereas adherents of the **objective worldview** would say that knowledge is gained from systematic observation. It seems plausible that belief in a range of paranormal phenomena may be rendered more likely by the adoption of a subjective worldview that relies less on the existence of hard data and observable facts.

A similar concept is the question of thinking styles – analytical versus intuitive – which was considered in Chapter 2. Lindeman (1998) suggested that preference for the intuitive thinking style would be associated with paranormal belief and evidence for this was discussed in Chapter 2.

Creativity

The evidence so far has tended to suggest that people who believe in paranormal phenomena have some kind of deficits in reasoning or perceptual or memory abilities. However, the picture is not all bad, and there is evidence of distinct advantages that tend to co-occur with paranormal belief. One of these is heightened creativity. Several researchers have found relationships between measures of creativity and belief in ESP (Joesting & Joesting, 1969; Moon, 1975), or belief in psi (Davis, Peterson, & Farley, 1974; Thalbourne, 1998; Thalbourne & Delin, 1994), or belief in the paranormal in general (Gianotti *et al.*, 2001). It is also worth noting that creativity may have some connection with fantasy-proneness, which is generally higher in believers than non-believers (see Chapter 2).

Transliminality and non-conscious processing

Non-conscious processing refers to the fact that vast amounts of mental activity (involved in perception, recognition, reasoning, decision-making, memory recall, and so on) occur without our conscious awareness. Our brains are naturally evolved computers carrying out multitudes of calculations every second so we cannot possibly become aware of all of the processing that is carried out. We become aware only of the outputs of processing and not the actual processing itself (Velmans, 2000). This raises the possibility that we may become confused about the origin of some of the perceptions and memories of which we become conscious. If we seem to know something, but have no recollection of how we came to know it, then we may attribute our knowledge to a paranormal cause rather than to a normal but non-conscious cause.

Copious evidence from psychological studies shows that we can be influenced by information of which we are unaware. Wilson (2002) gives a hypothetical example: imagine a woman who crosses over a suspension bridge each day on her way to work; then one day for no reason that she can think of she chooses a different route. Later she discovers that the suspension bridge collapsed that day. This could easily be interpreted as an example of precognition but it need not be if we consider other possibilities. Perhaps the bridge appeared different, maybe it swayed alarmingly, but the woman did not consciously notice this. Still, the knowledge could have been enough to persuade her to choose a different route the next day. There is direct evidence to support the possibility of this kind of event: for example, Rensink (2004) found that participants could sense that there was a difference between two visual images although the images were flashed so briefly they had no conscious awareness of them.

There is also direct evidence that participants may confuse subliminal perception (i.e. perception below the level of conscious awareness) with ESP (e.g. Miller, 1940). More recent evidence was offered by Crawley, French, and Yesson (2002) from an experiment they presented as a card-guessing task of ESP. Participants were shown the backs of a series of cards on the screen and had to guess which of five symbols was on the front of the card, the actual symbol having been randomly chosen by the computer on each turn. On some turns the image of the front of the card was flashed onto the screen very briefly before the back of the card appeared, a technique known as 'subliminal priming'. Participants were unaware of this briefly displayed image but nonetheless it did influence their decisions so that they made more correct guesses on trials which were primed than on unprimed trials. The number of correct guesses on primed trials was also related to a measure of transliminality.

The concept of transliminality was described in Chapter 5. Michael Thalbourne defined transliminality as 'a hypothesised tendency for psychological material to cross (*trans*) the threshold (*limen*) into or out of consciousness' (e.g. Thalbourne & Delin, 1994, p. 31). The idea is that some individuals have a more permeable threshold between content that is typically conscious and content that typically fails to reach consciousness. Such a person would often become aware of mental content – for example, thoughts, images, and emotions – which would normally remain below the threshold of conscious awareness.

Thalbourne and Delin (1994) proposed that transliminality might underlie a creative personality, because creativity is partially due to thoughts and ideas that arrive in the mind without conscious deliberation. It might also underlie belief in the paranormal, as a kind of creativity that makes associations between logically separate entities and events. Subjective paranormal or mystical experiences may be the result of dreams, imaginings, and fantasies, crossing from the unconscious realm into awareness.

There is empirical evidence to support this conception of transliminality. Thalbourne and Delin (1994) noted that scores on the measure of transliminality were related to other variables that suggested the individual was particularly interested in their subjective experience, believed their dreams were particularly relevant and worth paying attention to, and had subjective experiences of ESP. Thalbourne (1998) and Thalbourne et al. (1997) noted that transliminality is related to fantasy-proneness, absorption, and dissociativity, which are all related to belief in the paranormal and to subjective paranormal experience. Several studies have shown that transliminality is correlated strongly with belief in mental powers (e.g. Thalbourne, 2001, 2010b; Thalbourne & Houran, 2000, 2003), with belief in life after death and reincarnation (Thalbourne, 1998–9), and with subjective psi experiences in women (Houran & Lange, 2009). Several other examples of correlations between transliminality and paranormal belief and experience are described in Thalbourne (2009).

It is interesting to note the relationship between transliminality and temporal lobe activity (e.g. Thalbourne, Crawley & Houran, 2003; Thalbourne & Maltby, 2008). This supports the notion that transliminality may be caused by hyperconnectivity between the temporal lobe and sensory areas of the brain. Also, this may be why transliminality is often associated with mystical experiences, which are associated with activity in the temporal lobe. This line of research is still in the early stages so no firm conclusions can be drawn.

Conclusions

There are a number of biases and errors, and different styles of cognition, that can lead people to believe in paranormal phenomena or to think they may have had a paranormal experience. This chapter has covered many of them but by no means all. We have tried to illustrate how the features of our cognition can contribute to the inception and maintenance of belief in paranormal phenomena. The factors that seem to be reliably related to paranormal belief are weaknesses in critical thinking and particularly in reasoning about the causes of strange events; misperceptions of randomness; the tendency to perceive forms in random patterns; biases in memory and the ease of creation of false memories; and the trait of transliminality. Distorted perception and processing of evidence may be related to the maintenance rather than the formation of paranormal belief. Other potential features that might support paranormal belief seem plausible but are yet to be substantially tested by empirical investigation: the availability and representativeness heuristics; illusions of correlation and control; confirmation bias; and subjective validation. Believers in the paranormal, compared to non-believers, seem to have a lower level of education and in particular less scientific education. They tend to the subjective rather than the objective worldview and use intuitive thinking more often than non-believers. On the plus side, believers are more creative than non-believers.

Sutherland (1992) suggests ways in which we can try to improve our own thinking. First, we can try to keep an open mind and be willing to change our mind as a result of new information. Second, we can make sure we seek out information against our beliefs and consider it honestly and fairly. Third, we can objectively examine the flaws in the arguments that favour our own views. Fourth, we can try to avoid taking important decisions in a hurry. Fifth, we can suspend judgement where there is insufficient evidence to decide. Sixth, we can try to consider alternative explanations for events, even though they are inconsistent with our beliefs. Seventh, we can learn some basic statistics and probability theory and understand the situations where it can usefully be applied. If we become such paragons of virtue, then we are more likely to be protected against false beliefs – but nothing is guaranteed.

Suggested further reading

For discussions of general errors in reasoning:

Gilovich, T. (1991). *How we know what isn't so: The fallibility of human reason in everyday life*. New York, NY: Free Press.

Hutson, M. (2012). *The 7 laws of magical thinking: How irrationality makes us happy, healthy, and sane*. Oxford: Oneworld Publications.

Shermer, M. (1997). *Why people believe weird things: Pseudoscience, superstition and other confusions of our time*. London: Souvenir Press.

Sutherland, S. (1992). *Irrationality*. London: Pinter and Martin.

For an overview of cognitive biases associated with paranormal belief:

French, C. C. & Wilson, K. (2007). 'Cognitive factors underlying paranormal beliefs and experiences'. In S. Della Sala (ed.), *Tall tales about the mind and brain: Separating fact from fiction* (pp. 3–22). Oxford: Oxford University Press.

For more on ontological confusion:

Aarnio, K. & Lindeman, M. (2007). 'Superstitious, magical and paranormal beliefs: An integrative model'. *Journal of Research in Personality*, 41, 731–44.

For more on memory biases related to reports of ostensibly paranormal events:

French, C. C. (2003). 'Fantastic memories: The relevance of research into eyewitness testimony and false memories for reports of anomalous experiences'. *Journal of Consciousness Studies*, 10, 153–74.

French, C. C. & Wilson, K. (2006). 'Incredible memories: How accurate are reports of anomalous events?' *European Journal of Parapsychology*, 21, 166–81.

Social Perspectives

Introduction

There are many different social perspectives on paranormal belief. This chapter will concentrate on the most influential perspectives and those most important to understand the roles and functions of various paranormal beliefs in modern Western cultures (principally the UK and USA).

One perspective concerns the social transmission of paranormal belief, that is, how beliefs are passed from parents to children, or from peer to peer. A second perspective concerns the role of paranormal experts and practitioners, and the influence of the media, in informing and encouraging paranormal beliefs. A third perspective examines how people attempt to justify their belief or scepticism about the paranormal in their social interactions, and how conversations about the paranormal have a tendency to follow a particular form that could serve to perpetuate and foster belief. A fourth perspective looks at the role of cultural traditions in forming the particular types of paranormal belief that are commonly found in different cultures, and introduces the concept of the **meme** as a unit of cultural transmission. A fifth perspective is the sociocognitive approach to hypnosis, false memories, hidden memories (**cryptomnesia**), dissociative states, and multiple personality enactments. Finally, we will look briefly at an attributional model of hallucinations.

Chapter 1 presented information on the levels of paranormal belief in the general population in the USA. Typically, the proportion of the population that reports belief in the paranormal is much higher than the proportion that claims to have had personal experience of the paranormal. The absence of personal experience in the majority of cases begs the question from whence these beliefs originate. The answer seems likely to involve other people, the media, and the surrounding culture in general – in other words, various forms of social learning.

Hill (2011) points out that the pursuit of the paranormal is usually a social activity – for example, an interview with a psychic consultant, storytelling with friends, joining a ghost-hunting group, or attending a mediumistic séance or a stage show. This contrasts with anomalous experience which is generally a solitary event – for example, an alien abduction experience, an OBE, or a precognitive dream. Joining a ghost-hunting group event may be a way of transforming the personal experience of seeing a ghost into a shared and social experience. Indeed, the converse may also be true, and belonging to a ghost-hunting group may facilitate a personal anomalous experience.

Before we start to examine the social origins of paranormal belief we should pause to make sure we understand how this is defined. Irwin (2009) observed that an unjustified and anomalous belief owned by one person alone is commonly regarded as a delusion and is often thought of as being pathological. Irwin's contention is that a paranormal belief must be shared by a sizeable community in order to be considered a belief rather than a delusion. For example, if someone believes that they can make their car go faster by talking to it soothingly and playing it classical music, this might be generally regarded as a delusion (albeit a relatively harmless one) since no one else shares this opinion. On the other hand, the idea that talking soothingly to plants and playing them classical music makes them grow better is shared by many other people and so might qualify as a paranormal belief, although it is a relatively rare one.

Having said this, there are exceptions to every rule, and certainly there are examples of collective delusions where whole crowds of people have believed that they have seen something that was extremely unlikely to have been real (Irwin, 2009). One example is the apparition of the Virgin Mary that was seen by over 100,000 people between April 1968 and May 1971 above a Coptic Orthodox Church at Zeitoun in Egypt. It is more likely that what the witnesses actually saw were lights in the sky which they interpreted as visions of Mary, and these lights have been tentatively attributed to micro-seismic activity which peaked during these years (Bartholomew & Goode, 2000). This event was regarded as a collective delusion because of its spontaneous beginning, its rapid spread, its relatively swift ending, and its geographic localization, although it was shared by many people. Although the distinction between a 'belief' and 'delusion' can sometimes be difficult to make, in this book we are generally discussing paranormal beliefs rather than individual delusions.

We agree with Irwin (2009) that a paranormal belief is a belief that is shared with many others and we also say that it must last for a substantial period of time. Quite apart from the desirability of having a good definition, it is inevitably the case that the more common and long-lived types of belief have attracted the most substantial body of research (as pointed out by Irwin, 2009).

More recently, Irwin has refined his position somewhat and now argues that, although paranormal beliefs should not be considered to be *psychotic* delusions, it is legitimate to classify them as *nonpsychotic* delusions (Irwin, Dagnall, & Drinkwater, 2012). This view is based upon the collection of data by Irwin, Dagnall, and Drinkwater from 207 respondents indicating that level of paranormal belief correlated with various cognitive dysfunctions that are known to be associated with the development of clinical delusions. Firstly, paranormal belief was found to correlate with a tendency towards inferential confusion, that is, a reasoning style based upon 'a basic mistrust of the senses in favour of a mere possibility or imagination' (p. 109). Secondly, a correlation was found between paranormal belief and confirmation bias as assessed by Rassin's (2008) Confirmation Inventory (which includes items such as 'I only need a little information to reach a good decision'). Finally, a link was found between paranormal belief and various metacognitive beliefs, that is, beliefs about one's own thought processes and experiences. Specifically, some paranormal beliefs were found to be associated with a tendency to focus attention on thought processes as well as to believe that thoughts could be uncontrollable and dangerous. The authors concluded that 'paranormal beliefs and delusions share a common cognitive aetiology' (p. 116).

Irwin, Dagnall, and Drinkwater (2012) reject the idea that paranormal beliefs should be considered to be psychotic delusions on the grounds that they do not share a number of characteristics with the latter. Specifically, paranormal beliefs typically are not associated with other dysfunctional symptoms, are often not held with absolute certainty, and do not typically cause distress, anxiety, or depression. Furthermore, paranormal beliefs are endorsed by such a high proportion of the general population that it would clearly be ridiculous to classify all paranormal belief as psychotic.

Box 7.1 Mass crazes

It is interesting to look at Shermer's (1997) explanation of the rise and fall of mass crazes. See if you can spot how this relates to, for example, the witch trials of the seventeenth century or the popular fear of satanic cults.

1. The victims are a disempowered group, being poor, or disabled, or women, or children.
2. Sex is involved, via allegations of inappropriate activity or sexual abuse.
3. Accusation are made and followed by the assumption of guilt.
4. Those accused who deny their guilt are assumed to be lying.
5. Claims attract publicity which attracts more claims, until …
6. … many people are involved as either a victim or a perpetrator.
7. The accused start to fight back and the evidence is challenged; scientific experts cast doubt on the nature and quality of the evidence.
8. The movement fades away, the public loses interest, and the proponents of the belief are marginalized.

Does this sound familiar?

Learning from parents

A key form of social learning is the transmission of knowledge, values, and attitudes within families from parents to children. Because of the time spent in close proximity within the family environment, and the potential for strong and consistent communication over a period of many years, children have ample opportunity to observe and learn to imitate the attitudes and beliefs of their parents.

Despite the obvious possibility of parental influence, to date there have been few direct investigations of the parental transmission of paranormal beliefs. Early studies (Conklin, 1919; Emme, 1940; Maller & Lundeen, 1933) found that participants cited their parents as a major source of superstitious beliefs. This view of the contribution of parents is supported by more recent research based on interviews in which people cited their parents as important sources of paranormal belief in general (Preece & Baxter, 2000; Schriever, 2000).

As mentioned in Chapter 4, one particularly interesting study by Maller and Lundeen (1933) asked schoolchildren for the sources of their superstitious beliefs. A large set of 50 superstitions typical of the period was listed and participants were asked to say where they learnt of each superstition (e.g. home, school, or friends) and whether the superstition was presented to them as true or false. They calculated a 'corrective index' for each source as the number of superstitions presented as false divided by the number of superstitions presented as true. For example, if friends said that 15 of the superstitions were false and 30 were true, then the corrective index for friends would be 0.5 exactly. The findings of the 1933 study were that the home environment appeared to be a strong source for learning superstitions with a corrective index of 0.95, so more superstitions were acquired than lost at home. This does not necessarily pinpoint parents as the source of the beliefs as siblings are another possibility. Nonetheless, it does not seem that parents were particularly influential in discouraging superstitions beliefs. Of course, this study is dated and it would be interesting to see more recent data along the same lines.

There is a shortage of recent empirical research investigating the extent of correspondence between parental and offspring levels of paranormal belief. This lack of knowledge about how closely children adopt their parents' paranormal beliefs makes it hard to evaluate the role of social learning within the home. However, we can call on indirect evidence, when we consider the similarities between paranormal belief and religious belief; both types of belief are taught at home and in other environments approved by parents more than in formal education. Many researchers have noted that parents are important in influencing the religious beliefs of their children (e.g. Clark & Worthington, 1990; Dudley & Dudley, 1986; Gunnoe & Moore, 2002; Hunsberger, 1985; Martin, White, & Perlman, 2003; Milevsky, Szuchman, & Milevsky, 2008; Ozorak, 1989; Parker & Gaier, 1980) which suggests that the same may be true for paranormal beliefs.

How might parents influence the paranormal beliefs of their children? Perhaps this may happen through direct instruction, but perhaps also through observation and imitation. Children would have ample opportunity every day to observe their parents and to perceive their attitudes and values as well as their behaviours (e.g. Bandura, 1969). In the same way that parents who attach more importance to religion are more likely to have religious children (e.g. Bader & Desmond, 2006; Suziedelis & Potvin, 1981), it is plausible to think that parents who attach importance to a particular type of paranormal belief may have children who follow the same belief. The process by which children may come to acquire their parents' beliefs is sometimes known as 'internalization' (e.g. Altemeyer & Hunsberger, 1997; Argyle, 2000; Gunnoe & Moore, 2002) and it can happen automatically, without conscious intent. Zusne and Jones (1989) noted that most of our attitudes are learnt from others, and in particular parents and older siblings, via internalization.

An important question in all of this is whether the paranormal beliefs acquired by children tend to persist into adulthood. As reviewed in Chapter 2, the evidence for age differences in paranormal beliefs is weak and somewhat inconsistent which might tend to suggest that early-acquired beliefs are persistent throughout adult life. On the other hand, it is quite possible that different sources become more influential as people grow though different life stages. For example, Zusne and Jones (1989) noted that as people grow older the influence of parents may become weaker and other people may become more influential – for example, friends, teachers, religious authorities, and the media.

Taking these considerations into account, although it appears plausible that parents might transmit their paranormal beliefs to their children, there is a shortage of recent empirical evidence to support this proposition. It is also unclear to what extent any paranormal beliefs acquired in childhood would be maintained into adult life.

Genetic transmission from parents to children

Paranormal belief may be transmitted within a family by means other than social learning, for instance by genetic inheritance. One way in which this might occur is that genes can influence the development of certain personality factors that predispose the individual towards higher levels of paranormal belief (Makasovski & Irwin, 1999). For example, substantial evidence was presented in Chapter 3 that anxiety is related to level of paranormal belief and trait anxiety is known to be inherited to a considerable degree (e.g. Elev & Gregory, 2004). Socio-economic status may also be partly inherited from parents – though not genetically – and may have some influence on levels of paranormal belief, although the evidence is inconclusive (see Chapter 2).

Other personality traits, linked with paranormal belief and experience, have been reported to have moderate heritability, that is, to be inherited to an appreciable degree from parents. Dissociation (discussed in Chapter 3) has been reported in large-scale twin studies to have a moderate genetic influence, including those by Jang *et al.* (1998; over 300 twin pairs) and Becker-Blease *et al.* (2004; nearly 400 twin pairs), and Pieper *et al.* (2011). The picture is not entirely clear, however, as Waller and Ross (1997) failed to find any heritability for dissociation as a personality trait.

Absorption has been reported to be moderately heritable: for example, Tellegen *et al.* (1988; 400 twin pairs) and Finkel and McGue (1997) who also reported that absorption was more strongly heritable in women than in men. Similarly, the trait of openness to experience, which has been deemed to be strongly related to fantasy-proneness, is substantially heritable according to Bergeman *et al.* (1993). Finally, sensation seeking has been reported to be moderately heritable by Koopmans *et al.* (1995; 1591 twin pairs) and by Stoel, De Geus, and Boomsma (2006) with similar heritability for females and males.

Another type of inherited characteristic that might dispose the individual towards some forms of paranormal belief is the tendency to experience strange or anomalous perceptions, not shared with all other members of the community, for which the individual seeks some kind of explanation. As described in Chapter 5, Cohn (1999) investigated the phenomenon of 'second sight' (the ability to see things that are occurring at a distance or that will happen in the future) in Scotland in a large-scale community questionnaire survey. There did appear to be some familial transmission of 'second sight' so that offspring resembled their parents more than random chance would predict. By way of explanation, Cohn proposed that some people may have sensory systems which are more likely to generate spontaneous vivid imagery and this tendency is partly heritable. Family tradition in some cases interprets these anomalous sensory experiences as glimpses of distant or future events. So there are two sources of familial transmission of 'second sight': the genetically inherited tendency to have anomalous sensory experiences, and the socially transmitted tendency to interpret these in a particular way.

Also of interest was the observation that women reported more 'second sight' than men and were more likely than men to discuss 'second sight' within the family. Please refer to Chapter 2 on individual differences for more discussion of gender differences in paranormal belief and experience.

Learning from peers

Several sources report that peers and friends are believed to be an important source of paranormal beliefs. Back in 1919, Conklin noted that superstitions tend not to be taught deliberately as part of formal education but rather people learn them as children from their families and peers. Other researchers have supported this view, including Vyse (1997) who proposed that children are particularly good at absorbing superstitious beliefs from their friends and playmates. Schriever (2000) interviewed adults about the sources of their paranormal beliefs and discovered that friends were often cited as an important source. Similarly, Saunders and van Arsdale (1968) noted that a friend's account of a UFO sighting would be convincing for many people, and Messer and Griggs (1989) reported that the belief of peers was a major factor in personal paranormal beliefs. Auton, Pope, and Seeger (2003) noted that high paranormal believers in their sample were likely to have friends who held similar beliefs. The corrective index for friends calculated by Maller and Lundeen (1933) was 0.54, suggesting that friends were responsible for teaching and confirming twice as many superstitions as they were responsible for disconfirming. There is more on this topic in the section *Superstition from Childhood to Adulthood* in Chapter 4.

Clarke (1995) found that the experience of friends and family was cited as a source of belief in UFOs, ghosts, and the Loch Ness monster more often than was personal experience. He also noted that sometimes participants in a questionnaire study might include the experience of close others in answer to a question asking about personal experience of the paranormal, suggesting that the experience of others became interpreted as a personal experience. Similar evidence was offered by Patry and Pelletier (2001) who collected questionnaire responses from 400 participants about their belief in UFOs and alien abductions. Their participants were guided in their beliefs by what they thought other people believed, so only 5% said they had seen a UFO, but 24% said they knew someone who had seen a UFO, and 48% believed in UFOs from media reports. Interestingly, they also said that they would be more likely to believe a story reported by a friend than a story reported by the authorities or in the media, and were more likely to report their experience to a friend than to the authorities or the media. In contrast, according to Clarke (1995), personal experience was cited more often than the experience of others for psi-related beliefs (e.g. astral projection, clairvoyance, precognition, psychic healing, or telepathy) and astrology.

It is interesting to note that Paramount Pictures used social media (Twitter) to involve fans in a marketing strategy for the picture *Paranormal Activity* (Hampp, 2010). It seems they were well aware of the role of peer influence in generating an interest in entertainment on a paranormal theme – although it should be noted that peer influence is used to market films from a variety of genres and this is not unique to paranormal-themed films.

Superstitious beliefs appear to flourish particularly strongly within certain kinds of peer group. Several researchers have noticed that superstitions are common among sportsmen and -women, being indulged in by up to three-quarters of the participants in some studies (e.g. Bleak & Frederick, 1998; Burger & Lynn, 2005; Todd & Brown, 2003), which tends to point to peer-to-peer transmission of these beliefs. Bleak and Frederick (1998) noted that some rituals are shared within a team and are agreed by all members of the team. It does seem likely that the observation of other team members or opponents carrying their lucky charms or observing their lucky rituals would have the effect of legitimizing these behaviours and making them seem more socially acceptable, or even socially expected. As Burger and Lynn (2005) commented, superstitious behaviour might be normative in a baseball locker room, which would have the effect of encouraging players to be open about their rituals and charms. It would also encourage an ethos of acceptance and respect for each other's superstitions.

Other researchers have noted that social environment can enhance the likelihood or the perception of an anomalous experience. Hill (2011, p. 98) emphasizes the social nature of some ghost-hunting groups and how social bonding is promoted within the group by the sharing of experience. Cardeña *et al.* (2009) point out that we automatically imitate other people's emotional expressions and this leads us to experience their emotions to a certain extent. In a situation where a group of people anticipate the experience of anomalous sensations, this fosters a sense of arousal and expectation. Ghost-hunting team leaders are aware of this and encourage rapport, reactivity, and emotional empathy in a group. In this way, the members of a group can help to raise each other's level of arousal and any anomalous experience becomes shared and magnified within the group. Gordon (1997) agrees that ghosts and hauntings are a social phenomenon: 'haunting is a constituent element of modern social life' (p. 7).

All of these are examples of indirect evidence for peer-to-peer transmission of paranormal beliefs. But there is stronger evidence from experiments in which the influence of peers was manipulated, thus allowing us to make a causal inference that peer influence can promote paranormal belief. For example, Markovsky and Thye (2001) stored two bananas for a week, one under a box and the other under a pyramid. Participants were told about the theory that storing fruit under a pyramid helps to keep it fresh and were then asked to rate both bananas. A confederate sometimes posed as another participant and offered the opinion that the banana stored under the pyramid was fresher and better preserved. At other times the influence of the confederate was not made directly, but was delivered as a verbal report from the experimenter. The participants clearly showed the effect of social influence by rating the banana stored under the pyramid as fresher and better preserved than the other banana – but only if they had heard the confederate give this opinion. There was a slightly stronger effect when the confederate was actually present in the room to deliver their opinion in person and a noticeably stronger effect when the confederate was depicted as someone with a higher status – for example, a professor at the university, compared to someone of a lower status. Both of these variations are consistent with what we already know about the effects of social influence. Interestingly, when the judgement was to compare a banana stored in a plastic container compared to a cardboard container, the effect of social influence was stronger than in the pyramid version of the experiment. That is, the participant was more likely to agree with the opinion of the confederate when it did not require the adoption of a belief in the fruit-preserving power of pyramids. This suggests that there was some resistance to adopting a paranormal belief. Nonetheless, participants were still somewhat prepared to believe that a banana stored under a pyramid stayed fresher when a confederate offered the same opinion, showing the influence of peers on paranormal belief.

Gilovich (1991) points out that it is sensible to allow our judgements, opinions, and decisions to be influenced by others. In this way we utilize the knowledge and skills of other people to help us to make better decisions. So it makes sense for us to allow our beliefs and values to come to resemble those we perceive to be held by the people around us. However, there is evidence that we are systematically biased in our estimates of the extent to which other people agree with us, so that we think they agree with us more than they actually do. This is known as the **false consensus effect** (e.g. Ross, Greene, & House, 1977). The false consensus effect says that someone with a particular stance on an issue – for example, someone who believes in ghosts – would give a higher estimate of the proportion of the general population who believe in ghosts than another person who does not believe. (It is not necessarily a perception that a majority of people believe in ghosts, just that the number of people who believe in ghosts is estimated to be higher by a believer than by a non-believer.) The false consensus effect is thought to depend on a number of factors including our desire to feel that we are right and the desire to feel that other people would approve and agree with our decisions. If we think that our beliefs stem from rational thinking, then we would naturally think that others, as long as they are rational, would agree with us.

The false consensus effect can be fostered and maintained by selectively associating with people who share our beliefs so that our personal observations will tell us that the majority of people around us agree with us. Selective attention to media and cultural representations that agree with our beliefs would also help to maintain the apparent consensus.

Another factor that can maintain a false consensus is inadequate feedback from others. Gilovich (1991) points out that people do not generally question other people's beliefs or openly disagree with them and that such challenge would be considered impolite in conversation. Similarly, Hill (2011, p. 43) notes that people usually declare moderate positions and that extreme disbelief (or extreme belief) would be less well respected and considered less socially acceptable. As an example of failure to give negative feedback, members of the audience during a 'psychic' stage show do not shout out where the performer has made an incorrect statement (Shermer, 1997). The lack of accurate feedback will help to sustain a false consensus that many other people agree with our attitudes and beliefs (please refer to Chapter 6 for a discussion of *groupthink*).

A recent experiment serves as an example of the influence of the perceived popularity of belief (Ridolfo, Baxter, & Lucas, 2010). Participants were informed that ESP was a popular or an unpopular belief and then watched a short video that appeared to present evidence of ESP. Those participants who had been told that ESP was a popular belief were more likely to express belief themselves after watching the video, compared to those who were told that ESP was an unpopular belief.

A special kind of peer-to-peer transmission would, of course, come from the conjugal partner, but unfortunately no research could be located that addresses the influence exerted by one conjugal partner on another concerning paranormal beliefs. There is, however, some evidence that people tend to pair up with a partner who shares their beliefs to start with. For example, as already stated, Cohn (1999) reported that people prefer a partner with similar beliefs in psychic abilities. It seems commonsensical that a relationship will run more smoothly if both people have similar points of view but the extent to which this is true for paranormal beliefs in general is not known.

Considering the evidence from self-reports in interview and questionnaire studies, and experimental evidence of the causal effect of peer belief, there is substantial evidence that peers can exert a strong influence on personal paranormal beliefs.

Learning from observation of experts and practitioners

Many people may become convinced about the existence of psychic powers as a result of an individual reading with a psychic, fortune-teller, or spirit medium. If a psychic consultant appears to know items of personal information to which they have no known obvious means of access, then it is easy to believe that they have some special ability to obtain such information. However, as many people have pointed out (e.g. Hines, 2003, Chapter 10, pp. 331–50; Hyman, 1977, 1981; Shermer, 1997, 2008), there is a simple non-paranormal explanation for why a consultant may appear to have privileged access to personal information. You may have heard of this before: the answer is cold reading. This is covered in the next section.

Shermer (1997) notes that some people may be convinced about the existence of telepathy or communication with the spirits of dead people by a stage show in which another person in the audience validates a piece of information revealed by the psychic. Leaving aside the question of outright trickery, if a stage performer throws out enough random pieces of information, they are likely to strike a hit with some members of the audience. This would be an example of a coincidence, not a demonstration of psychic power or spirit mediumship. It may be convincing, though, to members of the audience, and Hill (2011, p. 157) explains how a psychic performer draws in the audience and holds their attention in order to manipulate their interpretations of events. The audience becomes involved in a social experience in which they collaborate to produce belief.

It appears that sometimes simple suggestion may suffice to enable a psychic performer to persuade their audience that something paranormal is occurring. For example, Wiseman, Greening, and Smith (2003) reported how suggestion from an actor playing the part of a spirit medium could influence participants in a séance to report (incorrectly) that they had seen objects moving without any visible cause. Similarly, Wiseman and Greening (2005) showed that a suggestion from a fake psychic could influence participants to report (incorrectly) seeing a key continuing to bend after a demonstration of supposed psychokinesis.

Paranormal investigators are another category of perceived experts who may be influential in promoting forms of paranormal belief. A study by Brewer (2013), for example, showed that paranormal investigators were perceived as being more convincing if they were presented as scientific authorities. This experiment presented a paranormal investigator in one of three ways: as a scientist, by using technical jargon and scientific-appearing equipment and highlighting a careful approach; in terms of traditional supernaturalism, referring to strange experiences as a child and being open to non-scientific possibilities; or with a rebuttal from a scientist saying that the investigator was non-scientific. In the scientist condition, participants rated the investigator as more scientific and credible, and reported higher belief in the paranormal. These outcomes were lower in the rebuttal condition. Interestingly, the amount of paranormal TV viewed by participants was associated with finding the investigator more scientific and credible.

As well as the influence of individual experts, there is also the influence of larger social groupings to consider, such as New Age communities, psychic colleges, or Wiccan covens. How much influence do they have on the paranormal beliefs of members of the public? Are they preaching only to those who are already believers? Merriam, Courtenay, and Baumgartner (2003) interviewed 20 witches belonging to several different covens to discover how they were affected by being members of their covens. The covens can be viewed as a 'community' of practice, a term coined by Lave and Wenger (1991) to describe a group of people engaged in a common practice who learn through their shared practice and who come to share common beliefs, attitudes, and values. Joining a coven was not easy as they don't advertise publicly and so new members had joined their coven only after a personal invitation. Initial contacts were typically made through a bookshop or an alternative newspaper or website. Then the individual was approached by someone who was checking whether they were serious before they were invited to a meeting. It appears from this that such communities would generally tend to have little influence on the general public.

Cold reading

This technique may be used by fraudulent psychics, fortune-tellers, and spirit mediums to convince a client that they have a special source of knowledge about their life, their problems, and their future. Cold reading may be used in an individual consultation or as part of a stage show.

One aspect of cold reading is to produce general statements or questions and pay careful attention to the body language of the client to see which items strike a chord. The client, if sufficiently cooperative, will explicitly acknowledge the 'hits' so there may be less need to rely on reading the body language. For example, a psychic consultant might observe that the client appears to be troubled by a personal relationship and the client might confirm, 'Yes, I'm having some trouble with my mother'. Wooffitt (2000) describes how a psychic often takes care to pose questions that can later be turned into statements if the implied information is accepted by the client, so as to avoid the appearance of offering incorrect or irrelevant information. Only if the client accepts the information presented in the form of a question does the psychic turn it into a statement. The client probably does not realize that they are feeding information to the psychic and would tell you that the psychic had obviously known about this particular relationship problem already. After all, a person who consults a psychic is almost certainly already a believer and so ready and willing to give credit to the psychic and unprepared to adopt a cautious, sceptical approach. With a psychic consultation typically costing around £30 per half hour (Wooffitt, 2000, p. 458) only the convinced will wish to part with their cash.

Shermer (2008) gives ten easy steps to becoming a successful 'psychic' consultant (see also Hyman, 1977; Roe & Roxburgh, 2013; Rowland, 2002). One of the key steps is to encourage the client to cooperate by explaining that a psychic reading is a joint effort. With luck, this will persuade the client to give up items of personal information that the psychic can remember and reproduce later when the client has forgotten mentioning them. A cooperative client will also acknowledge the lucky guesses and will either forgive the misses or help to reinterpret them to yield a hit.

Shermer (2008) advises the psychic consultant to explain that people come to them with matters that weigh heavily on their heart (not their head – you don't want people to start using their head!) and then suggest a few areas where the client may be experiencing difficulties – being careful to watch out for telltale body language. Most people will consult a psychic because of troubles or concerns about their relationships, their work, or their health, so these are some key areas to start off with. The consultant is advised to throw out a few vague statements and questions and see which ones the client picks up on. A useful technique is to ask questions disguised as statements. For example: Does that sound right? Who might this refer to? Does this sound significant to you? Does this make sense? Remember that a key step is to explain that a psychic reading is a joint effort.

Wooffitt (2008) explained how a question can be converted into a statement if it turns out to be correct. First the consultant poses a question, then if the client makes a positive response the consultant firms up the question into a statement accompanied by a claim that the knowledge was gained from a paranormal source. He gives an example (p. 65):

Practitioner: '... is your mother in spirit please?'
Client: 'Yes'
Practitioner: 'Cause I have your mother standing right over here ...'

A technique sometimes used by a spirit medium to cover for an incorrect statement is to act as though receiving a new and demanding communication from the spirit world as a means of changing the subject. All of these techniques are facilitated by the social custom of softening areas of disagreement. It is not usual to state too bluntly where information given by a conversation partner is incorrect. Rather, in conversation it is considered polite to soften a refusal or a denial in order to continue the smooth flow of conversation and not offend the speaker.

A consultant can seem to know a lot about a client by throwing out general items of information that tend to be true for a substantial proportion of the population. There are several seemingly specific pieces of personal information that happen to be true for many people although this is not widely appreciated. For example, look at the items in Box 7.2 and see if you can estimate for what proportion of the population these items would be true. Please make your estimates before you look at the answer.

Box 7.2   Endorsement of items of personal information (Blackmore, 1997)

Blackmore (1997) conducted a survey of over 6000 *Daily Telegraph* readers to see how many would endorse specific items of personal information. How many people do you think said that these items were true for them?

- Their back was giving them trouble.
- They were one of three or more children.
- They had a tape or CD of Handel's *Water Music*.
- They lived in a household with at least one cat.
- They had a scar on their left knee.

It may surprise you to learn that over 30% of Blackmore's (1997) sample endorsed each of her items. So a psychic consultant throwing out these snippets at random could generally expect to score one or two correct hits. A client might be impressed by this rate of success, especially if the psychic talked fast so there was little time to register the misses.

There are other pieces of personal information which sound quite specific and unusual but in fact they are true for many people. Have a look at the items in Box 7.3 (adapted from Rowland, 2002) and see how many you would endorse.

It is important to note that cold reading is probably often used unconsciously by people who genuinely believe they have a special talent and that their knowledge stems from some sort of paranormal ability. Although this may seem unlikely it is a natural result of the social setting of the consultation. The client may enthusiastically endorse the pieces of information revealed by the psychic to such an extent that the psychic may cease to think that their accuracy could be the result of luck or guessing and therefore it must stem from a special gift. It is no wonder that some psychics claim they do not know how they perform their readings and the information just seems to come to them.

A question which is sometimes asked is whether all of this is beneficial or harmful to the clients. A study by Lester (1982) in the United States asked

---

Box 7.3   Endorsement of items of personal information (adapted from Rowland, 2002)

These statements tend to be true for many people. See how many of these are true for you:

- You have a piece of jewellery from a deceased family member.
- You have a watch or a clock that no longer works.
- You used to wear your hair longer than you do now.
- You were involved in a childhood accident involving water (think how many ways you could interpret this one).
- You have an item of clothing you bought but you have never worn.
- The number 2 is associated with your house (house number, post code, phone number, car registration, etc.).

---

precisely this question. He suggested that there are four important elements to a therapeutic consultation: patient confidence in the therapist's powers, a location designated as a place of healing, a rationale to explain the client's troubles, and a system of therapy. He noted that there are many 'invisible' therapists in our society, including doctors, attorneys, and teachers, and also that astrologers and similar figures may play such a role. One person might consult an astrologer where another would go to a psychotherapist with questions about work and relationships. Lester found that the astrologers and others he looked at behaved empathically with their clients, as would a therapist. Their advice was 'pertinent, useful and sensible' and their services could appeal to those who would feel stigmatized by going to see a psychotherapist.

Before concluding that there is no harm done, we should note that there is an alternative view that sees astrology as a delusional system used to impose superficial order on a chaotic situation. Whereas psychotherapists aim to free their clients from their delusion and to enable them to see the world more accurately, astrologers encourage their clients to persist in their delusions and reinforce their personal helplessness. Not 'know thyself' but rather 'know thy stars'. On balance, it seems likely that many astrologers, psychics, palm readers, and the like offer generally good advice and empathic acceptance, and thus do more good than harm. However, they are less likely to offer a structured programme of consultations and personal work leading to the independence of the client. Their help is more of a sticking plaster and is unlikely to lead to genuine long-term improvement in the well-being and social functioning of the client (Dean, 1991).

Another negative note was sounded by Wiseman and Greening (2010). They employed an actress to visit five psychics with a story that she had experienced much bad luck recently and was seeking psychic help. All five of the psychics charged a significant amount of money for their help, ranging from £450 to £900. Most of them used techniques to prevent the 'client' from talking to anyone at all, even her closest friends, which seems likely to have been designed to stop more sensible advice from coming between the psychic and the large fee. None of the five psychics suggested that the 'client' should seek professional help or mainstream counselling, despite her obvious distress. And finally, none of them seemed to be aware that she was an actress playing a part.

On balance, it seems likely that little harm is being done by these practitioners of cold reading though opinions are mixed as to whether they do more harm than good. It does appear that there are some less scrupulous practitioners around who may ask for significant sums for their services. On the plus side, generally useful advice can be obtained reliably and reasonably cheaply from many psychics and mediums, though of course the same advice can be had freely from friends and relatives.

The influence of the media

The paranormal has become increasingly popular in the media in recent years and in particular the pastime of ghost-hunting is supported by TV programmes, films, and numerous websites collecting reports of ghost sightings and hosting homemade videos. There are thousands of ghost-hunting groups in the UK along with ghost-walks in historic towns and ghost-hunting weekends in old castles and hotels (Hill, 2011, p. 9). The popularity of ghost-hunting calls for some explanation. Perhaps people living through times of economic hardship and uncertainty are seeking comfort in familiar forms of entertainment and old-fashioned themes; after all, ghosts have been a part of popular culture for centuries. Or maybe people are seeking to find meaning and connection in their lives and seeking spiritual comfort under circumstances that threaten their livelihoods (e.g. Hill, 2011, p. 10).

Whatever the reason for the recent increase in media representations of paranormal themes, it seems clear that their influence is an important area for investigation. Three different types of evidence all combine to suggest that the media are an influential source of paranormal beliefs. These are questionnaire studies asking people to identify the sources of their paranormal beliefs; analyses of the content of media representations (e.g. films, newspaper articles, etc.); and experimental evidence showing how media representations can influence level of belief in a specific phenomenon.

A contrary note has been raised (e.g. Whittle, 2004) to suggest that although the media provide input and substance to paranormal beliefs, it is likely that childhood experiences and storytelling have already laid the foundations. Hence the media may influence the direction but not the tendency to paranormal belief. Mousseau (2003a) reported that there are equivalent levels of irrational belief in the UK and France, even though research into parapsychology receives much media coverage in the UK and is almost completely ignored in France. So it seems that media coverage cannot be the only factor fostering a belief in the paranormal in the UK.

Questionnaire studies

Questionnaire studies typically ask people to identify the paranormal and superstitious beliefs that they personally hold to be true, and then ask them to identify the sources of these beliefs. Such studies have supported the role of the media in promoting belief in children (e.g. Preece & Baxter, 2000), college students (e.g. Clarke, 1995; Maller & Lundeen, 1933), young people (e.g. McClenon, 1994), undergraduate students (e.g. Otis & Alcock, 1982), and the general adult population (e.g. Blackmore, 1994b; Irwin, 1985a; Lett, 1992; Otis & Alcock, 1982; Schriever, 2000). Lett (1992) offers a plausible explanation for the influence of the media by pointing out that the media are a major source of information in general for people who have finished their formal education.

Regarding the relative importance of the media, Clarke (1995) reported that the media were a less important source of belief than personal experience or the experience of friends and family, but it is worth noting that the media were virtually never cited as a source of disbelief. That is, the media were regarded as doing nothing to challenge or discourage belief in the paranormal. In contrast, Maller and Lundeen (1933) suggested that newspapers and books tended to deny and disconfirm rather than to promote superstitions, although not by a wide margin (and by no margin at all in the case of books; their 'corrective index' was 1.11 for newspapers and 1.00 for books). However, this dated study does predate the arrival of a huge wave of TV programmes and cinema films on paranormal themes, so the corrective index for the media might be much lower today.

Given this substantial evidence that children and adults regard the media as an important source of their paranormal beliefs, it is relevant to explore how the influence of the media might operate. Several mechanisms will be explored, including the role of the media in making paranormal concepts seem familiar, the *availability heuristic*, and the role of celebrity endorsement.

Researchers have pointed out that the media, and especially television, reaches many people and makes paranormal concepts familiar to the general population (e.g. Irwin, 2009; Sanghera, 2002). There are numerous TV series and films on a paranormal theme in the average week (e.g. Hill, 2011, p. 7) and magazines aimed at women, though not those for a male readership, carry frequent articles on paranormal themes (Sherriff, 2010). As well as making paranormal concepts seem familiar, Klare (1990) proposed that the reported experiences of others serve to validate the individual's own subjective paranormal experiences.

There is evidence that people who watched more TV programmes on paranormal themes had higher levels of belief (e.g. Auton, Pope, & Seeger,

2003; Sparks & Miller, 2001; Sparks, Nelson, & Campbell, 1997) although it must be noted that the causal direction is uncertain and it is perfectly possible that those people who already tend to be believers are more likely to watch paranormal TV programmes.

Nisbet (2006) conducted a systematic survey comparing the frequency of newspaper articles (from *The New York Times* and *The Washington Post*) referring to UFOs, psychics, or spirit mediums with levels of belief in UFOs, telepathy, and communication with the dead (from Gallup poll data). He observed that levels of belief declined between 2001 and 2006 along with a decline in the number of newspaper articles over this period. He invoked the *availability heuristic* (explained in Chapter 6) to explain the power of the media. This explanation runs along the following lines: images and depictions that are vivid and visual will have a big impact on the viewer and will be highly memorable. Frequent repetition will increase the likelihood that a particular image will be recalled. These well-remembered images, especially if they are recent, are readily called to mind when the individual is trying to judge the credibility of a subsequent event. So the media presentation and repetition of vivid and memorable images can bias the judgement of ambiguous information that is encountered in real life.

It is sometimes claimed that celebrity endorsement can promote interest in the paranormal (Sanghera, 2002). For example, Gwyneth Paltrow, Naomi Campbell, and Kylie Minogue have all consulted psychics and this can make the practice seem more plausible and desirable in the eyes of the celebrity-watching public. However, Clarke (1995) did not find that celebrities were cited by participants as a source of belief in the paranormal, so perhaps their influence is limited to putting topics in the public eye rather than encouraging belief as such.

The content of media representations

The second major source of evidence for the influence of the media on paranormal belief concerns a critical analysis of the way in which popular media present paranormal concepts. There is widespread agreement that the media tend to sensationalize stories on a paranormal theme in order to make them more appealing to the general public (e.g. Alcock, 1981; Klare, 1990; Kurtz, 1985b; Meyer, 1986; Sutherland, 1992; Zusne & Jones, 1989). A paranormal story is often a human-interest story included in a programme in order to balance out the objective news items (e.g. Klare, 1990; Sanghera, 2002). According to Klare (1990), the typical paranormal story is more suited to the feature-story format, which concentrates on telling a narrative from the viewpoint of an eyewitness, rather than a news story with its strict format of defining who, what, why, when, where, and how.

The danger is that people will often assume that a story would not be printed or broadcast if there were not some truth in it. Hence, a sensational story may perhaps attract attention and be regarded as being closer to the truth (and less exaggerated) than is in fact the case. Meyer (1986) explains how the old maxim 'Don't let the facts get in the way of a good story' seems to be applied strongly to stories of paranormal events or people who claim psychic powers.

Irwin (2009) regarded much of the media presentation of paranormal phenomena as misleading. He pointed out that TV channels need to achieve their target viewing figures and therefore they need to woo the viewing public, which leads to the presentation of entertainment rather than information. A TV programme will seldom include a truly balanced picture with equal time given to sceptics as well as to believers. More often, a programme that lasts for an hour may have just a few minutes near the end for the presentation of a sceptical perspective. The danger is that information, once it has been presented, is very difficult to ignore. Numerous studies into the decision-making processes of juries have shown that people cannot simply ignore information with which they have been presented and that the information continues to influence their decisions even where the individual tries to combat and remove such influence (see, for example, Lieberman & Arndt, 2000 for a review). Thus the judgement of the viewer can be biased by the deliberate presentation of information designed to entertain and the viewer may not realize how strongly they have been influenced. The brief presentation of a sceptical perspective near the end of a programme cannot counteract the influence of the material that has already been taken on board.

A similar warning was given by Goldacre (2010) who explains in his newspaper column how a pseudo-scientific story may present a misleading impression in its first few paragraphs, corrected by a statement at the end of the article that is much less likely to be read. He cites evidence from a large-scale study by the Poynter Institute in 2008 that once a story reaches 12 to 18 paragraphs in total length, readers will only read an average of half of the story. Only half of readers would get as far as paragraph 19 of a newspaper article. Goldacre claims that it is common practice to print a caveat or a dissenting voice right at the end of the piece and that this practice misleads the average reader.

Sutherland (1992) had a detailed look into the role of the media in sensationalizing claims of paranormal phenomena. He noted that in the media the paranormal is news but its absence is not, so an event that looks paranormal will be more likely to be reported than one that debunks a paranormal claim. There are several factors contributing to this situation. One factor is that a news item debunking a paranormal claim will often lack the entertainment value of the claim itself, and so is less likely to be reported or broadcast. Another factor is that in order to understand why a claim is unproven may require a more substantial level of detail to be absorbed than the claim itself, and may be too much effort for the readers or viewers to engage with. It will often require more cognitive effort to understand a scientifically plausible explanation for events than a paranormal explanation, often because a paranormal explanation has only a very vague and woolly description (see also Meyer, 1986 for a similar view). Thirdly, the scientific explanation is usually offered by a person who doesn't claim to have been present when the anomalous events occurred, and so their position appears to lack the authentic viewpoint of a witness. And finally, destroying a paranormal explanation for an anomalous event will remove an element of mystery and wonder from the world – and this is likely to be unpopular.

Another factor contributing to the uncritical reporting of paranormal stories was explained by Lett (1992) who proposed that journalists typically lack the knowledge, training, and experience to critically evaluate paranormal claims. Science journalists may have these abilities but paranormal stories are usually written by general journalists and not by specialist science journalists (see also Klare, 1990). Kurtz (1985b) explains that science involves hypothesis testing, in which data are systematically gathered that could support or challenge a potential explanation, and replication, in which different research groups present similar findings. An essential part of the scientific method is an attitude of scepticism, paying careful attention to new and surprising data but neither accepting them nor rejecting them out of hand. In this way, science is never absolutely fixed or final but is constantly changing and, importantly, is self-correcting.

The problem is that many people do not understand this approach and that journalists do not follow it. Instead, non-science journalists adhere to a different standard of *journalistic objectivity*, according to which every involved party can be allowed to present their case. Lett (1992) quotes Meyer as saying, 'It doesn't make any difference what the facts are – if somebody with an impressive sounding degree or title says something interesting, then it's a story.' Thus, as long as a single person claiming relevant qualifications can be found to support a paranormal claim, it can be presented as a legitimate viewpoint, however strong the contrary evidence or however overwhelming the proportion of scientists who do not support the claim. In this way, journalists who do not have a strong scientific background may allow minority opinions to have more prominence than perhaps they deserve. Thus journalistic objectivity is not the same thing as *scientific objectivity*. To a scientist, the stance of objectivity has more to do with presenting a fair and reasonable analysis of the conclusions reached by the majority of qualified experts in the relevant field. Kurtz (1985b) recommends that journalists writing about science topics should adhere to scientific standards rather than journalistic standards.

According to Lett (1992), the news media are only slightly more sceptical than the entertainment media. A good example is the Tamara Rand hoax, in which a faked prediction of the assassination attempt on Ronald Reagan that was actually recorded after the event was accepted uncritically by three of the four major news networks in the USA. It was not an example of good journalism for such an extraordinary claim to be accepted without checking its authenticity. It is unlikely that a good political journalist, or a financial journalist, would attempt to publish an extraordinary claim without verifying the facts first, but that is what happened in the Tamara Rand hoax.

There are objective data to establish the extent of this problem. Klare (1990) analysed the content of paranormal stories in four newspapers (*The New York Times*, *The Washington Post*, and two regional papers) and this is what he found. In all, 46% of stories were credulous, that is, having no critical or questioning content. A further 31% were neutral, having some critical or questioning content, and only 16% were sceptical, that is, predominantly critical or questioning (the remaining stories could not be categorized). This situation looks even less balanced when we consider that even in the 'neutral' stories the proportion of the items contributed by different types of contributor were as follows: sceptics, 8%; scientists, 5%; paranormal researchers (parapsychologists), 26%; practitioners, 18%; and experiencers, 16%. Feature stories were more credulous than news stories.

In the USA, the *National Enquirer* magazine, notorious for inventing stories, has a weekly circulation of over one million. In contrast the sceptical organization Committee for Skeptical Inquiry publishes a bimonthly journal, *Skeptical Inquirer*, with a peak circulation of around 50,000. In the UK, the *News of the World* (also frequently accused of supplementing stories with unverified details) had a circulation of over 2.5 million prior to its closure as a result of the phone-hacking scandal in 2011. In contrast, the *Skeptic* magazine has a three-monthly circulation of several hundred. It is clear that there is much more of a market for events that are sensational, even where their accuracy is in doubt, than for factual and sceptical viewpoints. Similarly, Gilovich (1991) noted that there are more books on the paranormal than on science subjects in the average bookstore.

A particular example of a 'human interest' feature story comes from the BBC1 *Breakfast* programme broadcast on Tuesday 2 November 2010. This was a story that talking to plants can make them grow faster. While this particular idea has been around for a while (e.g. Alleyne, 2009), the new twist was that the speaker's accent mattered – and a Liverpool accent was most effective. This conclusion was based on a study in which an actor talked to plants using different regional accents and the plant that received a Liverpool accent grew tallest. The major, and very obvious, flaw was that only one plant received each accent so that random variation in the natural growth rates of the plants could easily provide an explanation. This obvious flaw was not clearly pointed out by the presenter. Although a cautionary note was sounded each time the item appeared – for example, 'This is not a scientific experiment...' and 'This is very unscientific, nonetheless ...' – after each warning the presenter went on to describe the work very much as though it had been a scientific experiment and stated the findings with no further warning. If the BBC had thought it desirable to report only science stories resulting from properly designed and conducted research, then this item could not have been shown. The BBC is widely regarded in the UK as a serious broadcaster.

A typical example of a programme for a regional theatre shows three 'psychic' stage shows, or one every couple of months. Here is a typical description of an event (please note the disclaimer at the end):

X and Y are two highly celebrated Psychic Mediums and their new show will deliver messages of comfort and love from beyond the grave.

You will be amazed by their uncanny accuracy and warmed by their humanity as they devote their energies to delivering messages from your loved ones.

X of television's *Psychic TV* and *Psychics Performing Live* has previously appeared alongside his spiritual female counterpart Y in *Psychics on TV.*

The psychic event with X and Y is experimental and investigational. Please note that the show is for entertainment and results are not guaranteed.

The tiny disclaimer at the bottom of the advert is clearly not designed to compete with the extravagant claims made on behalf of the 'psychics'. The frequency of this type of stage show stands in contrast to the near absence of stage shows devoted to science or psychology, or any that refer to the results of controlled experimental studies into psychic mediumship. It seems that claims are being made in popular media where no dissenting voice is given an equivalent degree of publicity.

Of course, there is a question of cause and effect, and it must be noted that books, websites, TV programmes, films, and stage shows would not exist if it were not for their public popularity. So it is not clear whether media representations of paranormal phenomena are the cause of high levels of belief in the general public or merely a reflection of those levels of belief. To illuminate this question we need direct empirical evidence of the influence of media items on the beliefs of experimental participants.

It should also be noted that psychic content of TV programmes is largely accepted by the public in the UK as long as it is aimed at adults rather than children, is shown after the watershed, is presented as entertainment, and depicts phenomena perceived as psychic – for example, astrology, clairvoyance, talking to spirits, and tarot – rather than the occult – for example, satanism, voodoo, black magic, **Ouija boards** (Sancho, 2001). It was also considered that psychic advice should not be shown on the most popular channels because this would validate and normalize an unregulated fringe practice. Current codes of practice state that psychics may not give advice on health, medical, or financial issues. With these conditions, the 3000 members of the viewing public who participated in the study had no major concern about the depiction of paranormal phenomena. Indeed, they regarded many aspects of the paranormal as mainstream, familiar, and comfortable. Regarding the practitioners, they were regarded as benign and harmless if they were amateur, and still benign but financially motivated if they were professionals.

Experimental evidence

As it turns out, there is substantial experimental evidence that the way in which an ostensibly paranormal event is depicted can bias people's interpretations of the event and their belief in the paranormal in general. Several examples will be considered here.

Sparks, Pellechia, and Irvine (1998) showed participants a news clip about UFOs presented by a US TV presenter who was considered to possess at least a moderate degree of credibility. The clip was preceded by an introduction in which a group of UFO believers discussed searching for UFOs. In one condition the introduction also included scientists offering an alternative explanation (jet air craft) and in the other condition it did not. Participants were asked for their level of belief in UFOs both before and after viewing the news clip. The results showed that participants who viewed the one-sided message increased their belief in UFOs while those who viewed the two-sided message decreased their belief. This example gives clear evidence both of the influence of the media in promoting belief in UFOs and also of the potential for the inclusion of a sceptical message at an early point to reduce levels of belief. It should be noted that the participants in this experiment had moderate levels of belief in UFOs to start with, and so were likely to have been open to influence. Media messages may have less influence on a topic on which people have strong prior beliefs.

Sparks, Hansen, and Shah (1994) showed participants a recorded episode of the series *Beyond Reality* that depicted re-enacted versions of supposed paranormal events. Participants were divided into four groups and each group was given a different introduction to the re-enactment: Group 1 was told that it was an accurate description; Group 2 was told that it was purely fictitious; Group 3 was told that it was scientifically impossible; and Group 4 was given no introduction. The participants in Group 4 showed higher levels of general paranormal belief after watching the programme and again three weeks later, and those in Group 3 showed lower levels of paranormal belief. Interestingly, those in Groups 1 and 2 showed no significant difference in paranormal belief. This might suggest that a strong statement – for example, that a particular phenomenon is scientifically impossible – is needed to warn viewers that the events they are viewing should be treated with caution. Otherwise, in the absence of any such statement, it seems that viewers may be encouraged to believe in the paranormal.

A similar caution was voiced by Sparks and Pellechia (1997). They asked participants to read a news story about UFOs in which the story was either supported or challenged by either general commentary or a notable scientist. Those participants for whom the story was confirmed by a notable scientist showed a higher level of belief in UFOs than the others. Interestingly, those for whom the story was disconfirmed by a scientist did not show a lower level of belief. The authors speculated that possibly the mere presence of a scientist offered credibility to the story and that a much stronger challenge would be required to overturn this effect.

Sparks, Sparks, and Gray (1995) showed some of their participants a video about UFOs taken from the programme *Unsolved Mysteries* while the remainder watched another video clip unrelated to UFOs. Those who watched the *Unsolved Mysteries* video had higher levels of belief in UFOs after watching it, confirming the effectiveness of this type of medium in promoting belief in UFOs. The particularly interesting aspect of this experiment is that the researchers also measured participants' mental imagery abilities. The theory was that if the video contained no explicit images of UFOs, the participants who had stronger imagery would find it easier to invent their own images and so would find the video more convincing than those with weaker imagery. Those participants who saw explicit images of UFOs would have no need to create their own images and so there would be no relationship between participants' imagery ability and how convincing they found the video. This was indeed what they found: participants with strong imagery found the video more convincing and had higher levels of belief in UFOs (measured after watching the video) than participants with weak imagery, but only in the condition in which there were no explicit images of UFOs. When images of UFOs were shown, the level of belief in UFOs and the rated convincingness of the video were not related to participants' imagery abilities. This is reminiscent of the evidence (reviewed in Chapter 2; please see the section on *The Fantasy-Prone Personality*) that imagery ability is associated with paranormal belief. Perhaps individual differences in the ability to create visual imagery of a narrated account can explain some of the individual differences in paranormal belief.

We have reviewed different types of evidence suggesting that the media are an influential source of paranormal beliefs. Before we leave this section, it is appropriate to consider the question of whether all this media activity does any harm. Does it matter that the media present biased and credulous accounts? Is anybody likely to be damaged if they are encouraged to entertain too much belief in unproven phenomena?

Is any harm done?

There is an argument that promoting belief in the paranormal undermines public understanding of science in general, and more specifically promoting bogus treatments and remedies can divert people from seeking proper medical help and cost them time and money. When it comes to talking to plants, one could argue that very little harm is done, except perhaps to the dignity and credibility of the gardener. When it comes to medical treatment, the consequences can be more severe. An example was offered by Philip Meyer who reported on the consequences of an uncritical report he wrote as a young journalist about a new cure for asthma discovered by a physician in Florida. For years afterwards he received phone calls from distressed individuals who had read the story and as a result paid the Florida physician large sums of money – without enjoying any improvement in their condition (Meyer, 1986).

Sherriff (2010) particularly takes exception to the tendency of women's magazines in the UK to publish articles about unsubstantiated areas of pseudoscience, without critical comment, among serious articles about major health issues. She cites an article about learning to see one's aura and how important this is to one's health in a magazine that regularly warns women about the importance of regular testing for early detection of breast cancer. Another magazine published a series of 'spooky' coincidences from readers (e.g. predictive dreams and the like) alongside an article warning of the dangers of sexually transmitted diseases. Is there a risk that readers might take these articles equally seriously? Sherriff (2010) complains that the paranormal is still seen as a fitting topic for women's magazines, but not for men's magazines. She finds it 'insulting to have equal coverage given to breast cancer and aura tutorials' (p. 142) and asks how she is supposed to know that articles about Rohypnol are serious when they are intermixed with this kind of junk. There does seem to be a risk that the uncritical presentation of paranormal stories is a particular concern for the readers of women's magazines.

The role of formal (scientific) education

Several older research studies have reported that formal school education serves to decrease levels of superstitious belief (Conklin, 1919; Emme, 1940; Maller & Lundeen, 1933). The 'corrective index' calculated by Maller and Lundeen (1933) was 1.81 for schools, which is relatively high, and suggests that schools are effective in reducing levels of superstitious belief. This is believed to happen partly as a result of formal instruction and partly through the observation of social norms suggesting that superstitions may not always be socially acceptable or widely shared. However, this observation is not universal and other studies have found that levels of paranormal belief in general can sometimes increase over the course of a college education. Chapters 2 and 6 consider this topic in more detail.

Lett (1992) observed that the methods and principles of science are not always taught particularly well in schools while Yates and Chandler (2000) reported moderate levels of New Age belief among a sample of over 232 pre-service primary schoolteachers. This shortcoming in scientific education could leave the general public vulnerable to pseudoscientists who adopt the superficial appearance of science. For example, consider the example of the 'news' item on talking to plants that was described earlier in this chapter. People who do not understand the impact that random variation can have in a scientific experiment may have been more impressed than was warranted by this particular 'news' item, failing to appreciate the lack of rigour in the research.

The frequent observation that women are under-represented and under-engaged in science (relative to men) may help to explain why women's magazines, but not men's magazines, carry articles on paranormal themes. This topic was also considered in detail in Chapter 2.

The role of narrative convention

The concept of narrative convention (as used here) broadly refers to the standards and expectations governing the stories we tell each other and the manner of their telling. There are several ways in which the rules of narrative convention may help to foster and strengthen paranormal beliefs (e.g. Gilovich, 1990) and these will be briefly described here.

How we tell stories

The needs of a speaker, or writer, or TV broadcaster are primarily to capture and hold the attention of the audience, while the needs of the listener, or reader, or TV viewer are to be entertained and – perhaps – to be informed (Gilovich, 1990). Thus, the desire to tell a good story can lead to the exaggeration and dramatization of the events in the story.

In order for a story to be interesting and captivating it should be comprehensible in terms of the background knowledge held by the listener and so the story must conform to commonly held knowledge. If there is a widespread cultural belief in a particular type of paranormal phenomenon – for example, astrology, telepathy, or ghosts – this can be invoked to enhance the ease of comprehension of the story. The repetition of the paranormal concept may help to reinforce general levels of belief and so the system of storytelling both reinforces and is supported by widespread cultural beliefs.

Narrative convention says that too much detail would detract from the interest of the story, and so unnecessary detail should be left out. People typically do not remember all the details of a story but only the gist, that is, the meaning and the central events and characters. In retelling the story of an event it is natural to emphasize the gist of the story and to de-emphasize what is considered to be unnecessary detail. The risk, of course, is that what is considered to be unnecessary detail by a paranormal believer (and who else would recount the story of a supposedly paranormal event?) may contain the information that would allow a plausible alternative, non-paranormal account of events. We saw in Chapter 6 that eyewitnesses to an ostensibly paranormal event could give accounts that are inaccurate and incomplete in important details. Perhaps the narrative convention that says that unnecessary detail should be excluded is responsible for this tendency. If a person already believes that an event had a paranormal cause, then any detail that would suggest an alternative possibility is an unnecessary detail and can be omitted in the interest of good storytelling. This will, of course, make it harder for anyone with a sceptical perspective to offer an alternative account that does not rely on paranormal phenomena.

In order to make a story seem more immediate and compelling, it is a common practice to move the story closer to the speaker. Thus, something that actually happened to a distant friend-of-a-friend-of-a-friend 20 times removed becomes something that happened to a friend-of-a-friend. This is problematic because we know that we need to discount stories that have passed through too many hands. If we are deceived about how many hands a particular story has passed through, then we may give the story a level of credibility it does not actually deserve. All of these tendencies can apply generally to our acquaintances and to the media as sources of accounts of paranormal events. This would suggest that we should be cautious and conservative when listening to any such personal testimony.

Another interesting source of examples of narrative conventions is the area of alternative medicines and 'miracle' remedies. Diamond (2010), in a posthumous publication, described how, during the course of treatment for cancer, he received many letters from well-wishers recommending a variety of alternative remedies with testimonies of people supposedly cured by these remedies. He was struck by how often certain phrases appeared in the testimonies and he analysed a few of these phrases. One example is the type of phrase 'the doctors gave her only x months to live' as a preamble to the story of an alternative remedy that resulted in the patient surviving much longer than the quoted estimate. Diamond's point is that doctors seldom give estimates with any degree of certainty and it is not unusual for a doctor to give several different estimates depending on whether particular courses of treatment prove efficacious. The purpose of this type of narrative phrase would seem to be to heighten the drama of the patient's survival and so, by association, to heighten the apparent efficacy of the alternative remedy. But it is often a deceptive comparison against the worst-case medical estimate.

Another type of phrase that frequently occurred was 'This isn't an alternative cure: it's been proved to have worked' and a common example was Essiac therapy for cancer, supposedly offered in Canadian hospitals. As Diamond points out, hospitals in Canada offer Essiac therapy in much the same way that hospitals in Britain offer a place to pray; it comforts patients and does no serious harm. A third example of a common phrase was 'Although the doctors won't say he's cured ...' cited as proof of the reluctance of mainstream medical people to give any credit to alternative remedies. A more plausible explanation is simply that many conditions, including cancer, are not 'cured' at all but simply in remission. For the patient, of course, this is good news – but a doctor would prefer to be cautious and not proclaim a complete cure because of the chance that a condition might return.

We have seen how some of the common rules governing our narrative accounts can help to bolster belief in a variety of paranormal phenomena. The next section will examine in some detail how a particular type of narrative account can help to make a personal account of a supposedly paranormal event more convincing to the audience.

Avowals of prior scepticism and related techniques

A belief is a position that is not only held internally but is also defended and explained in social interaction. Because of the need to be able to explain or defend one's beliefs in conversation, we can regard the maintenance of paranormal belief as a social discursive process. An important part of this process is the 'avowal of prior scepticism'.

The avowal of prior scepticism refers to the practice of beginning a narrative account of an ostensibly paranormal event by explaining that the narrator used to be a sceptic until this particular event occurred. The avowal emphasizes how compelling the event must have been in order to convince the previously sceptical narrator. Especially if the narrators are explaining that they are now a believer, it is important to present themselves as someone who has been convinced to change their mind by the strongest of evidence. James Alcock is quoted as saying, 'Even the strongest proponents of paranormal claims often preface their remarks by reference to their initial scepticism about the reality of the phenomena' (Lamont, 2007). An avowal of prior disbelief can serve to make both the event itself, and the interpretation of the event as paranormal, seem more plausible (Lamont, 2007; Wooffitt, 1992).

A claim to prior disbelief or scepticism is an example of the phenomenon known as 'stake inoculation' (e.g. Potter, 1996) that refers to the practice of preparing to resist a predictable counter-argument: for example, if the narrator is a believer and wants to convince others they have a stake in making the account seem more plausible. Knowledge of this vested interest might make the audience more wary of the truth of the account. The obvious counter-argument would be that the narrator is gullible and so has been deceived by false appearances. A statement of prior scepticism inoculates or defends against this type of counter-argument so that the current state of belief can be presented as the product of the experience itself. Then the experience seems more compelling to the audience.

Lamont (2007) illustrates the point with the 1998 biography of Uri Geller written by Jonathan Margolis. The first extract, taken from the introduction, shows how Margolis employs the technique of avowal of prior scepticism. The second extract, taken from the final chapter, shows a remarkable contrast with the author's initial position:

> Readers are entitled, of course, to know from what sort of position I started my voyage round Uri Geller. The answer is, one of considerable scepticism. I was the last writer I would have expected to spend two years researching a book on Uri Geller. (Margolis, 1998, p. 5)

> The evidence for Uri Geller, I submit, is utterly compelling. (Margolis, 1998, p. 288)

Lamont (2007) goes on to show how reviewers of the book took on board the avowals of prior scepticism to highlight the conversion of the author. For example, in *The Sunday Telegraph* (1 August 1999), a reviewer explicitly acknowledged that Margolis started writing the biography from a position of 'considerable scepticism' before discovering 'compelling evidence' of Geller's supernatural powers. And a reviewer may themselves employ an avowal of prior scepticism to show how reading the book has convinced them that Uri Geller possessed paranormal powers. For example, one reviewer from *The Sunday Telegraph* (1 August 1999) explained how they approached Margolis's book from a personal position of 'extreme scepticism' but became a near convert by the end of the book.

It is worth noting that the opposite phenomenon can also occur – that an avowal of prior belief can make a claim of current scepticism seem more convincing (Lamont, 2007). A good example of this would be the intellectual journey taken by the notable scientist Susan Blackmore. She describes how she started as a believer, but after ten years of research that uncovered no evidence for paranormal phenomena, she became a sceptic. This serves to establish the qualities of open-mindedness and critical evaluation that are just as important to underscore the evidence against paranormal phenomena as they have been in the hands of believers trying to promote the evidence for paranormal phenomena. A particularly telling quotation is this (Blackmore, 2000, p. 55):

> It was just over thirty years ago that I had the dramatic out-of-body experience that convinced me of the reality of psychic phenomena and launched me on a crusade to show those closed-minded scientists that consciousness could reach beyond the body and that death was not the end. Just a few years of careful experiments changed all that. I found no psychic phenomena – only wishful thinking, self-deception, experimental error and, occasionally, fraud. I became a sceptic.

There are other narrative techniques that help to bolster the credibility of an account of an ostensibly paranormal event. For example, Wooffitt (1992, p. 117) identified the narrative format that runs along the lines of 'I was just doing [something very ordinary and unexciting] when [something strange] happened'. This serves to confirm that the individual was sober and sensible and so was a competent and believable witness. This is a common form of narrative even though the audience do not solicit information about what the narrator was doing immediately prior to the anomalous event.

Another narrative technique is to describe attempts to investigate potential rational explanations for the phenomenon (e.g. Wooffitt, 1992, p. 82). This presents the narrator as a rational scientist taking a sensible approach to try to find an explanation within the realms of normal events. Our society generally expects individuals to act in a rational manner and to be somewhat sceptical about paranormal phenomena, so it is important for the narrator to present this image to enhance their personal credibility. The narrator may also cite the experiences of other people to support their claims.

The narrator often does not define their experience as paranormal but rather they allow the audience to reach that conclusion. If the members of the audience decide for themselves what the phenomenon was, they are likely to be more convinced than if they are told what to believe (e.g. Childs & Murray, 2010). The narrator does emphasize the non-normality of the events, though, to make it clear that something very unusual has occurred. Wooffitt (1992) points out that naming the event too soon would make it look as though the narrator had a pre-existing interest in the particular phenomenon and this is not the impression the narrator is seeking to convey.

Finally, if the narrator occupies a more authoritative position and has higher credibility, then their account is likely to be more convincing. For example, in the study by Ramsey, Venette, and Rabalais (2011), scientists were more convincing than university students, who in turn were more convincing that children.

The problems facing the non-believer in social interaction

Scepticism about the paranormal is a personal position arising from contemplation of the issues and the evidence, just as much as belief in the paranormal, but scepticism can be harder to defend and to explain. A friend may relate an account of an ostensibly paranormal event such that there is no apparent normal explanation that springs readily to mind. So it can be difficult for a sceptic to justify a position of doubt about the paranormal causes of a particular event. Sometimes a person who expresses scepticism may be challenged to offer an alternative explanation but this is often not possible, because, as described previously, an account of an ostensibly paranormal event is seldom related in sufficient detail to permit the identification of a plausible normal explanation.

To illustrate this problem, Lamont, Coelho, and McKinlay (2009) asked focus groups of three to six people to attend a 'psychic' show. The show presented demonstrations of possibly psychic phenomena and offered some alternative explanations so as to leave open the question of causality between psychic powers and conjuring tricks. Participants all said the show was trickery but they all felt that their lack of a specific alternative explanation was problematic. They appealed to magic tricks in general although they could not provide a precise explanation, along the lines that other people might be able to say how the trick was done but they themselves could not be specific. It is easy to see how it could be difficult, in conversation with a friend who holds strong beliefs, to hold to the position that a demonstration of 'psychic' powers was mere trickery if a convincing alternative account could not be offered.

It is interesting to note that spirit mediums, for example, often deny that they have any special powers and attribute everything to the spirits. By not claiming to have any special powers, they get themselves off the hook of having to provide an explanation for the phenomena they appear to demonstrate.

Cultural traditions of paranormal belief

Irwin (2009) explains that the particular form of paranormal belief held by an individual is likely to be a product of the sociocultural environment they experienced while they were growing up. We are less likely to adopt a set of beliefs that were not present at all during our formative years. People can, of course, change their beliefs as adults, but this is less likely. So the particular beliefs held by an individual are likely to be those that are relatively common within their society and culture, or were common within the culture in which they were raised. For example, in the UK the lucky number is three but the lucky number in Hong Kong is eight; the unlucky number is 13 in the UK but four in Hong Kong. In the UK some buildings do not have a 13th floor; lucky numbers commanded a much higher price on a car licence plate in Hong Kong between 1989 and 1991 (Woo & Kwok, 1994).

Another example of cultural influence is the different interpretations placed on the physical and mental phenomena that can be experienced during sleep paralysis (see Chapter 9). In previous centuries, and in many countries today, the paralysis and its accompanying hallucinations were attributed to demons or ghosts, whereas now, and especially in the USA, these symptoms are much more likely to be attributed to alien abduction.

The classification of beliefs into two types proposed by Sperber (1990) is interesting in this respect. Sperber explained that the 'intuitive' type of belief is inspired by an automatic inference which is shaped into a particular verbal expression by the information widely available in the culture. So, for example, sleep paralysis and its accompanying hallucinations may inspire the intuitive belief that one has been visited by strange beings and then the cultural tradition of demons or UFOs shapes the verbal expression of this belief into an account that will be most readily accepted in the particular culture. Another example concerns the finding of Dambrun (2004) that individuals with a stronger belief in astrology were more prejudiced towards ethnic and stigmatized groups. Perhaps the intuitive belief in this case is the belief that social disadvantage is the product of stable internal characteristics and the attribution to the influence of one's stars is the cultural expression of this belief. In this way popular culture offers people the verbal labels to describe and share their experiences.

In contrast, the 'reflective' type of belief, according to Sperber (1990), is acquired through a rational process of examining the evidence and listening to relevant authorities. So, in previous centuries, a religious leader might have encouraged the belief in a demonic cause of sleep paralysis, but today many Internet websites will offer alien abduction as the cause.

A selection of other examples of cultural variations in paranormal beliefs will be offered to illustrate the principle that what is considered alternative in one culture may be part of the mainstream cultural tradition in another. As one example, fortune-telling and divination are very popular in Korea and enjoy widespread and official acceptance (Kim, 2005). Believers are often well educated, young, and urban-living. In Korea, fortune-telling and divination are a central part of the cultural tradition and Koreans derive part of their national identity from these beliefs. They may even cling to these traditional beliefs to protect against becoming too Westernized and in order to maintain cultural distinctiveness (Kim, 2005).

Icelandic folklore and sagas involve a long tradition of experiencing contact with the dead, and belief in communication with people after death is stronger in Iceland (41% of the population) than in most other European countries (23%) and the USA (27%) according to Haraldsson (1985a).

The practice of Feng Shui, while it is known in Europe and the USA, is much more popular in China (Tsang, 2004) where Feng Shui experts are employed as consultants to business decision makers. Perhaps the Feng Shui practitioners help Chinese businessmen to cope with uncertainty by providing some sense of increased assurance of future outcomes and so relieving their anxiety (Tsang, 2004). Companies in Taiwan usually consult the lunar calendar to decide on the date, and a Feng Shui expert to decide on the location, of a new business or property purchase (*Economist*, 1993a). The going rate in Hong Kong for Feng Shui consultation about office space was two Hong-Kong dollars (about 25 US cents) per square foot (*Economist*, 1993b).

Beliefs about the purpose of superstitious rituals may also vary between cultures. For example, in the study by Burger and Lynn (2005), players from the USA believed that superstitious rituals helped their personal success while the Japanese players felt that it helped their team success, in an interesting example of difference between an individualist and a collectivist culture.

It is important to note that this does not mean that the paranormal beliefs of an individual are entirely dependent on social transmission. If this were the case then everybody in a given culture would hold the same beliefs and this is evidently not true. Indeed, as we have seen in other chapters (especially Chapter 2), there are personality influences and motivational influences on the levels and kinds of belief held by an individual.

Memes

The concept of memes is also relevant in the context of the cultural transmission of paranormal beliefs. A meme is a unit of cultural transmission, by analogy with a gene as a unit of genetic inheritance. A meme could be, for example, a skill, or a habit, or it could be a tune, an idea, a catchphrase, a fashion in clothing or design. The idea was first discussed by Dawkins in 1976 and has been extensively described by many theorists including Blackmore (2001) who describes a meme as 'information copied from person to person by imitation' (see also Blackmore, 1999). The idea is that memes and genes have co-evolved and have resulted in large human brains which are optimized for transmitting certain types of memes. The essential elements of evolution are present for memes: there is variation in the content of memes; some memes are better able to ensure their replication (passing from one person to another); and the aspect that makes a meme more replicable is contained when it is replicated. These three elements may be known as variation, selection, and heredity (Blackmore, 2001). The concept that genes and memes have co-evolved requires us to accept that aspects of human evolution are for the benefit of memes rather than for the benefit of genes or of the humans who replicate the memes, an idea which has proved to be rather controversial. Please refer to Chapter 8 for a fuller discussion of the evolutionary aspects of paranormal belief and experience.

Using this concept of the meme, it seems plausible that a meme could exist and ensure its own replication if it were perceived to be associated with survival and reproductive success even if it did not actually contribute to that success. For example, if a migrating tribe brought new technology into an area, then the people already resident would benefit from copying the technology. But they may not be knowledgeable about precisely what made the new tribe more successful and they may imitate incidental features that don't contribute

---

Box 7.4   Paranormal beliefs as memes

Thinking about the idea of memes, can you see how astrology might be considered to be a meme? How could it be introduced and spread by imitation? Does it fulfil the conditions of variation, selection, and heredity?

How about the various forms of alternative medicine? Or witchcraft?

You might like to try to apply the idea of a meme to your own example.

---

to survival. In this way, a meme could spread without necessarily having to convey any benefit to the imitator.

Some memes are better at getting themselves imitated than others. Those memes which are particularly memorable, or easy to visualize, or which make people feel more confident, or which appear to explain important questions that trouble people, would be likely to spread widely. This could apply to a number of paranormal beliefs (please see Box 7.4).

The socio-cognitive view of hypnosis, false memories, and multiple identities

An important social perspective is the socio-cognitive approach to understanding hypnosis and other related issues, including the creation of false memories, dissociative states, and the enactment of multiple personalities.

Special state versus socio-cognitive views of hypnosis

Hypnosis is a fascinating phenomenon about which many claims have been made: that people can be made to perform feats of which they would not ordinarily be capable, or remember events they thought they had forgotten. A widely held and influential view is that hypnosis is a 'special state' of consciousness in which the will of the individual is partly controlled by the hypnotist. According to the special state view, hypnosis is something that happens to people, rather than something in which they actively participate; the hypnotic trance is seen as a passive rather than an active state.

The special state view of hypnosis is held by many clinicians and therapists who work with patients to recover hidden memories of events that are believed to be the source of their present difficulties and emotional disturbances. The idea is that when the individual is hypnotized they will obey the request of the hypnotist and delve into memories which their conscious mind normally keeps under control – the phenomenon known as **repression**. The hypnotic trance weakens the control of the conscious mind so that the repressed memories can come to the surface and be accessible to recall. Many therapists believe that hypnotically recovered memories are likely to be accurate and true (see Spanos, 1996 for a review).

But how accurate is this view? Can hypnosis aid in the recall of hidden or repressed memories? And are the memories recalled under hypnosis always accurate and reliable? Before we consider this question, let us look at an alternative view of hypnosis.

An alternative to the special state view is the socio-cognitive approach to hypnosis (e.g. Barber, 1969; Lynn & Rhue, 1991; Wagstaff, 1981, 1999). According to this approach, hypnotic behaviour is not passive but active. The individual is trying to behave in accordance with their understanding of the role of the hypnotized subject. Hypnosis is not a special state of consciousness in which the individual's actions are directed by another, but a state in which the individual tries to act out the social role of a hypnotic subject. Hence the term 'socio-cognitive' refers to the social nature of the role and the cognitive and imaginative involvement in working out how to behave in the hypnotic situation. The individual's behaviour is dependent on picking up cues from the hypnotist and their ability to become absorbed in playing the role of a person under hypnosis. A person under hypnosis may perceive their behaviour as involuntary if that is how they interpret the requirement of the hypnotic role.

According to the socio-cognitive view, the memories that are 'recovered' under hypnosis are in fact imaginative constructions created by the hypnotic subject who is trying to comply with the instructions of the hypnotist. They may have some element of truth and indeed some 'recovered' memories may be almost entirely true, although others may not be. The danger is that any 'recovered' memory may be a fabrication created from general background knowledge by an exercise of the imagination. When the 'recovered' memory relates to events that occurred many years ago, there is often no way to gather objective information to verify the accuracy of the memory. This makes such 'recovered' memories very hard to validate.

To see how this process might work it is important to understand that memory is not like a tape recorder; it is not a precise, complete, and unchangeable record of past events. Far from it – memory is a reconstruction based on genuine fragments of memory, fleshed out with general knowledge, expectations, and clues provided by other people. Memory can be vague, incomplete, and subject to alteration depending on the cues and expectations present in the environment. Please refer back to Chapter 6 for a review of the ways in which memory can be biased.

Recovered versus false memories of childhood sexual abuse

When a recovered memory relates to childhood sexual abuse (CSA), then the impact on the individual and on their family can be very severe, so this is where we will focus our attention. The idea of repressed memory is part of the therapeutic technique of psychoanalysis. This technique holds that the key to current difficulties lies in childhood and that to overcome psychological problems one must understand the events of childhood and how they affect us today.

This concept is familiar to most people as is the idea that CSA must have an effect on adult life.

It is sometimes argued that recovered memories of CSA must be real because they are so painful that no one would create them. But an individual in therapy is seeking a reason for their present problems, and if they are looking for a reason in events of their childhood, then any recovered memory must be sufficiently traumatic to offer an explanation for current difficulties.

The attention focused on CSA has led to the development of a psychotherapeutic speciality for dealing with adult survivors. The danger is that a client who goes to one of these specialists may feel that their task is to try to conform to the therapist's idea of what has caused their problems. The goal of therapy then becomes to recover the repressed memories of CSA that are assumed to exist. Therapists often use hypnotic regression procedures (Spanos, 1996) and may offer strong encouragement to patients to find memories of abuse. A compliant and trusting client would then be able to construct memories of CSA to please the therapist, using knowledge of CSA gained from the popular media, websites, and self-help groups of survivors. Therapists usually validate any apparently recovered memories as real which helps the client to accept the memories (Fredrickson, 1992).

So what is the evidence for the recovery of repressed memories of CSA? We need to know whether there is any evidence that painful memories can be repressed so that there is an extensive period of time for which the memories are not accessible to the conscious mind. Two studies on this topic are particularly informative. Femina, Yeager, and Lewis (1990) interviewed 60 adults, all of them victims of CSA from official records, and reported that 18 of them denied any memory of the abuse, which would appear to support the possibility of repressed memories. However, some of the individuals were contacted and given a second interview that aimed at building rapport. All the individuals given a second interview now acknowledged abuse and said that they had previously denied it because it was too painful to talk about, or they wished to protect family members, or they were trying to forget it, or they felt a lack of rapport with the first interviewer. In a second study, Williams (1994) interviewed 129 women with documented histories of CSA that occurred between infancy and 12 years old. Only 12% had no recollection of any CSA at all and we do not know how old these were. If these women were those who were abused at a very young age of two or three or less, then their inability to recall is due to simple childhood amnesia. Most people cannot recall any events that occurred before about four years old.

So there seems to be a lack of solid evidence that memories of CSA can be repressed. There is also good evidence that children generally do not forget violent and dangerous events that occurred in their childhood (McNally, 2003a). For example, Rofe (2008) reviewed many studies of repression and concluded that there is poor empirical support for the concept that painful memories are repressed into the unconscious where they cause difficulties in adjustment and general life.

There is also direct evidence that suggests that memories recovered during hypnosis can be false. During hypnotic age-regression, in which clients are asked to return to a younger age of their life, a client typically does not behave like a child but according to an adult's view of a child. For example, O'Connell, Shor, and Orne (1970) showed that age-regressed adults would eat a lollipop coated in mud but children would not. That shows considerable dedication to playing the role! Further evidence for the unreality of some recovered memories lies in the observation that people have claimed to recover memories of past lives and of being abducted by aliens (see Chapter 9). Unless you accept these events as true, it seems pretty conclusive that recovered memories can be false memories.

Before we leave this chapter we will have a look at the related phenomenon of *dissociative identity disorder* (DID; formerly known as *multiple personality disorder*).

The socio-cognitive approach to dissociative identity disorder

People with a diagnosis of DID behave as if they have several separate personalities or 'alters', of which only one can be active at any time. Typically many of these alters appear to have amnesia for the existence of the others – for example, one alter may appear to be unaware that other alters exist and cannot recall any memories of events that occurred when one of the other alters was in charge. Nowadays most people diagnosed with DID are women, with psychological problems that pre-date the diagnosis of DID and they usually claim to have been sexually abused in childhood.

The theory is that the trauma of CSA causes the child to enter a hypnotic-like state and then split off (or dissociate) a part of themselves into an 'alter'. Then the main personality can carry on with no memory of the abuse, which is held in the memory of the alter. However, like the Freudian concept of repressed memory, the memory of the abuse causes psychological problems. The alters can be contacted using hypnotic age regression and they can be reintegrated into one personality.

The alternative socio-cognitive view is that DID is a disorder created by the therapist (a process known as iatrogenesis) with the compliance of the client. DID has become widely known and accepted as a legitimate way for people to explain their problems, assisted by films including *The Three Faces of Eve* and *Sybil*. Clients learn to construe themselves as possessing multiple personalities, each with its own personality and memories and to behave accordingly. They use the information available to them to construct a set of alters which are validated and confirmed by the reactions of the therapist. For example, questions like 'Do you ever feel as if you are not alone, as if there is someone else or some other part watching you?' encourage the view that one has separate identities, and some therapists may explicitly ask the other alters to come out and talk. The clients are asked to look into the back of their mind to see if there 'is anyone else there'. Self-help groups may also encourage the individual to display the enactment of multiple identities in order to win recognition and acceptance within the group. A lonely and unhappy person is easily swayed by a warm and welcoming group in their search for acceptance and social approval. This might sound far-fetched but consider that we all view ourselves as playing different roles in different parts of our lives, and as possessing different qualities and behaviour in these different roles.

Evidence relating to this view will be reviewed. First, DID was rare before 1980 (only 79 cases in the worldwide literature) but by 2000 there were around 40,000 cases, mainly in USA and Canada (Lynn & Deming, 2010). Was it previously rare because it was hard to diagnose (is it hard to diagnose a patient who calls themselves by different names and behaves like a different person on different occasions?) or because spontaneous cases are very rare and most of the modern cases are created by therapists? Second, the number of alters per client has grown from two or three before around 1970 to an average of 15 in the last 1980s (Ross, Norton, & Fraser, 1989). There is no apparent explanation for this phenomenon other than expectation and compliance on the part of the client. Third, clients typically have no memory of CSA when they enter therapy and 'recover' memory during therapy – but are the memories recovered or are they created during the therapeutic process? It is relevant that DID therapists are particularly likely to use hypnotic procedures (Spanos, 1996). Fourth, most cases are diagnosed by a small minority of therapists; is this because only a few therapists are able to identify DID or is it because these therapists are somehow creating the appearance of DID?

It is worth noting that one of the main influences on raising public awareness of multiple personality disorder was the publication, in 1973, of the best-selling book *Sybil* (Schreiber, 1973). This was the allegedly true story of a young woman who had apparently developed 16 different personalities as a consequence of severe abuse at the hands of her schizophrenic mother. The book has sold millions of copies and was the basis for two feature films of the same name. The true story behind this dramatic case was revealed by Debbie Nathan in 2011 in *Sybil Exposed*. Nathan's meticulous research proves beyond reasonable doubt that the alters in this case were the result of the bizarre and unethical treatment that she received at the hands of her therapist, Cornelia Wilbur.

The two distinct views on the causes of DID seem hard to reconcile. The socio-cognitive view says that memories recovered during hypnosis are likely to be constructions rather than genuine memories, and DID may be created by therapists, with the active cooperation of clients, who come to believe they possess multiple personality and learn to act accordingly. In contrast, the childhood trauma model of DID describes it as an involuntary condition arising from a mechanism for coping with repeated abusive and traumatic experiences of childhood. In our view, the evidence, as reviewed by Spanos (1996) and Mair (2013) for example, strongly favours the socio-cognitive view.

Houran and Lange's attributional model of paranormal belief and experience

Houran and Lange (2004) proposed their 'attributional model' to explain a possible source of hallucinations. The model contains several factors that influence the likelihood or the content of hallucinations and delusions.

Many people will have an anomalous perception at some time in their life. Anomalous perceptions may generate fear if there is no explanation readily at hand. The key point of the attributional model is that labelling an anomalous perception as a particular type of paranormal experience can provide an immediate explanation for the experience and that this can reduce the fear. This reduced fear is beneficial and so it sustains the belief in the particular paranormal phenomenon. The belief in this particular type of paranormal phenomenon makes it more likely that future anomalous perceptions will be interpreted in a similar light (Houran & Lange, 1996) thus sustaining the belief in a feedback loop.

However, a delusion or hallucination can be modified if the feedback loop is broken – for example, if the individual is offered an alternative explanation for the anomalous perceptual experience. This highlights the principle that people who have delusions or hallucinations are not ignoring the evidence of their own senses but rather they are interpreting the evidence in a way that makes sense to them. This is especially so if the anomalous event is perceived to have personal significance (Lange & Houran, 1998).

Lange et al. (1996) explained how contextual cues may influence the content of hallucinations. For example, cultural factors (e.g. belief in ghosts, a religious heritage) combined with certain situations (e.g. a séance or a supposedly haunted house) and an appropriate emotional or physical state of the individual (e.g. bereavement, temporal lobe stimulation) can make it more likely that a perceptual anomaly will be interpreted as a vision of a deceased loved one. In their study of many individual cases, they reported that 71% of experiences were congruent with contextual cues, only 3% were incongruent, and the congruence of the remainder of cases could not be assessed. Similar results were obtained by Houran and Lange (1997) in a study of deathbed visions.

Suggested further reading

For more on the media representation of ghosts and spirits:

Hill, A. (2011). *Paranormal media: Audiences, spirits and magic in popular culture.* London and New York: Routledge.
Lett, J. (1992). 'The persistent popularity of the paranormal'. *Skeptical Inquirer*, 16, 381–88.

For a general discussion of why we believe in the absence of reliable evidence:

Gilovich, T. (1991). *How we know what isn't so: The fallibility of human reason in everyday life.* New York, NY: Free Press.
Sutherland, S. (1992). *Irrationality.* London: Pinter and Martin.

For more information on cold reading:

Hyman, R. (1977). '"Cold reading": How to convince strangers that you know all about them'. *The Zetetic*, Spring–Summer, 1, 18–37.
Rowland, I. (2002). *The full facts book of cold reading*. 3rd edn. London: Ian Rowland Limited.

For a detailed discussion of how we tell each other stories:

Wooffitt, R. (1992). *Telling tales of the unexpected: The organisation of factual discourse*. Hemel Hempstead: Harvester Wheatsheaf.

For a detailed consideration of memes:

Blackmore, S. J. (1999). *The meme machine*. Oxford: Oxford University Press.

Evolutionary Perspectives

8

Introduction

Although the roots of evolutionary psychology can be traced back to Charles Darwin's seminal book *The Origin of Species*, there is no doubt that this approach has gained greatly in influence in the last few decades. The approach taken by modern evolutionary psychologists is to try to explain human psychological traits in terms of the evolutionary pressures of natural selection. Many evolutionary psychologists argue that the mind has a modular structure with different modules serving different functions. Each of these modules has evolved to solve different problems that have consistently faced humankind during our ancestral history. Some of these modular adaptations, as we will see, may well have some relevance in explaining a range of paranormal and supernatural beliefs.

This chapter will differ from most of the other chapters in this book in two important ways. Firstly, there will be considerably less presentation of the results of empirical investigations and considerably more speculation on the origins of various psychological traits than in other chapters. Even though the ideas of evolutionary psychologists have become more influential recently, evolutionary psychology is still a controversial subject. Critics sometimes accuse evolutionary psychologists of making up 'just-so' stories to explain the psychological traits we observe in modern humans; that is to say, if a trait is still common in the human species, it must have served some purpose in terms of helping the species to survive. The task then is simply to come up with a plausible explanation of what that purpose might have been. This criticism, although sometimes appropriate, is probably overstated. It is possible to derive and test new hypotheses on the basis of this approach that go well beyond simply re-describing the initial data. Having said that, much of evolutionary psychology is indeed quite speculative in nature as it is simply not possible to go back in time and observe the pressures that may or may not have played crucial roles in the evolutionary development of our species.

Secondly, this chapter tends to focus more upon the psychology of religious beliefs as opposed to other types of supernatural belief. This simply reflects the fact that, to date, more theorists in the area of the psychology of religion have applied the perspective of evolutionary psychology to their chosen subject matter than have anomalistic psychologists. As we shall see, however, much of the thinking behind these theories can be very easily applied to all kinds of supernatural belief, religious or otherwise. It is important to note, however, that the approach to the psychology of religion discussed in this chapter is only one approach within that field.

Among those who apply the principles of evolutionary psychology to the study of religion there is one important ongoing debate that, although it will not be discussed extensively in this chapter, the reader should be aware of. Some evolutionary psychologists believe that religion itself evolved through natural selection and that it is an adaptation that directly confers some advantages in evolutionary terms. Others argue that religion may simply be a by-product of the evolution of other psychological traits that conferred such direct advantages (interested readers may refer to Boyer & Bergstrom, 2008; Sosis, 2009).

Thinking, fast and slow

It is now generally accepted that human cognition can be best understood by conceiving of human thought as relying upon two different systems, each with its own characteristics. Nobel laureate Daniel Kahneman, one of the pioneers in developing this approach, follows Stanovich and West (2000) in referring to these two modes of thought by the convenient shorthand of *System 1* and *System 2* (e.g. Kahneman, 2011). System 1 is fast, automatic, involves no sense of voluntary control, and requires little or no effort. In contrast, System 2 is slower, requires conscious effort and feels as if it is under conscious control. Subjectively, we have little conscious awareness of the operation of System 1 whereas the operations of System 2 give rise to our sense of self. Although we may feel that our beliefs and decisions are based solely upon rational processing within System 2, in fact System 1 generates many of the impressions and feelings that influence our conscious reflections.

This way of thinking about human cognition provides the solution to what may appear at first sight to be a puzzle regarding the cognitive biases discussed in Chapter 6. Why are such biases still so pervasive throughout the human species if they systematically lead us astray in certain situations? Surely it is always better to accurately evaluate reality and therefore any such cognitive biases should have been selected out as a consequence of evolution? The truth is that our thinking is guided to a much greater degree than we realize by System 1 thinking – and the big advantage that System 1 has over System 2 is speed. Generally, we make decisions using System 1's quick and dirty rules of thumb known as *heuristics*. Fortunately, these quick decisions usually give us the right answer – or at least answers that, if incorrect, do not cost us a lot. In this context, the right answer is the one that is most likely to keep us alive so that we can pass on our genes to the next generation. Our minds have evolved to help us to maximize our chances of physical survival not of apprehending the truth about the world around us. In terms of the cost-benefit analysis of natural selection, it simply makes more sense for us to have evolved cognitive systems that most of the time quickly generate the right answer in terms of survival rather than slower, more reflective, decisions that might be right slightly more often.

The usual example that is presented to illustrate this point is that of the Stone Age man who hears something rustling in the bushes. In one hypothetical scenario, System 1 thinking almost instantly leads to the decision that there is a predator in the bushes and our hero makes a hasty exit. In the other hypothetical scenario, System 2 thinking takes control and our hero stands there pensively scratching his beard while he tries to decide if he really is in danger or not. Clearly, reliance on System 1 is going to maximize his chances of survival and therefore passing on his genes to the next generation. In the first scenario, the benefit if System 1 has delivered an accurate conclusion is enormous: our hero avoids becoming lunch. The cost of System 1 being wrong in this context is minimal: that is, simply wasting some energy in running away from a sabretooth that wasn't really there. Reliance on System 2 is not a sensible strategy in this context because of the huge cost potentially attached to taking too long to make a decision. Thus, in general, evolutionary pressures will have favoured reliance on System 1 thinking.

There are two kinds of error that can be made in the previous scenario. First, as described, our hero might have assumed there was a predator in the bushes when really there was not. This is an example of what is known as a Type I error (or a false positive). It is the equivalent of a scientist who wrongly rejects the null hypothesis and concludes that she has found an effect that isn't really there. Second, our prehistoric decision-maker might have disastrously concluded that there was no predator in the bushes when in fact there was one. This would be an example of a Type II error (or a false negative), the equivalent of the scientist who wrongly accepts the null hypothesis when, in fact, there really is an effect.

One of the reasons that the human species has been so successful is because we are very good at picking up on patterns in our surroundings even when the signals may be somewhat ambiguous and open to interpretation. Thus, in the past, survival depended upon the skills of hunters to both pick up on signs that led to prey as well as those that assisted in avoiding predators. In terms of the development of agriculture, it was essential that humans were able to capitalize upon the changing meteorological conditions and other cues from the natural environment associated with changing seasons. This required the ability to pick up on the signals that heralded such changes. The development of tools required the making of connections between cause and effect. Given the general evolutionary bias in favour of making Type I as opposed to Type II errors, the price that we pay for our impressive ability to recognize meaningful patterns and cause-and-effect relationships in the world around us is that sometimes we see meaning and significance in randomness and sometimes we perceive cause-and-effect relationships based upon nothing more than illusory correlations.

Patterns and meaning

Perhaps the most extreme form of seeing meaning in randomness is that which occurs during psychotic breakdown. The term **apophenia** is used to refer to the spontaneous perceiving of connections and meaning in randomness. Numerous examples can be found in first-hand accounts of schizophrenic breakdown, such as the following from the Swedish writer August Strindberg (1897/1979, quoted by Brugger, 2001, p. 203):

> I once found my pillow, which I had crumpled when taking my mid-day rest, so moulded that it looked like a marble head in the style of Michaelangelo ... These occurrences could not be regarded as acciden-tal, for on some days the pillows presented the appearance of horrible monsters, of gothic gargoyles, of dragons, and one night ... I was greeted by the Evil One himself.

We have all had the experience of seeing meaningful shapes in clouds, rocks, the grain of wood, and so on. During a psychotic episode, however, these pat-terns can appear to have tremendous meaning and significance.

Apophenia refers to our general tendency to make connections and find meaning in meaningless noise, a tendency that Michael Shermer (2011) has referred to as **patternicity**. This tendency is evident in a range of contexts including conspiratorial thinking, gamblers falsely believing they can perceive patterns in, say, a series of randomly drawn lottery numbers, and allegedly divining hidden meanings in holy texts. The term **pareidolia** refers to the spe-cific type of apophenia that applies in the perceptual domain whereby clear and distinct stimuli, such as faces, are perceived in random stimuli. Poole (2007) presents a number of the most notorious examples including a cinnamon bun bearing an uncanny likeness to Mother Teresa, an image of Rasputin inside a cat's ear, and the Virgin Mary on a grilled cheese sandwich!

Human beings are simply not very good at being able to recognize random-ness or at generating it spontaneously. Instead, we typically have to use dice or other mechanical means to achieve true randomness. Even those who have a reasonable grasp of the nature of randomness on an intellectual level still fall victim to our shared misleading intuitions about it. Consider the following runs of 30 heads and tails. Which of them is more likely?

Sequence A: HHHHHHHHHHHHHHHHHHHHHHHHHHHHHH
Sequence B: HTTHTHHTTTHTHTHTHTTHHTHHTTTHTHTT
Sequence C: THTTTHTHTHTTTHHTTHTHHTTTTTHHHHT

The truth is that *any* pre-specified sequence of a fixed length is equally likely; in this case, the probability of any row is 0.5^{30}. Many people, however, feel that Sequence B is more likely than A simply because it corresponds more to their idea of true randomness – it's all 'jumbled up'!

Now consider a different question: only one of those rows was actually produced by one of the authors (CCF) tossing a coin 30 times. He did that just once and recorded the results. Which sequence do you think that is? The answer is Sequence C which may be a bit surprising. To most people, we suspect that it looks random for the first 20 throws but then we have a run of five tails immediately followed by a row of four heads. How can that be random? The truth is that the simple laws of probability predict that a run of five in 30 flips should occur in almost two runs out of three (Bellos, 2010). This being followed by four heads was just a fluke – but that's the way randomness works. It's predictably unpredictable!

Our intuitions tell us that repetition should be rare in random sequences and our intuition is simply wrong. In a random sequence, every event is entirely independent of every other event and therefore repetitions will occur. But we tend to judge strings of digits that include repetitions as being less random than those that do not. Similarly, when asked to generate random sequences, we tend to avoid repetition more than we should – and interestingly, as described in Chapter 6, believers in the paranormal tend to do this more than non-believers (e.g. Brugger, Landis, & Regard, 1990).

Our tendency to read more meaning than we should into random sequences is also responsible for belief in the 'hot hand' in basketball. The idea is that for some games a particular player is 'hot' – when on a hot run, every shot they try seems to go in the basket. Conversely, the opposite can happen. Players can have games where every shot they try is a miss. This would make psychological sense. If your first shot goes in, it boosts your confidence and your next shot is more likely to go in too. If your first shot misses, your confidence goes down and anxiety goes up, resulting in poorer performance. Belief in the hot hand is shared by players, coaches, and fans. The only problem is that it is an illusion, as shown by Gilovich, Vallone, and Tversky (1985). The number of runs of hits for a particular player exactly corresponds to what the laws of probability would predict for a player of that level in terms of hit average. The hot hand hypothesis would predict more long runs (and the cold hand hypothesis, more short runs) than what actually occur.

Religious concepts

In many respects, religious beliefs and practices are, despite their prevalence, distinctly odd. Why does such a high proportion of the human race find religious ideas so easy to accept even in the absence of solid empirical evidence to support them? Indeed, why are such ideas so resistant to evidence that often appears to directly contradict them? As Wilson (2010) argues, religious ideas appear to have a natural appeal that scepticism simply does not possess for most people. The fact that religious beliefs are so pervasive in diverse cultures around the world strongly suggests to evolutionary psychologists that they are a product of mental systems that have evolved universally in the human species (for more detailed treatments, see Atran, 2002; Barrett, 2004; Bering, 2011; Boyer, 2001; Pyysiäinen, 2001; Pyysiäinen & Anttonen, 2002).

Pascal Boyer (2001) asked the question of what it was about supernatural concepts that makes them so amenable to sharing between members of a group. Were there some common characteristics of such concepts that explained this property? He argued that our ancestors would have been preoccupied with five basic domains of thought: people, animals, plants, artefacts, and natural (inanimate) objects. Thinking in terms of such ontological categories is very efficient, insofar as we would make many default assumptions about the properties of any new object from one of those categories that we encounter. Thus, we expect people and animals to behave in accordance with intentional goals, whereas we would not expect that of artefacts or other inanimate objects.

For a religious concept to be passed on between members of a society, it has to grab our attention, be easy to remember, and be easy to describe to others. Boyer (2001) proposes that the optimal formula for concepts with these properties is to be something that has all of the default values of a member of one of the five basic ontological categories, but with one or two counter-intuitive properties. Thus, religious concepts preserve most of the properties of an ontological category but violate just one or two. A commonly given example is that of a statue that people pray to. The statue will be assumed to possess many of the default properties of an artefact: it will be immobile; it would smash if we hit it with a hammer; and so on. But additionally it has a couple of properties that violate our assumptions for that category: it can hear and respond to our prayers.

Boyer's (2001) reasoning is supported by the fact that a wide range of supernatural concepts collected across disparate religions do indeed seem to comply with his description. By combining his five ontological categories with three possible types of violation of default assumptions (psychological, physical, and biological), Boyer was able to successfully categorize most religious concepts. Furthermore, there is empirical evidence that novel concepts which fit the formula are indeed interesting, memorable, and easy to describe. If more than a couple of counter-intuitive violations are applied, these properties are lost.

Anthropomorphism

Anthropologist Stewart Guthrie (1993) presented a wealth of evidence in support of his contention that **anthropomorphism** (i.e. our tendency to attribute human characteristics to non-human objects and events) is a pervasive aspect of human cognition. According to him, such anthropomorphism makes sense in evolutionary terms. In Guthrie's (1993, p. 3) words:

> I claim we anthropomorphize because guessing that the world is human-like is a good bet. It is a bet because the world is uncertain, ambiguous and in need of interpretation. It is a good bet because the most valuable

interpretations usually are those that disclose the presence of whatever is most important to us. That usually is other humans.

Scanning the world for humans and humanlike things and events, we find apparent instances everywhere. We later judge many of these interpretations mistaken, but those that are correct more than justify the strategy. Because betting on the most significant interpretations is deeply rooted, anthropomorphism is spontaneous, plausible, and even compelling.

One of the most obvious ways in which this tendency manifests itself is our readiness to see humanlike faces in random patterns, a tendency that is obviously linked to our general tendency to perceive patterns and meaning in randomness as described previously. Faces are incredibly important stimuli for us in a number of ways. In evolutionary terms, it was not only important for us to readily perceive other human beings in our surroundings but also to be able to quickly assess the likelihood that they were familiar or unfamiliar, a friend or foe. As a result, our brains are hard-wired to recognize faces and thus even very simple schematic stimuli, such as two dots for eyes and a couple of lines for nose and mouth, will readily be interpreted by us a face.

Inevitably, there is enough randomness in the world around us to regularly encounter stimulus configurations that look like faces (see, for example, Guthrie, 1993 and Poole, 2007 for numerous examples). Most of us, most of the time, do not attach much significance to such phenomena but a sizeable minority of the population find them so compelling that they assume that they must have greater significance beyond the simple accidental arrangement of stimuli. As already described, the images that are often found are those of religious figures such as Jesus or the Virgin Mary. Such images are routinely found in the patterns in the grain of wood, in stains on floors, in clouds, in rocks, in slices of fruit or vegetables, and so on. People often attach great significance to such images. For example, in 1994 a woman in Miami took a bite of her grilled cheese sandwich and saw what she took to be an image of the Virgin Mary on the sandwich staring back at her. She kept the rest of the sandwich in a clear plastic box on her nightstand for the next decade before selling it on eBay in 2004 – for $28,000! It was bought by an online casino company.

The tendency to attach significance to items such as these illustrates not only our tendency to perceive meaning in randomness but also our tendency to perceive agency where in fact there is none. Shermer (2011) refers to this tendency as **agenticity**. In other words, we often have a tendency not only to perceive a meaningful pattern in random stimuli but also to assume that someone or something must have intentionally made that pattern.

Agency

This tendency to assume that events happen because someone or something made them happen is another example of a bias that, from an evolutionary perspective, makes sense in terms of the cost-benefit analysis involved. As with our previous example of the Stone Age man and the rustling in the bushes, the cost of mistakenly concluding that there is an intentional agent (e.g. an enemy or a predator) in the bushes that caused the rustling when, in fact, there isn't is far lower than the cost of mistakenly concluding that there is no such agent when, in fact, there is.

This sense of agency is also related to Guthrie's (1993) notion that we tend to think anthropomorphically. We not only tend to see human forms and faces in our environment but also to assume that all events that happen in our environment are caused by humanlike agents. This is a consequence of our readiness to accept religious concepts that involve just one or two tweaks to the five basic domains of thought, as many supernatural concepts involve the assumption that a humanlike agent is involved but one with a couple of properties (e.g. invisibility) that ordinary humans do not possess.

Justin Barrett (2004) has developed the notion of what he calls our **hyperactive agency detection device (HADD)** on the basis of such thinking. Our HADDs have helped us to survive in evolutionary terms because it simply makes sense for us to assume that things that happen around us happen because someone or something made them happen. But the price that we pay is that we overgeneralize this attribution to inappropriate natural events. Thus our ancestors assumed that thunder and lightning, natural disasters, and failures of the harvest must all be caused by someone or something. The creation of gods to explain such occurrences was a direct consequence. Although many of the theorists involved in this area have focused primarily upon religious concepts, it is clear that such explanations can be readily applied to other supernatural and paranormal concepts, such as ghosts, fairies, witches, and so on.

It is easy to see how Barrett's (2004) notion of the HADD can be applied to a range of supernatural concepts. Our HADDs are likely to be at their most sensitive when we find ourselves in situations of inherent uncertainty and vulnerability. Thus we are much more likely to think in terms of potential intruders – or even ghosts – if we are woken up by an unexpected noise in the middle of the night rather than a similar noise in the middle of the day.

Jesse Bering (2011) argues that once we invoke agency to explain events occurring in our environment, we naturally think in terms of what is known as **theory of mind**: that is to say, we activate those mental processes that deal with social interaction generally. Whenever we successfully interact with others in a social context, we automatically and often unconsciously make assumptions about the other person's intentions and beliefs and modify our own behaviour accordingly. Evolutionary psychologists believe that we have evolved specific mental modules for dealing with such information, given its overriding importance for our survival. Thus we have to quickly make decisions regarding what the other person hopes to achieve by interacting with us. Do they intend to help us or to harm us? What are they trying to tell us? Can we trust them? Is their understanding of the situation accurate or do they hold false beliefs?

These same mental processes are brought into play whenever we believe our-selves to be interacting with any kind of supernatural agent. If we believe that there is such a thing as an omniscient, omnipotent being that created the uni-verse including all human life, it is quite natural for us to try to behave in ways of which we think this being would approve. We will assume that the being has similar moral values to our own but the fact that the being is all-knowing will give it a very powerful role in influencing our actions in the hope of obtaining rewards or of avoiding punishment for misdeeds. On a somewhat more mun-dane level, we will make similar assumptions regarding the perceived behav-iour of disembodied spirits. Whether we are dealing with God or a lesser spirit, we may often feel the temptation to interpret various natural events as signs or omens that are intended to give us an indication of how the spirit being wants us to behave. Thus, we are not simply attributing meaning and significance where perhaps we shouldn't; we also naturally assume that there is a purpose to that message. It has been deliberately put there by an intentional agent to tell us something.

Bering and Parker (2006) devised an ingenious method to study this phe-nomenon in children under controlled conditions. They invited children in dif-ferent age groups to come and play a guessing game in which they would have to try and guess in which of two boxes a ball had been hidden. In fact, there was a ball in each box, allowing the experimenters to determine in advance whether the child would get it 'right' or 'wrong'. Each child was tested indi-vidually for four trials. On each trial, the child would go into the corner of the room, cover his or her eyes for a short time, and then return and indicate which box they thought contained the ball by placing a hand on it. They were allowed a few seconds to make their decision, during which time they could change their mind if they wanted to and put their hand on the other box. When the experimenter announced that time was up, the child was either told that their final answer was right (and the box the child was touching was opened to show the ball) or wrong (and the other box was opened to show the ball).

Half of the children were randomly assigned to the control condition. These children were told that they were right on two trials and wrong on two tri-als, randomly determined. But children in the experimental condition were told something else before they began. They were told that there was a friendly, invis-ible, magic princess in the room named Alice. The child's attention was drawn to a picture of Alice (in her visible form, looking a lot like Barbie) on the inside of the door. The child was also told, 'Princess Alice really likes you, and she's going to help you play this game. She's going to tell you, somehow, when you pick the *wrong* box.' The children were reminded of this at the start of each trial.

During the game, the experimenters ensured that an unexpected event, such as a lamp flickering on and off or the picture of Alice falling off the door, would occur just as the child initially placed their hand on a box. The idea was that if a child in the experimental condition took the unexpected event as a sign from Alice that they were touching the wrong box, they would move their hand to the other box.

The results were interesting and somewhat unexpected. The children in the control condition, as expected, did not move their hands in response to the unexpected event, but the children in one age group in the experimental condition did. Following Piaget, one might have assumed that it would be the youngest children who would have been the ones to demonstrate this behaviour but in fact it was the oldest children, those in the seven- to nine-year-old group, who did so.

The children were asked afterwards what they thought had caused the unexpected events. The youngest children, aged three or four, did not link the events to Princess Alice at all, simply saying that maybe the picture had not been put up properly or the lamp was broken. The oldest children, aged seven to nine, clearly took the events as evidence that Princess Alice was telling them to change their answers. The middle group, aged five and six, reported that they did believe that Princess Alice had caused the events but clearly they did not interpret the events as a sign that Alice was telling them to change their answer. Why not?

Bering and Parker (2006) point out that such an interpretation requires a fairly advanced theory of mind. The children would have to be able to reason that 'Alice knows [that I don't know] where the ball is', which involves more advanced 'second-order' theorizing, that is, not just appreciating another person's beliefs but appreciating that they have beliefs about your beliefs. Although children appear to develop a theory of mind at around the age of three or four, such advanced understanding is unlikely to develop before age seven, explaining why it was only the oldest group who were capable of 'interpreting the signs'.

It is also worth noting that none of the children in the control condition, not even those in the oldest age group, spontaneously interpreted the unexpected events as 'signs'. The children needed to be primed by being told about Princess Alice in order for them to do so. Once again, the effects of context are all-important. At certain times in our lives, we will be more receptive to such 'signs' than others. Obvious examples are following a bereavement or when, at a particularly low point, a religious believer asks for a sign from God in order to 'show him the way'.

Ghost-hunting for beginners

A nice way to illustrate all of these biases in action is to consider some of the typical activities of amateur ghost-hunting groups. Such groups are extremely common in the UK and USA partly due to the popularization of ghost-hunting via numerous TV series. Although such groups often present themselves to the external world as being engaged in 'scientific investigations' of the paranormal, it is quite clear that they are actually engaged in little more than exercises in wishful thinking and overactive imagination. Although they often make use of various electronic gadgets to gather their data, this serves simply to impress and bamboozle the uninformed observer. Members of such groups rarely have any formal scientific training and, indeed, often embrace a range of pseudoscientific hypotheses in order to bolster their claims.

Typically, such groups will often spend one or more nights in a reputedly haunted location with various pieces of electronic apparatus suitably deployed. These include digital cameras, night cameras, motion detectors, sound recorders, thermometers, and so on. In this context, even slightly unusual events are taken as evidence of ghostly activity. Thus, if a piece of equipment fails to work properly or if an object is misplaced, this is generally interpreted as being due to the intervention of spirits even though in other contexts no such interpretation would be given. Often there will be some attempt to figure out what the ghost is trying to communicate by this 'sign'. This is a clear example of reading significance and meaning into events that are likely to occur from time to time in the natural course of events without any supernatural intervention. Our ghost hunters are behaving in exactly the same way as the seven- to nine-year-olds in the experiment described earlier.

Another nice example of seeing meaning and significance in a minor anomaly is the phenomenon of the so-called orbs. Many self-styled paranormal investigators are convinced that what appear to be small spheres of light that appear on many photographs, especially those taken using the flash on compact digital cameras, are in fact spirits. Experts in photography dismiss this interpretation, instead insisting that the effect is produced when a particle of dust or a water droplet is caught out of focus in the light from the flash. There is, of course, absolutely no logical connection between the phenomenon of these circular artefacts and 'spirit energy' and it is unclear how this association arose in the first place. But it is clear why it has become popular. Before the advent of digital cameras, ghost hunters would often spend many uncomfortable nights sitting in cold, dark, allegedly haunted buildings and have absolutely nothing to show for it. These days it is a pretty safe bet that photographs taken in such dusty environments will produce many images containing ghostly orbs, which are then taken as proof that the location was indeed haunted.

Many ghost hunters will attribute intentionality to the orbs, describing their 'behaviour' as indicating intelligence. If the orbs appear to be close to a person in the picture, they are described as 'friendly'. If they are distant or few in number, they are described as being 'shy'. Such observations are reminiscent of Albert Michotte's (1962) classic work on the perception of causality. Michotte showed that presenting participants with simple animations of shapes moving in particular ways was often sufficient to elicit descriptions of the scene such as the following:

> The little ball is trying to play with the big ball, but the big ball doesn't want to play so he chases the little ball away. But the little ball is stubborn and keeps bothering the big ball. Finally, the big ball gets mad and leaves.

This is a very clear demonstration of the readiness with which we attribute intentionality to objects on the basis of minimal cues.

Another phenomenon that beautifully illustrates the ghost hunters' tendency to perceive meaning in randomness and to assume that an intentional agent caused that meaning to be there is the so-called *electronic voice phenomenon (EVP)*. As you may recall from Chapter 1, this refers to the claim that it is possible to directly record spirit voices by leaving a recording device in an allegedly haunted location (e.g. Raudive, 1971). While it is likely that the techniques used sometimes result in the inadvertent recordings of voices of the living, it also appears to be the case that the recordings are often just random background noises that bear a superficial resemblance to speech. Although some paranormal investigators claim to be able to perceive clear messages in such recordings, most people cannot hear any such message unless they are told in advance what they are supposed to hear. As explained in Chapter 1, this is due to the effects of top-down processing. As you might expect, the messages that the ghost hunters report are heavily influenced by the context in which they are recorded.

Magical thinking as an adaptive cognitive tool

We have already seen in previous chapters, especially Chapter 3, that magical thinking appears to sometimes serve a protective function against the possible development of learned helplessness and depression and as a means to alleviate anxiety by providing a sense of control, albeit an illusory one. D. Thomas Markle (2010) discusses such observations from an evolutionary perspective.

He argues that humans are most likely to resort to magical thinking as a coping mechanism when faced with anything that threatens reproductive or survival fitness. However, some threats are unmanageable threats insofar as the threatened individuals lack either the resources or knowledge to deal with the threat effectively. Such unmanageable threats cause stress and anxiety that has three main survival costs: 'a reduction in task productivity due to a reduction in working memory, a physiological weakening of the body, and a loss of memory functions' (Markle, 2010, p. 19).

When faced with unmanageable threats, rational reflection is by definition of no use but magical thinking at least mitigates the survival costs, caused by anxiety and stress, that logical thinking cannot. Therefore, Markle (2010, p. 20) concludes,

[I]f we take the idea that magical thinking is found in arguably all of human culture, and combine that with the idea that it seems to be a unique cognitive ability well suited for dealing with the stress of unmanageable threats, the possibility of magical thinking being evolutionarily selected must at least be considered.

Clearly, much of the research reviewed in Chapter 3 (e.g. Dudley, 1999, 2000; Keinan, 2002) appears to fit in well with the framework described by Markle (2010). As further support for the idea that magical thinking is associated with lack of control, Markle cites the classic work of anthropologist Bronislav Malinowski (1922). Malinowski documented the fact that Melanesian islanders only engaged in magical rituals in connection with tasks involving a high degree of uncertainty and risk, such as deep-sea fishing. No such rituals were carried out in connection with routine tasks such as inland fishing, planting crops, or constructing boats and shelters.

Further support is provided by Padgett and Jorgenson (1982) on the basis of their analysis of the number of articles on superstitions and the occult published in German newspaper articles between 1918 and 1940. This was a period of severe economic decline in Germany with dramatic increases in inflation and levels of unemployment. As public anxiety increased, so did the number of articles on the occult and related topics.

Conclusions

The perspective provided by evolutionary psychology is persuasive and plausible, albeit more speculative than many of the other perspectives considered in this book. There is a vast amount of evidence in support of the idea that human cognition relies on two different systems, one of which is fast, automatic, and non-conscious, and another which is slower, effortful, and of which we are consciously aware. There is no doubt that much of our thinking is based upon heuristics – quick and dirty rules of thumb that usually deliver the right answer. Such a system, it can plausibly be argued, would serve us better in evolutionary terms than a slower, more reflective, system that was right slightly more often. Beyond this, many of the ideas presented in this chapter are more speculative, albeit quite plausible and supported by some limited empirical evidence. One of the tasks facing future researchers will be to devise direct experimental tests of the hypotheses proposed.

The notion that it would make sense in evolutionary terms for us to have a stronger bias towards Type I errors than Type II errors seems reasonable. Thus we would sometimes see patterns and meaning in randomness and perceive cause-and-effect relationships where none exist. Our tendency to see meaning in randomness combined with our postulated natural anthropomorphism leads us to perceive events around us in terms of being caused by intentional agents. From there, it is a short cognitive step to belief in gods, spirits, and a host of other supernatural beings.

Although it can be argued that magical thinking can be viewed as an adaptive and functional cognitive tool, this should certainly not be taken to indicate that superstitious thinking and behaviour are to be encouraged. While it may be true that magical thinking served an adaptive function during our evolutionary history and, indeed, can still sometimes do so in the present, it only serves a useful purpose when we are faced by unmanageable threats. It goes without saying that it is preferable to be faced by threats that we know how to handle. Thanks to advances in our scientific understanding, we live in a very different world to our distant ancestors. For them, everyday life was a struggle for survival, surrounded as they were by threats of many different kinds. We face far fewer threats in our daily lives. Wherever possible, we should rely upon rational analysis as the best means for dealing with those threats that still remain.

Suggested further reading

For a concise overview of some of the ideas presented in this chapter:

Wilson, S. (2010). 'The naturalness of weird beliefs'. *The Psychologist*, 23, 564–67.

For more detailed treatments of these ideas:

Hood, B. (2009). *Supersense: From superstition to religion – The brain science of belief.* London: Constable.
Shermer, M. (2011). *The believing brain: From ghosts and gods to politics and conspiracies – How we construct beliefs and reinforce them as truths.* New York: Times Books.

For arguments that religion is an intrinsic human trait that carries evolutionary benefits:

Bering, J. (2011). *The god instinct: The psychology of souls, destiny, and the meaning of life.* London: Nicholas Brealey Publishing.

Integrating the Different Approaches: Alien Contact Claims

9

Introduction

The previous chapters of this book have shown how each of the sub-disciplines of psychology can provide insights to help us to understand and explain a wide range of ostensibly paranormal experiences. However, they have also demonstrated that it is rarely the case that such experiences can be fully explained in terms of the perspectives of only a single psychological approach. In all but the simplest cases, it is much more likely that a number of different perspectives have something to offer in terms of approaching a full explanation of any particular type of phenomenon. This is not surprising given the complexity and variability of the phenomena with which we are dealing. Indeed, a full appreciation of many of these phenomena requires that we go beyond the insights provided by psychology and also take into account the perspectives provided by other disciplines, such as sociology and anthropology.

This chapter discusses the psychology of alien contact claims of various kinds. As we will see, some of the claims in this area can be explained in quite straightforward psychological terms but others, most notably alien abduction claims, can only be explained by considering findings from a wider range of psychological and related perspectives. The chapter will begin by considering the varied ways in which human beings claim to have experienced alien contact. The main focus will, however, be upon the psychology of alien abduction experiences.

Types of alien contact claim

Although there have been sightings of UFOs throughout history, a significant date in the modern era is 24 June 1947 when pilot Kenneth Arnold saw nine UFOs while flying near the Cascade Mountains in Washington (see, for example, Bartholomew & Howard, 1998). He described their motion as being 'like a saucer skipping over water' and thus the phrase 'flying saucer' was born. Following reports of Arnold's experience, other people began reporting sightings. There was a major wave of sightings in 1952, leading to the setting up of Project Blue Book that same year. This was a US Air Force project to determine if the UFOs constituted any kind of threat to national security. Bear in mind that this was at the height of the Cold War and the Americans were worried that the UFOs might actually be some kind of Russian monitoring device. On the basis of Project Blue Book and other investigations, the USAF concluded that there was no evidence to indicate that UFOs were of extraterrestrial (ET) origin. This conclusion was, however, dismissed by self-styled 'UFOlogists' as simply a cover-up. There is a widespread belief among UFOlogical groups that the governments and military forces of the world know all about the ET origins of UFOs but keep the truth from the public for their own reasons. It is even claimed that alien bodies have been recovered from crashed saucers, but the available evidence in no way supports such accounts.

Opinion polls show a widespread belief among the public that UFOs are evidence of visitations from another planet. Many people report having themselves seen UFOs. If by that they mean literally an '*unidentified* flying object', then there is no problem. Most people, however, mean ETs of some kind. It goes without saying that it is a huge inferential leap to jump from lights in the sky of unknown origin to visitations by aliens from another planet.

Back in the 1940s, astronomer J. Allen Hynek began his investigations of UFOs sceptical of the ET hypothesis, but gradually became a believer. He is the person who devised the classification system for UFO experiences made famous by Spielberg's film *Close Encounters of the Third Kind*. The most common type of UFO experience consists of a sighting with no physical evidence of any kind. This is known as a *close encounter of the first kind*. The vast majority of such sightings can be explained in terms of the constructive nature of human perception and memory.

Although both perception and memory are constructive processes, this is not generally appreciated by non-psychologists. For most people, if they saw something 'with their own eyes,' it may be inconceivable to them that their perception or memory of the event was inaccurate. The conditions of observation of UFOs are typically not good. For example, they usually occur at night and there are no cues available in the sky to assist in the estimation of size and distance. It is precisely under such conditions that top-down processing predominates and the viewer's own beliefs and expectations can become very potent in determining what is seen and remembered. Abundant evidence, much of it from studies by Elizabeth Loftus (e.g. 1979), shows the unreliability of eyewitness accounts and the ease with which subsequent questioning can distort memories.

Careful investigation following a UFO report will usually reveal it to have a prosaic explanation. This is accepted by UFOlogists themselves, although they are impressed by the small percentage of sightings that cannot be fully explained. Sceptics, on the other hand, view these as simply cases for which there is not enough evidence available to reach any valid conclusion. The most common cause of UFO reports is the bright planet Venus. Other common UFOs include aeroplanes (especially those carrying advertising displays), rocket launches, meteorites, and weather balloons. Such identifications can be made with some confidence when witnesses report seeing a 'UFO' in the direction of a known bright object at the relevant time and do not report seeing the bright object (e.g. Venus) itself. It might seem ridiculous to claim that anyone could mistake Venus for a spaceship but numerous accounts show that this can happen and that, furthermore, many elaborate details are added as a result of top-down processing.

Hines (2003) provides many illustrative accounts, including the case of two policemen in Ohio who, in 1966, chased Venus for an hour convinced that it was a UFO. In fact, a second police car joined the pursuit. As Hines (2003, p. 250) points out,

> [I]f two police cars really were chasing a large UFO only hundreds of feet above the road, one might reasonably expect that other independent witnesses would have seen the same object. In fact, the chase was twice slowed by early morning traffic. Yet none of the hundreds of people who saw the speeding police cars reported seeing the UFO they were chasing.

This case involved trained police officers. UFOlogists are fond of referring to the reliability of witnesses and seem to think that if the witness was a member of the police force or the military, or an airline pilot or a president, this somehow guarantees the validity of the claims in question. Of course, it does no such thing. Usually one is not doubting the sincerity of the witness, but we can all make mistakes. There are numerous well-documented cases of professional observers (including astronomers) misinterpreting lights in the sky.

Close encounters of the second kind are those that involve some kind of physical evidence in addition to a sighting. None of the evidence that has been produced provides convincing evidence of ET contact. Photographic evidence can usually be explained in terms of over-interpretation (e.g. of blemishes produced during processing or of naturally occurring phenomena of which the photographer was not aware at the time of taking the picture) or as hoaxes. It is worth noting that hoaxes are becoming much harder to detect with recent advances in computer graphics technology.

The so-called *close encounters of the third kind* are those in which contact is allegedly made between human and alien. The first report of contact between a human and an ET took place in 1952. George Adamski claimed to have met a visitor from Venus in the Californian desert (Bartholomew & Howard, 1998). Among other best-selling adventures, Adamski claimed that he was actually taken for a ride in the Venusian spaceship. One of the earliest claims of actual abduction, sometimes referred to as *close encounters of the fourth kind*, took place in 1957 in Brazil (Bartholomew & Howard, 1998). Working at night on his family farm, Antonio Villas Boas reported seeing what looked like a large star descend from the sky. The occupants emerged, and dragged him into their spaceship. He was then seduced by a female alien.

Such claims were not taken very seriously at the time even by UFOlogists, but in the 1960s one famous case was to change the attitude of many. The case of

Betty and Barney Hill contains many of the elements that characterize modern abductee claims (Bartholomew & Howard, 1998). The couple claim that while driving from Montreal to New Hampshire in September 1961, they spotted a UFO. Barney got out of the car to investigate, but, seeing alien faces through the windows of the UFO, he got scared and the couple drove home. They arrived home two hours later than expected and could not account for the missing time. About a week later Betty began to have dreams of being taken onto the spaceship and of being physically examined by the aliens.

Several years later, the Hills consulted a psychiatrist, Dr Benjamin Simon, with respect to marital problems. Under hypnosis, the Hills relived in detail their abduction experience. They claimed their car had been stopped at a roadblock put in place by the aliens. Barney had tried to run, but both were captured, taken on board the spaceship, and medically examined. Betty was even shown a map of the stars showing major trade routes used by the aliens, which she drew later from memory. It was subsequently confirmed that the map accurately showed the position of stars that Betty could not possibly have known about. That, at least, is how the UFOlogists tell it, particularly John Fuller who wrote a best-selling account of the experience (Fuller, 1966). The account contains many classic features, as stated: a UFO sighting, missing time, nightmares, hypnosis, and so on.

How can sceptics dismiss such an impressive case? For the details, see, for example, Klass (1989), but in summary: (i) the 'UFO' was in fact the planet Jupiter; (ii) the 'missing time' was reported inconsistently, was not noticed until weeks later (after questioning by UFOlogists), and, besides, the Hills had taken a tortuous route home; (iii) hypnosis is most emphatically not a reliable means for recovering memories (indeed, the psychiatrist who carried out the hypnosis in this case did not himself believe the accounts produced); and (iv) the star map does not actually bear any close resemblance to any particular group of stars.

The craze for abduction stories really took off in 1987 with the publication of two particular books. The first, *Communion*, was written as an allegedly true account of the author's own terrifying experiences (Strieber, 1987). It is worth bearing in mind, however, that the author, Whitley Strieber, had, until penning *Communion*, made his living as a writer of horror stories. His experiences with aliens began in December 1986 and include some bizarre and horrifying episodes including having needles inserted into his head and his anus by the aliens. Klass (1989) presented a critique of Strieber's claims, pointing out that Strieber reports a life filled with many bizarre experiences. Strieber is also a self-confessed liar. He often makes dramatic claims – for example, being present during a horrific real-life sniper attack – only to later admit that he was in fact making it up. He appears to have great difficulty distinguishing fantasy from reality. Strieber's wife acknowledges that he sees things that other people, including her, cannot see. Strieber also reports a long history of being obsessed with intruders.

Budd Hopkins's book *Intruders* also appeared in 1987. There was considerable rivalry between Hopkins and Strieber (sadly, Hopkins died in 2011), as described by Schnabel (1994). Hopkins claimed that alien abductions were much more common than generally believed and presented his own research with abductees to support his claim. He claimed that sexual abuse is a common element of such abductions, and that the aliens plan to cross-breed with humans. He placed a lot of significance upon the phenomenon of 'missing time,' whereby an individual may realize that they cannot account for some period of time. Sceptics, on the other hand, feel that, given what we know about the way memory works, it is not surprising that people often cannot account for every hour of every day. Hopkins frequently hypnotized his clients. Given that they approached him in the first place in the belief that they may have been abducted, it does not surprise sceptics that this is precisely what Hopkins usually found to be the case. The standard abduction scenario is now common knowledge in Western culture and the similarity in the stories produced can largely be explained by this. Hopkins sometimes insisted that a person had been abducted by aliens even if the person themselves was not convinced.

If we were to ask you to spend some time writing a story about being abducted by aliens, it is unlikely that your story would be identical to, say, the Hills's or Strieber's accounts, but the chances are that there would be some strong similarities. You might come up with something more like Susan Blackmore's (1994a, p. 30) account of a close encounter of the fourth kind, a composite based upon reports she had received from many abductees:

I woke up in the middle of the night and everything looked odd and strangely lit. At the end of my bed was a 4 feet high grey alien. Its spindly, thin body supported a huge head with two enormous, slanted, liquid black eyes. It compelled me, telepathically, to follow and led me into a spaceship, along curved corridors to an examination room full of tables on which people lay. I was forced to lie down while they painfully examined me, extracted ova (or sperm) and implanted something in my nose. I could see jars containing half-human, half-alien fetuses and a nursery full of silent, sickly children. When I eventually found myself back in bed, several hours had gone by.

Although there are many variations on the basic theme, alien abduction experiences typically include capture by the aliens and medical examination. These days, the aliens most often correspond to the now-classic description of the so-called greys described earlier. There used to be much more variation in the descriptions of aliens before greys became the norm. Other common, although not universal, elements in the classic scenario include tours of the aliens' ship, trips to other planets, and the receipt of messages to humanity, often involving dire warnings of the future destruction of the planet through pollution or nuclear war unless we mend our ways.

It is difficult to estimate how many people believe themselves to have been abducted by aliens (Appelle, Lynn, & Newman, 2000; French, 2001c) but the number is likely to run into at least the thousands. Strieber (1987) claimed to have received letters from almost a quarter of a million people who had had such experiences. Bear in mind, however, that UFOlogists maintain that the aliens are capable of wiping their victims' memories of the event and therefore they claim that the actual number of abductions is much higher than the number of people who have conscious memories of such episodes. This has led some UFOlogists to claim that the true number of alien abductees is staggering. For example, Jacobs (1992) claimed that as many as 15 million Americans may have been victims of alien abduction.

One of the most commonly quoted estimates was produced by Hopkins, Jacobs, and Westrum (1992) who claimed that up to that point in time around 3.7 million Americans had probably been abducted by aliens. Hopkins and colleagues started out by assuming that there was no point in simply asking respondents if they had ever been abducted by aliens because many of them would have no memory of the event even if they had been. Therefore, an indirect approach was required. Hopkins, Jacobs, and Westrum assumed that people who had been abducted may not be able to remember the abduction itself but that they would have telltale memories that something strange had happened to them. Therefore, they asked their respondents ($N = 5947$) to indicate, among other things, how often they had had each of the following key experiences (the percentages indicate how many respondents reported that they had had the experience in question at least once; item wording and percentages from Hopkins, Jacobs, & Westrum, 1992, pp. 26–8):

Waking up paralysed with a sense of a strange person or presence or something else in the room. [18%]
Experiencing a period of time of an hour or more in which you were apparently lost, but you could not remember why or where you had been. [13%]
Feeling that you were actually flying through the air although you didn't know how or why. [10%]
Seeing unusual lights or balls of light in a room without knowing what was causing them or where they came from. [8%]
Finding puzzling scars on your body and neither you nor anyone else remembering how you received them or from where you got them. [8%]

Hopkins and colleagues assumed that if respondents answered positively to four or more of the aforementioned five items, they had probably been abducted by aliens and then had their memories wiped. They extrapolated from the 119 individuals in their sample to the American population as a whole, leading them to claim that 2% of the population (i.e. 3.7 million Americans) had probably been abducted by aliens.

Such a claim is unjustified for a number of reasons, not least on the grounds of simple logic. As Stires (1997) points out, the authors made no attempt to justify their initial assumption that the key experiences listed are actually associated with alien abduction. How could they, given that there is no group of known abductees that could be used to provide the required data? But even if it was the case that people really were being abducted by aliens and that the only evidence was the key telltale signs that Hopkins, Jacobs, and Westrum had based their conclusions upon, their estimate would still only be valid if those key signs could *only* occur as a consequence of alien abduction. However, there are many other possible causes of the experiences listed. For example, if you have read Chapter 5, you probably recognized a couple of the experiences listed as being associated with sleep paralysis (about which more later). French (2001c, p. 105) illustrates their error in reasoning by demonstrating the absurd consequences that follow when similar invalid reasoning is used in a different context:

> Death is associated with lack of movement, failure to respond to mild distracting stimuli, and inability to solve simple problems. By the logic of Hopkins and colleagues, anyone who exhibits these three 'symptoms' is probably dead – whereas common sense suggests that they may be asleep or just watching television!

Furthermore, as Klass (1997) points out, if 3.7 million Americans really had been abducted by aliens at the time the survey was carried out and if we assume that the first such abduction was that of the Hills in 1961, this would mean that some 340 Americans had been abducted *every single day* without anyone noticing. Clearly, such figures strain credulity. To add insult to injury, the unjustified conclusions of the survey are often misquoted by journalists and documentary makers as being that 3.7 million Americans 'believe they were abducted by aliens'. In fact, at no point were the respondents in this survey ever asked if they believed that they had ever been abducted by aliens.

Why should psychologists bother examining such claims? The fact is that although the number of people who believe they have been abducted by aliens is probably much lower than the estimates discussed before, there are in all probability many thousands of individuals who do hold such beliefs, often based upon clear and detailed memories of the alleged event. They even have the support of some academics. For example, the late John Mack, then a professor of psychiatry at Harvard and a Pulitzer Prize winner, published a book (Mack, 1994) declaring that 'these accounts are not hallucinations, not dreams, but real experiences'.

Is there intelligent life elsewhere in the universe?

Before we consider possible explanations of the alien abduction experience, we should note that adopting a sceptical stance regarding alien abduction claims should not be confused with wholesale rejection of the possibility of life elsewhere in the universe. Many scientists who are dubious regarding the alleged ET causes of UFO sightings and alien abduction claims are very open to the possibility that life may have sprung up on other planets, the late Carl Sagan being a prime example. Although he was very sceptical regarding the idea of visitors from outer space, he was also a champion of the Search for Extraterrestrial Intelligence (SETI) programme that searches for signs of ET intelligence using both radio and optical telescopes.

The Drake equation was devised by Professor Frank Drake in order to estimate the likely number of detectable alien civilizations in our own galaxy, the Milky Way. The equation takes into account such factors as the average rate of star formation, the fraction of those stars that have planets, the average number of such planets that can potentially support life, and so on, in order to produce a number N which estimates the number of civilizations in the Milky Way with which communication might be possible. This equation has generated a great deal of debate and controversy and estimates of the factors that feed into the equation are constantly being updated as scientific knowledge improves. That said, many scientists believe that life, and even intelligent life, almost certainly will have evolved elsewhere in our galaxy. However, it is quite possible that even if alien civilizations are relatively common, they may well never make actual physical contact with each other given the huge distances that separate the stars.

Alien abductions: The ET hypothesis

Before we consider possible psychological explanations of the alien abduction phenomenon, we will briefly assess some of the evidence that has been put forward in support of the claim that people really are being abducted by aliens. This is known as the ET hypothesis and is the subject of a huge number of largely uncritical books, documentaries, websites, blogs, and newspaper and magazine articles. Supporters of the ET hypothesis typically claim that their view is not only supported by the testimony of the abductees themselves but also by other lines of evidence. A full discussion of all of these lines of evidence is beyond the scope of this chapter but interested readers may refer to Bartholomew and Howard (1998), Brookesmith (1996), Clarke and Roberts (1990, 2002), Clarke, Randles, and Roberts (2000), Devereux and Brookesmith (1997), Frazier, Karr, and Nickell (1997), Klass (1983) and Sheaffer (1998) for more detailed assessments. Suffice it to say that, as these sources make clear, the evidence is nowhere near as compelling as it is often claimed to be.

We will focus here on three claims that relate to the alien abduction phenomenon; specifically, the claim that aliens implant small devices into their unwilling victims, the claim that unexplained scars are evidence of alien abduction, and the claim that aliens are engaged in a sinister cross-breeding project. All of these claims are widely accepted within the UFOlogical community. The purpose of the alleged implants is unclear. Some believe that they are mind-control devices; others that they are simply tracking devices, comparable to the tracking devices that human scientists might use to monitor the movements of wild animals. Presumably the aliens would use such devices to locate their human victims in cases of repeated abduction.

Potentially, the scientific analysis of such implants, if they really exist, could produce extremely strong evidence in support of the ET hypothesis. If it were shown that the technology used to produce the implants was unknown on our planet, it would be very difficult for sceptics to dismiss such evidence. In practice, this has yet to happen. Despite repeated claims that such implants exist, very few have been handed over for proper scientific analysis. Of those that have, all have turned out to have perfectly terrestrial explanations, such as consisting of everyday organic material (e.g. cotton) that has somehow become encysted under the skin. In one notorious case, an alleged implant was shown to be nothing more mysterious than a dental filling (Blackmore, 1999). In lots of other cases, the alleged implant is said to mysteriously vanish before it can be subject to proper analysis, allegedly retrieved by the aliens themselves or else taken away by the mysterious 'MIBs' who supposedly turn up following alien encounters.

Some abductees claim that unexplained scars on their bodies provide proof of their encounter with aliens, the marks allegedly being the result of medical procedures inflicted upon them by their abductors. The most obvious objection to this argument is that most people could probably find marks of unknown origin somewhere on their bodies if they looked hard enough. Just because we cannot remember how we got a particular scar in no way proves that it was produced by an alien medical procedure. As with many other ostensibly paranormal phenomena, context is all-important here: any anomaly, no matter how minor, is interpreted within the paranormal framework and taken as further evidence in support of the claim. We must not forget, of course, that in a minority of cases where the claimants are deliberately engaged in a hoax, any such wounds might even be self-inflicted.

Hopkins (1987) and Jacobs (1998), among others, claimed that the main motivation for the aliens' activities on Earth was that they are engaged in a sinister cross-breeding project, with the intention of producing human–alien hybrids. It was claimed that this ongoing programme involved women reporting that they had somehow become pregnant even though they had no memory of having engaged in normal sexual intercourse. A few months later, however, they found themselves to be no longer pregnant, despite having no memory of having miscarried or having had an abortion. The explanation offered by the UFOlogists is that the women became pregnant as a consequence of being abducted by aliens and artificially inseminated. Subsequently, the women are again abducted and the hybrid embryo is removed and brought to full-term outside the womb. The aliens are, it is claimed, able to wipe the memories of their victims for these episodes although they can be recovered using hypnotic regression. Indeed, some abductees report that they have not only recovered memories of their initial abductions but also subsequent occasions where they were briefly reunited with their strange offspring. Despite claims that there are dozens of documented cases in support of such claims, not a single case has been presented supported by convincing medical documentation (Randle, Estes, & Cone, 1999). To sum up, the available evidence does not support the claim that people really are being abducted by aliens.

Alien abductions: Psychological factors

A number of commentators have considered a range of psychological factors that might lead people to believe that they had had an alien encounter (e.g. Appelle, 1996; Appelle, Lynn, & Newman, 2000; Baker, 1992; Bartholomew & Howard, 1998; Blackmore, 1994a; Brookesmith, 1998; Clancy, 2005; Devereux & Brookesmith, 1997; French, 2001c; Holden & French, 2002; Klass, 1989; Newman & Baumeister, 1996a; Randle, Estes, & Cone, 1999; Rutkowski, 2000; Showalter, 1997; Spanos, 1996).

Several studies have addressed the possibility that alien contact claims may be associated with psychopathology. It is certainly the case that many members of the general public assume that anyone who reports any kind of alien encounter must be 'crazy'. In general, the available studies do not support this view. For example, Parnell and Sprinkle (1990) used the Minnesota Multiphasic Personality Inventory to assess the personality profiles of 225 people who had reported UFO experiences and concluded that the group as a whole showed no evidence of serious psychopathology. This is the same conclusion as that reached by Bloecher, Clamar, and Hopkins (1985; nine abductees), Rodeghier, Goodpaster, and Blatterbauer (1991; 27 abductees), and Mack (1994; 76 abductees). Similarly, no differences were found on measures of psychopathology by Spanos et al. (1993) between those who reported intense UFO experiences (such as seeing and communicating with aliens), those who reported non-intense experiences (such as seeing unidentified lights in the sky), and those who reported no UFO experiences. Bartholomew, Basterfield, and Howard (1991) concluded their biographical analysis of 152 subjects claiming abduction or repeated UFO contact by stating that the sample was 'remarkably devoid of a history of mental illness' (p. 215).

Although, in general, those claiming alien contact do not appear to show higher levels of psychopathology than control samples, some interesting differences have been noted suggesting that the former group are not representative of the population as a whole. Some case studies (e.g. Fisman & Takhar, 1996; Powers, 1997) have reported that abductees display symptoms of posttraumatic stress disorder. Both Mack (1994) and Ring and Rosing (1990) report high levels of reported childhood trauma among abductees and Rodeghier, Goodpaster, and Blatterbauer (1991) reported poor sleep patterns, and high levels of loneliness and unhappiness among their sample. Stone-Carmen (1994) reported that 57% of her sample of abductees had attempted suicide. Parnell and Sprinkle (1990; see also, Parnell, 1988) reported that their sample of individuals who claimed to have communicated with aliens 'had a significantly greater tendency to endorse unusual feelings, thoughts and attitudes; to be suspicious or distrustful; and to be creative, imaginative, or possibly have schizoid tendencies' (p. 45). French *et al.* (2008) reported that a group 19 volunteers claiming alien contact showed higher levels of tendency to hallucinate that a matched control group as assessed by the Launay-Slade Hallucination Scale (Launay & Slade, 1981).

One obvious possibility to explain reports of alien contact is that the claimants are simply making the whole thing up, either as attention-seeking behaviour, for possible financial gain from book and film rights, or just for the sheer hell of it. It is certainly the case that a number of claimants have indeed attained celebrity status within the UFOlogical community and, as a result, are invited onto TV chat shows and get to attend UFO conferences around the world. There is also little doubt that one or two high-profile UFO cases are almost certainly hoaxes, starting with the early claims from contactees, with their trips to planets that we now know could not sustain life, to more recent cases (see, for example, Klass's 1989 critique of the Travis Walton case which became the subject of a 'true story' feature film *Fire in the Sky*).

Having said that, it appears that most claimants are sincere in the claims that they make. The vast majority shun publicity and are very reticent about telling others of their experiences as they are fully aware that many people will dismiss them as being 'crazy'. One of the things that convinces many observers that the experiences recounted are based upon real events and are not just deliberate falsehoods is the fact that when the claimants are describing their memories of the alleged abduction, they appear to be reliving the sheer terror of the encounter. Many UFOlogists argue that the abductees are either telling the truth or they deserve an Oscar for their acting ability.

The intensity of the emotions that abductees feel when remembering their alien encounters is supported by the results of a study carried out by McNally *et al.* (2004). People suffering from post-traumatic stress disorder typically demonstrate very high levels of psychophysiological arousal when they recount their experiences under laboratory conditions. McNally and colleagues had a group of ten self-reported alien abductees provide details of a number of different personal experiences. These details were used to record a number of personalized scripts: two relating to the abduction experiences, and three that were unrelated (one stressful, one positive, and one neutral). Recordings of these scripts were then played back to the abductees, as well as to a control group, while their heart rate, skin conductance, and electromyographic responses were monitored. As hypothesized, the arousal levels indicated by the psychophysiological indices were higher for the abduction and stressful scripts than for the positive and neutral scripts, and this effect was stronger in the abductee sample than in the control sample.

This result is clearly consistent with the idea that the abductees really had had terrifying encounters with aliens and that even the memory of this trauma was sufficient to produce extreme fear in them. Indeed, this is exactly how these findings were interpreted by some commentators, including the late Professor of Psychiatry, John Mack, McNally's colleague at Harvard. But this is not the conclusion that McNally and his team drew from this study. As McNally fully appreciated, given his position as one of the world's leading experts on memory, there was another possibility to consider in addition to the possibilities that either the alien encounters really happened or the claimants were deliberately lying. It seemed more likely to McNally and his team that the abductees were suffering from false memories of an alien encounter and that it is sufficient for an individual to sincerely *believe* that they have had such an experience for them to experience extreme emotion upon 'recalling' the details.

Given the inherent implausibility of alien abduction and contact claims and the apparent sincerity of the majority of claimants, it appears likely that many such claims are based upon false memories and there are several lines of evidence that support this hypothesis. French (2003; French & Wilson, 2006) discussed the relevance of false memory research for reports of a range of anomalous experiences including alien abduction claims. Memory researchers have developed a wide range of techniques for implanting false memories and have thus been able to investigate psychological factors that are associated with susceptibility to false memories. Although results have varied across studies, a number of individual difference measures have been shown to correlate with such susceptibility, including dissociativity, absorption, and fantasy-proneness. It should be noted that these three personality factors overlap considerably in conceptual terms and are known to intercorrelate significantly (e.g. Glicksohn & Barrett, 2003). As noted by French (2003), these factors have also been shown to correlate with paranormal belief and the general tendency to report paranormal experiences, raising the possibility that at least some reports of paranormal experiences may be based upon false memories. It is thus of considerable interest to evaluate the extent to which the personality profile of those reporting alien contact corresponds to that described previously.

Wolfradt (1997, p. 15) defines dissociation as 'a structured separation of mental processes (e.g., thoughts, emotion, conation, memory and identity) that are ordinarily integrated'. Less formally, individuals who score highly on measures of dissociativity often appear to others to be a bit 'spaced out' or, to put it in even more colloquial terms, 'away with the fairies'. As discussed in Chapter 3, dissociativity correlates with paranormal belief generally and a number of studies (e.g. Powers, 1994; French et al., 2008) have shown that those claiming alien contact score higher on measures of dissociativity than control groups.

Tellegen and Atkinson (1974) define absorption as 'openness to absorbing and self-altering experiences, a trait related to hypnotic susceptibility'. Individuals who score highly on this measure are likely to psychologically block out the external world when they are engaged in an absorbing task such as watching a film, reading a novel, or solving a mathematical puzzle. A number of studies (e.g. Clancy et al., 2002; French et al., 2008) have reported higher levels of absorption in those reporting alien contact compared to control groups.

The picture with respect to fantasy-proneness is less clear-cut. As described previously, fantasy-proneness was first described by Wilson and Barber (1983) who were investigating the personality profiles of a group of female volunteers who scored at the high extreme in terms of hypnotic susceptibility. All were found to be fantasy-prone. Such individuals have very rich and detailed fantasy lives and spend much of their time daydreaming. By their own admission, as a consequence of the vividness of their mental imagery, they sometimes believe that events that they have only imagined have actually taken place in reality. They report a wide range of paranormal experiences and often claim to possess psychic powers, such as healing. Wilson and Barber also noted that they were prone to a range of unusual physiological symptoms, including a very high proportion that reported phantom pregnancies (13 out of 22). This observation may be particularly relevant to the preceding discussion of the so-called missing embryo syndrome. Similarly, Hough and Rogers (2007–8) reported that almost half of their sample of 20 female abductees claimed to have been impregnated by aliens.

Two different approaches have been taken in addressing the issue of whether or not those claiming alien contact are fantasy-prone – and, in general, they have reached different conclusions. Studies that have produced evidence in support of the idea that abductees are fantasy-prone have tended to be those that have carried out biographical analyses. For example, Bartholomew and Howard (1998) analysed 152 reported cases in terms of the number of characteristics of fantasy-proneness present in each case. Although some cases were described in a single paragraph while others were the subjects of entire books, Bartholomew and Howard found that 132 of their cases showed evidence of one or more features of fantasy-proneness. These features included reports of hypnotic susceptibility, psychic phenomena, OBEs, apparitions, healing, and physiological effects. Similarly, Nickell (1996) concluded that all 13 of the detailed cases presented by Mack (1994) showed signs of fantasy-proneness.

A different picture emerges though when we consider those studies that have compared groups claiming alien contact with control groups using questionnaire measures of fantasy-proneness. Of three such studies that have used the Inventory of Childhood Memories and Imaginings (Myers, 1983) to assess fantasy-proneness, only French *et al.* (2008) reported a small but significant difference between the groups with the 'experiencer' group scoring higher. Rodeghier, Goodpaster, and Blatterbauer (1991) found no differences between groups and neither did Spanos *et al.* (1993), although the latter team did find that scores on the questionnaire correlated positively with the intensity of the experience (e.g. communicating with aliens as opposed to merely seeing lights in the sky). Hough and Rogers (2007–8) compared a group of abductees with a control group using the Creative Experiences Questionnaire (Merckelbach, Horselenberg, & Muris, 2001) to assess fantasy-proneness, once again finding no differences between the groups.

Ring and Rosing (1990) used a measure of their own design to assess fantasy-proneness and concluded that those reporting UFO-related experiences were not in general more fantasy-prone than the rest of the population. However, they did report that the experiencers, as children, were more sensitive to 'non-ordinary realities' than other people, as assessed by items dealing with seeing 'into "other realities" that others didn't seem to be aware of' and being 'aware of non-physical beings'. As proposed elsewhere (French, 2001c), in the absence of any evidence to support the objective existence of non-physical beings and non-ordinary realities, it might be more parsimonious to assume that some people are so fantasy-prone that they do not even realize that some of their experiences are based upon pure imagination.

It is worth noting here that people who report alien contact experiences typically have very high levels of paranormal belief generally and report having many paranormal experiences and abilities compared to the general population. Initially, this observation was primarily supported by anecdotal evidence (e.g. Basterfield, 2001; Bullard, 1987; Druffel & Rogo, 1980; Evans, 1983, 1998; Gotlib, 1994; Mack, 1994; Randles, 1988; Schwarz, 1983; Spencer, 1994; Vallee, 1977) but was confirmed by more systematic research using standardized measures by Basterfield and Thalbourne (2002) and French et al. (2008).

Thus we can see that, in general, abductees and others claiming alien contact do appear to have personality profiles consistent with a heightened susceptibility to false memories. To date, only two studies have attempted to directly measure susceptibility to false memories in such groups. Clancy et al. (2002) used a version of the so-called DRM task (Deese, 1959; Roediger & McDermott, 1995) to assess susceptibility to false memories in three groups of volunteers. The first group consisted of individuals who had allegedly 'recovered' memories of being abducted by aliens. The second group consisted of people who believed that they had been abducted by aliens but had no conscious memories of the event. Those in the third group did not believe that they had ever been abducted by aliens. The DRM technique involves testing memory for lists of words. Several lists of words are presented and within each list all of the words are strongly semantically associated with a critical lure word which is itself not presented. For example, the list might consist of the words *pin, sow, prick, injection, jab, thread*, and so on, but the word *needle* is not presented. When memory is tested either by recall or recognition, a substantial proportion of respondents wrongly report that the lure word was presented. The number of lure words incorrectly reported over a series of lists provides one indication of susceptibility to false memories. Clancy and colleagues found that their volunteers who reported conscious memories of being abducted by aliens showed the greatest susceptibility to false memories while those who did not believe themselves to have been abducted by aliens showed the least. However, a follow-up study by French et al. (2008) did not find any significant differences in performance on the DRM task between a group claiming to have had alien contact experiences and a matched control group, despite the fact that the experiencers were found to score more highly on measures of dissociativity, absorption, and fantasy-proneness.

Another line of evidence that strongly supports the idea that most claims of alien contact are probably based upon false memories is the widespread use of hypnotic regression as a means to 'recover' memories of such encounters. Although this practise is widely endorsed by such leading figures as Hopkins

(1987) and Mack (1994), it is based upon a profound misunderstanding of the relationship between memory and hypnosis. The popular view of hypnosis, portrayed in Hollywood movies and other works of fiction, is that it provides an almost magical key to unlock hidden or 'repressed' memories. In fact, hypnosis provides a context in which information derived from various sources is woven together to produce a narrative account often accompanied by vivid mental imagery and strong emotional reactions (Baker, 1988, 1992; Clancy, 2005; French, 2001c; Klass, 1989; Newman & Baumeister, 1996a, 1996b, 1998; Randle, Estes, & Cone, 1999). The sources that feed into this narrative include mental phenomena such as imagination, expectation, dreams, and so on, along with fragments of memories of unusual real-life experiences and of UFO-related material from films, books, magazines, TV programmes, and so on. A number of commentators have noted that abductees typically produce accounts of their experience that correspond to the expectations of the hypnotist carrying out the hypnotic regression procedure, suggesting that those carrying out the procedure are unintentionally leading their subjects by the questions that they ask and their responses to the answers produced (e.g. Matheson, 1998).

What are the grounds for believing that hypnotically recovered memories are unlikely to correspond to events that really took place? There are a number of lines of evidence to support such scepticism. Contrary to the picture painted in Hollywood crime thrillers, the idea that hypnosis is useful in improving the memory of eyewitnesses in forensic contexts is greatly exaggerated. In the movies, it appears that hypnosis enables the eyewitness to relive their observation of the crime and even allows them to mentally zoom in on crucial details, such as the registration number of, say, the getaway car used in a bank robbery. In fact, hypnotic regression is no more effective than various other techniques in attempting to recover such details and often carries risks of encouraging confabulation, that is, subjects will tend to fill in any gaps in their account with whatever comes to mind and then believe that what they said really happened (see, for example, Wagstaff, 1989; Kebbell & Wagstaff, 1998). It is for this reason that evidence obtained from eyewitnesses using hypnotic regression is rarely admissible in court.

Many people are convinced of the power of hypnosis to recover detailed memories even from early childhood because they have witnessed hypnotic age regression, perhaps as part of a hypnotist's stage age. Such demonstrations do appear to be quite impressive to the casual observer. The hypnotic subject not only appears to be able to remember details of, say, their fifth birthday, they actually appear to be reliving the day, accompanied by appropriate changes in behaviour, mannerisms, vocabulary, voice, and emotional responses. The emotional responses in particular can be so compelling that observers conclude that the subject is not simply 'putting on an act' – in just the same way that observers often conclude that alleged abductees must be reliving a terrifying experience that really took place because of the genuine terror they show during regression. In fact, however, more detailed analysis shows that such subjects are not actually behaving as real children do. They are behaving as typical adults *think* that real children do. Detailed analysis of the cognitive abilities displayed and the language used shows this conclusively (see, for example, Colman, 1987).

Some hypnotherapists endorse other unfounded claims relating to the alleged relationship between hypnosis and memory, such as that 'memories obtained through hypnosis are more likely to be accurate than those simply recalled, and that hypnosis can be used to recover accurate memories even from as far back as birth' (Yapko, 1994, p. 163; see also Ost *et al.*, 2013). A minority go yet further, claiming that hypnosis can be used to recover memories of life in the womb and, indeed, even memories of previous incarnations. The available evidence strongly suggests that any such memories are false memories (Baker, 1992; French, 2003; Spanos, 1996).

With respect to hypnotically retrieved past-life memories, evidence of two main types shows them to be false: evidence from individual case studies and evidence from experimental studies. With respect to individual case studies, most cases of apparent past-life memories lack detail and what information is provided is either common knowledge of life in the relevant historical period or, more likely, of the Hollywood version of that historical period. Such cases clearly support the notion that past-life memories are fantasy-based constructions. However, occasionally cases arise in which a large amount of supporting detail is provided, such as the famous case of Bridey Murphy, the subject of the best-selling book *The Search for Bridey Murphy* (Bernstein, 1956). Bridey Murphy was apparently a past-life incarnation of Virginia Tighe, a Colorado housewife, who made her first appearance in the twentieth century as a result of hypnotic regression. Bridey spoke with a thick Irish brogue, quite unlike Virginia's accent, and gave numerous details of her life in Cork, Ireland, in 1806. This amazing story was depicted in a popular Hollywood movie, convincing even more people of the reality of reincarnation.

Despite the popularity of the story, subsequent investigation totally undermined any possibility that Bridey Murphy had ever actually existed. No records could be found in Ireland that Bridey or any of her alleged relatives lived in Cork in the 1800s. Further investigation into Virginia's past provided further clues to solve the mystery. It turned out that Virginia was an imaginative child and a talented actress who would often deliver monologues in a well-rehearsed Irish accent. She had an Irish aunt and had had an Irish neighbour as a teenager – whose name just happened to be Bridey Murphy Corkell (see Gardner, 1957 and Harris, 1986 for further details).

A similar case is reported by Wilson (1987), this time of a woman who claimed, under hypnosis, that she had been tried as a witch in Chelmsford in 1556. Her performance was dramatic and compelling, as she provided details in what appeared to be fluent archaic English. She even appeared to relive being forced to hold a red hot metal bar. The details of her trial were generally historically accurate according to a contemporary sixteenth-century pamphlet. However, an expert on archaic English quickly realized that the woman was in fact speaking a Hollywood version of archaic English, not the real thing.

Furthermore, it turned out that the real date of the trial was 1566 but that a printer's error had led to it being commonly misquoted as 1556, proving that the woman had picked up the information about the trial from a secondary source.

A similar explanation applies in the case of the initially impressive series of past-life reincarnations reported by Iverson (1977). These regressions had been carried out by Arnall Bloxham, a Cardiff-based hypnotherapist. In each case, his subjects had produced a wealth of historical detail, much of it fairly obscure, which historical experts had confirmed as accurate. His star case was a Welsh housewife referred to as Jane Evans who produced details of no less than six previous incarnations. In one past life, Evans claimed to be the maid of a fifteenth-century French merchant named Jacques Couer. She knew extensive details of his life but insisted that he was single whereas the historical record showed conclusively that he was married and had five children. This was the clue that allowed Melvin Harris (1986) to solve the case. Couer was the subject of the historical novel *The Moneyman* by Thomas B. Costain. In the interests of plot development, Costain had taken the liberty of omitting Couer's family from the story. It appears that many of the details Evans produced relating to Couer came from this book.

Another of Evans's incarnations was explained in a similar manner. In this life, she was apparently a woman living during the Roman occupation of England. Again, many of the details she provided were historically accurate. However, it turned out that this time her story was based upon the historical novel *The Living Wood*. This is supported by the fact that her account not only included historically accurate details relating to real historical figures but also completely fictional characters that the author had included in his story purely to aid the plotline.

It is possible, of course, in all of these cases, as well as in cases of hypnotically recovered memories of alien abduction, that the subjects are deliberately and consciously simply making up stories based upon information that they have picked up from other sources. It is generally believed, however, that these accounts are not deliberate hoaxes but are instead examples of the phenomenon of *cryptomnesia* (literally, 'hidden memories'; Baker, 1992). Information from various sources is combined together during hypnotic regression but the original source of the material may not be remembered.

There are numerous cases of alien abduction narratives that contain details that may well have originated in films and TV programmes. One notable example of probable media influence is Barney Hill's description of the strange 'wraparound' eyes that he claims his abductors had, eyes that the aliens used for telepathic communication (Brookesmith, 1998). As pointed out by Martin Kottmeyer, this description was first given during a hypnotic regression that took place on 22 February 1964. On 10 February that year, less than two weeks earlier, the science fiction series *The Outer Limits* had featured aliens with exactly such unusual telepathic 'wraparound' eyes. This would appear to be more than just a coincidence.

In addition to the evidence from individual case studies of hypnotic past-life regression, we can also gain insights into the relationship between hypnosis and memory by considering experimental studies of past-life regression, such as the series of studies reported by Spanos *et al.* (1991). Spanos and colleagues reported that volunteers who exhibited past-life identities in response to hypnotic regression suggestions scored higher on measures of hypnotic susceptibility and fantasy-proneness but not on measures of psychopathology, generally in line with the personality profile of abductees.

Two of the studies in the series showed how subjects' expectations could influence the content of the recovered memories. In one study, some subjects were told before the session began that past-life identities often involved being of a different gender and race to themselves as well as living in exotic cultures. The remaining subjects were not fed such information prior to the regression. As predicted, subjects in the former group were more likely to incorporate the suggestions into their reports compared to those in the latter group. In a separate study, subjects were informed that during the hypnotic regression they would be questioned about their past-life childhoods in order to gain information regarding child-rearing practices in earlier times. One group was explicitly told that child abuse was common in the past whereas the other group were not primed in this way. As expected, the former group were more likely to report childhood abuse during their past-life. In the context of recovered memories of alien abduction, it is clear that expectations will also influence the details of these memories. Such expectations could either arise from culturally shared knowledge or from the direct influence of the hypnotist involved.

Whether participants in these studies accepted their memories of past lives as evidence for the reality of reincarnation as opposed to products of their own imaginations depended upon at least two factors: their personal prior belief in reincarnation and whether they were led to believe by the experimenters that reincarnation was a scientifically credible notion. Extrapolating to the context of recovered memories of alien contact, we can see that it is very likely that abductees will accept their recovered memories as being genuine memories for real events. They already suspect that they are victims of alien abduction, otherwise they would not be seeking the services of a hypnotist specializing in the use of regression to recover such memories. Furthermore, the hypnotist in question is also convinced of the veracity of the memories recovered using this technique.

The most telling piece of evidence on this issue comes from a study carried out by Alvin Lawson (1984). Lawson selected eight volunteers with minimal prior knowledge of UFOs and no belief whatsoever that they had ever experienced alien contact. He hypnotized them and asked them to simply imagine that they had been abducted by aliens. The accounts they produced were then compared to accounts produced by people who genuinely believed that they had been abducted by aliens. The accounts produced by the 'imaginary abductees' caused quite a stir among traditional UFO researchers. In the words of Thomas E. Bullard (1989, pp. 27–8), 'Not only did the subjects readily respond to an initial suggestion with an elaborate and detailed story, with little need for prodding along the way, but the contents bore striking similarities to alleged real abductions, both in more obvious matters and in odd, minute details.' Following further analysis, however, Bullard concluded that the imaginary abductions were not as coherent as the allegedly 'real' cases and that this indicated that the latter were most likely based upon events that had really taken place. As French (2001c) points out, a more likely explanation of any difference in coherence between the two sets of accounts is that Lawson's subjects were deliberately chosen because of their 'minimal prior UFO knowledge' whereas those who believed that they had experienced genuine alien contact would, no doubt, have sought out as much information on alien abduction as they could find prior to their regression. Lawson's subjects, in contrast, would be relying solely on generic, widely available, cultural stereotypes of the experience that they would then have elaborated upon.

Although a strong case can be made that many accounts of alien abduction are probably based upon false memories produced by hypnotic regression, we must still explain why such individuals came to believe that they were victims of alien abduction in the first place. After all, prior to apparently recovering their memories of alien encounters via hypnosis, most of these people had no conscious memories of such contact. In such cases, the individual comes to believe that they are victims of alien abduction because that hypothesis appears to them to offer the best explanation for unusual experiences that they have had. Typically, these experiences would include one or more sightings of UFOs and unusual physiological conditions (such as inexplicable scars or symptoms of pregnancy), as described previously in this chapter. Other examples would include sleep paralysis episodes and periods of the so-called missing time.

Sleep paralysis episodes provide a plausible explanation for a wide range of ostensibly paranormal experiences (Adler, 2011; French & Santomauro, 2007; Santomauro & French, 2009). Sleep paralysis is a very common experience that occurs either just as someone is drifting off to sleep or as they wake up. Although estimates vary widely, surveys show that typically between 25% and 40% of the general population will report having experienced it at least once in their lives. It may only occur once or twice in a lifetime or it can be experienced on a regular basis.

In its most common form, an episode may consist of little more than a slightly disturbing period of bodily paralysis lasting at most a few seconds. However, in a sizeable minority of sufferers it may be accompanied by other symptoms that result in an altogether more terrifying experience. The sufferer may experience an overwhelming sense of presence. Even though they may not be able to see anyone else in the room, they are certain that there is someone or something in the room with them. They may also experience a range of visual, auditory, and/or tactile hallucinations. They may see strange lights or dark shadows moving around the room or even grotesque figures staring down at them. They may hear voices, or footsteps or strange mechanical sounds. They may feel that someone is lying next to them on the bed or even that that they are being dragged, unable to move, from their bed. People often report a sense of pressure on their chests and great difficulty breathing.

To give but one example (for more, see Adler, 2011; French & Santomauro, 2007; Santomauro & French, 2009), consider the experiences of British student Jeremy Deane who suffers from regular attacks, particularly if his regular sleep cycle is disrupted (French, 2011a). On some occasions, he experiences multiple episodes in a single night, including hallucinatory symptoms such as feeling his whole body vibrate and seeing objects around him transform themselves in nightmarish ways. In his own words:

> Common images are bearded, goblin-like demons laughing or whispering sinister speech, a faceless girl (usually covering her face with hair, moving around in bed moaning and feeling my body), hands appearing from the wall and attempting to strangle me. A hung man talking in the corner of the room, and some of the most bizarre experiences may include up to a dozen 'critter' entities (think *Gremlins* movie) laughing and talking about me.

Such experiences, although clearly terrifying, do not explicitly include imagery corresponding to classic alien encounter scenarios. However, many self-appointed UFO experts, such as Budd Hopkins and John Mack, insist that such experiences are a strong indication that the individual concerned has been a victim of alien abduction. The aliens, they argue, have wiped their victims' memories for most of the details of the abduction and all that remains are bizarre and confusing 'screen memories', such as those reported previously.

In fact, there is an extensive scientific literature on sleep paralysis and we have a reasonably good understanding of how to explain these experiences without needing to resort to such unlikely explanations as alien interference. In fact, the vast majority of us are subject to sleep paralysis virtually every night – albeit that we are not consciously aware of it. The normal sleep cycle involves gradually passing through different stages of sleep, each of which are characterized by changes in brain waves, breathing rate, heart rate, and so on. Part of this cycle is referred to as 'rapid eye movement' (or REM) sleep and this is the phase of sleep that is associated with vivid dreaming. During REM sleep, the muscles of the body are actually paralysed, presumably to stop the dreamer acting out the actions of the dream. Of course, you are not usually aware of this paralysis because you are only conscious of what you are dreaming about. But sometimes the mechanism that controls this cycle can go slightly awry and we regain something like normal wakeful consciousness while still in the REM state. The result is a unique altered state of consciousness that is a mix of normal waking consciousness and dream consciousness. The sufferer may be fully aware that they are lying in bed and can see the bedroom clearly but at the same time they cannot move a muscle and are experiencing hallucinations as the mind does its best to make sense of the dream imagery that has seeped through into waking consciousness. A number of studies (e.g. Blackmore & Cox, 2000; French *et al.*, 2008; McNally & Clancy, 2005) have shown that individuals reporting alien contact and abduction experiences also report higher levels of sleep paralysis than control groups.

There is little systematic research into the phenomenon of 'missing time' but once again it would appear that alien interference is an unlikely explanation. The concept of missing time refers to situations in which an individual cannot account for what happened to them over an extended period of time. There are a number of mundane explanations for such reports. It may well be that the person involved simply got the time wrong at some point and hence, say, a journey appeared to take longer than it actually did. Another possibility is that people tend to overestimate how much detail they should be able to remember about past events. Try thinking back to events of this time last week. In all probability, if it was a typical day, you would almost certainly struggle to give a minute-by-minute account of how you spent the day. Finally, there is the possibility that the person giving the report may have entered a mild dissociative state. Such states are known to alter time perception. One familiar example of such a state is known as 'highway hypnosis', the name given to the experience on long monotonous drives of suddenly 'coming to' after a long period of driving on 'automatic pilot'.

Although the factors discussed before provide a plausible and empirically supported account of many alien contact and abduction claims, we must be wary of claiming that we have a 'one size fits all' explanation for all such reports. It is possible that most accounts are based upon false memories that resulted from an attempt to explain unusual experiences of some sort. But the triggering experience is not always sleep paralysis, as we have seen (as Spanos *et al.*, 1993 showed only 60% of 'intense' UFO experiences were sleep-related). Furthermore, it may be that hypnosis was not used to 'recover' memories of the alien encounter. Hypnotic regression is by no means the only way for false memories to be produced. Simply imagining events that never took place can be enough to produce false memories for those events, a phenomenon known as 'imagination inflation' (Loftus, 2001).

It is always possible, of course, that some reports of alien encounters may be based upon more or less accurate memories of hallucinatory experiences. For example, very occasionally, a sleep paralysis episode might include explicit alien-related imagery. Moreover, as described in Chapter 5, Persinger (e.g. Persinger & Makarec, 1987; Persinger & Valliant, 1985) has proposed that unusual patterns of activity in the temporal lobes of the brain of susceptible individuals might result in a wide range of hallucinatory experiences. This is an intriguing albeit controversial hypothesis that certainly warrants further investigation. Even more controversially, Persinger (1989, 1990) has argued that unusual patterns of firing in the temporal lobes might be triggered by unusual activity in the earth's natural electromagnetic field caused by movements in tectonic plates. Persinger (1990, p. 105) has even gone so far as to declare that 'most UFO phenomena (not due to frank misobservation) are natural events, generated by the stresses and strains within the earth's crust'.

Tectonic strain theory has, however, been criticized by many commentators (e.g. Braithwaite, 2011; Jacobs, 1990; Long, 1990; Rutkowski, 1984, 1990, 1994). Furthermore, neither Spanos *et al.* (1993) nor Blackmore and Cox (2000) found any evidence of heightened temporal lobe lability in volunteers reporting alien encounters as assessed using Persinger and Makarec's (1987) Temporal Lobe Signs Inventory subscale of the Personal Philosophy Inventory. Regardless of the validity or otherwise of Persinger's tectonic strain theory, there are several cases on record of individuals reporting alien contact experiences when third parties were able to observe that they had never physically gone anywhere (see, for example, Schnabel, 1994). Instead, they appeared to have either temporarily lost consciousness or to be in a trance state, supporting the general contention that such experiences are best explained as purely mental events rather than events taking place in the real world.

As shown by the history of folklore, unusual human experiences have always been interpreted in the context of whatever belief system predominated at the time. Nocturnal visitation, abduction, transformation, and the acquisition of strange powers are themes that recur in all such tales. In days gone by, the agents behind such experiences were said to be angels, demons, fairies, or spirits but in our modern technological era, advanced aliens may be preferred. Following Jung (1959), a number of commentators have proposed symbolic interpretations of alien abduction narratives. For example, Lawson (1984) perceived in the imagery of abduction echoes of birth memories; Newman and Baumeister (1996a, 1996b, 1998; Newman, 1997) discerned parallels with sadomasochism; Matheson (1998) felt that the aliens represented both our hopes and fears regarding modern technology. French (2001c) argued that, as so many more or less plausible interpretations of this multifaceted phenomenon could be proposed, no definitive account of the specific details of the modern abduction myth is ever likely to emerge.

Concluding comment

As stated at the outset of this chapter, several different psychological perspectives are required if we are to approach complete understanding of alien contact and abduction claims, given their inherent complexity. As such claims appear to be generally based upon false memories, we must draw upon insights and techniques from cognitive psychology to explore this aspect. As many of these false memories appear to be a consequence of the use of hypnotic regression, theoretical models of hypnosis and empirical findings from studies based upon the sociocognitive approach to hypnosis are relevant. As those claiming to have alien contact experiences appear to tend towards a particular personality profile, we must also consider evidence relating to individual difference variables. As part of this, we examined possible associations with psychopathological variables, even though the conclusion drawn from this consideration was that those claiming alien contact experiences did not, in general, show signs of serious psychopathology. In considering the types of anomalous experience that might lead an individual to suspect that they had been abducted by aliens, attention was paid to both sleep paralysis and possible unusual activity in the temporal lobes, thus drawing upon psychophysiological factors. Finally, further insights can be gained by considering research carried out by anthropologists and historians of folklore that allows us to place alien contact experiences in a wider cross-cultural context.

Suggested further reading

Appelle, S., Lynn, S. J., & Newman, L. (2000). 'Alien abduction experiences'. In E. Cardeña, S. J. Lynn, & S. Krippner (eds), *Varieties of anomalous experience: Examining the scientific evidence* (pp. 253–82). Washington, DC: American Psychological Association.

Clancy, S. A. (2005). *Abducted: Why people come to believe they were kidnapped by aliens.* Cambridge, MA: Harvard University Press.

French, C. C. (2001c). 'Alien abductions'. In R. Roberts & D. Groome (eds), *Parapsychology: The science of unusual experience* (pp. 102–16). London: Arnold.

Holden, K. J. & French, C. C. (2002). 'Alien abduction experiences: Clues from neuropsychology and neuropsychiatry'. *Cognitive Neuropsychiatry*, 7, 163–78.

Klass, P. J. (1989). *UFO abductions: A dangerous game.* Updated edition. Buffalo, NY: Prometheus.

Parapsychological Perspectives

10

Introduction

As stated in Chapter 1, anomalistic psychology 'attempts to explain paranormal and related beliefs and ostensibly paranormal experiences in terms of known (or knowable) psychological and physical factors'. *Parapsychology* was defined as, 'The scientific study of certain paranormal or ostensibly paranormal phenomena' with the word *paranormal* being defined as follows: 'Term for any phenomenon that in one or more respects exceeds the limits of what is deemed physically possible according to current scientific assumptions'. Whereas anomalistic psychologists typically adopt the working hypothesis that paranormal forces do not exist and attempt to develop and test explanations for ostensibly paranormal experiences in terms of psychological factors, parapsychologists are generally more open to the possibility that some phenomena may be genuinely paranormal, that is, beyond explanation in terms of current scientific assumptions. It is important that we assess the evidence produced by parapsychologists that at least some anomalous phenomena may be the result of genuine paranormal forces.

What kind of anomalous phenomena are we talking about here? If you creep up quietly behind someone and shout 'boo', you can make their heart beat faster, but this is not paranormal. But if you simply stare at a CCTV image of a person in another room and this makes their heart beat faster, this is an anomalous phenomenon. If you look out of your window and see a woman walking past, this is perfectly normal. But if the woman is ten miles away, or will walk past tomorrow but not today, or she died last week, these are all anomalous experiences suggestive of paranormal processes.

In 1949, Broad published an article in which he outlined a set of 'basic limiting principles' which he described like this:

> There are certain limiting principles which we unhesitatingly take for granted as the framework within which all our practical activities and our scientific theories are confined. Some of these seem to be self-evident.

Others are so overwhelmingly supported by all the empirical facts which fall within the range of ordinary experience and the scientific elaborations of it (including under this heading orthodox psychology) that it hardly enters our heads to question them. Let us call these Basic Limiting Principles. Now psychical research is concerned with alleged events which seem *prima facie* to conflict with one or more of these principles.

These basic limiting principles (BLPs) include the idea that causes must occur before their effects (no backward causation); that we can perceive objects and events only via our senses (no perception unmediated by sensation); that a mind cannot produce a change directly in the material world; and that the brain is necessary for any mental event (no disembodied consciousness). These BLPs seem to rule out the apparently paranormal phenomena of telepathy, clairvoyance, precognition/premonition, and psychokinesis, as well as consciousness surviving death, which are collectively known as *psi*. Therefore, if any of these paranormal phenomena can be reliably demonstrated to exist, it would be necessary to re-examine in a fundamental way our understanding of the universe. For this reason, we should ask for a very high standard of proof before accepting psi as real; the principle is that 'extraordinary claims require extraordinary proof'. Indeed, Bem (2011) and Morris (2001), both well-known proponents of psi, concur that extraordinary evidence would be required to establish the reality of any alleged psi phenomenon.

Broad (1949) notes that, in seeking to explain an anomalous event, one should first try to explain the event with reference to already known agents and laws. If this cannot be done, then one should seek to explain the event with new laws or agents that fall within the framework of the BLPs. The step of considering a change to any of the BLPs should only be taken in the light of very good evidence of a paranormal event which cannot be explained in any other way. **Occam's razor**, the principle that the simplest explanation is always to be preferred, implies that we cannot suppose the existence of paranormal processes without exhausting all the alternatives: remember that 'extraordinary claims require extraordinary proof'.

This chapter will examine the strongest evidence that currently exists in support of the paranormal causation of anomalous experience. There have been very many studies over the decades which have claimed to find evidence for psi, and space does not permit a comprehensive review of all the previous research (see, for example, Irwin & Watt, 2007). Therefore, attention will be focused on those studies conducted according to the most rigorous standards and using the most complete controls to guard against error. By and large, these are also the more recent studies as, in any area of science, practical experience allows researchers to develop more sophisticated methodologies. We will be examining proof-oriented research which is aimed at establishing the reality of paranormal processes, rather than process-oriented research which is aimed at discovering the mechanisms of these processes. While the debate rages about the reality of paranormal processes, it seems wise to establish their reality first.

There are some general rules about good experimental design that are particularly important for investigating anomalous psi processes (Morris, 2001). Random selection of the target on each trial in telepathy and clairvoyance studies means that any tendency of the participant to guess one answer rather than another cannot influence the result. The participant should be isolated from the location at which the targets are presented in order to reduce the possibility of **sensory leakage** in which the participant might be aware of the correct answer via perfectly normal sensory channels. The participant's response should be permanently recorded to minimize the chance of biased interpretation, and the correct answer on each trial should also be recorded permanently and unambiguously. The process of matching the participant's responses with the potential targets should be done by an independent judge with no knowledge of the actual targets. Finally, there should be a clear-cut means of establishing whether anything out of the ordinary has occurred, such as a statistical test that can decide whether the participant has performed at a level unlikely to be the result of random chance.

There is debate about whether it is appropriate to test for psi in the general population. Some theorists maintain that psi is a natural consequence of the physical structure of the universe (e.g. Radin, 2006) and that psi abilities are widespread in the population (e.g. Radin, 1997b, p. 153). Others suppose that only a few people have psi abilities. If the latter is true then many studies will not happen to recruit any participants with the abilities and will achieve a null result. Other studies may recruit, by chance, some gifted individuals, and so may produce positive results. This would predict that the observation of psi effects in experimental studies using randomly selected participants will be inconsistent and unreliable, which is problematic for research in a scientific field where reliability and consistency are held to be important. As Radin (1997b) notes: 'If a phenomenon is highly unstable, we can't be sure whether we are measuring a real effect, some other effect, or just random variations.' This debate seems hard to resolve in the absence of any knowledge about the mechanism of psi. If we knew how it worked, then we might be able to devise appropriate tests to find the gifted individuals, but we do not yet have the knowledge to do this. So we are left with a circular argument: the inconsistencies in the research literature may be explained if psi abilities are restricted to a few individuals, but we can only suppose this by observing the inconsistent effects.

One solution to the problem of psi ability being unevenly distributed in the population may lie in the use of meta-analysis to gather up data from many studies and look for an overall effect. If no effect is apparent in a combination of studies involving thousands of participants, then it is reasonable to conclude that probably no one has such ability.

The alternative would be to advertise for people who believe they have psi abilities and verify their claims, with the aim of working only with a few gifted individuals (e.g. Braude, 1986). This carries its own risks, as detailed by

Wiseman and Morris (1994) who warn of the techniques that psychic frauds may use to deceive a researcher. Wiseman and Morris (1995b) explain the methods that may be used to minimize the chances of fraud and point out that if it can be verified that there are no opportunities for deceit, the results of such research should be taken seriously. This protects the genuine psychic from accusations of possible fraud and protects the researcher from wasted time and effort. By and large, the studies that aimed to recruit participants with particular psi abilities have not yielded convincing results and, given the concerns about fraud, the best of the research has tended to used standard experimental techniques and random selection of participants.

Another problem is the uncertainty about which particular process might be operating in any one demonstration of an anomalous phenomenon (Irwin & Watt, 2007). For example, suppose a person sitting in one room is able to describe the image appearing on a computer screen in another room observed by a second person. This could be clairvoyance if the information is obtained from the image on the computer screen; telepathy if the information is obtained from the mind of the other person; precognition if the participant knew in advance which image was going to appear; or psychokinesis if the participant caused a particular image to appear. If a series of trials are conducted and the participant's descriptions are written down, to be checked later on by an independent judge against the actual targets, then perhaps the judge could be using PK to change the descriptions to match the targets, or using retroactive PK to change the targets to match the descriptions. So it is impossible to say for certain which particular paranormal process might be responsible for a given anomalous observation. For this reason, the sections of this chapter are organized according to the experimental procedure followed and the anomalous phenomenon observed rather than the nature of the supposed paranormal process.

Can you tell who has sent you a message?

Some people claim to be able to tell, when the phone rings, who is on the other end of the line before they answer. This could be an example of telepathy, if the information is obtained from the mind of the caller, or precognition, if the receiver senses the voice of the caller before hearing it. It is also possible to conduct experiments by using text messages on mobile phones. In a typical study, there are several potential senders in one place with one experimenter, and the receiver sitting in a different room or a different building with a second experimenter. The first experimenter randomly selects one of the senders to send a brief message to the receiver. As soon as the message arrives at the receiver's mobile phone they must guess who the sender is without looking to see. This type of experiment can employ many of the principles of good design: random selection of the sender on each trial; the sender and receiver can be isolated to reduce the possibility of 'sensory leakage'; the receiver can be asked to write down their response on a permanent record; the experimenter can be asked to write down the identity of the sender on each trial; and statistical tests can detect whether performance differs from chance.

Sheldrake and Beharee (2009) invited participants to guess which of four senders had sent a message. Two of the senders were real and two were virtual, that is, the message was generated by a computer. The hit rate was 26.7% which was significantly above the chance level of 25% in 6000 trials, but with a very small effect size. Unfortunately, when high-scoring participants were tested again, their scores fell back towards the chance level of performance. This observation raises the possibility that the initial high scores were just the product of random variation (in any group of people, some will happen to do better than others) or perhaps some of the participants (who were acquaintances) were cheating and had arranged in advance a system of illicit communication. The possibility of cheating was discounted by videotaping some participants, but a videotape may not have captured all the possibilities. Notably, the experimenter did not remain in the room with the sender.

Another problem is that the hit rates were almost the same for actual and virtual senders, yet no telepathic effect was predicted for the virtual sender. This could be due to clairvoyance perhaps, but this was not the prediction, which weakens the impact of the results. Finally, the effect size was much smaller than previous studies which had used a similar methodology but had fewer controls to guard against illicit communications (e.g. Sheldrake, Godwin, & Rockell, 2004; Sheldrake & Smart, 2005). This pattern of results becoming weaker as controls are tightened is very much as one might expect if the previous results had been due to unintended communication flow.

Of course, it is not possible to be sure what actually occurred in any particular experiment. But given the problems observed in the experimental database, it appears there is as yet no convincing evidence of the ability to detect the sender of a message.

Can you tell if someone is staring at you?

It is sometimes said that some people can tell when a person is staring at them. This has been tested by having one person sitting in a room while another person stares at them, perhaps through a one-way mirror or via CCTV from another room.

In the early 1990s, a noted sceptic, Richard Wiseman, and a proponent, Marilyn Schlitz, each performed a series of studies to test whether a participant can detect when they are being stared at. The method chosen to detect staring was to record the participant's skin conductance response (a measure of autonomic nervous system arousal) which is potentially more sensitive than a simple 'yes/no' response. The theory is that if the participants knew they were being stared at, even subconsciously, then they would become slightly more aroused. The interesting result was that Wiseman obtained null results while Schlitz observed a significant effect (Schlitz & LaBerge, 1994; Wiseman & Smith, 1994; Wiseman et al., 1995) using very similar procedures.

To try to resolve this discrepancy and discover why different results were obtained, they collaborated on a joint project in which they each ran an experiment in 1997 in Wiseman's laboratory and another experiment in 1999 in Schlitz's laboratory. They both used the same experimental protocols, they both obtained participants from the same pool, and each served as the experimenter and starer (Wiseman & Schlitz, 1997, 1999). The surprising result was that, again, Schlitz found evidence for the detection of remote staring in both laboratories while Wiseman did not.

There are a few possible interpretations for this puzzling phenomenon: perhaps Schlitz was more skilled at eliciting psi from her participants; perhaps the more gifted participants came to the researcher known to be a proponent of psi; or perhaps it was the experimenter's own psi that was responsible for the results.

It was also noted that the experimenter met and greeted the participants and also did all of the staring. To try to understand their different results, they ran another experiment in which the person who did the staring may or may not have been the person who met and greeted the participant (Schlitz et al., 2006). No significant effects were found and the results did not replicate Schlitz's earlier results. There is no way of being certain why this study did not find a significant result, but the authors did note that the experimental procedures and the statistical analysis were superior in this study compared to the previous studies in important ways. Following a natural process of gradual improvement, the equipment used to measure skin conductance was better and there were improved safeguards against sensory leakage compared to the previous studies. Another point worth mentioning is that all of the authors regarded this as a productive form of collaboration. Forging an agreement in advance helped to limit the post-experimental disagreement about how to interpret the results.

Schmidt et al. (2004) conducted a meta-analysis looking at the results of several previous experiments and concluded that there was a small overall effect of remote staring. Unfortunately, it is a cause for concern that they also noted that effect size was inversely correlated with study quality so that the better-controlled studies had the smaller effect sizes. Their recommendation was that more studies should be conducted. Two of these have produced null results (Muller, Schmidt, & Walach, 2009; Wehr, 2009).

On balance, it appears that there is no convincing evidence of the ability to detect if one is being stared at.

Some researchers speculate about psi-conducive and psi-permissive experimenters (e.g. Schmeidler, 1997). The former are those who have some psi gift and who temporarily transfer the gift and so enable their participants to show some evidence of psi ability. The latter are those who simply create a warm and friendly climate in the experimental situation and so encourage their participants to do their best and utilize their own psi abilities. The experimenter effects of Wiseman and Schlitz (1997, 1999) do seem to have been replicated to at least some extent and so they are worthy of note, though as yet we do not know how a psi-conducive effect might work.

There is also a concept of psi-inhibitory researchers (e.g. Palmer, 1997) who are presumed to have some ability, probably unconscious, to inhibit the psi abilities of their experimental participants and prevent these abilities from being manifest in a positive experimental result. This is problematic as it creates a non-falsifiable situation in which any failure to observe an effect of psi can be attributed to the presence of a psi-inhibitory researcher (e.g. Parker & Brusewitz, 2003).

How do you think the concept of psi inhibition might be investigated in a falsifiable way?

Can you see an image or video shown to another person in a remote location?

Many parapsychologists (e.g. Honorton, 1978) argue that clairvoyance and telepathy are based upon weak information signals which are usually drowned out by other perceptions and cognitions. However, if the participant is in a relaxed state so that internal physiological noise is low, and if there is homogenous external input, there is a better chance of detecting the weak signal. This is why anomalous cognitions are theorized to occur more often in dreaming states and also why the **ganzfeld technique** was introduced. In the ganzfeld ('total field') procedure, the *receiver* relaxes in a comfy chair with half ping-pong balls over their eyes to create a homogenous visual field and wears headphones playing white noise. A *sender* looks at a randomly selected photograph or video clip at a remote location and the receiver simultaneously describes out loud any thoughts and images that come into their head which are recorded for later transcription. Often, an experimenter (who is blind with respect to the actual target) will review what the receiver said immediately at the end of the trial in order to clarify any unclear statements.

Later, a judge, who is also blind to the target, (or sometimes, the receiver) listens to the recording (or reads the transcript) and chooses which one of four stimuli, the target and three decoys, best matches the receiver's impressions. If the actual target is selected, this is counted as a hit and so the chance level of performance is one in four or 25%. This type of study can be conducted according to a rigorous protocol with randomly chosen targets, permanent recording of the receiver's responses, independent judging, and a clear way of detecting whether psi (anomalous information transfer) has occurred, that is, above chance performance in a statistical test.

A series of such studies was subjected to meta-analysis separately by Honorton (1985), a proponent of psi, and Hyman (1985b), a noted sceptic. These authors came to differing conclusions, with Honorton announcing an overall psi effect and Hyman suggesting that methodological flaws rather than psi were responsible for the apparent information transfer. However, this was a productive exchange and in 1986 these two researchers issued a joint communiqué in which they agreed that there were some empirical data that required explanation but disagreed that it necessarily offered proof of psi. They preferred to withhold a conclusion until they could see the results of new studies conducted according to an even more rigorous protocol which they published jointly (Hyman & Honorton, 1986).

The methodology included strict controls against sensory leakage (so that information could not be transmitted by conventional means); testing and documentation of the methods of selecting random targets and decoys (so that the selection process could not inadvertently bias the results); procedures for statistical analysis (to prevent overly generous interpretation); and advance specification of each study as a pilot or a full experiment (to prevent the researcher from stopping when a desired result was achieved). This was a good step forwards as it laid out the grounds for future collaboration and joint analysis by sceptics and believers and should have reduced the scope for people from different sides of the spectrum of belief to disagree about the evidence.

Unfortunately, the Hyman and Honorton (1986) agreement on a rigorous methodology was not sufficient to prevent future disagreement and much the same situation arose again with a new series of studies. Proponents (Bem, 1994; Bem & Honorton, 1994) and sceptics (e.g. Hyman, 1994) could not agree on whether the results of this new series of studies offered evidence for psi. Hyman noted that the new studies found different effects from the old studies so it was not clear that there was replication. For example, the old studies found significant effects from still photographs, while the new studies found nothing from still photographs but significant effects from video clips. Is this sufficiently similar to count as a replication? Perhaps the phenomenon – if it is real – is unreliable? Hyman (1994) was also concerned that the new studies may not have followed the agreed methodology in all respects and he wanted to see more replications in a wider range of independent laboratories. After all, in normal science, an effect should be capable of being observed by any competent researcher following an appropriate procedure in any adequately equipped laboratory. If evidence for psi could be found in a large number of laboratories this would be much more convincing.

The story continues. Milton and Wiseman (1999) reviewed a set of 30 ganzfeld studies from a variety of different laboratories that complied with the methodological guidelines and failed to find an overall effect of psi. Soon after, Bem, Palmer, and Broughton (2001) updated the data set used by Milton and Wiseman with ten new studies and found a significant overall effect of psi (and see also Storm & Ertel, 2001), though this was contested by Milton and Wiseman (2001, 2002). More recently, Storm, Tressoldi, and Di Risio (2010) again reviewed the ganzfeld studies and reported evidence for psi, but still failed to convince critics such as Hyman (2010).

Can you describe remote locations without using the known senses?

Targ and Puthoff (1974) caused a stir when they reported apparently impressive results using a technique called **remote viewing**. In this paradigm, which is conceptually similar to the ganzfeld technique, the receiver again sits in the laboratory with an experimenter. Another experimenter, accompanied by one or two other people (the *senders*), visits randomly selected sites such as bridges, parks, airports, etc. This team tries to telepathically transmit information about the site to the receiver at predetermined times. The receiver describes any impressions that he or she picks up. These impressions are transcribed and given to independent judges who visit each site and rate the degree to which the site matches the transcribed impressions. The receiver may also subsequently visit the site to assess the degree of match. In a variation of this basic design, in some studies no senders are used and the remote viewer is simply given map coordinates and asked to describe what is at that location. If successful, this would be a demonstration of clairvoyance whereas the standard technique might involve either clairvoyance or telepathy.

Targ and Puthoff's (1974) experiments produced results that suggested that the descriptions matched the sites to a highly statistically significant degree. It turned out, however, that this effect was probably based upon two flaws in the experiment. Firstly, the judges were given a list of targets which were in the same order as they had been when used in the experiment. Secondly, the investigators had not edited out cues in the transcripts that gave clues to the position of the response in the sequence. Although it took a great deal of effort to obtain copies of the transcripts, as Targ and Puthoff had refused to release them, David Marks and Richard Kammann (Marks, 2000) were eventually successful in obtaining them. They discovered that they could match the poorly edited transcripts and sites without even visiting the sites.

Remote viewing experiments have been published since, some claiming significant results, others not. Methodological problems still arise. This was vividly demonstrated when Hansen, Utts, and Markwick (1992), all respected parapsychologists, criticized the remote viewing studies carried out by the Princeton Engineering Anomalies Research (PEAR) group. The PEAR group, led by Professor of Engineering Robert Jahn, was generally highly regarded within parapsychology. Hansen, Utts, and Markwick, however, summed up their remote viewing studies in the following terms:

> The research departs from criteria usually expected in formal scientific experimentation. Problems occur with regard to randomization, statistical baselines, application of statistical models, agent coding of descriptor lists, feedback to percipients, sensory cues, and precautions against cheating. ... It is concluded that the quoted significance values are meaningless because of defects in the experimental and statistical procedures. (p. 97)

Elsewhere (p. 107), they described the work as 'undoubtedly some of the poorest quality ESP experiments published in many years'. Needless to say, the PEAR group rejected these criticisms (see Dobyns *et al.*, 1992 for details). It is worth noting, however, that when such strong criticism can arise from within the parapsychological community it does not inspire confidence in the findings in those outside it.

Having said that, it should be noted that one of the authors of this critique of PEAR's remote viewing work, Jessica Utts, subsequently strongly endorsed the positive results produced over a 30-year period by researchers at SRI International and Science Applications International Corporation (SAIC). Hers was one of two evaluations commissioned by the American Institutes for Research (AIR) at the request of the Congress and CIA. This work had been sponsored by the US government with a view to possible intelligence applications. Her conclusions were as follows (Utts, 1996, p. 3):

> Using the standards applied to any other area of science, it is concluded that psychic functioning has been well established. The statistical results of the studies examined are far beyond what is expected by chance. Arguments that these results could be due to methodological flaws in the experiments are soundly refuted. Effects of a magnitude similar to those found in government-sponsored research at SRI and SAIC have been replicated at a number of laboratories around the world. Such consistency cannot be readily explained by claims of flaws or fraud.

Whereas Utts is a respected proponent of the paranormal, the other evaluation was produced by Ray Hyman, a well-known critic. Hyman (1996) agreed with Utts that the SAIC research was methodologically superior to previous remote viewing research and that real effects were occurring, but he was not convinced that the statistical departures from chance expectation necessarily reflect psi. As he pointed out, the work was carried out under conditions of extreme secrecy and therefore only received limited external scrutiny. Also the consistency across laboratories is only to be found in terms of average effect sizes. The effect sizes pertaining to individual experimenters and conditions within a study vary considerably. Hyman believed that Utts's conclusion was premature.

Back in the 1970s, the general attitude of informed sceptics appeared to be that there was nothing in the experimental psi database that could not easily be explained away in terms of shoddy methodology, failure to replicate, and occasional fraud by participants or experimenters. In the 1980s, many informed sceptics went so far as to admit that there was *something* interesting in the data which required explanation but stopped short of actually endorsing the psi hypothesis. For example, consider this statement from Hyman (1996, p. 39):

> I agree with Jessica Utts that the effect sizes reported in the SAIC experiments and in the recent ganzfeld studies probably cannot be dismissed

as due to chance. Nor do they appear to be accounted for by multiple testing, file-drawer distortions, inappropriate statistical testing or other misuse of statistical inference.

He went on, 'Having accepted the existence of non-chance effects, the focus now is upon whether these effects have normal causes' (p. 39).

His overall assessment of the state of evidence within parapsychology was also quite positive:

> I admit that the latest findings should make [parapsychologists] optimistic. The case for psychic functioning seems better than it ever has been. The contemporary findings along with the output of the SRI/SAIC program do seem to indicate that something beyond odd statistical hiccups is taking place. I also have to admit that I do not have a ready explanation for these observed effects. Inexplicable statistical departures from chance, however, are a far cry from compelling evidence for anomalous cognition. (Hyman, 1996, p. 43)

However, not all subsequent assessments were quite so positive. Marks (2000), for example, argued that the experimental protocols employed in the SAIC studies were not actually as tight as the published accounts may have led one to believe. In particular, Wiseman and Milton (1998; see also May, 1998) examined the protocol used in the first SAIC remote-viewing experiment and discovered a number of potential pathways for information leakage. The SAIC team then had difficulty in reconstructing the actual details of the protocol, producing no less than five different versions. As Wiseman and Milton (1999) point out,

> These difficulties not only make an assessment of Experiment One extremely difficult, but also call into question whether the assessors commissioned to write a US-government sponsored report on the other studies in the SAIC program [i.e. Utts and Hyman] would have been given accurate information about their unrecorded details. (p. 3)

More recently, a simple and elegant experiment by Wiseman and Watt (2010) used Twitter to invite members of the public to identify a location using their mind power. On each day for four days, Wiseman sent a tweet from one of five possible locations in Edinburgh and invited anyone interested to send their thoughts and impressions about the location. Judges were given five photographs, the target and four decoys, and asked to select the target based on the information received from members of the public. All four trials were misses. The believers performed no better than the sceptics, although in an earlier, less formal study, the believers had reported finding stronger correspondences between their impressions and the actual targets than did the sceptics. So there was no evidence for remote viewing – but some suggestion that believers are better at seeing correspondences between their impressions and the actual target even when these correspondences are not apparent to others.

Consistently inconsistent findings?

Although space does not permit a thorough consideration, it is interesting to look at the inconsistency among studies with respect to factors said to affect the results of studies of anomalous information transfer. Some researchers have reported that emotional links between sender and receiver – for example, when both are friends or relatives – may facilitate the flow of information transfer; however, others have found contradictory evidence or no effect (e.g. Perez-Navarro, Lawrence, & Hume, 2009; Sherwood *et al.*, 2005). Prior personal experience of psi has been associated with positive experimental results in some studies (e.g. Bierman *et al.*, 1993; Parker, Frederiksen, & Johansson, 1997) but other studies have found no relationship with belief in psi (e.g. Bem, 2011; Goulding, 2005b; Putz, Gassler, & Wackermann, 2007; Sherwood *et al.*, 2005; Wiseman & Watt, 2010).

The practice of mental disciplines such as meditation has sometimes been associated with successful psi effects (e.g. Bierman *et al.*, 1993; Edge *et al.*, 1986) and this is attributed to a general interest in inner experience and a tendency to pay attention to inner states and sensations. Other studies, however, have failed to find this factor to be of influence or have found a negative relationship (e.g. Bem, 2011; Goulding, 2005b; Perez-Navarro, Lawrence, & Hume, 2009). An adjustment to the hypothesis might theorize that participants could be paying attention to the wrong inner states and that this disguises the weak psi signal, but there is a danger that this might render the hypothesis non-falsifiable. If we assume that a person who meditates regularly and scores above chance is paying attention to the correct inner signal, while a person who meditates regularly and scores at chance must be paying attention to the wrong inner signal, then we need a way of determining to which inner signal each person is attending. But there is no independent way of confirming this except to look at performance in the experimental task, which makes a circular argument.

Overall, there has been a history of claim and counterclaim and one might be forgiven for seeing no end in sight. Despite a good attempt to establish a means of settling the argument – the methodology agreed between Hyman and Honorton (1986) – there continues to be debate about whether studies have followed the methodology correctly and about how the results should be analysed. It seems that neither side, the believers or the sceptics, are going to be easily convinced. In the light of the principle that extraordinary claims require extraordinary proof, and the lack of sufficiently convincing evidence in the form of a demonstration that can be reliably reproduced on demand (Hyman, 2010), perhaps it is still premature to conclude that there exists a genuinely anomalous process of information transfer.

Box 10.1   What is the underlying process?

Bem, Palmer, and Broughton (2001) assert that the observed heterogeneity of results could be due to variations in the experimental procedure. This is an interesting argument but it is impossible to be sure because we don't know how the putative anomalous process of information transfer is theorized to work, and so we don't know what the crucial factors are.

Several factors have been investigated (see text for details) that may influence the ability to transfer information between a sender and a receiver or the ability of a receiver to detect information from the environment at a distance. Some of these are procedural factors – for example, the use of moving versus still images. Many factors relate to the participant – for example, extraversion versus introversion; the practice of mental disciplines– for example, meditation; tolerance of ambiguity; prior belief in psi; an emotional link between sender and receiver (if they are already friends); and relaxed versus tense state of arousal.

These factors have all given inconsistent results so we are no nearer to knowing under what conditions an anomalous process of information transfer is most likely to be observed. This is unlike more conventional areas of psychology, in which effects and processes are reliably observed to occur more often or more strongly under some conditions, and for some people, than others. Is this a problem? Do you think it is reasonable to expect consistent results from a process we do not understand?

Box 10.2   Should this have resolved the argument?

The methodology proposed jointly by Hyman and Honorton (1986) was intended to provide the basis for an agreement that any study conducted according to the methodology would be taken seriously. However, it seems that there is still an argument about whether there might have been methodological flaws in some studies following the agreed methodology.

Do you think it was acceptable to add new criteria after the joint communiqué was published?
How far should a researcher have to stick to a specified protocol?
How large does a flaw have to be in order to render the results of a study invalid?
Are sceptics obliged to respect the results of research conducted according to the agreed methodology or are they right to point out if the research contains new flaws?

Can you obtain information about events before they occur?

Precognition is the process of acquiring information about a future event that could not reasonably be predicted from information available at the time. *Premonition* refers to the process of experiencing an affective (emotional) response to a future event without any known means of acquiring such a response. Various experimental paradigms have been used to investigate precognition and premonition and some of the more popular paradigms will be described here.

Many studies have looked at whether participants can have accurate premonitions for arousing stimuli. Radin (1997a) presented participants with a series of images including some with violent or erotic themes, selected to invoke arousal, and others chosen to exert a calming influence (e.g. sunsets). Various physiological measures including heart rate and electrodermal activity (skin conductance) were recorded before, during and after the targets were shown. The results suggested that these measures distinguished between calm and arousing stimuli one second before the targets were displayed, implying that participants had experienced premonitions of the stimuli. Unfortunately, this study illustrates a number of the problems that can arise with this type of research. The first problem is the observation of small and uneven sample sizes across experiments (n = 8, n = 3, n = 16, n = 4) where it is preferable to have larger and consistently sized samples to provide assurance that the studies were conducted according to a predefined plan. The second problem is that the results may have been due to an anticipatory orienting response, that is, participants may have gradually increased their expectation of an extreme image until one appeared, and then anticipated a calming stimulus on the next trial. This would produce an average effect of a larger orienting response on the extreme trials if such trials were in a minority. The authors tried to rule out this explanation with a detailed statistical exploration but perhaps this possibility should still be admitted (and this was acknowledged by Bierman & Radin, 1997). The third problem is the lack of an explanation for the mechanism of the premonitory effect that has been noted before. Finally, Parkhomtchouk *et al.* (2002) disagreed with the method of analysis. In their own study they were not able to fully replicate the results of Radin (1997a) so the problem of replication failure arises again.

Along similar lines, but using auditory instead of visual stimuli, Spottiswoode and May (2003) divided up their experimental session into a series of equal time intervals and presented participants with either an auditory stimulus or no stimulus during each interval. Participants were more likely to show an increase in skin conductance in the three-second wait before an auditory stimulus was played as against the three seconds before a no-stimulus interval, suggestive of a premonition. Again, however, there were some problems with this research, including that the significant results were obtained only by using a different method of analysis than was used in previous studies (e.g. Bierman & Radin, 1997; Radin, 1997a) so this does not offer a wholly convincing replication.

Robinson (2009) noted that the majority of precognitions are believed by the receiver to arise while dreaming (Drewes, 2002) and decided to run an experiment to examine dream precognition. He asked participants to keep a dream diary for one night, then the next day come to the laboratory and choose which of two passages most resembled their dream. The passages each described a video clip and one of these clips, chosen at random, was subsequently shown to the participant. Precognition would be demonstrated by the previous chance selection of the descriptive passage that referred to the video clip subsequently shown to the participant; this would suggest that the participant had acquired knowledge of the video clip before it was chosen. Unfortunately, there was no psi effect.

Habituation refers to the gradual weakening of the response to a stimulus if it is repeatedly exposed without any consequence. Precognitive affective habituation (or presentiment) occurs when participants show weaker reactions to an emotional picture that is later exposed repeatedly without consequence than to a picture that is not later exposed. That is, the habituation allegedly works retroactively and the picture creates habituation before it is exposed. In a typical experiment, a pair of pictures is displayed in which either both pictures arouse negative emotion, both arouse positive emotion, or both are neutral. The participant is asked to select the picture they prefer. Subsequently one of each pair of pictures is chosen to be repeatedly exposed. A hit is scored if the participant prefers the negative picture which is later repeatedly exposed (because a negative picture becomes less unlikeable with familiarity) or the neutral picture which is later exposed (because a neutral picture becomes more likeable with familiarity) or the positive picture which is not later exposed (because a positive picture becomes less likeable with familiarity).

Bem (2003) reported a statistically significant effect, but it was observed only among the more emotionally reactive participants and especially males. This effect was partially replicated by Batthyany, Kranz, and Erber (2009) who observed an effect of precognitive habituation for the more emotionally reactive participants, males and females, but only for high-arousal negative stimuli. Savva, Roe, and Smith (2006) failed to replicate the precognitive habituation effect at all. Parker and Sjoden (2010) reported an effect only among a subset of the participants selected after the experiment was completed and there was no difference in precognitive habituation between the more and less emotionally reactive participants. Finally, two successful replications were reported by Bem (2011, Experiments 5 and 6).

The last two aforementioned experiments were reported in an important series of studies published by Bem (2011) in the influential *Journal of Personality and Social Psychology* (*JPSP*). Bem and his research assistants conducted nine studies in all with over 1000 participants in an attempt to demonstrate that future events can retroactively affect responses in the present. Bem is a noted supporter of the psi hypothesis and an experienced researcher and his aim was to produce solid empirical evidence from simple experimental studies that there is a phenomenon worth investigating. Most of the nine studies yielded significant positive results, suggesting that events in the future can indeed influence responses made before the event occurs. The strongest evidence came from an experiment looking at the 'retroactive facilitation of recall' for words: if you take a list of words, and rehearse half of them, these will be recalled better than the words which were not rehearsed. Bem put this paradigm into reverse, so that participants were presented with a set of words once each, then tested on recall of the words, and only then were half of the words randomly chosen to be rehearsed. These randomly selected words were later found to have been better recalled than the non-rehearsed words although there is no conventional means by which this could have occurred. Bem thinks that the participants were, in some way, able to 'feel the future'.

Publication in the prestigious *JPSP* guaranteed a wide audience for the Bem (2011) article. It therefore had a much larger impact than the many previous works along similar lines that were published in less well-known, specialist parapsychology journals. The article also picked up a lot of general media attention, partly because of its surprise value, and partly because it was published in such a well-regarded journal. Perhaps mindful that this is a controversial topic, the editors, Judd and Gawronski (2011), explained their decision to publish the article in an editorial. They noted that the Bem paper went through a rigorous review process with a large set of reviews by 'distinguished experts in social cognition'. They noted that they had invited a commentary from a group of sceptics which was published in the same issue of the journal. They noted:

> Our obligation as journal editors is not to endorse particular hypotheses but to advance and stimulate science through a rigorous review process. It is our hope and expectation that the current two papers will stimulate further discussion, attempts at replication, and critical further thoughts about appropriate methods in research on social cognition and attitudes.

It is therefore most unfortunate that, despite the editors' declared hope that the publication would inspire attempts at replication, the *JPSP* itself refused to publish any such replications, including three independent studies carried at Goldsmiths, University of London (Chris French), and the Universities of Hertfordshire (Richard Wiseman) and Edinburgh (Stuart Ritchie), citing the editorial policy of refusing to publish straight replications. Two prestigious journals *Science Brevia* and *Psychological Science* also refused to publish this series of replication attempts without even sending out the paper for peer review. This is a problem for this whole field of research because replicability is one of the cornerstones of science – without successful replication we simply do not know whether there is an effect at all. Now, many journals will publish a replication and extension – that is, some small difference in the procedure or an additional hypothesis – but not an exact replication. The problem here is that parapsychologists could claim that any difference in the procedure could have been responsible for the failure to replicate and so an exact replication is necessary (French, 2012a). As it turned out, Ritchie, Wiseman, and French (2012a) were ultimately successful in getting their paper accepted for publication in the high-impact online journal *PLoS ONE*. Their paper received a similar amount of media coverage to that generated by the original controversial claims, thus providing a degree of balance.

However, in general, the difficulty in publishing a failed replication attempt in a journal with an equally large readership to *JPSP*, ensuring equal publicity in the general media, could leave psychology and parapsychology researchers and the general public with a misleading impression of the strength of the evidence base for precognition and premonition. Goldacre (2011) even noted that in this instance the *JPSP* seems to have behaved somewhat like a tabloid newspaper, preferring an eye-catching story of premonition and precognition to the more sober, but more plausible, reality of failures to replicate and null effects (see also Carey, 2011).

Mention should be made here that specialist parapsychological journals typically do publish failures to replicate in an attempt to present a complete and honest picture of the current state of research. The problem is that they do not have the large readership of, for example, the *JPSP*, and cannot command the same level of attendant publicity.

As has happened so often in the past, there were serious criticisms of the Bem (2011) studies. Wagenmakers *et al.* (2011) reviewed the method of analysis used in the Bem paper and found two main problems. One was the observation that the data analysis appeared to be at least partly exploratory rather than fully specified in advance when best practice would be for the method of analysis of a controversial claim to be fully specified in advance. The second problem was that the use of one-sided probability values might have overstated the evidence in favour of psi. Wagenmakers *et al.* (2011) reanalysed the data using their preferred method of analysis (Bayesian *t*-tests) and reported that there was nearly no evidence at all under this new method of analysis. Their conclusion was that changes are needed in the way that psychologists frame their hypotheses, conduct experiments, and analyse the results.

Alcock (2011) also raised concerns about the statistics and the methodology. He noted that the published article did not contain sufficient detail of the methodology to be sure of the details, but in order to be sure that there was no opportunity for unintentional data leakage or other forms of bias, the methodology should have been more fully specified. He also noted that some changes to methodology seem to have been made, and some stimuli altered, partway through an experiment, which is not very good practice. There was also some suggestion of inaccuracy in the documentation of these studies; for example, footnote 1 (p. 409) states that the minimum number of participants in each study was 100 and yet Experiment 9, which yielded the largest effect size, had only 50 participants.

As it happens, Bem's (2011) controversial results and attempts to replicate them fed into a controversy relating to the role of replication and publication bias in psychology in general that is of great relevance to parapsychology and will be discussed further in Chapter 12. For now, it is enough to note that many of the problems highlighted by this controversy would be eliminated if psychology and parapsychology adopted the practice of pre-registering studies, especially in the case of controversial claims. Such pre-registration means that all of the details of data collection and analysis are specified in advance.

In the case of Bem's studies, Richard Wiseman and Caroline Watt set up such a registry and the results of six attempts to replicate Bem's retroactive facilitation of recall experiment were subsequently available for a meta-analysis (Wiseman & Watt, submitted). Overall, the results of the studies did not replicate Bem's controversial finding.

Can your thoughts influence the physical state of another person?

This phenomenon is also known as Direct Mental Interaction with Living Systems (DMILS). Psychokinesis (also sometimes known as telekinesis) is the apparent process by which thoughts or intentions may exert a physical influence on an object or a biological process without any known mechanism of effect. So DMILS would be an example of thoughts and intentions exerting an influence on a biological system.

In the basic procedure a *sender* in one room is asked to try to make the *receiver* in another room either relaxed or tense during defined time periods. The psychophysiological state of the receiver is typically detected via skin conductance (sweat detection or electro-dermal analysis, EDA), heart rate, blood pressure, or electroencephalogram (EEG) to measure changes in state of arousal.

Braud and Schlitz (1991) asked their participants to use specific mental imagery to produce specific physiological changes in other participants sitting in a different room, with no apparent means of communication between them. The first participant was asked to use imagery to either increase or decrease the sympathetic nervous system activity of the second participant which was measured by skin conductance response. Changes in the skin conductance response were judged by a researcher who was blind to the attempts of the first participant. The predicted effect was apparent on 40% (six of 15) of the studies, which is better than would be expected by chance. Positive results in a DMILS paradigm have been found by other researchers (e.g. Radin, Taylor, & Braud, 1995), though replication failures have also been reported (e.g. Wolfgang, 2008, using EEG patterns). Braud (1994) and Delanoy (2001) each reviewed a series of studies in which an agent attempted to interact with the psychophysiological state of another person in a different room with no direct communication or contact. The conclusion was that there is replicable evidence for this phenomenon, although Braud (1994) notes the lack of a satisfactory theoretical model.

Schlitz and Braud (1997) performed a meta-analysis of 30 studies involving more than 400 self-selected volunteer participants, typically healers and psychics. The overall results showed a strongly significant effect of distant intentionality, that is, their participants appeared to be able to influence the physical state of another person at a distance. Key aspects of these studies were well-controlled – for example, the influencer and the influencee were physically separated, the influencee was blind to the timing of each attempted influencing period of time, and the starting and stopping points of influence periods were randomly chosen. Of the 30 studies, 14 gave statistically significant results while 16 did not. This below-50% success rate for individual studies does raise the possibility of a 'file-drawer' problem, that is, the positive results counted of individual studies in this meta-analysis could conceivably be balanced by a number of non-significant results that were never published. It is, however, consistent with the existence of a process whose moderating variables have yet to be identified and which is accordingly perceived to be unreliable in practice.

Schmidt *et al.* (2004) performed a meta-analysis of 30 studies on direct mental interaction, using electro-dermal activity as the dependent measure. Again, there was a small but significant combined effect in the meta-analysis, though the authors note that more replications and the development of a theoretical model are required before the putative effect will become convincing.

A more recent and similarly positive meta-analysis was performed by Schmidt (2012) including 576 separate sessions in 11 studies. In these studies the intention was to promote focused attention in the recipient, so this represented a different measure but a similarly beneficial intent. Although the studies were reported to be of 'remarkable similarity' (p. 531) in their methodological approach, the effect sizes were more variable than would be expected by chance. Also, Schmidt noted that the significance level of the combined results was 0.03, so only a couple of negative results would move this over the criterion value of 0.05 and demand a different interpretation. A further problem, also noted by other researchers (e.g. Braud, 1994; Schmidt *et al.*, 2004), was the lack of a theoretical model to account for the results. Schmidt did point to the similarity in effect size between this and other previous meta-analyses as supporting evidence – but in the absence of a theoretical model this might seem somewhat less than convincing.

The apparent success of this paradigm might beg the question of why DMILS is not more commonly appreciated and used by, for example, the medical profession. Perhaps the absence of any known mechanism hampers the adoption of this means of interacting with another person's nervous system or perhaps the replication failures render the potential applicability less certain. It may be that the useful adoption of this kind of technique will have to wait until the causal pathway is delineated at a neural level and the technique can be reliably reproduced.

Can you influence a physical object using only your mind?

A typical procedure uses a random event generator (REG) – for example, a computer – to generate a random sequence of ones and zeros, each of which constitutes one trial. Participants are asked to try to influence the process so as to produce more ones or more zeros. Feedback can be given, for example by causing lights to flash in a different sequence, or sound to be played from one speaker or another, depending on whether the outcome of each trial is a one or a zero. REGs are useful for research into **micro-PK** for several reasons: they can easily generate large samples, they are not biased, and the output can be automatically stored on a computer to aid the analysis (Bösch, Steinkamp, & Boller, 2006; Radin, 1997b). Radin (1997b, p. 149) also commends the use of REG because 'random systems are psychologically "easier" to influence mentally than are massive objects'.

Robert Jahn of Princeton Engineering Anomalies Research Laboratory has performed a substantial series of experiments into micro-PK using this type of procedure and claimed many significant findings (and there was an earlier series of studies by Helmut Schmidt). Alcock (1990) was less convinced and wrote a thorough critique in which he detailed concerns about the methodology and the statistical results. He noted peculiarities in the baseline condition, which is problematic because the existence of PK would be detected by deviations from the baseline condition and the chance of detecting such deviations could be influenced by characteristics of the baseline condition. He also noted that a single participant provided much of the data that were responsible for the significant results and without those data some of the experimental conditions became non-significant and others only just reached statistical significance. This is problematic because a genuine effect should not be so highly dependent on one individual. This individual was believed to be a person who worked in the laboratory and it would be preferable in some respects for the micro-PK effect to be demonstrated by a range of individuals not connected with the researcher. This brings us to the debate about whether testing the general population is appropriate if abilities exist only in a few individuals (see Box 10.1).

Bösch, Steinkamp, and Boller (2006) conducted a review and meta-analysis of 380 micro-PK studies using REGs, all of which passed criteria regarding the quality of their methodology. They observed a very small overall effect size, 0.500035 against the chance level of 0.5, which reached statistical significance because of the very large number of trials in some studies. However, there are several problems which prevent a firm conclusion at this time. These problems are mostly connected with the observation of a very variable (heterogeneous) effect size such that the smaller studies had larger effects. This raises the possibility that some successful pilot studies (which are typically small studies) might have been published as formal experiments. The problem here is that an unsuccessful pilot study would be less likely to be published and so this practice could bias the literature in favour of successful studies. This could be prevented by specifying in advance whether a study is a pilot study or a formal experiment, but the database does contain some earlier studies whose status may be a little uncertain. Second, the number of trials should be specified in advance to prevent the possibility of a researcher deciding to stop at a point when a 'lucky streak' appears in an otherwise random pattern of results (which is more likely to happen in a smaller study). Third, the earlier studies tended to be the smaller studies and to have the larger effect sizes, which is of some concern in view of the general trend for methodological rigour to improve over time.

Fourth, there is the 'file-drawer' problem, referring to the bias in favour of publishing positive findings. A researcher with a negative finding might not find the time to write it up, reasoning that it is less likely to be published, and that the failure to find a significant result might suggest a study with inappropriate methodology. If a paper reporting a negative finding is submitted to a journal, it is less likely to be published. So the literature may contain a disproportionate number of positive findings and this can bias the conclusions of a meta-analysis (see Chapter 12). In this instance, Bösch, Steinkamp, and Boller (2006) concluded that the number of experiments with negative results that would be needed to balance out the number of published experiments with positive results was a little over 1500 over a period of 20 years, and this was regarded as feasible. So the 'file-drawer' problem poses a potential explanation for the results of the meta-analysis.

Wilson and Shadish (2006) were even more critical of the published research into micro-PK. They were of the opinion that the methodological problems were too great to draw any conclusions, and that effects of the size reported were too small to be meaningful. It is hard to argue that an effect of the size of 0.500035 – which represents 35 extra hits over one million trials – could ever amount to anything meaningful in the real world. They suggested that proponents of micro-PK should attempt to offer research designs capable of producing larger effects.

Other researchers – for example, Radin et al. (2006) – disagreed and proposed that the effects are both real and important. Certainly, if it is possible to influence a physical object using only the power of the mind, this would be a very important effect and would necessitate changes to our understanding of the physical nature of the universe. However, as has been observed before, the mechanism by which the micro-PK effect is exerted remains to be explained. One particular issue is that we don't know quite where the participant was exerting their supposed mental influence: was it exerted on the REG itself, or on the feedback display, or on the recorded data offered to the judge (Irwin & Watt, 2007)? If the participant is unclear about what exactly they were trying to influence, then it becomes harder to understand the nature of the effect.

It is hard to draw a definite conclusion regarding the micro-PK research. There are some interesting findings which, if genuine, would be worth pursuing. However, there are still some issues of concern and it is not clear that an extraordinary level of proof has been offered. If we remember the saying 'extraordinary claims require extraordinary proof', then perhaps we should withhold judgement for the moment.

The survival hypothesis

The survival hypothesis refers to the possibility that some aspect of a person's consciousness may be able to exist independently of their body and may be able to survive the death of the body. So support for the survival hypothesis might be found in evidence that an OBE involves genuine separation of the mind from the body or that it is possible to communicate with the spirits of dead people.

It is very difficult to demonstrate that an OBE involves a genuine separation of consciousness from the body. To do this, it would be necessary for the person who claims to have experienced an OBE to provide information available at the location to which they travelled in the OBE which they could not have acquired or inferred by any conventional means and could not be the result of coincidence. But this is virtually impossible to prove in practice unless a specific experimental situation is set up. There are some individuals who claim to be able to induce OBEs more or less at will as a result of engaging in various mental exercises. It would require only one such individual to be able to reliably demonstrate the ability to pick up information from remote locations to put an end to the arguments over whether mind could be separated from brain. It is extremely telling that despite many decades of such claims, no one has yet been able to provide such evidence.

The other main type of evidence for the survival hypothesis would be the provision of information received from a deceased person via a spirit medium when there was no conventional way that information could have been provided. Many studies have carried out controlled tests of spirit mediums by asking the medium to give a reading for a number of different sitters, and then asking each sitter to select which reading applies most strongly to them. If the spirit medium is genuinely receiving information from beyond the grave, then the sitters should be able to pick out the reading that applies to them more accurately than guesswork. Typical results show that sitters cannot select the reading that applies to them (e.g. French, 2012b; Jensen & Cardeña, 2009) offering no support for the survival hypothesis.

Many people claim to have seen a ghost, but this is inherently difficult to prove. I may genuinely believe that I have seen a figure where no living person is present, but there are many ways in which my perception may have been mistaken. An apparitional experience may be the result of sleep paralysis (French & Santomauro, 2007), as described in Chapter 5. Most ghostly sightings occur in dark places with plenty of shadows and Houran, Wiseman, and Thalbourne (2002), for example, explain how the layout of an old building, with low lighting and shadowy corners, can contribute to perceptual illusions. Also, the power of suggestion and prior expectation could lead someone to believe they have seen a ghost (e.g. Braithwaite, 2011; Houran, Wiseman, & Thalbourne, 2002).

As discussed in Chapter 5, Persinger (e.g. 2001) offered a possible explanation for the appearance of ghostly apparitions. He proposed that fluctuations in the earth's background magnetic field can stimulate neural overactivity in someone with an especially sensitive temporal lobe, which can produce a sense of a presence and a visual hallucination. Some support for his hypothesis was offered by Braithwaite and Townsend (2008) although there have also been failures to replicate (e.g. French *et al.*, 2009; Granqvist *et al.*, 2005).

Conclusion and the way ahead

One of the main problems with all of the ostensibly paranormal forces considered in this chapter is that there is no known mechanism for their operation. Back in 1986, Edge *et al.* noted that we need a theory of psi; now a generation later we still do not have a theory recognized outside the field of parapsychology. This is not entirely unusual in science. Indeed, as Bem (2011) points out, it is frequently the case that a phenomenon is observed and measured before a theoretical explanation is proposed. However, before an explanation can be developed, it is necessary to explore the parameters of the phenomenon and to understand under what circumstances it occurs. This enables the phenomenon to be fully described so that its source can be determined. In the absence of any reliable means of producing the effect, and with no clear picture of when and where it occurs, it is very hard to make progress in understanding the mechanism of the phenomenon. Thus we seem to be stuck in a loop: without knowing the mechanism, it is difficult to predict how to produce the phenomenon reliably, and without consistent observations of the circumstances under which the phenomenon occurs, it is hard to start to posit a mechanism.

Bem (2011) supposes that precognitive and premonitory abilities would confer a survival advantage. This benefit seems very likely – if the abilities are real – but Bem does not really come close to offering a mechanism. Other researchers speculate that a mechanism for psi may reside in some property of quantum mechanics (e.g. Radin, 2006) though acknowledging that this view does not yet offer a satisfactory explanation for psi.

The question of replicability is often regarded as a cornerstone of the scientific process (e.g. Beyerstein, 1995; Smith, 2010). Indeed, Radin, a vocal proponent of psi, acknowledges that replication is 'fundamental for making the scientific case for psi' (Radin, 1997b, p. xix). No observation is taken seriously, or regarded as reliable, if it cannot be replicated most of the time when a specific methodology is followed. It seems that for many, if not all, of the parapsychological phenomena reviewed here, the demand for replicability is simply not met (for more on replicability, see Chapter 12).

This leaves parapsychology in a difficult situation. Funding tends to be offered to fields where there is a reasonable chance of success and parapsychology does not look like one of these fields. With limited ability to attract funding, the chances of making much progress are diminished. Unless there is a clear breakthrough which should involve substantial progress in understanding the mechanisms lying behind paranormal forces, it is hard to see much future in parapsychological research. Irwin and Watt (2007, p. 59) state that there 'is and can be no definitive experiment on the authenticity of ESP' but this seems unnecessarily negative. If an experiment were devised that could be replicated most of the time by a researcher of a sceptical viewpoint, then this could become a definitive experiment. To date no such experiment has become apparent.

Another hallmark of science is connectivity: one branch of science connects with other branches and advances in one field lead to advances in another field. In the case of psi and the paranormal it does not appear to have offered anything to other fields of science. Psi will probably not be taken seriously until it does start to offer this kind of benefit to the wider scientific community (Edge *et al.*, 1986).

One possible way to make progress was suggested by Kennedy (2004) and similar points were made by Watt (2005). He proposed that studies should be planned in advance, according to a methodology agreed by a group of parapsychologists, sceptics, and statisticians, and conducted by different researchers in different laboratories. Such replication by different groups of researchers is essential in case of an unintentional methodological weakness in one individual study. The only such attempt to do this to date appears to be the registry set up by Wiseman and Watt (submitted) described earlier. As pointed out by Hyman (1996), it is impossible to be sure that any individual experiment is entirely free from flaws. The results of such a programme of studies, if demonstrating a replicable effect, would command respect. With a clearly replicable effect, attention could be turned to exploring the conditions under which the effect is more likely to be observed, which leads to the possibility of discovering the underlying mechanisms. Sadly, at the present moment we have yet to discover an empirical demonstration psi that can reliably be replicated by neutral researchers.

Radin (1997b) points out that even though flaws might be shown to exist in particular experiments, and these flaws could have produced the outcome, that does not prove that the outcome was necessarily due to the flaws rather than genuine psi. This is true, but the principle that extraordinary claims require extraordinary proof still applies. A demonstration of anomalous results from a replicable experiment demonstrably free from flaws is still required. It may not be possible to convince all the sceptics, but there are many open-minded researchers who are prepared to accept evidence if it is sufficiently convincing. Extraordinary claims require extraordinary proof and we are still waiting for that extraordinary proof.

Suggested further reading

For thorough coverage of parapsychological research:

Irwin, H. J. & Watt, C. (2007). *An introduction to parapsychology*. 5th edn. Jefferson, NC: McFarland & Co.

For a discussion of good experimental design in parapsychology:

Morris, R. L. (2001). 'Research methods in experimental parapsychology: Problems and prospects'. *European Journal of Parapsychology*, 16, 8–18.
Wiseman, R. & Morris, R. L. (1995b). *Guidelines for testing psychic claimants*. Hatfield: University of Hertfordshire Press.

For the Bem study and one of the attempted replications:

Bem, D. J. (2011). 'Feeling the future: Experimental evidence for anomalous retroactive influences on cognition and affect'. *Journal of Personality and Social Psychology*, 100, 407–25.

Ritchie, S. J., Wiseman, R., & French, C. C. (2012a). 'Failing the future: Three unsuccessful attempts to replicate Bem's "retroactive facilitation of recall" effect'. *PLoS One*, 7, e33423. doi:10.1371/journal.pone.0033423.

Philosophical Perspectives

11

Introduction

It is not surprising that many of the experiences described in this book have a tremendous impact upon the people who experience them. The nature of the experiences is such that they often appear to have profound implications in terms of our understanding of the universe and our place in it. Attempts to address such issues have traditionally been the domain of philosophers, although most scientists and theologians also have strong, often opposing, views in this area.

We cannot provide a detailed discussion of all of the philosophical issues that are related to parapsychology and anomalistic psychology in one short chapter. Instead, we will focus upon two issues that have both been topics for heated debate for a very long time. The first is the scientific status of parapsychology. Many critics of parapsychology have condemned it as being nothing more than a pseudoscience that should be relegated to the scrapheap along with phlogiston theory, astrology, and homeopathy. We will consider the arguments for such a position and offer our own verdict on the scientific status of the discipline.

The second topic that will be considered in this chapter is the implications of parapsychology for one of oldest philosophical puzzles in existence: the so-called **mind–body problem**. Ever since human beings were first able to reflect upon their own existence, the nature of consciousness itself has defied explanation. The standard view of most neuroscientists is one that implies that consciousness cannot become detached from the underlying neural substrate of the brain but clearly a number of alleged paranormal phenomena would appear to contradict such a position. If OBEs are taken at face value, this would imply that a fundamental assumption of modern neuroscience is simply wrong, as would any convincing evidence for life after death.

The scientific status of parapsychology

Critics of parapsychology often dismiss parapsychology as being nothing more than pseudoscience. They imply that although parapsychologists may present themselves to the outside world as studying their subject matter in a scientific manner, close inspection reveals that this is just a sham. In fact, they argue, parapsychology does not meet the criteria of true science and can safely be rejected along with other crackpot claims. To give but one example, Mario Bunge (1991, p. 136) wrote, 'Parapsychology, a prime example of magical thinking, has no future as a science.' Are such critics justified in their assertion?

Before we can consider the scientific status of parapsychology, we need to take a step back and ask how is it possible to ever distinguish between science and non-science. This is known as the **demarcation problem** and is arguably the most fundamental question at the heart of the philosophy of science. Clearly, one cannot begin to answer such questions unless one is able to unambiguously define what constitutes a true science. Although this may sound like a fairly straightforward task, it turns out to be deceptively complex (Chalmers, 1999). Is it possible to specify exactly what it is that distinguishes true science from other approaches?

A naive approach might be to assert that science is about discovering universally true laws of nature and that this is achieved by a process of induction. Our hypothetical scientist observes the world around her and notices what she takes to be certain consistencies, for example, that the time it takes for a pendulum to swing back to its original position when released is constant, regardless of the initial angle of displacement. She then states her hunch as a formal hypothesis and sets about testing it by repeatedly timing the swings of the pendulum over a long series of trials using a range of angles of displacement. If her hypothesis is supported over a large number of observations, she announces to the world that she has discovered a new, universally true, scientific law: The period of a pendulum is constant regardless of the initial angle of displacement.

But there is a logical problem here: no matter how many trials she has observed that supported her hypothesis, this offers no absolute guarantee that the next trial will also support it. One influential solution to this problem with the inductive approach was proposed by the late Sir Karl Popper (1963). He argued that although one could never show that a hypothesis was universally true, no matter how many observations one made that were consistent with it, it only took a single observation that contradicted the hypothesis to demonstrate that it was not universally true. In other words, Popper argued that scientists should proceed not by attempting to verify hypotheses but by attempting to falsify them. If they were unable to do so, they would be justified in provisionally accepting that their hypothesis, and the theory from which it was derived, might be true, given that it was consistent with all of the available evidence.

If, however, new observations were made that contradicted the hypothesis (and thus the theory from which it was derived), the scientist should produce a revised theory that was consistent with both the original data as well as the new observations. Ideally, the new theory might also generate interesting new hypotheses that could be investigated by subjecting them to tests that might potentially falsify them. For as long as the new theory was not falsified, it would be tentatively accepted as being our best guess about the way things are. It is important to note that Popper believed that science was never about certainty. No matter how well supported a particular theory or hypothesis was, it was always possible that new observations might be made that would undermine it. The classic example of this from the history of science was the paradigm shift from Newtonian physics, once thought to explain absolutely everything, to Einsteinian physics. Although Newton's theory explained virtually all of the data available in his day, Einstein's theory could explain all of those data as well as some observations that had persistently defied explanation in Newtonian terms. Popper viewed the progress of science in terms of the generation and testing of increasingly powerful guesses about the nature of reality.

Thus, Popper proposed that falsifiability provided the solution to the demarcation problem. If a hypothesis or theory is in principle open to falsification, it can be deemed to be scientific. If no observation could ever be made that would lead to the rejection of the hypothesis or theory, it is not scientific. Although this view was highly influential and has much merit, it is now generally accepted that falsifiability alone is not sufficient to solve the demarcation problem.

To give but one objection, it would never be advisable to reject any but the simplest hypothesis on the basis of a single apparent falsification. Although almost all experiments are aimed at testing one or a few primary hypotheses, closer consideration usually reveals that their rationale rests on numerous supporting hypotheses. For example, suppose that you hypothesize that paranormal belief correlates with susceptibility to false memories and you collect data to test your hypothesis. You do not find a statistically significant relationship between your two variables. Should you then reject your hypothesis? Perhaps there really is no such relationship and therefore you would be right to reject your hypothesis. But it is also possible that the hypothesis is true (and, indeed, evidence is presented in Chapter 6 suggesting that it is) but that one of your supporting hypotheses is false. Did you use a valid measure of paranormal belief? Did you use an appropriate measure of susceptibility to false memory? Was your experiment powerful enough in statistical terms to reveal an effect or should you have run more participants? The list goes on.

Does that mean falsifiability is useless as an indicator of the scientific status of a hypothesis or theory? On the contrary, as argued elsewhere (Holt *et al.*, 2012), there are situations where it is helpful to consider falsifiability in assessing hypotheses or theories. If a hypothesis or theory is *in principle* non-falsifiable, then it cannot be scientific. Thus, some creationists argue that God created the world just a few thousand years ago, a claim that is totally at odds with scientific evidence suggesting that our planet is, in fact, billions of years old. The creationists in question dismiss such evidence by arguing that

God created the world with these signs of prior aging, such as fossils in rocks, already in place. Their hypothesis thus becomes non-falsifiable.

In fact, despite a great deal of debate and discussion, it has not proved possible to produce a definitive criterion or set of criteria to distinguish science from non-science. Many commentators would instead agree with Edge *et al.* (1986, p. 311) that, 'although there is no easy definition and although there are no hard and fast criteria by which we can easily judge whether a discipline is scientific, there do seem to be benchmarks of good science'. These benchmarks include such features as replicability, core knowledge and core procedures, use of control conditions, connections with other branches of science, and so on. These benchmarks should not be thought of as absolute criteria but instead as indicators of the extent to which any particular discipline might be judged to be truly scientific.

Given that it has not proven possible to produce a definitive set of criteria to distinguish science from non-science, it will probably come as no surprise that the attempt to produce a definitive set of criteria to characterize pseudoscience has also proven to be problematic (Holt *et al.*, 2012). One definition of 'pseudoscience' is simply 'claims and methods that are falsely presented as science' but this clearly begs the question, 'What is science?' which, as stated, is not an easy question to answer.

This has led to different commentators proposing different sets of characteristics as being indicative of an area of intellectual activity being a pseudoscience. Thus Mario Bunge argued that a pseudoscience has the following features (as summarized by Alcock, 1981, p. 117):

- Its theory of knowledge is subjectivistic, containing aspects accessible only to the initiated.
- Its formal background is modest, with only rare involvement of mathematics or logic.
- Its fund of knowledge contains untestable or even false hypotheses which are in conflict with a larger body of knowledge.
- Its methods are neither checkable by alternative methods nor justifiable in terms of well-confirmed theories.
- It borrows nothing from neighbouring fields; there is no overlap with another field of research.
- It has no specific background of relatively confirmed theories.
- It has an unchanging body of belief, whereas scientific enquiry teems with novelty.
- It has a worldview admitting elusive immaterial entities, such as disembodied minds, whereas science countenances only changing concrete things.

Radner and Radner (1982) presented their nine 'marks of pseudoscience', arguing that such signs are only ever found in 'crackpot work and never in genuine scientific work'. These marks included anachronistic thinking, the tendency to 'look for mysteries', a 'grab-bag approach to evidence' (ignoring the actual quality of the evidence), irrefutable hypotheses, the use of the 'argument from spurious similarity', and refusal to revise theories in the light of criticism.

An alternative list of features was proposed by Scott O. Lilienfeld (2005). He proposed that pseudosciences tend to have the following features:

- A tendency to invoke ad hoc hypotheses, which can be thought of as 'escape hatches' or loopholes, as a means of immunizing claims from falsification.
- An absence of self-correction and an accompanying intellectual stagnation.
- An emphasis on confirmation rather than refutation.
- A tendency to place the burden of proof on sceptics, not proponents, of claims.
- Excessive reliance on anecdotal and testimonial evidence to substantiate claims.
- Evasion of the scrutiny afforded by peer review.
- Absence of 'connectivity' ... that is, a failure to build on existing scientific knowledge.
- Use of impressive-sounding jargon whose primary purpose is to lend claims a façade of scientific respectability.
- An absence of boundary conditions ... that is, a failure to specify the settings under which claims do not hold.

Several other such lists have been proposed and it is immediately obvious that although there is a lot of overlap between them, there is also considerable variation. This should come as no surprise given that it is unlikely that a universally agreed definitive set of criteria for separating science from pseudoscience exists given the inherent difficulty of definitively defining science in the first place.

Some of the commentators who have put forward such lists have argued that if an area of activity meets even one of the criteria proposed, it should be condemned as a pseudoscience (e.g. Radner & Radner, 1982). Others have taken a more nuanced approach, arguing that it is more realistic to think of science and pseudoscience as being extremes on a continuum (e.g. Lilienfeld, Lynn, & Lohr, 2003). A few prototypical sciences (e.g. physics and chemistry) may well score very highly on virtually all of the benchmarks of 'good science' and a few prototypical pseudosciences (e.g. homeopathy and astrology) may score highly on most of the benchmarks of pseudoscience. But many disciplines, including parts of psychology, will score somewhere in between. Thus a more nuanced approach is called for, acknowledging that each discipline must be assessed for the degree to which it meets the proposed criteria of science and pseudoscience and then an overall judgement made. We find ourselves in sympathy with the latter approach.

A few commentators (e.g. McNally, 2003b; Truzzi, 1996) have gone so far as to argue that the fuzziness of the concept of pseudoscience means that it would be preferable to simply stop using it. Once again, however, we feel more sympathy for the view of Lilienfeld, Lynn, and Lohr (2003, p. 5) who argue:

> As psychophysicist S. S. Stevens observed, the fact that the precise boundary between day and night is indistinct does not imply that day and night cannot be meaningfully differentiated ... From this perspective, pseudosciences can be conceptualized as possessing a fallible, but nevertheless useful, list of indicators or 'warning signs.' The more such warning signs a discipline exhibits, the more it begins to cross the murky dividing line separating science from pseudoscience.

Having set the stage, we are now in a position to address the question posed at the beginning of this chapter: what is the scientific status of parapsychology? Is it really a science or simply a pseudoscience posing as true science? How does it measure up against some of the most commonly presented indicators of pseudoscience? Marie-Catherine Mousseau (2003b) adopted an empirical approach in addressing this question. She compared the contents of a sample of mainstream journals, such as *Molecular and Optical Physics* and the *British Journal of Psychology*, with the contents of a sample of 'fringe' journals, such as the *Journal of Parapsychology* and the *Journal of Scientific Exploration*. Contrary to what many critics of parapsychology might have expected, the 'fringe' journals came out rather well from the comparison.

For example, unlike many pseudosciences, parapsychology does not have a greater emphasis on confirmation in contrast to refutation. In fact, she found that 'almost half of the fringe articles report a negative outcome (disconfirmation). By contrast, no report of a negative result has been found in my sample of mainstream journals' (Mousseau, 2003b, p. 274). There was also little evidence of 'an unchanging body of belief' in parapsychology with 17% of the 'fringe' articles dealing with theory and proposing new hypotheses.

Was there evidence of an 'excessive reliance on anecdotal and testimonial evidence to substantiate claims' as seen in other pseudosciences? No. '43% of articles in the fringe journals deal with empirical matters and almost one-fourth report laboratory experiments' (Mousseau, 2003b, p. 273). Was there an 'absence of self-correction'? No. Parapsychology seems to score higher on this criterion than mainstream sciences: '29% of the fringe-journal articles ... discuss progress of research, problems encountered, epistemological issues. This kind of article is completely absent from the mainstream sample' (p. 275). What about connections to other fields of research? Mousseau (2003b) found that over a third of citations in fringe journals were of articles in mainstream science journals, such as physics, psychology, and neuroscience journals. In contrast, mainstream science articles overwhelmingly cited articles in the same field (90% of the time in the sample as a whole but 99% in the physics journals).

Similar results were found by Mousseau (2003b) with respect to a number of other commonly presented criteria of pseudoscience. Parapsychology fell a little short on some of them but often appeared to do rather better than mainstream science on others. It would therefore appear to be unjustified to classify parapsychology as a pseudoscience. The main point is that science, however we may define it, is not an established body of certain facts; it is a method for approaching the truth. Parapsychology, at its best, appears to adhere to scientific methodology and therefore there is little reason to dismiss it as a pseudoscience. It should be noted that this is probably a minority view among critics of parapsychology. It may appear to be slightly odd for us to be arguing that parapsychology is a legitimate science when it is clear from the other chapters in this book that we ourselves are far from convinced that paranormal forces even exist. However, in terms of the most commonly presented indicators of science and pseudoscience, this appears to us to be the correct verdict.

Parapsychology and the mind–body problem

The mind–body problem is one of the most fundamental problems in philosophy. It has challenged the greatest thinkers for centuries and for this reason is nowadays often referred to as the **hard problem**, a term first coined by philosopher David Chalmers (1995). In his words, 'The hard problem ... is the question of how physical processes in the brain give rise to subjective experience' (Chalmers, 1995, p. 63). There have been many books written attempting to provide solutions to this puzzle but to date no one has provided a solution that has received general acceptance and approval. It looks like the hard problem will be with us for a long time to come. Although in one sense we all know what consciousness is as a result of simply being a living human being, in another sense none of us really understands it (for a more detailed discussion of attempts to solve the hard problem, see Blackmore, 2004).

Essentially, the problem relates to the fact that, for most people, the idea of *dualism* is intuitively very appealing. We naturally make a distinction between the physical world out there and our own inner subjective mental experience. They seem to be very different things. Objects out in the real world have various properties such as colour, movement, degrees of solidity, and so on, and other people can experience these objects in, we assume, more or less the same way that we do. Most of us take it for granted that there is a real objective universe out there that we all live in. But our mental experiences are not like that at all. No one else can experience our thoughts, our emotions and our sensations in the same way that we do. They are private and unsharable. We can try to describe them to others in words but that does not come close to how it feels to actually experience them.

Such intuitions have led many people, perhaps most notably the great French philosopher and mathematician René Descartes (1596–1650), to argue that there are indeed two fundamental sorts of stuff in our universe: the physical and the mental. The physical world is the world out there consisting of matter and energy, including rocks, trees, animals, stars, light – and even human brains. In contrast, the mental world is not located in a specific physical space. Descartes described it as non-spatial and indivisible. This unextended 'thinking stuff' is what minds are made of.

It is easy to see why dualism is appealing. We might be willing to accept that certain sets of neurons fire in a certain way in our brains whenever we experience the colour red but most of us do not feel comfortable with the idea that the pattern of neural firing is *identical* to our subjective experience of seeing the colour red. They appear to be two different kinds of things. The big problem for dualism is to explain how the physical world can have any effect on an immaterial mind and *vice versa*. How could light of a particular wavelength reflecting off the surface of a red apple into your eye, causing particular cells to fire in your visual system, ultimately produce the subjective experience of redness in an immaterial mind? Conversely, how could your subjective mental desire to eat that apple cause a pattern of neural impulses within your physical brain to ultimately result in movements of your physical body as you grab and eat the apple?

There have been, as stated, numerous attempts to solve the mind–body problem. One approach has been to posit some special mechanism whereby the mental and the physical can indeed interact. Descartes, for example, suggested that such interaction might take place in the pineal gland. More recently, philosopher Sir Karl Popper and neurophysiologist Sir John Eccles proposed a version of dualist interactionism, arguing that critical processes in certain parts of the brain are so finely poised that they can, indeed, be affected by a non-physical self (Popper & Eccles, 1977). But like Descartes, they completely failed to explain exactly how this could happen. This apparently insurmountable problem of explaining how two fundamentally different types of stuff could ever interact has resulted in dualism having very few supporters nowadays among philosophers and scientists.

But if dualism does not work, how are we to explain the mystery of consciousness? If there is no conceivable way in which the mental and the physical as conceived of by Descartes could possibly interact, might it be the case that the universe contains only one kind of substance, either the mental or the physical? Attempts to solve the hard problem by taking such approaches are examples of **monism** and, as you might expect, come in two main categories. At one extreme are those approaches that argue that ultimately only the mental really exists. Such a view is often referred to as **idealism** and one of its most famous proponents was Bishop Berkeley (1685–1753). One difficulty for such idealist approaches is that they make it 'very hard to understand why physical objects seem to have enduring qualities that we can all agree upon – or indeed how science is possible at all' (Blackmore, 2004, p. 9).

In contrast, materialists reject the mental and argue that all is physical. In this view, the whole universe, including our brains, is subject to the same laws of nature and there is simply no place for immaterial entities such as minds to influence events. There are different varieties of this *materialist* approach, including **identity theory** (which argues that mental states are literally identical to physical states) and **functionalism** (which equates mental states with functional states). One difficulty with this viewpoint is the basic objection that subjectively mental states appear to be qualitatively different to patterns of neural activity as already discussed.

Another approach to solving the problem is **epiphenomenalism**, the argument that mental states are indeed caused by physical changes in the brain but that they have no causal role to play. In other words, our subjective sense of consciousness is a mere by-product of the interactions of physical and chemical processes in our brains despite our strong impressions that we are, for example, capable of acting through our own free will. This approach was championed by English biologist and palaeontologist Thomas Henry Huxley (1825–95). Suffice it to say that neither this approach nor any other has satisfactorily solved the hard problem in the eyes of most philosophers and scientists.

Most modern neuroscientists would probably classify themselves as materialists, albeit while still recognizing that the hard problem has not yet been solved. In general, they would assume that consciousness is entirely dependent upon the underlying neural substrate of the brain. There is indeed a vast amount of empirical evidence that is consistent with that viewpoint, including the effects of drugs, brain stimulation, and brain damage on the mind and behaviour. Neuroscientists would also, in general, argue that consciousness cannot become separated from the brain. But several claims within parapsychology would appear to be at odds with that position. People who have OBEs are convinced that they have experienced at first hand precisely such a separation. Indeed, they often report that they can view their physical bodies beneath them as they view the scene from above.

All evidence in favour of life after death is also evidence against this fundamental assumption of modern neuroscience. Clearly, if some aspect of our consciousness survives the destruction of the physical brain, then consciousness cannot be entirely dependent upon the brain. Note that it would be possible in principle for mind and body to be separable without this necessarily proving that consciousness (or, if you prefer, 'the soul') survives death. It is possible to conceive of scenarios in which the mind can become separated from the brain but only while the brain is alive. There is no doubt, however, that proof that mental states are not entirely dependent upon brain states would go a long way towards making the idea of *post-mortem* survival more plausible.

Let us just reflect for a moment on some of the many ways in which paranormal claims often appear to support the notion that consciousness is separable from the physical brain and thus potentially provide support for a strongly dualist position. The most obvious example is the OBE. If OBEs really are what they appear to be to the person having the experience, then it follows that our sense of subjective awareness of our surroundings is not, as commonly assumed, entirely dependent upon our physical sensory systems but that instead it is possible to see without using our eyes, to hear without using our ears, and so on. If your consciousness (or your 'soul', as some readers might prefer) can leave your physical body under certain circumstances, the idea that whatever leaves your body during OBEs might also survive your own physical death appears to be much more likely.

As discussed in Chapter 5, there are alternative explanations for OBEs that explain them as being a complex hallucinatory experience that does not involve consciousness actually leaving the physical body. The evidence in favour of such explanations continues to accumulate but it is worth noting that OBEs potentially provide a very direct way to prove that such separation is possible. It is difficult to evaluate the true nature of such experiences in the context of NDEs because of the spontaneous and unpredictable nature of NDEs. But it is not impossible. A number of hospitals around the world have taken part in studies for a number of years involving the placing of concealed target pictures on hospital wards, typically coronary care units. These target pictures can only be viewed from a position above the picture near to the ceiling. The idea is that if a patient suffers a heart attack and has an OBE as part of an NDE, they may be able to report back the nature of the target image upon recovery. Such evidence would be very difficult to explain away from a sceptical perspective and would indeed provide reasonably strong *prima facie* evidence that consciousness could be separated from the brain. To date, no reports of success in identifying the hidden targets have been reported from such studies, despite several reports of NDEs.

In Chapter 10 it was pointed out that some individuals claim to be able to induce OBEs more or less at will by means of various mental exercises. In principle, therefore, it would be much easier to investigate the true nature of OBEs using such individuals rather than via NDEs. It would take only a single individual who could reliably report under properly controlled conditions upon events or objects at remote locations via the use of OBEs to establish once and for all that a fundamental assumption of modern neuroscience is mistaken. Despite over a century of anecdotal claims to the contrary, there is no convincing evidence that anyone actually has such an ability.

The idea that our minds do somehow survive our bodily death is inherent in most major world religions and is believed by the vast majority of the inhabitants of our planet – despite the fact that most neuroscientists, the people who know most about the workings of the brain, would probably reject it. As described in Chapter 5, there are a few scientists who take a different approach, arguing, for example, that NDEs provide strong evidence that consciousness can not only leave the body but may even provide a glimpse of an afterlife. Such arguments should not be taken seriously, however, for the simple reason that the person reporting the experience did not, in fact, die – they must have survived to tell the tale!

A few neuroscientists have argued that NDEs simply cannot be explained in terms of current neuroscientific assumptions because modern neuroscience cannot explain how higher cognitive functions such as perception and memory can take place in the absence of cortical activity. Thus van Lommel *et al.* (2001, p. 2044) ask, 'How could a clear consciousness outside one's body be experienced at the moment that the brain no longer functions during a period of clinical death with flat EEG?' (van Lommel *et al.*, 2001, p. 2044). Similarly, Parnia and Fenwick (2002, p. 8) write,

> The occurrence of lucid, well structured thought processes together with reasoning, attention and memory recall of specific events during a cardiac arrest (NDE) raise a number of interesting and perplexing questions regarding how such experiences could arise. These experiences appear to be occurring at a time when cerebral function can be described at best as severely impaired, and at worst absent.

Such claims have been severely criticized on a number of grounds, some of which were presented in Chapter 5. In addition to the arguments presented there, Crislip (2008) points out that it is grossly misleading to describe the patients being referred to as 'clinically dead'. In his words (Crislip, 2008, p. 14): 'Having your heart stop for 2 to 10 minutes and being promptly resuscitated doesn't make you "clinically dead". It only means your heart isn't beating and you may not be conscious.'

In the most comprehensive rebuttal of such claims to date, Braithwaite (2008b) points out that, among many other objections, such arguments appear to be based upon over-reliance on the power of surface EEG recordings as indicating brain activity within different regions of the brain. Isoelectric surface EEG recordings (i.e. the so-called flatlining) is not necessarily an indication of total brain inactivity, as there may still be activity in deeper brain areas such as the amygdala and hippocampus. Complex and meaningful hallucinations can be generated by discharges in these areas without the involvement of any cortical activity (Gloor, 1986). Toa *et al.* (2005) present convincing data to show that high-amplitude seizure activity may be taking place in deep brain regions but be undetectable by surface EEG recordings. Kobayashi *et al.* (2006), in a study comparing the fMRI blood-oxygen-level dependent (BOLD) response with surface EEG recordings, showed that surface EEG could sometimes even fail to detect seizure activity that was taking place in the cortex.

The interested reader is referred Crislip (2008), Braithwaite (2008b), and French (2009b), who raise many other telling objections to the arguments currently being put forward to suggest that NDEs take place during a period of 'brain death' and thus constitute a major challenge to neuroscience. Although it would be premature to claim that we have a complete explanation of NDEs, it is certainly the case that the evidence available is consistent with the fundamental assumption that consciousness cannot, in fact, become separated from the physical brain.

Most of the scientists who would disagree with this conclusion are presumably basing their opinions upon their assessment of the NDEs of other people, but at least one based his opinion upon his own personal NDE. Neurosurgeon Dr Eben Alexander experienced a very vivid NDE in 2008 after he contracted a rare form of bacterial meningitis. He subsequently wrote an account of his experience in a best-selling book, *Proof of Heaven: A Neurosurgeon's Journey into the Afterlife* (Alexander, 2012). The book was very well received and many favourable commentators seemed to assume that the claim that NDEs provide a genuine glimpse of an afterlife was somehow a lot more plausible simply because the person making the claim was a neurosurgeon. This is a common logical fallacy referred to as the *argument from authority*. Any claim should be assessed on its own merits in terms of reasoning and evidence – and on that basis, Dr Alexander's claims were woefully inadequate (for critiques, see, for example, Blakemore, 2012; Harris, 2012).

There are many other paranormal claims that relate to the possibility of life after death, many of which have been examined in previous chapters of this book. For example, if reincarnation claims were supported by compelling evidence, this would prove beyond reasonable doubt that consciousness could not only be separated from the physical brain and survive the death of the physical body but that it could somehow then survive in limbo for a while before becoming attached to a new physical brain. It goes without saying that no one has ever come close to proposing exactly what processes this would involve. On balance, the evidence very strongly supports the idea that apparent past-life memories are, in fact, false memories.

Many people believe that ghosts are spirits of the deceased, but the vast majority of the evidence put forward in support of the existence of ghosts can easily be accounted for in terms of such factors as the imperfections of human perception and memory, anomalous experiences such as sleep paralysis and other forms of hallucination, sincere misinterpretation of natural phenomena, and occasional deliberate hoaxes (see, for example, French, 2013).

The claims of mediums to be able to communicate with the dead generally do not seem to fare well when tested under properly controlled conditions and their apparent abilities appear to be explicable in terms of cold reading, either deliberate or unintentional, and hot reading (i.e. obtaining information about sitters by non-paranormal means). In fact, all of the various types of evidence that have been put forward to support the idea of life after death do not survive close critical scrutiny. At least for the time being, parapsychological evidence is incapable of proving the dualists right.

Suggested further reading

For useful guidelines on distinguishing science from pseudoscience:

Lilienfeld, S. (2005). 'The 10 commandments of helping students distinguish science from pseudoscience in psychology'. *Observer*, 18, 39–40 & 49–51.

For specific consideration of the scientific status of parapsychology:

Holt, N., Simmonds-Moore, C., Luke, D., & French, C. C. (2012). *Anomalistic Psychology*. Basingstoke: Palgrave Macmillan. Chapter 5, pp. 77–88.

For a comprehensive introduction to the topic of consciousness:

Blackmore, S. J. (2004). *Consciousness: An introduction*. Oxford: Oxford University Press.

Future Prospects of Anomalistic Psychology and Parapsychology

12

Introduction

Although we still have much to learn regarding many of the topics covered in this book, we feel justified in asserting that anomalistic psychology has made real progress in providing plausible, empirically supported, non-paranormal accounts of a wide range of ostensibly paranormal experiences. As shown in the previous chapters, each of the sub-disciplines of psychology provides a perspective that gives insight into understanding anomalous experiences and related beliefs. Typically, however, a full understanding of all but the simplest phenomena in this field requires consideration from several perspectives and thus there is a real need for more integrated theories in many areas. We hope that this book contributes in some small way to the development of such theories. The remainder of this short chapter will give our personal perspective on the future prospects for anomalistic psychology and parapsychology.

Future prospects of anomalistic psychology

As argued elsewhere, we feel that anomalistic psychology has a bright future (French, 2011b). It is fair to say that, in one sense, anomalistic psychology has quite a long history. For example, two centuries ago, Dr John Ferriar was arguing that reports of ghosts were based upon optical illusions (Ferriar, 1813) and 40 years later French physician Alexandre Jacques François Brière de Boismont put forward an explanation of the same phenomenon in terms of hallucinations (Brière de Boismont, 1853). In 1886, British psychiatrist Henry Maudsley argued that so-called supernatural experiences could be explained in terms of disorders of the mind, along with misperceptions and misinterpretations of naturally occurring phenomena (Maudsley, 1886). A century ago, Karl Jaspers argued that all ostensibly paranormal experiences were based upon psychiatric symptoms (Jaspers, 1913).

Although we would question such heavy emphasis upon explanations of ostensibly paranormal experiences in purely psychiatric terms, these early contributions are notable for attempting to provide non-paranormal explanations for such phenomena. Several other such contributions could also have been cited. It remains the case, however, that such publications appeared sporadically at best until fairly recently. The term *anomalistic psychology* was first used by Leonard Zusne and Warren H. Jones in 1982 in their textbook with that title (a second edition followed in 1989). From that point on, the number of papers in academic journals and books on anomalistic psychology has increased steadily, along with conference presentations and media coverage. Several recent popular science bestsellers have been devoted exclusively to the subject matter of anomalistic psychology (e.g. Hood, 2009; Hutson, 2012; Shermer, 2011; Wiseman, 2011), thus bringing the findings and insights of recent research to a wider audience. Anomalistic psychology is now offered as an option at an increasing number of universities in the UK and elsewhere and is even offered as an option on the UK's most popular A2 syllabus (French, 2009a, 2009c; Holt *et al.*, 2012).

Why is anomalistic psychology such a popular subject among students and the general public? There are several reasons (French, 2001a). Among them is the wide range of topics covered. These include, at one extreme, highly entertaining and informative topics such as the psychology of magic (e.g. Kuhn, Amlani, & Rensink, 2008; Lamont & Wiseman, 1999; Macnick & Martinez-Conde, 2010) and the techniques used by deliberate con artists to fool others into thinking that they, the con artists, have genuine psychic ability (e.g. Hyman, 1977; Keene, 1976; Randi, 1982a, 1982b, 1987; Rowland, 2002). As well as providing genuine insights into human psychology, such publications also serve a purpose in terms of consumer protection by informing readers of telltale signs of trickery.

At the other extreme, both anomalistic psychology and parapsychology touch on some of the most profound issues facing us as human beings. Do we survive bodily death? What is the nature of consciousness? Is the mind simply 'what the brain does' or can the mind become separated from the physical brain? If so, how could an immaterial mind interact with an immaterial brain? Needless to say, the answers to these questions have obvious implications for other issues deemed to be of central importance to human beings, not least those relating to religious issues.

Anomalistic psychology also focuses upon challenging issues relating to the nature of evidence and enquiry. How can we distinguish between science and pseudoscience? Why should we give more weight to some forms of evidence than others? In particular, why is direct personal experience, contrary to what most people believe, often an unreliable form of evidence? All of these questions and more are addressed in anomalistic psychology with reference to such fascinating topics as ESP, PK, ghosts, aliens, reincarnation, psychics, and so on. These are topics that most people, whether believers or sceptics, find inherently intriguing as shown by the widespread media coverage they receive. They are the stuff of many conversations in the pub or arguments at dinner parties. Thus they make a great 'hook' for getting people thinking about more general issues relating to what is real and what is not.

Many of the topics covered in anomalistic psychology courses implicitly provide excellent training in critical thinking. There is an emphasis upon basing claims on solid evidence and sound reasoning as opposed to anecdote, intuition, or appeals to authority. Many critical thinking courses at schools and universities make use of examples from anomalistic psychology as case studies to illustrate the cognitive pitfalls that await the unwary in assessing controversial claims. Furthermore, many of the topics covered provide striking and persuasive examples of the biases in memory, perception, and reasoning that afflict human cognition.

With respect to research, anomalistic psychology has a reciprocal relationship with the rest of psychology. It is one of those branches of psychology that is defined in terms of its subject matter, like forensic or consumer psychology, as opposed to its general approach and perspective, as in developmental, social, or cognitive psychology. As the chapters in this book illustrate, each of these perspectives can offer different and useful insights with respect to our attempts to understand anomalous experience and belief. Experiments in anomalistic psychology often involve the application of a theory or concept developed in another branch of psychology to a specific phenomenon in the anomalistic realm. Thus we might investigate whether post-event misinformation can lead to people misremembering the details of a psychic reading (Wilson & French, 2008–9) or whether some people might be influenced by non-consciously processed information in such a way that it could lead them to believe they themselves were psychic (Crawley, French, & Yesson, 2002). Such studies are valuable insofar as they provide solid empirical evidence in support of the claim that many ostensibly paranormal experiences may be adequately explained in non-paranormal terms. It is not enough for those who are sceptical of paranormal claims to merely provide speculative, albeit plausible, non-paranormal explanations for such phenomena. They should always, wherever possible, back up such speculation with empirical evidence. The burden of proof always rests with those making a claim, whether that claim is paranormal or non-paranormal in nature.

The lessons learned and conclusions drawn from anomalistic psychology often have great relevance to wider issues within psychology. One of the themes that runs through anomalistic psychology is that of the pervasive effects of belief upon other aspects of cognition. In the case of anomalistic psychology, we are typically considering the effects of paranormal or related beliefs upon cognition and behaviour but the lessons learned are likely to also apply to other forms of belief including political and religious beliefs – and even our attitudes towards celebrities and sports stars!

It is often the case that knowledge from anomalistic psychology is of relevance in evaluating controversial claims that, on the surface, appear to be entirely unrelated to the topics covered in this book. For example, back in the mid-1970s an Australian teacher named Rosemary Crossley invented a new technique that was intended to allow those suffering from autism, cerebral palsy, and other disorders that prevent speech to communicate with the outside world. The basic idea was simple. It was claimed that if another person, referred to as a *facilitator*, held the hand of the impaired individual over a computer keyboard or letter board, the patient could then spell out messages letter by letter. The technique was known as **facilitated communication** and it appeared to be a major breakthrough. Children and adults who had previously been completely unable to communicate with the outside world suddenly had a means whereby they could express themselves, sometimes even producing poetry. The technique was introduced into the US by sociologist Douglas Biklen and spread around the world. From the outset, however, there were doubters. The breakthrough appeared to many to be simply too good to be true (Brugger, 2001; Jacobson, Mulick, & Schwartz, 1995; Spitz, 1997; Wegner, 2002). For example, most of the patients involved had never had any training in written language. What is more, they often appeared to be typing out their messages without even looking at the keyboard!

Turning to a seemingly unrelated news story, in January 2010, a report by the BBC's *Newsnight* programme informed viewers that the Iraqi government had spent around $85 million (£52 million) on British-made devices known as ADE-651s (Hawley & Jones, 2010). The devices were used as bomb detectors, at a cost of $40,000 each, and were in use not only in Iraq but also in Afghanistan and many other countries around the world. They consisted of a swivelling metal rod connected to a handheld grip and were said to work on a similar principal to dowsing, a centuries-old technique said to enable the detection of water using branches or metal dowsing rods. The company that manufactured the ADE-651 claimed that under ideal conditions, it could detect explosives up to 1 kilometre away. Amazingly, by changing a card within the device, it was claimed that it could also be used to detect people, elephants, and even $100 bills!

What do these two stories have in common, apart from the fact that they are both promoting techniques that appear to verge on the miraculous? Familiarity with anomalistic psychology provides the answer: both claims are based upon the **ideomotor effect**. This is an effect whereby suggestions, beliefs, or expectations cause unconscious muscular movements. The ideomotor effect provides the explanation for a number of ostensibly paranormal phenomena. For example, at the height of the Victorian popularity of séances, an initially American craze caught on in Britain and Europe – that of so-called table tilting. In these sessions, sitters would sit around a table resting their hands upon its upper surface. After a period of time, the table would, it was claimed, move, apparently of its own volition. Initial movements might simply be slight jerks but in a successful session, sitters might find themselves chasing around the room trying to keep up with the table. Naturally, all of the sitters would deny that they were simply pushing the table. It was claimed that the movements of the table could be used as a means of communicating with the spirit world, and indeed its movement was generally thought to be brought about by the actions of spirits. This phenomenon has a special place in the history of anomalistic psychology insofar as it attracted the attention of Michael Faraday, the famous English physicist (Hyman, 1985a). He carried out a series of ingenious experimental investigations that established that, despite the protestations of the sitters to the contrary, it was in fact the case that unintentional muscular movements caused the table to move. This was one of the first systematic studies of the ideomotor effect.

The ideomotor effect also explains a number of other ostensibly paranormal phenomena including Ouija boards and dowsing. Ouija boards, which are also sometimes referred to as *spirit boards*, typically consist of a round board marked with all of the letters of the alphabet, the digits one to nine, and the words 'yes' and 'no'. Sitters place their fingers lightly on a specially constructed heart-shaped piece of wood known as a *planchette* and proceed to address questions to the spirit world. The technique also works simply by using letters and numbers written on pieces of paper and arranged in a circle on a smooth table, along with an upturned wine glass in place of a planchette. Amazingly, in response to questions, the planchette (or wine glass) often appears to move around pointing to various letters and numbers to relay the responses back from the spirits – although this only seems to work if at least some of the sitters have their fingers in contact with the pointing device. Once again, we are dealing with an example of the ideomotor effect. Although the illusion that the pointer is being moved by some outside force is extremely strong, the truth is that the sitters are actually moving it without realizing it.

Dowsers claim to be able to locate water or other substances by using Y-shaped twigs, L-shaped dowsing rods, or pendulums. They claim that the dowsing instrument will suddenly move, apparently of its own accord, when held in the vicinity of the target substance. Some dowsers go further and claim that dowsing can be used to locate pretty much anything – and some go further still by claiming that the dowser does not even need to be physically near the target and can instead use the technique to locate the target on a map!

Sadly, properly controlled double-blind tests of dowsing repeatedly show that if dowsers are unaware of the correct target location, their performance is no better than guesswork (e.g. Randi, 1982a; French, 2012c). However, on trials where the dowser is aware of the target location (or else is able to guess it thanks to available cues), the dowsing reaction takes place as expected. The illusion can be very strong that the reaction is due to some external force, but in fact it is once again due to non-conscious muscular activity on the part of the dowser.

The reader has probably guessed by now what the *Newsnight* exposé revealed. Not surprisingly, as the ADE-651 was based upon the same principles as dowsing, it had the same level of effectiveness – that is to say, absolutely none. These expensive bits of allegedly hi-tech kit were in fact nothing more than junk and had never once been proven capable of detecting explosives (let alone elephants) under properly controlled conditions. The real tragedy here, of course, is that in all probability hundreds of lives were lost in terrorist explosions because Iraqi security forces were relying on a technique that is nothing more than pseudoscience. In May 2013, James McCormick, who is thought to have made around £50 million from the sale of these devices, was jailed for ten years.

How does this relate to the use of facilitated communication? Sadly, it turned out that the doubters were correct. Facilitated communication simply did not work, despite the apparently amazing results that had been achieved. The messages were not from the patients at all – they were the result of non-conscious muscular movements on the part of the facilitators. This was proven quite conclusively to be the case in well-controlled double-blind tests where either the facilitator knew the correct answer to a question and the patient did not or *vice versa*. In the former case, if the facilitator thought the patient knew the right answer, it would be given. In the latter case, the correct answer was never forthcoming (Brugger, 2001; Jacobson, Mulick, & Schwartz, 1995; Spitz, 1997; Wegner, 2002). These are but two cases where knowledge of the findings of anomalistic psychology would have averted tragic outcomes. Many others could be cited.

Although anomalistic psychology has a long history – and, as the aforesaid illustrates, valuable insights can still be gained from studying the findings of pioneering early studies in the field – it is undoubtedly the case that anomalistic psychology is still a small and specialized sub-discipline within psychology as a whole. However, there are many indications, as described, that it is a steadily growing sub-discipline that, in addition to being inherently fascinating and a fantastic tool to teach critical thinking skills, also provides important insights into understanding a range of phenomena beyond the boundaries of the sub-discipline itself.

Future prospects of parapsychology

What then are the future prospects of parapsychology? Inevitably, answers to this question will reflect the biases of the respondents and readers should bear this in mind in reading our own personal assessment. Neither of the co-authors of this book is persuaded by the currently available evidence that psi exists but we do believe that a properly scientific and sceptical attitude must acknowledge the theoretical possibility that future research findings may prove our position to be mistaken. Furthermore, we believe that the currently available evidence is sufficiently complex and ambiguous that both proponents and critics of the psi hypothesis can be considered to be defending intellectually respectable positions. Real progress depends upon an honest and open dialogue between proponents and critics as argued by Morris (2000) and is not helped by the kind of *ad hominen* attacks that all too often characterize the comments of those at either extreme of the spectrum of opinions. One admirable attempt to facilitate such dialogue is the collection of chapters edited by Krippner and Friedman (2010).

We will begin our discussion with the views of one well-known and vocal proponent of the paranormal, those of Dean Radin (1997b, 2006). Radin argues strongly that the evidence in support of the existence of psi is over-whelming and that only ignorance and prejudice on the part of most scientists stands in the way of the universal acknowledgment of this fact. In his words (Radin, 1997b, p. 275):

> [T]he effects observed in a thousand psi experiments are not due to chance, selective reporting, variations in experimental quality, or design flaws. They've been independently replicated by competent, convention-ally trained scientists at well-known academic, industrial, and govern-ment-supported laboratories worldwide for more than a century.

If Radin is correct in his assessment, the future prospects for parapsychology are good. It may take some time for the wider scientific community to catch up with the forward-thinking parapsychologists, but the history of science shows repeatedly that sometimes ideas that are rejected at the time they are first pro-posed are eventually accepted when the accumulated empirical evidence in their favour is simply too overwhelming to ignore. Radin appears to believe that such a tipping point is imminent.

It will not have escaped the reader's notice, however, that Radin's assessment of the current state of the evidence in parapsychology is considerably more positive than our own (see Chapter 10). How is it that different commentators can examine the same body of research findings and yet come to such radically different conclusions? The answer, of course, is that the processes involved in judgement are affected by prior beliefs every bit as much as those involved in perception and memory. Confirmation bias will be at play for both believers and sceptics when they attempt to get to grips with the confusing and contra-dictory findings reported in parapsychology journals. Ultimately, all we can do in these pages is to present our reasons for disagreeing with Radin and other proponents and readers must draw their own conclusions regarding where the truth lies.

Elsewhere, one of us (French, 2010a, 2010b) reflected on what it would take to change his opinion from believing that psi probably does not exist to believ-ing that it probably does. Among other suggestions, it was pointed out that any kind of practical application of psi would be sufficient to silence sceptics. In the same volume, Dean Radin (2010, p. 25) made the following brave prediction:

> Before 2015, we may see a few psi applications in common use for enhancing intuition, and psi-based methods may be used to improve the efficiency of some electronic, biochemical and biological processes. It is also conceivable that the Western world will be shocked one day when long-simmering rumors about psi applications in China are officially unveiled and found to be true.

At the time of writing (March 2013), no such applications appear to be on the immediate horizon.

The truth is that the history of parapsychology appears to be a history of false dawns. The elusive goal of a robust and replicable demonstration of psi is often promised but to date has never been delivered. For example, there is not a single demonstration of a psi effect that could be used as the basis for a first-year practical psychology class with a reasonable chance that the alleged psi effect would actually be demonstrated. In contrast, there are dozens of psychological effects relating to memory, perception, and attention that rarely fail to be reliably demonstrated on demand. However, that is not to say that it is only parapsychology that has problems with replication. In fact, psychology itself is currently going through a healthy period of critical self-examination with respect to such issues as replication problems and publication bias and many of the issues raised are of direct relevance to parapsychology.

As described in Chapter 10, Ritchie, Wiseman, and French (2012a) initially found that their failed attempts to replicate Bem's (2011) controversial results were rejected by three high-impact journals without even being sent out for peer review. This highlighted the problem of publication bias within psychology. The fact is that currently most high-impact journals simply refuse to consider direct replications despite the fact that it is often claimed that 'replication is the cornerstone of science'. Furthermore, such journals are highly unlikely to publish non-significant findings. The result is that many of the 'top' psychology journals give a grossly misleading impression of the state of research within the discipline insofar as there is a strong bias towards publishing significant and novel findings (Ritchie, Wiseman, & French, 2012b; see also French, 2012a, 2012d). It is highly likely, therefore, that many of the novel (and often counter-intuitive) effects reported in such journals are of questionable robustness. Many of them may have arisen as a result of spuriously significant results due to *post hoc* trawling of data for any kind of departure from chance expectation, inappropriate statistical analysis, or as a result of unidentified methodological flaws.

Such concerns have resulted in a number of reflective papers and special sections in publications dealing specifically with the issue of replication in psychology (e.g. Ritchie, Wiseman, & French, 2012b, and associated commentaries; special section of *Perspectives on Psychological Science*, edited by Pashler & Wagenmakers, 2012). Many of the issues raised are directly relevant to parapsychology. For example, Simmons, Nelson, and Simonsohn (2011) present a compelling case to show that false-positive findings must actually be reported at a much higher rate than the 5% level implied by the alpha level typically taken to be the critical level for statistical significance. This is because of the flexibility that researchers have in terms of data collection, selection and analysis. This flexibility is usually not apparent from the final published article. For example, researchers may choose to test for significance after running 20 observations per condition in an experiment with two conditions. If a significant effect is found, the researchers cease data collection and report their findings. If not, they run another ten observations per condition and again test for significance. This seemingly trivial departure from best practice will raise the false-positive rate by approximately 50%. By using computer simulations to investigate the effects of combining a number of such small departures from best practice, Simmons, Nelson, and Simonsohn were able to show that one could quite quickly end up with a false-positive rate of 61%. In other words, it is often the case that it becomes more likely than not that a false-positive result will be found!

Simmons, Nelson, and Simonsohn (2011) went further in hammering their message home by presenting the results of two actual experiments 'that demonstrate how unacceptably easy it is to accumulate (and report) statistically significant evidence for a false hypothesis' (p. 1359). In their first study, they demonstrated that an unlikely hypothesis was supported by real data: that listening to a children's song can make participants feel older. In their second study, they demonstrated that an *impossible* hypothesis was supported by real data: that listening to a particular song can actually reduce participants' age! In their words, 'These two studies were conducted with real participants, employed legitimate statistical analyses, and are reported truthfully'. How is this possible?

Simmons, Nelson, and Simonsohn (2011) went on to reveal the things that were not reported in their entirely truthful (but incomplete) initial account that made clear the shortcomings of their contrived studies. For example, their original report failed to mention a long list of additional variables that the researchers had collected data upon, thus allowing for various analyses to be carried out until an apparently significant result was found. It is worth noting here that Bem (2011) collected data upon a wide range of variables in his retroactive facilitation of recall studies that were not reported in his published paper but were apparent from the software he used to run the experiments (including how much the experimenter liked each participant, how enthusiastic the participant appeared, whether the participant engaged in meditation and/or biofeedback, etc.). Furthermore, Bem's stimulus words were divided into common and uncommon words, presumably to test some specific hypothesis, but no mention is made of this in the final published report.

Another trick revealed by Simmons, Nelson, and Simonsohn (2011) is the use of *optional stopping*, that is, not deciding in advance how many participants to run but instead analysing the results every so often as you go along and stopping data collection once a significant effect is found. Once again, there is suggestive evidence that Bem may have engaged in this practice insofar as the effect sizes reported across his nine studies are inversely proportional to his sample sizes. He even reports his largest effect size for a study involving 50 participants (Experiment 9) despite having explicitly stated that all experiments would involve at least 100 participants.

There are many other aspects of undisclosed flexibility (also referred to as *researcher degrees of freedom*) that might not be apparent to a reader of a published article (e.g. choices regarding selective exclusion of outliers, whether or not to use covariates or various data transformations). The idea that researchers exploit this undisclosed flexibility is further supported by the fact that p-values just below the conventionally accepted significance level of .05 are more common in the published literature than they should be (Masicampo & Lalande,

2012). Researchers know that their findings are unlikely to be accepted for publication if they fail to reach this arbitrary level of significance and reviewers are indeed less likely to accept such papers for publication thus resulting in another type of publication bias. Furthermore, Wicherts, Bakker, and Molenaar (2011) showed that researchers were especially unlikely to share their data if their published findings were only just significant, possibly because they were concerned that inappropriate statistical practices might be revealed. John, Loewenstein, and Prelec (2012) present data showing that many psychologists admit to sometimes engaging in the questionable research practices described by Simmons, Nelson, and Simonsohn (2011).

Within psychology and other sciences, steps are being taken to try to rectify these problems. For example, the Open Science Collaboration (2012) is a large-scale collaborative project which aims to empirically estimate the reproducibility of effects reported in psychology experiments by systematically replicating studies published in 2008 in three high-impact psychology journals. Simmons, Nelson, and Simonsohn (2011) have published sets of guidelines to researchers and reviewers to minimize the problem of undisclosed flexibility described previously. Specific suggestions have been proposed to make the publication of replication attempts more rewarding for researchers than it currently is (e.g. Koole & Lakens, 2012; Simons, 2012). Within psychology and beyond, many commentators are arguing that all studies should be preregistered in advance, including details of the planned analyses (e.g. Wagenmakers et al., 2012). Such a practice would eliminate many of the problems discussed earlier.

At first glance, it might appear that the issues relating to replication in psychology that are causing such concern for the field might provide some comfort for parapsychologists. After all, many of them have argued for a long time that theirs is not the only science with replication problems. Are double standards in operation here? Why should parapsychology be singled out among the sciences on the basis of replication problems when the preceding discussion makes it clear that psychology also suffers from such problems? Furthermore, so do other sciences, as made clear by the title of a classic article by Ioannidis (2005) on this issue: 'Why most published research findings are false'.

In one sense, it is true that double standards are operating here – but there is a good reason for this. There are very few findings in psychology that are of such tremendous importance that we would be required to revise our entire scientific worldview if we were to accept them. But findings reported by parapsychologists would, in the eyes of most scientists, require precisely such revision. In the famous words of Carl Sagan, 'Extraordinary claims require extraordinary evidence.' Furthermore, other disciplines may have their problems with the issue of replication but none have them as severely as parapsychology. For example, as already pointed out, there are dozens and dozens of highly robust and replicable effects within psychology in contrast to not one single such effect in parapsychology.

Further reflection on the preceding discussion will, however, reveal an even gloomier implication for parapsychology. It is clear that there is emerging a general consensus within the scientific community that many of the findings published in respected scientific journals may well be spurious effects that cannot be replicated. The task facing all sciences is to find ways to identify true signals against a background of noisy data but clearly the noise is often mistaken for a true signal resulting in another published spurious finding. What would a science look like in which there were, in fact, no true signals at all, only noise? Is it possible that it would look something like parapsychology? If this is really the case, the future prospects for parapsychology are grim indeed.

Many critics of parapsychology believe that such a gloomy diagnosis for the field is the correct one. Wiseman (2010) has described a number of ways in which he believes that some parapsychologists 'nullify null results'. He maintains that parapsychologists have a strong tendency to repeatedly propose new procedures to test for psi. Because there are few, if any, theoretical constraints upon psi-related hypotheses, almost any new procedure can be tried. Occasionally, for the reasons described before, a significant effect will be reported but new procedures that fail to produce significant results will typically never be reported. Attempts to replicate any reported effects using slightly different procedures are deemed as supportive if positive significant results are obtained but any failures to replicate may be dismissed as being due to the minor changes in procedure that were introduced.

Parapsychologists will often claim evidence for psi on the basis of any significant departure from chance expectation in their data even if the pattern of results is completely different to that previously reported. Wiseman also criticizes parapsychologists for misusing meta-analyses. Alcock (2003) has appealed to parapsychologists to 'give the null hypothesis a chance,' raising the issue of what, if anything, would convince those who believe strongly in the paranormal that perhaps psi simply does not exist (see also Alcock, 2010a, 2010b).

If the critics are wrong and psi really does exist, there are many ways in which parapsychologists could prove that and silence their critics forever. A single robust and replicable psi effect or a reliable practical application of psi would go a very long way towards achieving this goal. If the critics are right, however, there is a real danger that parapsychology will limp on indefinitely as a discipline from one false dawn to another unless it adopts the recommendations that are currently being put forward to improve replicability in psychology. In fairness, many of these issues have been recognized within parapsychology for a considerable time, but the field has never properly come to grips with them.

Wiseman (2010, p. 176) made a specific proposal to 'move forward and rapidly reach closure on the issue' of whether psi exists or not:

> To achieve this, researchers should change the way in which they view null findings. They might stop trying numerous new procedures and cherry-picking those that seem to work, and instead identify one or two that have already yielded the most promising results. They could stop

varying these procedures, and instead have a series of labs carry out strict replications that are both methodologically sound and incorporate the most psi-conducive conditions possible. They could avoid the haunting spectre of retrospective meta-analysis by pre-registering the key details involved in each of the studies. And finally, they might agree to stop jumping ship, and instead have the courage to accept the null hypothesis if the selected front-runners do not produce evidence of a significant and replicable effect.

It will be interesting to see whether the parapsychological community is willing to rise to this challenge in as direct a way as psychologists are currently tackling similar issues relating to replicability.

It is often said that it is impossible to prove a negative. Logically, this is complete nonsense as many kinds of negative statement can easily be proved (e.g. this book is not an elephant). But some negative statements are indeed, to all intents and purposes, impossible to prove and one of these is: 'Psi does not exist'. Even if the evidence put forward to date in favour of the psi hypothesis is not compelling, it is always possible that proof lies around the next corner. Parapsychologists have, with some justification, bemoaned the fact that the cumulative efforts of all the parapsychological researchers that ever lived are the equivalent of only a couple of weeks of research in other disciplines. This is because, relatively speaking, they are so few in number. However, until recently anomalistic psychologists were even fewer in number and yet they have, within a couple of decades, produced several empirically supported explanations for ostensibly paranormal experiences and several of the effects reported replicate reliably. Although no amount of evidence supporting such non-paranormal explanations for ostensibly paranormal events could ever logically prove that psi does not exist, as long as such evidence continues to accumulate in the absence of any replicable psi effects, the psi hypothesis becomes increasingly untenable.

Suggested further reading

For discussion of replication issues:

Pashler, H. & Wagenmakers, E-J. (2012). 'Editors' introduction to the special section on replicability in psychological science: A crisis in confidence?' *Perspectives on Psychological Science*, 7, 528–30. (See also associated articles, pp. 531–654.)

Ritchie, S. J., Wiseman, R., & French, C. C. (2012b). 'Replication, replication, replication'. *The Psychologist*, 25, 346–8. (See also associated commentaries, pp. 349–57.)

For debate between advocates and critics of the psi hypothesis:

Krippner, S. & Friedman, H. L. (eds). (2010). *Debating psychic experience: Human potential or human illusion?* Santa Barbara, CA: Praeger.

Glossary of Terms

Absorption: The disposition to have episodes of total immersion in an experience that occupies all of one's senses, thoughts, and imagination and to be resistant to distraction. Absorption is related to hypnotic susceptibility, dissociation, and fantasy-proneness.

Agency (or **Agenticity**): The tendency to assume that events happen because some intentional agent makes then happen.

Alien abduction: The claim that a person has been taken on board an extraterrestrial spaceship against their will and (usually) has been subjected to medical examination and experimentation.

Alternative medicine: A wide range of largely unproven and/or untested practices based upon principles that are not accepted by conventional science, believed by some to be able to treat a wide range of diseases; to be used in place of conventional medical treatments (cf. *complementary medicine*).

Analytical thinking style: Style of thinking characterized as being deliberative, slow, reflective, under conscious control, and primarily verbal.

Angels: Allegedly, spiritual beings that serve God.

Anomalistic psychology: Branch of psychology that attempts to explain paranormal and related beliefs and ostensibly paranormal experiences in terms of known (or knowable) psychological and physical factors.

Anthropomorphism: Tendency to attribute human characteristics to non-human objects and events.

Apophenia: The spontaneous perception of connections and meaning in randomness; also referred to as *patternicity*.

Astrology: The belief that the course of an individual's life, including personality and aptitudes, is influenced by the position of celestial bodies at the moment of birth.

Aura: An alleged energy field surrounding all living things which certain gifted individuals claim to be able to see (despite the fact that the field is not generally thought to be detectable by scientific instruments). Aura readers claim that they can discern information such as emotional state and physical health by examining the size, shape, and colour of the aura.

Availability heuristic: The tendency to make judgements about frequency and probability on the basis of how easy we find it to bring examples to mind.

Barnum effect: Tendency to accept vague and general statements as having specific relevance to one's own life and circumstances.

Bermuda Triangle: Triangular area in the Atlantic Ocean where a large number of ships, planes, and people are said to have mysteriously disappeared.

Bible Code: A code supposedly embedded in the Bible by God which allegedly predicted many historical events which took place after this version of the Bible was written.

Bigfoot: A large ape-like creature allegedly seen in many countries around the world.

Bipolar disorder: Psychiatric disorder characterized by extreme mood swings between periods of deep depression and manic elation. Also known as *manic depression*.

Channelling: The claim that certain gifted individuals have the ability to allow their physical bodies to be temporarily taken over by discarnate entities such as spirits of the deceased, extraterrestrials, or beings from other dimensions, thus allowing the entities to communicate with ordinary human beings.

Clairvoyance: The alleged ability to obtain visual information from remote locations without the use of the known sensory channels.

Cold reading: The technique of discovering information about a person by interacting with them although the information is not explicitly stated, used by deliberate con artists to give the impression that they know all about complete strangers, and also unintentionally used by people who may genuinely believe they have psychic powers.

Complementary medicine: A wide range of largely unproven and/or untested practices based upon principles that are not accepted by conventional science, believed by some to be able assist in the treatment of a wide range of diseases; to be used alongside conventional medical treatments (cf. *alternative medicine*).

Confirmation bias: Pervasive cognitive bias that leads us to favour evidence that is congruent with our pre-existing beliefs.

Crop circles: Patterns of flattened cereal crops, usually wheat and usually in England, thought by some to be produced by aliens and by others to be the product of unusual meteorological conditions. Many, perhaps all, are in fact the work of hoaxers and some are complex and highly artistic.

Cross-sectional: Research conducted on people of different ages at the same point in time.

Cryptomnesia: Literally meaning 'hidden memories'; this is the phenomenon whereby a memory occurs without the person concerned being aware of the original source of the memory.

Crystal power: Pseudoscientific belief that crystals can be used to store and channel energy that can be used for healing.

Demarcation problem: In the philosophy of science, specifying how science can be distinguished from non-science.

Dermo-optical perception: Alleged ability to see with the sensory receptors in the skin.

Differential item functioning: The tendency of different groups of people to interpret the same question in different ways; poses a threat to the validity of questionnaire data.

Dissociation: A separation of mental processes, including thoughts, emotions, conation, memory, and identity, which are normally integrated. Believed by many to be used as a means of distancing oneself from an aversive experience. Associated with absorption, fantasy-proneness, and hypnotic susceptibility.

Dissociative identity disorder: Formerly known as *multiple personality disorder*, a disputed psychiatric diagnosis referring to an alleged condition in which an individual appears to take on several distinct personalities, each with their own set of preferences, abilities, and memories.

Dissociativity: Tendency to slip into dissociated states of consciousness.

Divination: The practice of attempting to foretell the future by paranormal means (e.g. reading tea leaves, tarot cards, or horoscopes).

Dowsing: The alleged ability to be able to locate water, oil, or other substances, or even obtain other kinds of information (e.g. the sex of an unborn child) using various devices (such as rods and pendulums), the movement of which provides the required answers.

Dualism: The belief that the universe consists of two fundamentally different types of stuff: the mental and the physical.

Electronic voice phenomenon (EVP): The alleged recording of sprit voices using various electronic devices.

Epiphenomenalism: In philosophy, the view that mental states are caused by physical events in the brain but that mental states have no causal role to play.

Exorcism: Procedure whereby allegedly an external spirit is forced to leave the mind and body of a person who has been possessed.

Extrasensory perception (ESP): Acquisition of information about an external object or event (past, present, or future) without the use of the known sensory channels.

Extraversion: The tendency to be outgoing, sociable, and assertive, and to enjoy thrills and excitement; the opposite of *introversion*. Extraverts like to be around other people and become bored by themselves.

Facilitated communication: Controversial technique intended to allow individuals with severe communication problems to communicate with the outside world. Essentially, the technique involves another individual, referred to as a 'facilitator', supporting the arm or hand of the impaired individual while the latter uses a keyboard or some other device. Controlled double-blind studies generally indicate that the messages produced originate from the facilitator not from the patient.

Fairy: Small, beautiful, winged being with magical powers. Although mainly believed in only by children in modern Western societies, belief in fairies was common among adults in the West in the past.

False consensus effect: The tendency to believe that one's own views are shared more widely than they really are.

False memory: An apparent memory of an event that either never took place at all or else a highly distorted memory of an event that did take place.

Fantasy-proneness: Having a rich fantasy life and frequently being able to construct a vivid daydream that seems like reality (and may become confused with reality). Associated with various types of psychic and paranormal experiences and with absorption, dissociation, and hypnotic susceptibility.

Feng Shui: The practice of arranging one's surroundings in line with the principles of an ancient Chinese philosophy based upon yin, yang, and the flow of mysterious energies (such as chi) in order to live harmoniously within one's environment.

Functionalism: In philosophy, the view that mental states equate to functional states within the brain.

Ganzfeld technique: Experimental technique used to investigate extrasensory perception that involves having the receiver relax in conditions of mild perceptual deprivation when attempting to telepathically transmit target information to a receiver at a remote location.

Ghost: Disembodied spirit of a deceased person (or, rarely, an animal or a structure: e.g. a ghost ship) that allegedly haunts a particular location or individual.

Glossolalia: Also known as 'speaking in tongues'; the practice of speaking meaningless babble during certain types of religious ritual.

Groupthink: Tendency displayed by members of a group to reach incorrect conclusions due to placing too much emphasis on the need to avoid conflict within the group.

Habituation: The gradual weakening of the response to a stimulus if it is repeatedly exposed without any consequence.

Hallucination: A perceptual experience in the absence of appropriate external stimulation.

Hard problem: See *mind–body problem*.

Heuristic: This is a mental routine for generating an approximate solution to a problem quickly and with little effort. It will seldom come up with the very best answer but will usually produce an answer that is good enough. Life consists of a multitude of decisions and to ponder each carefully would leave us no room for living, so heuristics are vital to our everyday life. The downside is that occasionally a heuristic can lead us into error, that is, a decision or a belief that is a long way short of being the best. See *availability heuristic* and *representativeness heuristic*.

Hindsight bias: The tendency to believe in retrospect that events were more predictable than they actually were.

'Hundredth monkey' phenomenon: The claim, made by Dr Lyall Watson, that when enough people or animals know about a particular new idea or piece of behaviour, it suddenly becomes known to others by some mysterious mechanism which does not involve direct instruction or imitation. The name derives from an alleged incident in which monkeys on an island learnt how to wash sweet potatoes. When a sufficient number had mastered the skill, the habit spontaneously appeared among monkeys on other islands even though they had no direct contact with monkeys on the original island.

Hyperactive agency detection device (HADD): Hypothetical mental module that attributes agency to events that occur around us. It is argued that the HADD confers a survival advantage in evolutionary terms despite being oversensitive.

Hypnagogic: Relating to the state just before entering sleep.

Hypnopompic: Relating to the state just before fully waking from sleep.

Hypnosis: Procedure used to allegedly induce a particular type of altered state of consciousness during which the subject's mind operates in a markedly different way to the way it would operate during normal consciousness.

Hypnotic regression: The procedure whereby an individual is instructed, following a hypnotic induction procedure, to mentally 'go back in time' to retrieve allegedly repressed memories (or memories of a previous life in past-life regression).

Hypnotic susceptibility: The ability to easily enter into a hypnotic state. Associated with fantasy-proneness, dissociation, and absorption.

Iatrogenic: Inadvertently caused by those providing treatment.

I Ching (**Book of Changes**): An ancient Chinese text used for divination.

Idealism: In philosophy, the view that ultimately only the mental really exists, the physical universe being an illusion.

Identity theory: In philosophy, the view that mental states are literally identical to physical states in the brain.

Ideomotor effect: Phenomenon whereby unconscious muscular activity causes movement which is then mistakenly attributed to an external source.

Illusion of control: The tendency for people to perceive that they have control over events when in fact they have no such control.

Illusory correlation: The phenomenon of perceiving a correlation between two sets of stimuli or events when in fact no such correlation truly exists.

Introspection: The examination of one's own internal mental processes.

Introversion: The tendency to be reserved and to prefer one's own company or that of a few close friends or relatives rather than large groups. The opposite of *extraversion*. Introverts enjoy solitary activities and mental stimulation.

Intuitive thinking style: Thinking style characterized as being fast, non-conscious, driven by emotion, automatic, and holistic.

Kirlian photography: A technique discovered in 1939 by Semyon Kirlian which involves producing images of objects subject to high-voltage electrical fields while in contact with a photographic plate. This is said to reveal the aura (or life force) of the object.

Learned helplessness: A condition in which a person (or an animal) has learned to behave helplessly in an aversive situation over which they have no control. Even when control over the situation is restored, the victim may make no effort to escape the situation or improve it.

Ley lines: Lines along which it is claimed mysterious energy flows leading to them often being used as sites for religious ceremonies and structures, not to mention UFO visitations.

Loch Ness monster: A large aquatic animal, supposed to live in Loch Ness, Scotland, and often known affectionately as 'Nessie'. It is believed by some to be a descendant of a prehistoric Plesiosaur surviving to the present day. There have been many reported sightings but its existence cannot be firmly established.

Locus of control: The perceived source of major influences on the events and outcomes in one's life – may be internal (events and outcomes are caused by one's own actions and behaviours) or external (outcomes depend on destiny, fate, luck, powerful external forces, or other people).

Longitudinal: Research that examines the same group of people over an extended period of time, often many years.

Lycanthropy: The belief, common during the Middles Ages, that a person can turn into a wild creature, most often a werewolf.

Macro-PK: The movement of objects visible to the naked eye.

Magical thinking: Thinking that one's thoughts, wishes, and intentions can have a direct effect on the material world.

Manic depression: See *bipolar disorder*.

Materialism: In philosophy, the view that ultimately only the physical universe really exists.

Medium: A person claiming to be able to communicate with the dead.

Mediumship: The practice of allegedly communicating with the dead.

Meme: A hypothetical unit of cultural transmission (e.g. ideas, jokes, songs) that is transmitted via non-genetic means such as imitation.

Men in Black (MIBs): Mysterious visitors, possibly government agents or aliens, who allegedly visit witnesses to UFO incidents in order to ensure that they do not speak about what they have seen.

Micro-PK: The movement of objects that cannot be directly observed but must be inferred from other visible effects.

Mind–body problem: The as yet unresolved question of whether and, if so, how mind can interact with matter, particularly with respect to explaining the relationship between consciousness and the brain. Also known as the *hard problem*.

Missing time: The experience that a period of time has passed for which one has no memory despite being fully conscious at the time.

Monism: The philosophical position that the universe consists entirely of only one type of stuff, either the physical or the mental.

Multiple personality disorder: See *dissociative identity disorder*.

Myers-Briggs Type Indicator®: A commonly used instrument for measuring a person's preferences using four basic scales with opposite poles, based upon the theorizing of psychoanalyst Carl Jung.

Narcissism: The personality trait of being high in self-importance, tending to value the self above others, and believing in one's superior abilities or worth.

Near-death experience (NDE): An apparently transcendental experience, often experienced by individuals who are, or believe themselves to be, near death. The components of the NDE can include: feelings of peacefulness and bliss, an *out-of-body experience (OBE)*, travelling down a tunnel towards a white light, entering the light, meeting spiritual beings (such as religious figures or deceased loved ones), a life review, and a boundary of some sort where the decision is made that the individual is to carry on living.

Neurosis: Term once used to describe a number of mental problems, including phobias and *obsessive-compulsive disorder (OCD)*, which, although distressing, do not involve any loss of contact with reality.

Neuroticism: A tendency to experience negative mood, especially anxiety, depression, or anger, and to be susceptible to stress.

Non-state theories of hypnosis: Theories that maintain that the full range of the so-called hypnotic phenomena can be explained in terms of fairly mundane psychological processes (such as compliance, imagination, relaxation, etc.) without any need to invoke a unique altered state of consciousness (cf. *state theories of hypnosis*).

Objective worldview: View that knowledge about the world is gained from systematic observation.

Obsessive-compulsive disorder (OCD): Psychological disorder involving intrusive anxiety-provoking thoughts and repetitive behaviour intended to allay the anxiety although any relief is only short-lived.

Occam's razor: Also known as Ockham's razor (after friar and philosopher, William of Ockham, c. 1287–1347), it is the principle that among competing hypotheses or theories, the one that makes the fewest assumptions is to be preferred.

Openness to experience: The tendency to have an active imagination, to be open to new aesthetic and intellectual experiences, and to have a desire for variety and new ideas.

Ouija board: Board with the letters of the alphabet, numbers from zero to nine, and words 'yes' and 'no' arranged in a circle used to allegedly communicate with spirits. Sitters place their fingers lightly on a heart-shaped wooden 'planchette' that appears to move around the board of its own volition in response to questions (or else an upturned wine glass on a smooth table can be used).

Out-of-body experience (OBE): An experience during which an individual subjectively feels as if their centre of consciousness has left their physical body, often involving the sensation that one is looking down upon one's physical body from above.

Paranormal: Beyond explanation by conventional science as currently understood. Some people include traditional religion within this definition.

Parapsychology: The scientific study of evidence and claims relating to extrasensory perception, psychokinesis, and 'post-mortem' survival.

Pareidolia: The perception of clear images and sounds in random stimuli.

Patternicity: See *apophenia*.

Possession: The alleged phenomenon whereby an external spirit takes control of a person's mind and body.

Prana: All-pervading life energy of the universe according to Hindu beliefs (cf. the Chinese concept of chi).

Precognition: The alleged ability to directly obtain information about future events other than by the use of the known sensory channels and inference.

Premonition: The alleged process of experiencing an affective (emotional) response to a future event without any known means of acquiring such a response.

Presence, sense of: The feeling that another being is in one's immediate environment even though this conviction is unsupported by sensory input.

Pseudoscience: Theories, assumptions, and methods that, although adopting the superficial trappings of science, are not truly scientific.

Psi: A general term used to refer to paranormal forces of any kind.

Psychic: (*adjective*) pertaining to the paranormal; (*noun*) one claiming to possess paranormal powers.

Psychic healing: The alleged ability to cure or treat diseases by mental influence alone without the use of physical curative substances or procedures.

Psychodynamic functions hypothesis (PFH): The hypothesis, first proposed by Irwin (1992), that paranormal belief is an attempt to impose a sense of control over life events by people who have feelings of helplessness, insecurity, and lack of control resulting from some childhood trauma.

Psychokinesis (PK): The alleged ability to mentally move or influence objects in the outside world without the mediation of any known physical energy.

Psychosis: Severe mental disorder involving loss of contact with reality.

Psychoticism: Personality trait characterized by aggressiveness and hostility towards others.

Reality monitoring: The process of distinguishing between mental events and events occurring in external reality.

Reflexology: A form of alternative or complementary medicine which involves massaging the feet in order to diagnose and treat ailments in all parts of the body.

Regression to the mean: Statistical phenomenon whereby if a variable is extreme when first measured it will probably be closer to the average when measured a second time.

Reincarnation: The belief that following death one's soul survives and goes on to inhabit a new physical body.

Remote viewing: Technique used to investigate extrasensory perception typically by sending one or more agents (also known as 'senders') to a randomly selected location at prearranged times from whence they attempt to telepathically transmit information about the location to a receiver. Some studies do not involve one or more agents at a distant location but instead simply the provision to the remote viewer of map coordinates of a distant location thus testing for clairvoyance.

REM sleep: Short for 'rapid-eye-movement sleep', this is the phase of sleep associated with vivid dreaming. It can be recognized on the basis of a number of psychophysiological characteristics, most notably rapid movements of the eyes beneath closed eyelids.

Representativeness heuristic: The tendency to base probability judgements on the degree to which an event or object is representative of its parent population.

Repression: The questionable notion, derived from psychoanalytic theory, that when an individual experiences a traumatic event, the memory for that traumatic event may be automatically pushed into a non-conscious part of the mind.

Reverse speech theory: The pseudoscientific theory, proposed by David Oates, that whenever a person speaks two messages are produced. The first is the one consciously perceived by the listener which is produced by the speaker's left hemisphere. The second can only be heard consciously when the speech is played backwards, but is perceived unconsciously by the listener and is produced by the speaker's right hemisphere. The latter message always reveals the speaker's true feelings and intentions.

Runes: Characters of ancient alphabets sometimes used in divination.

Schizophrenia: Psychotic disorder characterized by severely impaired thinking, behaviour, and emotions, involving symptoms such as hallucinations, delusions, and social withdrawal.

Schizotypy: The tendency to experience symptoms typically associated with schizophrenia although not necessarily in such extreme form as to be considered of clinical significance.

Séance: Social gathering, especially popular in the Victorian era, at which communication with the dead was said to occur via a *medium*. Phenomena reported included levitation of objects, disembodied voices, materializations, and so on.

Sensation seeking: A personality trait that includes the tendency to seek out novel, varied, exciting, or intense experiences, and the willingness to take risks in pursuit of these experiences, as well as a tendency to be interested in unusual ideas which are not part of the scientific mainstream and to be motivated to explore strange, and maybe mystical, forces.

Sensory leakage: Ways in which imperfect control in experiments testing for extrasensory perception could allow targets to be known via information obtainable through the ordinary sensory channels.

Shroud of Turin: Allegedly the shroud used to wrap Christ's body after the crucifixion which bears a mysterious image of a Christ-like figure. Reliably dated to the fourteenth century CE.

Sleep paralysis: A commonly reported altered state of consciousness which occurs at the threshold between sleep and wakeful consciousness, the central symptom of which is temporary inability to move. Symptoms which are often associated with episodes of sleep paralysis include auditory and visual hallucinations, a sense of presence, difficulty breathing and intense fear.

Social marginality hypothesis: The hypothesis that members of socially marginalized groups, such as the poor and less well educated, women, the elderly, and ethnic minorities, will be more susceptible to paranormal beliefs.

Spiritualism: A system of belief based upon the notion that *mediums* are able to communicate with the dead.

Spontaneous human combustion: Phenomenon whereby people allegedly spontaneously burst into flames for no apparent reason.

State theories of hypnosis: Theories that maintain that hypnotic induction procedures produce a unique altered state of consciousness (cf. *non-state theories of hypnosis*).

Subjective validation: The tendency to find correspondences between two unrelated sets of stimuli or events because a belief, hypothesis, or expectation leads one to assume that such correspondences are there to be found.

Subjective worldview: View that knowledge about the world is gained through introspection and reflection.

Syllogistic reasoning: A form of reasoning that involves drawing conclusions from pairs of premises.

Tarot cards: Particular type of cards used in a common system of divination.

Tectonic strain theory: Controversial theory proposed by Michael Persinger which argues that the intense electromagnetic field produced near fault lines preceding earthquakes, due to the movement of the earth's tectonic plates, causes (a) luminous effects that might be reported as UFOs and (b) abnormal activity in the temporal lobes of susceptible individuals causing hallucinatory experiences.

Telepathy: Direct mind-to-mind contact without the use of known sensory channels.

Theory of mind: The ability to attribute mental states (such as beliefs, intentions, and so on) to others and to appreciate that these mental states may differ from our own.

Thinking styles: There are two main thinking styles that can be understood as habitual ways of thinking. The 'analytical' thinking style uses words and logic, is deliberate and intentional, requires some effort, is relatively slow, and takes place with full awareness. It analyses data gathered by observation in an objective manner. In contrast, the 'intuitive' thinking style uses non-verbal symbols and metaphors, is holistic, is automatic and unintentional, is fast and relatively effortless, and often takes place subconsciously. People seem to have a facility and a preference for one style over the other and will tend to use one style more often. This is not to say that people cannot use both styles and will in appropriate circumstances, just that people will have a tendency to use one more than the other.

Transliminality: Hypersensitivity to psychological material originating in either the unconscious or the external environment.

UFOlogists: Self-appointed 'experts' on evidence relating to the claim that the earth is frequently visited by extraterrestrial spacecraft.

Vampires: Mythical creatures that feed on human blood, leading their victims to also become vampires.

Witch: Female who claims to be able to perform magic spells by the use of various potions and rituals.

Worldview: There are two main worldviews that can be understood as a set of beliefs about how knowledge of the world is acquired. The 'subjective' worldview is characterized by the belief that knowledge is gained through introspection and reflection. What is important is that new knowledge should be integrated with existing knowledge to make a coherent whole; hence, any new information is tested for internal consistency with other beliefs, and may be accepted if it satisfies the criterion of consistency. The 'objective' worldview, in contrast, is characterized by the belief that knowledge is gained from systematic observation of the world. This is a materialistic view that relies on data generated from scientific observation and controlled research. New information is accepted if it satisfies scientific criteria of being valid, reliable, and replicable – that is, other researchers can obtain similar results and build a consensus of experts.

Zombie: A soulless yet moving dead body produced by means of black magic.

References

Aarnio, K. & Lindeman, M. (2005). 'Paranormal beliefs, education, and thinking styles'. *Personality and Individual Differences*, 39, 1227–36.

Aarnio, K. & Lindeman, M. (2007). 'Superstitious, magical and paranormal beliefs: An integrative model'. *Journal of Research in Personality*, 41, 731–44.

Adler, S. R. (2011). *Sleep paralysis: Night-mares, nocebos, and the mind-body connection*. Piscataway, NJ: Rutgers University Press.

Alcock, J. E. (1981). *Parapsychology: Science or magic?* Oxford: Pergamon Press.

Alcock, J. E. (1990). 'Parapsychology: Science of the anomalous or search for nonmaterial aspects of human existence'. *Behavioral and Brain Sciences*, 13, 390–1.

Alcock, J. E. (2003). 'Give the null hypothesis a chance: Reasons to remain doubtful about the existence of psi'. In J. E. Alcock, J. E. Burns, & A. Freeman (eds), *Psi wars: Getting to grips with the paranormal* (pp. 29–50). Exeter, UK: Imprint Academic.

Alcock, J. E. (2010a). 'Attributions about impossible things'. In S. Krippner & H. L. Friedman (eds), *Debating psychic experience: Human potential or human illusion?* (pp. 29–41). Santa Barbara, CA: Praeger.

Alcock, J. E. (2010b). 'Let's focus on the data'. In S. Krippner & H. L. Friedman (eds), *Debating psychic experience: Human potential or human illusion?* (pp. 129–32). Santa Barbara, CA: Praeger.

Alcock, J. E. (2011). 'Back from the future: Parapsychology and the Bem affair'. *Skeptical Inquirer*. Retrieved 30 December 2011 from http://www.csicop.org/specialarticles/show/back_from_the_future.

Alcock, J. E. & Otis, L. P. (1980). 'Critical thinking and belief in the paranormal'. *Psychological Reports*, 46, 479–82.

Alexander, E. (2012). *Proof of heaven: A neurosurgeon's journey into the afterlife*. New York: Simon & Schuster.

Allen, J. & Lester, D. (1994). 'Belief in paranormal phenomena and an external locus of control'. *Perceptual and Motor Skills*, 79, 226.

Alleyne, R. (2009). 'Women's voices "make plants grow faster" finds Royal Horticultural Society'. *The Daily Telegraph*, 22 June.

Altemeyer, B. & Hunsberger, B. (1997). *Amazing conversions: Why some turn to faith and others abandon religion*. Amherst, NY: Prometheus Books.

Alvarado, C. (2000). 'Out-of-body experiences'. In E. Cardeña, S. J. Lynn, & S. Krippner (eds), *Varieties of anomalous experience: Examining the scientific evidence* (pp. 183–218). Washington, DC: American Psychological Association.

American Psychiatric Association (1994). *Diagnostic and statistical manual of mental disorders*. 4th edn. Washington, DC: American Psychiatric Association.

Anastasi, A. & Urbina, S. (1997). *Psychological testing*. 7th edn. Upper Saddle River, NJ: Prentice Hall.

Appelle, S. (1996). 'The abduction experience: A critical evaluation of theory and evidence'. *Journal of UFO Studies*, 6, 29–79.

Appelle, S., Lynn, S. J., & Newman, L. (2000). 'Alien abduction experiences'. In E. Cardeña, S. J. Lynn, & S. Krippner (eds), *Varieties of anomalous experience: Examining the scientific evidence* (pp. 253–82). Washington, DC: American Psychological Association.

Arcangel, D. (1997). 'Investigating the relationship between Myers-Briggs Type Indicator and facilitated reunion experiences'. *Journal of the American Society for Psychical Research*, 91, 82–95.

Argyle, M. (2000). *Psychology and religion: An introduction*. London: Routledge.

Atkinson, R. P. (1994). 'Relationships of hypnotic susceptibility to paranormal beliefs and claimed experiences: Implications for hypnotic absorption'. *American Journal of Clinical Hypnosis*, 37, 34–40.

Atran, S. (2002). *In gods we trust: The evolutionary landscape of religion*. Oxford: Oxford University Press.

Auton, H. R., Pope, J., & Seeger, G. (2003). 'It isn't that strange: Paranormal belief and personality traits'. *Social Behavior and Personality*, 31, 711–20.

Ayeroff, F. & Abelson, R. P. (1976). 'ESP and ESB: Belief in personal success at mental telepathy'. *Journal of Personality and Social Psychology*, 34, 240–7.

Bader, C. D. & Desmond, S. A. (2006). 'Do as I say and as I do: The effects of consistent parental beliefs and behaviours upon religious transmission'. *Sociology of Religion*, 67, 313–29.

Baker, R. A. (1988). 'The aliens among us: Hypnotic regression revisited'. *Skeptical Inquirer*, 12, 147–62.

Baker, R. A. (1992). *Hidden memories: Voices and visions from within*. Buffalo, NY: Prometheus.

Bandura, A. (1969) 'The role of modelling processes in personality development'. In D. M. Gelfand (ed.), *Social learning in childhood* (pp. 185–95). Monterey, CA: Brooks/Cole Publishing.

Banks, J. (2001). 'Rorschach audio: Ghost voices and perceptual creativity'. *Leonardo Music Journal*, 11, 77–83.

Banks, J. (2012). *Rorschach audio: Art & illusion for sound*. London: Strange Attractor Press.

Barber, T. X. (1969). *Hypnosis: A scientific approach*. New York: Van Nostrand Reinhold.

Barrett, J. L. (2004). *Why would anyone believe in God?* Plymouth: Alta Mira Press.

Bartholomew, R. E., Basterfield, K., & Howard, G. S. (1991). 'UFO abductees and contactees: Psychopathology or fantasy-proneness?' *Professional Psychology: Research and Practice*, 22, 215–22.

Bartholomew, R. E. & Goode, E. (2000). 'Mass delusions and hysterias: Highlights from the past millennium'. *Sceptical Inquirer*, 24, 20–8.

Bartholomew, R. E. & Howard, G. S. (1998). *UFOs and alien contact: Two centuries of mystery*. Amherst, NY: Prometheus.

Baruss, I. (2001). 'Failure to replicate electronic voice phenomenon'. *Journal of Scientific Exploration*, 15, 355–67.

Basterfield, K. (2001). 'Paranormal aspects of the UFO phenomenon: 1975–1999'. *Australian Journal of Parapsychology*, 1, 30–55.

Basterfield, K. & Thalbourne, M. A. (2002). 'Belief in, and alleged experience of, the paranormal in ostensible UFO abductees'. *Australian Journal of Parapsychology*, 2, 2–18.

Batthyany, A., Kranz, G. S., & Erber, A. (2009). 'Moderating factors in precognitive habituation: The roles of situational vigilance, emotional reactivity and affect regulation'. *Journal of the Society for Psychical Research*, 73, 65–82.

Beck, R. & Miller, J. P. (2001). 'Erosion of belief and disbelief: Effects of religiosity and negative affect on beliefs in the paranormal and supernatural'. *Journal of Social Psychology*, 141, 277–87.

Becker-Blease, K.A., Deater-Deckard, K., Eley, T., Freyd, J., Stevenson, J., & Plomin, R. (2004). 'A genetic analysis of individual differences in dissociative behaviours in childhood and adolescence'. *Journal of Child Psychology and Psychiatry*, 45, 522–32.

Belanger, A. F. (1944). 'An empirical study of superstitions and unfounded beliefs'. *Proceedings of the Iowa Academy of Science*, 51, 355–9.

Bellos, A. (2010). *Alex's adventures in Numberland: Dispatches from the wonderful world of mathematics*. London: Bloomsbury.

Bem, D. J. (1994). 'Response to Hyman'. *Psychological Bulletin*, 115, 25–7.

Bem, D. J. (2003). 'Precognitive habituation: Replicable evidence for a process of anomalous cognition'. *Proceedings of presented papers: The Parapsychological Association 46th Annual Convention*, 6–20.

Bem, D. J. (2011). 'Feeling the future: Experimental evidence for anomalous retroactive influences on cognition and affect'. *Journal of Personality and Social Psychology*, 100, 407–25.

Bem, D. J. & Honorton, C. (1994). 'Does psi exist? Replicable evidence for an anomalous process of information transfer'. *Psychological Bulletin*, 115, 4–18.

Bem, D., Palmer, J., & Broughton, R. (2001). 'Updating the Ganzfeld database: A victim of its own success?' *Journal of Parapsychology*, 65, 207–18.

Bentall, R. & Slade, P. (1985). 'Reality testing and auditory hallucinations: A signal-detection analysis'. *British Journal of Clinical Psychology*, 24, 159–69.

Bergeman, C. S., Plomin, R., Pedersen, N. L., McClearn, G. E., Nesselroad, J. R., Costa, P. T., Chipuer, H. M., & McCrae, R. R. (1993). 'Genetic and environmental effects on openness to experience, agreeableness, and conscientiousness. *Journal of Personality*, 61, 159–79.

Bering, J. (2011). *The god instinct: The psychology of souls, destiny, and the meaning of life*. London: Nicholas Brealey Publishing.

Bering, J. M. & Parker, B. D. (2006). 'Children's attributions of intentions to an invisible agent'. *Developmental Psychology*, 42, 253–62.

Bernstein, M. (1956). *The search for Bridey Murphy*. Garden City, NY: Doubleday.

Beyerstein, B. L. (1995). 'Distinguishing science from pseudoscience'. Retrieved 12 January 2012 from http://www.sld.cu/galerias/pdf/sitios/revsalud/beyerstein_cience_vs_pseudoscience.pdf.

Beyerstein, B. L. (1999). 'Investigating anomalous subjective experiences: Believing is seeing is believing'. *Rational Enquirer*, 10, 1–5.

Bhushan, R. & Bhushan, L. I. (1987). 'Superstition among college students'. *Asian Journal of Psychology and Education*, 19, 11–16.

Bierman, D. J., Bosga, D., Gerding, H., & Wezelman, R. (1993). 'Anomalous information access in the Ganzfeld: Utrecht-novice series I and II'. *Proceedings of the Parapsychological Association 36th Annual Convention*, Toronto, Canada, 192–203.

Bierman, D. & Radin, D. (1997). 'Anomalous anticipatory response on randomised future conditions'. *Perceptual and Motor Skills*, 84, 689–90.

Blackmore, S. J. (1982). *Beyond the body: An investigation of out-of-the body experiences*. London: Heinemann.

Blackmore, S. J. (1984). 'A postal survey of OBEs and other experiences'. *Journal of the Society for Psychical Research*, 52, 225–44.

Blackmore, S. J. (1993). *Dying to live: Science and the near-death experience*. London: Grafton.

Blackmore, S. J. (1994a). 'Alien abduction: The inside story'. *New Scientist*, 144, 29–31.

Blackmore, S. J. (1994b). 'Are women more sheepish? Gender differences in belief in the paranormal'. In L. Coley & R. A. White (eds), *Women and parapsychology* (pp. 68–89). New York: Parapsychology Foundation.

Blackmore, S. J. (1996). 'Near-death experiences'. In G. Stein (ed.), *The encyclopedia of the paranormal* (pp. 425–41). Amherst, NY: Prometheus Books.

Blackmore, S. J. (1997). 'Probability misjudgment and belief in the paranormal: A newspaper survey'. *British Journal of Psychology*, 88, 683–9.

Blackmore, S. J. (1999). *The meme machine*. Oxford: Oxford University Press.

Blackmore, S. J. (2000). 'First person – into the unknown'. *New Scientist*, 4 November, 55.

Blackmore, S. J. (2001). 'Evolution and memes: The human brain as a selective imitation device'. *Cybernetics and Systems*, 32, 225–55.

Blackmore, S. J. (2004). *Consciousness: An introduction*. Oxford: Oxford University Press.

Blackmore, S. J. & Cox, M. (2000). 'Alien abductions, sleep paralysis, and the temporal lobe'. *European Journal of UFO and Abduction Studies*, 1, 113–18.

Blackmore, S. J. & Moore, R. (1994). 'Seeing things: Visual recognition and belief in the paranormal'. *European Journal of Parapsychology*, 10, 91–103.

Blackmore, S. J. & Rose, N. (1997). 'Reality and imagination: A psi-conducive confusion?' *Journal of Parapsychology*, 61, 321–35.

Blackmore, S. & Troscianko, T. (1985). 'Belief in the paranormal: Probability judgments, illusory control, and the "chance baseline shift"'. *British Journal of Psychology*, 76, 459–68.

Blagrove, M., French, C. C., & Jones, G. (2006). 'Probabilistic reasoning, affirmative bias and belief in precognitive dreams'. *Applied Cognitive Psychology*, 20, 65–83.

Blakemore, C. (2012). 'Is the afterlife full of fluffy clouds and angels?' Retrieved 13 February 2013 from http://www.telegraph.co.uk/comment/9598971/Is-the-afterlife-full-of-fluffy-clouds-and-angels.html.

Blanke, O. & Arzy, S. (2005). 'The out-of-body experience: Disturbed self-processing at the temporo-parietal junction'. *Neuroscientist*, 11, 16–24.

Blanke, O., Landis, T., Spinelli, L., & Seeck, M. (2003). 'Out-of-body experience and autoscopy of neurological origin'. *Brain*, 127, 243–58.

Blanke, O., Mohr, C., Michel, C. M., Pascual-Leone, A., Brugger, P., Seeck, M., Landis, T., & Thut, G. (2005). 'Linking out-of-body experience and self-processing to mental own-body imagery at the temporoparietal junction'. *Journal of Neuroscience*, 19, 550–7.

Blanke, O., Ortigue, S., Landis, T., & Seeck, M. (2002). 'Stimulating illusory own-body perceptions'. *Nature*, 419, 269–70.

Bleak, J. L. & Frederick, C. M. (1998). 'Superstitious behaviour in sport: Levels of effectiveness and determinants of use in three collegiate sports'. *Journal of Sport Behaviour*, 21, 1–15.

Bloecher, T., Clamar, A., & Hopkins, B. (1985). *Summary report on the psychological testing of nine individuals reporting UFO abduction experiences*. Mount Rainier, MD: Fund for UFO Research.

Blum, S. H. (1976). 'Some aspects of belief in prevailing superstitions'. *Psychological Reports*, 38, 579–82.

Bolton, D., Dearsley, P., Madronal-Luque, R., & Baron-Cohen, S. (2002). 'Magical thinking in childhood and adolescence: Development and relation to obessive compulsion'. *British Journal of Developmental Psychology*, 20, 479–94.

Booth, J. N., Koren, S. A., & Persinger, M. A. (2005). 'Increased feelings of the sensed presence and increased geomagnetic activity at the time of the experience during exposures to transcerebral weak complex magnetic fields'. *International Journal of Neuroscience*, 115, 1053–79.

Bösch, H., Steinkamp, F., & Boller, E. (2006). 'Examining psychokinesis: The interaction of human intention with random number generators. A meta-analysis'. *Psychological Bulletin*, 132, 497–523.

Boyce, T. E. & Geller, E. S. (2002). 'Using the Barnum effect to teach psychological research methods'. *Teaching of Psychology*, 29, 316–18.

Boyer, P. (1997). 'Further distinctions between magic, reality, religion and fiction'. *Child Development*, 68, 1012–14.

Boyer, P. (2001). *Religion explained*. London: Vintage.

Boyer, P. & Bergstrom, B. (2008). 'Evolutionary perspectives on religion'. *Annual Review of Anthropology*, 37, 111–30.

Braithwaite, J. J. (2008a). 'Putting magnetism in its place: A critical examination of the weak intensity magnetic field account of anomalous haunt-type experiences'. *Journal of the Society for Psychical Research*, 72, 34–50.

Braithwaite, J. J. (2008b). 'Towards a cognitive neuroscience of the dying brain'. *The Skeptic*, 21(2), 8–16.

Braithwaite, J. J. (2011). 'Magnetic fields, hallucinations and anomalous experiences: A sceptical critique of the current evidence'. *The Skeptic*, 22.4/23.1, 38–45.

Braithwaite, J. J., Broglia, E., Bagshaw, A. P., & Wilkins, A. J. (2013). 'Evidence for elevated cortical hyperexcitability and its association with out-of-body experiences in the non-clinical population: New findings from a pattern-glare task'. *Cortex*, 49, 793–805.

Braithwaite, J. J., Samson, D., Apperly, I., Broglia, E., & Hullerman, J. (2011). 'Cognitive correlates of the spontaneous out-of-body experience (OBE) in the psychologically normal population: Evidence for an increased role of temporal-lobe instability, body-distortion processing, and impairments in own-body transformations'. *Cortex*, 47, 839–53.

Braithwaite, J. J. & Townsend, M. (2006). 'Good vibrations: The case for a specific effect of infrasound in instances of anomalous experience has yet to be empirically demonstrated'. *Journal of the Society for Psychical Research*, 70, 211–24.

Braithwaite, J. J. & Townsend, M. (2008). 'Sleeping with the entity: Part II – Temporally complex distortions in the magnetic field from human movement in a bed located in an English castle's reputedly haunted bedroom'. *European Journal of Parapsychology*, 23, 90–126.

Brandon, R. (1983). *The spiritualists: The passion for the occult in the nineteenth and twentieth centuries*. London: Weidenfeld and Nicolson.

Braud, W. G. (1994). 'Can our intentions interact directly with the physical world?' *European Journal of Parapsychology*, 10, 78–90.

Braud, W. & Schlitz, M. (1991). 'Conscious interactions with remote biological systems: Anomalous intentionality effects'. *Subtle Energies*, 2, 1–46.

Braude, S. (1986). *The limits of influence*. New York: Routledge and Kegan Paul.

Bressan, P. (2002). 'The connection between random sequences, everyday coincidences, and belief in the paranormal'. *Applied Cognitive Psychology*, 16, 17–34.

Brett, C. M. C., Peters, E. R., Johns, L. C., Tabraham, P., Valmaggia, L. R., & McGuire, P. (2007). 'Appraisals of Anomalous Experiences Interview (AANEX): A multidimensional measure of psychological responses to anomalies associated with psychosis'. *British Journal of Psychiatry*, 191 (suppl. S1), s23–s30.

Brewer, P. R. (2013). 'The trappings of science: Media messages, scientific authority, and beliefs about paranormal investigators'. *Science Communication*, 35, 311–33.

Brière de Boismont, A. J. F. (1853). *Hallucinations, or, the rational history of apparitions, visions, dreams, ecstasy, magnetism, and somnambulism*. Philadelphia: Lindsay and Blakiston.

Britton, W. B. & Bootzin, R. R. (2004). 'Near-death experiences and the temporal lobe'. *Psychological Science*, 15, 254–8.

Broad, C. D. (1949). 'The relevance of psychical research to philosophy'. *Philosophy*, 24, 291–309.

Brookesmith, P. (1996). *UFO: The government files*. London: Blandford.

Brookesmith, P. (1998). *Alien abductions*. New York: Barnes & Noble.

Brugger, P. (2001). 'From haunted brain to haunted science: A cognitive neuroscience view of paranormal and pseudoscientific thought'. In J. Houran & R. Lange (eds), *Hauntings and poltergeists: Multidisciplinary perspectives* (pp. 195–213). Jefferson, NC: McFarland and Company, Inc.

Brugger, P. & Baumann, A. T. (1994). 'Repetition avoidance in responses to imaginary questions: The effect of respondents' belief in ESP'. *Psychological Reports*, 75, 883–93.

Brugger, P. & Graves, R. E. (1997a). 'Right hemispatial inattention and magical ideation'. *European Archives of Psychiatry and Clinical Neuroscience*, 247, 55–7.

Brugger, P. & Graves, R. E. (1997b). 'Testing vs. believing hypotheses: Magical ideation in the judgements of contingencies'. *Cognitive Neuropsychiatry*, 2, 251–72.

Brugger, P., Landis, T., & Regard, M. (1990). 'A "sheep-goat" effect in repetition avoidance: Extra-sensory perception as an effect of subjective probability?' *British Journal of Psychology*, 81, 455–68.

Brugger, P., Regard, M., & Landis, T. (1991). 'Belief in extrasensory perception and illusory control: A replication'. *Journal of Psychology*, 125, 501–2.

Brugger, P., Regard, M., Landis, T., Cook, N., Krebs, D., & Niederberger, J. (1993). '"Meaningful" patterns in visual noise: Effects of lateral stimulation and the observer's belief in ESP'. *Psychopathology*, 26, 261–5.

Brugger, P., Regard, M., Landis, T., & Graves, R. E. (1995). 'The roots of meaningful coincidence'. *Lancet*, 345, 1306–7.

Brugger, P. & Taylor, K. I. (2003). 'ESP: Extrasensory perception or effect of subjective probability?' *Journal of Consciousness Studies*, 10, 221–46.

Bullard, T. E. (1987). *UFO abductions: The measure of a mystery*. Mount Rainier, MD: Fund for UFO Research.

Bullard, T. E. (1989). 'Hypnosis and UFO abductions: A troubled relationship'. *Journal of UFO Studies*, 1, 3–40.

Bunge, M. (1991). 'A skeptic's beliefs and disbeliefs'. *New Ideas in Psychology*, 9, 131–49.

Burger, J. M. & Lynn, A. L. (2005). 'Superstitious behaviour among American and Japanese professional baseball players'. *Basic and Applied Social Psychology*, 27, 71–6.

Byrne, T. & Normand, M. (2000). 'The demon-haunted sentence: A skeptical analysis of reverse speech'. *Skeptical Inquirer*, 24(2), 46–9.

Callaghan, A. & Irwin, H. J. (2003). 'Paranormal belief as a psychological coping mechanism'. *Journal of the Society for Psychical Research*, 67, 200–7.

Canetti, D. & Pedahzur, A. (2002). 'The effects of contextual and psychological variables on extreme right-wing sentiments'. *Social Behavior and Personality*, 30, 317–34.

Cardeña, E., Terhune, D. B., Lööf, A., & Buratti, S. (2009). 'Hypnotic experience is related to emotional contagion'. *International Journal of Clinical and Experimental Hypnosis*, 57, 33–46.

Carey, B. (2011). 'Journal's article on ESP is expected to prompt outrage'. *The New York Times*, 5 January.

Carr, D. B. (1982). 'Pathophysiology of stress-induced limbic lobe dysfunction: A hypothesis relevant to near-death experiences'. *Anabiosis: The Journal of Near-Death Studies*, 2, 75–89.

Carroll, R. T. (2003). *The skeptic's dictionary: A collection of strange beliefs, amusing deceptions and dangerous delusions*. Hoboken, NJ: John Wiley & Sons.

Chalmers, A. F. (1999). *What is this thing called science?* 3rd edn. Queensland: University of Queensland Press.

Chalmers, D. J. (1995). 'The puzzle of conscious experience'. *Scientific American*, December, 62–8.

Chandler, M. (1997). 'Rescuing magical thinking from the jaws of social determinism'. *Child Development*, 68, 1021–3.

Chequers, J., Joseph, S., & Diduca, D. (1997). 'Belief in extraterrestrial life, UFO-related beliefs, and schizotypal personality'. *Personality and Individual Differences*, 23, 519–21.

Cheyne, J. A. & Girard, T. A. (2009). 'The body unbound: Vestibular-motor hallucinations and out-of-body experiences'. *Cortex*, 45, 201–15.

Cheyne, J. A., Newby-Clark, I. R., & Rueffer, S. D. (1999). 'Relations among hypnagogic and hypnopompic experiences associated with sleep paralysis'. *Journal of Sleep Research*, 8, 313–17.

Childs, C. & Murray, C. D. (2010). '"We all had an experience in there together": A discursive psychological analysis of collaborative paranormal accounts by paranormal investigation team members'. *Qualitative Research in Psychology*, 7, 21–33.

Chorpita, B. F. & Barlow, D. H. (1998). 'The development of anxiety: The role of control in the early environment'. *Psychological Bulletin*, 124, 3–21.

Clancy, S. A. (2005). *Abducted: Why people come to believe they were kidnapped by aliens*. Cambridge, MA: Harvard University Press.

Clancy, S. A., McNally, R. J., Schacter, D. L., Lenzenweger, M. F., & Pitman, R. K. (2002). 'Memory distortion in people reporting abduction by aliens'. *Journal of Abnormal Psychology*, 111, 455–61.

Claridge, G. A. (1997). *Schizotypy: Implications for illness and health*. Oxford: Oxford University Press.

Claridge, G. A. (2010). 'Spiritual experience: Healthy psychoticism?' In I. Clarke (ed.), *Psychosis and spirituality: Consolidating the new paradigm*. 2nd edn (pp. 75–87). Chichester: John Wiley and Sons.

Clark, C. A. & Worthington, E. L. (1990). 'Family variables affecting the transmission of religious values from parents to adolescents: A review'. In B. K. Barber & B. C. Rollins (eds), *Parent–adolescent relationships* (pp. 154–84). Lanham, MD: University Press of America.

Clarke, D. (1991). 'Belief in the paranormal: A New Zealand survey'. *Journal of the Society for Psychical Research*, 57, 412–25.

Clarke, D. (1993). 'Self-actualization and paranormal beliefs: An empirical study'. *Journal of the Society for Psychical Research*, 59, 81–8.

Clarke, D. (1995). 'Experience and other reasons given for belief and disbelief in paranormal and religious phenomena'. *Journal of the Society for Psychical Research*, 60, 371–84.

Clarke, D., Randles, J., & Roberts, A. (2000). *The UFOs that never were*. London: London House.

Clarke, D. & Roberts, A. (1990). *Phantoms of the sky: UFOs, a modern myth?* London: Robert Hale.

Clarke, D. & Roberts, A. (2002). *Out of the shadows: UFOs, the establishment and the official cover-up*. London: Piatkus.

Clarke, I. (ed.). (2010). *Psychosis and spirituality: Consolidating the new paradigm*. 2nd edn. Chichester: John Wiley and Sons.

Cohen, G. (1989). *Memory in the real world*. Hillsdale, NJ, England: Lawrence Erlbaum Associates.

Cohn, S. A. (1999). 'Second sight and family history: Pedigree and segregation analyses'. *Journal of Scientific Exploration*, 13, 351–72.

Coleman, M. & Ganong, L. H. (1987). 'Sex, sex roles and irrational beliefs'. *Psychological Reports*, 61, 631–8.

Colman, A. M. (1987). *Facts, fallacies and frauds in psychology*. London: Hutchinson.

Conklin, E. S. (1919). 'Superstitious belief and practice among college students'. *American Journal of Psychology*, 30, 83–102.

Cook, C. M. & Persinger, M. A. (1997). 'Experimental induction of the "sensed presence" in normal subjects and an exceptional subject'. *Perceptual and Motor Skills*, 85, 683–93.

Cook, C. M. & Persinger, M. A. (2001). 'Geophysical variables and behaviour: XCII. Experimental elicitation of the experience of a sentient being by right hemispheric, weak magnetic fields: Interaction with temporal lobe sensitivity'. *Perceptual and Motor Skills*, 92, 447–8.

Costa, P. T., Jr & McCrae, R. R. (1992). *The NEO Personality Inventory Manual*. Odessa, FL: Personality Assessment Resources, Inc.

Costa, P. T., Jr & McCrae, R. R. (1995). 'Domains and facets: Hierarchical personality assessment using the revised NEO Personality Inventory'. *Journal of Personality Assessment*, 64, 21–50.

Council, J. R. & Huff, K. D. (1990). 'Hypnosis, fantasy activity and reports of paranormal experiences in high, medium and low fantasizers'. *British Journal of Experimental and Clinical Hypnosis*, 7, 9–15.

Crawley, S. E., French, C. C., & Yesson, S. A. (2002). 'Evidence for transliminality from a subliminal card-guessing task'. *Perception*, 31, 887–92.

Crislip, M. (2008). 'Near death experiences and the medical literature. [US] *Skeptic*, 14(2), 14–15.

Curtis, J. T. & Wilson, J. P. (1997). 'Sensation-seeking and ESP test performance: A preliminary investigation'. *Journal of the Society for Psychical Research*, 62, 1–21.

Dag, I. (1999). 'The relationships among paranormal beliefs, locus of control and psychopathology in a Turkish college sample'. *Personality and Individual Differences*, 26, 723–37.

Dagnall, N., Parker, A., & Munley, G. (2007). 'Superstitious belief – Negative and positive superstitions and psychological functioning'. *European Journal of Parapsychology*, 22, 121–37.

Dagnall, N., Parker, A., & Munley, G. (2008). 'News events, false memory and paranormal belief'. *European Journal of Parapsychology*, 23, 173–88.

Dambrun, M. (2004). 'Belief in paranormal determinism as a source of prejudice towards disadvantaged groups: "The dark side of stars"'. *Social Behaviour and Personality*, 32, 627–36.

Davies, M. F. (1988). 'Paranormal beliefs in British and southern USA college students'. *Psychological Reports*, 62, 163–6.

Davies, M. F. & Kirkby, H. E. (1985). 'Multidimensionality of the relationship between perceived control and belief in the paranormal: Spheres of control and types of paranormal phenomena'. *Personality and Individual Differences*, 6, 661–3.

Davis, G. A., Peterson, J. M., & Farley, F. H. (1974). 'Attitudes, motivation, sensation seeking, and belief in ESP as predictors of real creative behaviour'. *Journal of Creative Behaviour*, 8, 31–9.

Dawkins, R. (1976). *The selfish gene*. Oxford: Oxford University Press.

Dean, G. (1991). 'Does astrology need to be true? Part 1: A look at the real thing'. In K. Frazier (ed.), *The hundredth monkey and other paradigms of the paranormal* (pp. 279–96). Buffalo, NY: Prometheus.

Deese, J. (1959). 'On the prediction of occurrence of particular verbal intrusions in immediate recall'. *Journal of Experimental Psychology*, 58, 17–22.

Delanoy, D. (2001). 'Anomalous psychophysiological responses to remote cognition: The DMILS studies'. *European Journal of Parapsychology*, 16, 30–41.

Denman, C. (2010). 'A look at probability and coincidence'. In W. M. Grossman & C. C. French (eds), *Why statues weep: The best of the Skeptic* (pp. 119–24). London: The Philosophy Press Ltd.

De Ridder, D., Van Laere, K., Dupont, P., Menovsky, T., & Van de Heyning, P. (2007). 'Visualising out-of-body experience in the brain'. *New England Journal of Medicine*, 357, 1829–33.

Devereux, P. & Brookesmith, P. (1997). *UFOs and ufology: The first 50 years*. London: Blandford.

Diamond, J. (2010). 'Miracle cures: Only believe'. In W. M. Grossman and C. C. French (eds), *Why statues weep: The best of the Skeptic* (pp. 67–70). London: Philosophy Press.

Dobyns, Y. H., Dunne, B. J., Jahn, R. G., & Nelson, R. D. (1992). 'Response to Hansen, Utts and Markwick: Statistical and methodological problems of the PEAR remote viewing (*sic*) experiments'. *Journal of Parapsychology*, 56, 115–46.

Donahue, M. J. (1993). 'Prevalence and correlates of new age beliefs in six protestant denominations'. *Journal for the Scientific Study of Religion*, 32, 177–84.

Donovan, J. M. (1998). 'Reinterpreting telepathy as unusual experiences of empathy and charisma'. *Perceptual and Motor Skills*, 87, 131–46.

Drewes, A. A. (2002). 'Dr. Louisa Rhine's letters revisited: The children'. *Journal of Parapsychology*, 66, 343–70.

Druffel, A. & Rogo, D. S. (1980). *The Tujunga Canyon contacts*. Englewood Cliffs, NJ: Prentice Hall.

Dudley, R. L. & Dudley, M. G. (1986). 'Transmission of religious values from parents to adolescents'. *Review of Religious Research*, 28, 3–15.

Dudley, R. T. (1999). 'The effect of superstitious belief on performance following an unsolvable problem'. *Personality and Individual Differences*, 26, 1057–64.

Dudley, R. T. (2000). 'The relationship between negative affect and paranormal belief'. *Personality and Individual Differences*, 28, 315–21.

Dudley, R. T. (2002). 'Order effects in research on paranormal belief'. *Psychological Reports*, 90, 665–6.

Dudley, R. T. & Whisnand, E. A. (2000). 'Paranormal belief and attributional style'. *Psychological Reports*, 86, 863–4.

Easton, S., Blanke, O., & Mohr, C. (2009). 'A putative implication for fronto-parietal connectivity in out-of-body experiences'. *Cortex*, 45, 216–27.

Eckblad, M. & Chapman, L. (1983). 'Magical ideation as an indicator of schizoptypy'. *Journal of Consulting and Clinical Psychology*, 51, 215–25.

Economist, The (1993a). 'Play your cards right'. 378 (7830), 76.

Economist, The (1993b). 'The splash of the cockerel'. 326 (7795), 75.

Edge, H. L., Morris, R. L., Rush, J. H., & Palmer, J. (1986). *Foundations of parapsychology: Exploring the boundaries of human capability*. Boston, MA: Routledge and Kegan Paul.

Einstein, D. A. & Menzies, R. G. (2006). 'Magical thinking in obsessive-compulsive disorder, panic disorder and the general community'. *Behavioural and Cognitive Psychotherapy*, 34, 351–7.

Elev, T. C. & Gregory, A. M. (2004). 'Behavioural genetics'. In T. L. Morris & J. S. March (eds), *Anxiety disorders in children and adolescents* (pp. 71–97). New York: Guildford.

Ellis, D. J. (1975). 'Listening to the "Raudive voices"'. *Journal of the Society for Psychical Research*, 48, 31–42.

Emme, E. E. (1940). 'Modification and origin of certain beliefs in superstition among 96 college students'. *Journal of Psychology*, 10, 279–91.

Emme, E. E. (1941). 'Supplementary study of superstitious beliefs among college students'. *Journal of Psychology*, 12, 183–4.

Emmons, C. F. & Sobal, J. (1981). 'Paranormal beliefs: Testing the marginality hypothesis'. *Sociological Focus*, 14, 49–56.

Epstein, S., Pacini, R., Denes-Raj, V., & Heier, H. (1996). 'Individual differences in intuitive-experiential and analytical-rational thinking styles'. *Journal of Personality and Social Psychology*, 71, 390–405.

Eudell, R. & Campbell, J. B. (2007). 'Openness to experience and belief in the paranormal – A modified replication of Zingrone, Alvarado, and Dalton (1998–99)'. *European Journal of Parapsychology*, 22, 166–74.

Evans, D. W., Milanak, M. E., Medeiros, B., & Ross, J. L. (2002). 'Magical beliefs and rituals in young children'. *Child Psychiatry and Human Development*, 39, 43–58.

Evans, H. (1983). *The evidence for UFOs*. Wellingborough: Aquarian.

Evans, H. (1998). *From other worlds: The truth about aliens, abductions, UFOs and the paranormal*. London: Carlton.

Eysenck, H. J. (1964). *Crime and personality*. London: Routledge and Kegan Paul.

Eysenck, H. J. (1967). 'Personality and extra-sensory perception'. *Journal of the Society for Psychical Research*, 44, 55–71.

Eysenck, H. J. & Eysenck, S. B. G. (1975). *Manual of the Eysenck Personality Questionnaire*. London: Hodder and Stoughton.

Eysenck, M. (ed.). (1998). *Psychology: An integrated approach*. Harlow, England: Longman.

Farha, B. & Steward, G. (2006). 'Paranormal beliefs: An analysis of college students'. *Sceptical Inquirer*, 31, 37–40.

Femina, D. D., Yeager, C. A., & Lewis, D. O. (1990). 'Child abuse (adolescent records vs. adult recall)'. *Child Abuse & Neglect*, 13, 227–31.

Fenwick, P. (2001). 'The neurophysiology of religious experience'. In I. Clarke (ed.), *Psychosis and spirituality: Exploring the new frontier* (pp. 15–26). London: Whurr Publishers.

Ferriar, J. (1813). *An essay towards a theory of apparitions*. London: Cadell and Davies.

Fichten, C. S. & Sunerton, B. (1983). 'Popular horoscopes and the "Barnum effect"'. *Journal of Psychology*, 114, 123–34.

Finkel, D. & McGue, M. (1997). 'Sex differences and nonadditivity in heritability of the Multidimensional Personality Questionnaire Scales'. *Journal of Personality and Social Psychology*, 72, 929–38.

Fisman, S. & Takhar, J. (1996). 'Alien abduction in PTSD'. *Journal of the American Academy of Child and Adolescent Psychiatry*, 34, 974–5.

Fitzpatrick, O. D. & Shook, S. L. (1994). 'Belief in the paranormal: Does identity development during the college years make a difference? An initial investigation'. *Journal of Parapsychology*, 58, 315–29.

Flavell, J. H., Green, F. L., & Flavell, E. R. (1986). 'Development of knowledge about the appearance–reality distinction'. *Monographs of the Society for Research in Child Development*, 51(1), Serial No. 212, 1–87.

Fong, G. T. & Nisbett, R. E. (1991). 'Immediately and delayed transfer of training effects in statistical reasoning'. *Journal of Experimental Psychology: General*, 120, 34–45.

Fontana, D. (2003). *Psychology, religion, and spirituality*. British Psychological Society and Blackwell: Leicester and Oxford.

Fox, J. W. (1992). 'The structure, stability and social antecedence of reported paranormal experiences'. *Sociological Analysis*, 53, 417–31.

Fox, J. & Williams, C. (2000). 'Paranormal belief, experience, and the Keirsey Temperament Sorter'. *Psychological Reports*, 86, 1104–6.

Francis, L. J., Williams, E., & Robbins, M. (2010). 'Personality, conventional Christian belief and unconventional paranormal belief: A study among teenagers'. *British Journal of Religious Education*, 32, 31–9.

Frazier, K., Karr, B., & Nickell, J. (eds). (1997). *The UFO invasion: The Roswell incident, alien abductions, and government coverups*. Amherst, NY: Prometheus.

Fredrickson, R. (1992). *Repressed memories*. New York: Fireside/Parkside.

French, C. C. (1992a). 'Factors underlying belief in the paranormal: Do sheep and goats think differently?' *The Psychologist*, 5, 295–9.

French, C. C. (1992b). 'Population stereotypes and belief in the paranormal: Is there a relationship?' *Australian Psychologist*, 27, 57–8.

French, C. C. (2001a). 'Why I study anomalistic psychology'. *The Psychologist*, 14, 356–7.

French, C. C. (2001b). *Paranormal perception? A critical evaluation*. London: Institute for Cultural Research. Monograph Series No. 42.

French, C. C. (2001c). 'Alien abductions'. In R. Roberts & D. Groome (eds), *Parapsychology: The science of unusual experience* (pp. 102–16). London: Arnold.

French, C. C. (2001d). 'Dying to know the truth: Visions of a dying brain or false memories?' *Lancet*, 358, 2010–11.

French, C. C. (2003). 'Fantastic memories: The relevance of research into eyewitness testimony and false memories for reports of anomalous experiences'. *Journal of Consciousness Studies*, 10, 153–74.

French, C. C. (2005a). 'Scepticism'. In J. Henry (ed.), *Parapsychology: Research into exceptional experiences* (pp. 80–9). London: Routledge.

French, C. C. (2005b). 'Near-death experiences in cardiac arrest survivors'. *Progress in Brain Research*, 150, 355–72.

French, C. C. (2009a). 'Anomalistic psychology'. In M. Cardwell, L. Clark, C. Meldrum, & A. Wadeley (eds), *Psychology A2 for AQA A*. 4th edn. (pp. 472–505). London: Collins.

French, C. C. (2009b). 'Near-death experiences and the brain'. In C. Murray (ed.), *Psychological scientific perspectives on out-of-body and near-death experiences* (pp. 187–203). New York: Nova Science Publishers.

French, C. C. (2009c). 'Spoon-bending for beginners: Teaching anomalistic psychology to teenagers'. Retrieved 28 February 2013 from http://www.guardian.co.uk/science/2009/aug/11/anomalistic-psychology-paranormal-parapsychology.

French, C. C. (2010a). 'Reflections of a (relatively) moderate skeptic'. In S. Krippner & H. L. Friedman (eds), *Debating psychic experience: Human potential or human illusion?* (pp. 53–64). Santa Barbara, CA: Praeger.

French, C. C. (2010b). 'Missing the point?' In S. Krippner & H. L. Friedman (eds), *Debating psychic experience: Human potential or human illusion?* (pp. 149–51). Santa Barbara, CA: Praeger.

French, C. C. (2011a). 'The waking nightmare of sleep paralysis'. In K. Sturgess and the Young Australian Skeptics (eds), *Skeptical blog anthology* (pp. 103–7). Young Australian Skeptics.

French, C. C. (2011b). 'The rise of anomalistic psychology – and the fall of parapsychology?' Retrieved 28 February 2013 from http://blogs.nature.com/soapboxscience/2011/12/19/the-rise-of-anomalistic-psychology-%E2%80%93-and-the-fall-of-parapsychology.

French, C. C. (2012a). 'Precognition studies and the curse of the failed replications'. Retrieved 9 January 2013 from http://www.guardian.co.uk/science/2012/mar/15/precognition-studies-curse-failed-replications.

French, C. C. (2012b). 'Halloween challenge: Psychics submit their powers to a scientific trial'. Retrieved 13 January 2013 from http://www.guardian.co.uk/science/2012/oct/31/halloween-challenge-psychics-scientific-trial.

French, C. C. (2012c). 'Doubting dowsers'. *The Skeptic*, Summer, p. 6.

French, C. C. (2012d). 'Peering into the future of peer review: A curious case from parapsychology'. *Psychology Review*, 18(2), 26–9.

French, C. C. (2013). 'The psychology of ghosts and haunting'. *The Skeptic*, 24(2), 31–4.

French, C. C., Haque, U., Bunton-Stasyshyn, R., & Davis, R. (2009). 'The "haunt" project: An attempt to build a "haunted" room by manipulating complex electromagnetic fields and infrasound'. *Cortex*, 45, 619–29.

French, C. C. & Santomauro, J. (2007). 'Something wicked this way comes: Causes and interpretations of sleep paralysis'. In S. Della Sala (ed.), *Tall tales about the mind and brain: Separating fact from fiction* (pp. 380–98). Oxford: Oxford University Press.

French, C. C., Santomauro, J., Hamilton, V., Fox, R., & Thalbourne, M. A. (2008). 'Psychological aspects of the alien contact experience'. *Cortex*, 44, 1387–95.

French, C. C. & Wilson, K. (2006). 'Incredible memories: How accurate are reports of anomalous events?' *European Journal of Parapsychology*, 21, 166–81.

French, C. C. & Wilson, K. (2007). 'Cognitive factors underlying paranormal beliefs and experiences'. In S. Della Sala (ed.), *Tall tales about the mind and brain: Separating fact from fiction* (pp. 3–22). Oxford: Oxford University Press.

French, C. C., Wilson, K., & Davis, L. (2012). 'Is the correlation between paranormal belief and susceptibility to false memories due to acquiescence bias?' Invited presentation to Ninth Symposium of the Bial Foundation, Porto, Portugal, 28–31 March.

Frost, R. O., Krause, M. S., McMahon, M. J., Peppe, J., Evans, M., McPhee, A. E., & Holden, M. (1993). 'Compulsivity and superstitiousness'. *Behaviour Research and Therapy*, 31, 423–5.

Fuller, J. (1966). *The interrupted journey*. New York: Dial.

Gallagher, C., Kumar, V. K., & Pekala, R. J. (1994). 'The anomalous experiences inventory: Reliability and validity'. *Journal of Parapsychology*, 58, 402–28.

Gardner, M. (1957). *Fads and fallacies in the name of science*. New York: Dover.

Garry, M., Manning, C. G., Loftus, E. F., & Sherman, S. J. (1996). 'Imagination inflation: Imagining a childhood event inflates confidence that it occurred'. *Psychonomic Bulletin and Review*, 3, 208–14.

Gaynard, T. J. (1992). 'Young people and the paranormal'. *Journal of the Society for Psychical Research*, 58, 165–80.

Genovese, J. E. C. (2005). 'Paranormal beliefs, schizotypy, and thinking styles among teachers and future teachers'. *Personality and Individual Differences*, 39, 93–102.

Gianotti, L. R. R., Faber, P. L., & Lehmann, D. (2002). 'EEG source locations after guessed random events in believers and sceptics of paranormal phenomena'. *International Congress Series*, 1232, 439–41.

Gianotti, L. R. R., Mohr, C., Pizzagalli, D., Lehmann, C., & Brugger, P. (2001). 'Associative processing and paranormal belief'. *Psychiatry and Clinical Neurosciences*, 55, 595–603.

Gibson, R. L. & Hartshorne, T. S. (1996). 'Childhood sexual abuse and adult loneliness and network orientation'. *Child Abuse and Neglect*, 20, 1087–93.

Gilovich, T. (1990). 'Differential construal and the false consensus effect'. *Journal of Personality and Social Psychology*, 59, 623–34.

Gilovich, T. (1991). *How we know what isn't so: The fallibility of human reason in everyday life*. New York, NY: Free Press.

Gilovich, T., Vallone, R., & Tversky, A. (1985). 'The hot hand in basketball: On the misperception of random sequences'. *Cognitive Psychology*, 17, 295–314.

Glicksohn, J. (1990). 'Belief in the paranormal and subjective paranormal experience'. *Personality and Individual Differences*, 11, 675–83.

Glicksohn, J. & Barrett, T. R. (2003). 'Absorption and hallucinatory experience'. *Applied Cognitive Psychology*, 17, 833–49.

Gloor, P. (1986). 'Role of the limbic system in perception, memory, and affect: Lessons from temporal lobe epilepsy'. In B. K. Doane & K. E. Livingston (eds). *The limbic system: Functional organisation and clinical disorders* (pp. 159–69). New York: Raven Press.

Goldacre, B. (2010). 'The caveat in paragraph number 19'. Retrieved 27 November 2012 from http://www.badscience.net/2010/10/the-caveat-in-paragraph-number-19/.

Goldacre, B. (2011). 'Backwards step on looking into the future'. Retrieved 30 December 2011 from http://www.guardian.co.uk/commentisfree/2011/apr/23/ben-goldacre-bad-science.

Golomb, C. & Galasso, L. (1995). 'Make believe and reality: Explorations of the imaginary realm'. *Developmental Psychology*, 31, 800–10.

Gordon, A. (1997). *Ghostly matters: Haunting and the sociological imagination*. Minneapolis, MN: University of Minnesota Press.

Göritz, A. S. & Schumacher, J. (2000). 'The WWW as a research medium: An illustrative survey of paranormal belief'. *Perceptual and Motor Skills*, 90, 1195–206.

Gotlib, D. (1994). 'Comments, questions on Keith Basterfield's talk "Abductions: The paranormal connection"'. In A. Pritchard, D. Pritchard, J. E. Mack, P. Casey, & C. Yapp (eds), *Alien discussions: Proceedings of the abduction study conference held at MIT* (p. 50). Cambridge, MA: North Cambridge Press.

Goulding, A. (2004). 'Schizotypy models in relation to subjective health and paranormal beliefs and experiences'. *Personality and Individual Differences*, 37, 157–67.

Goulding, A. (2005a). 'Healthy schizotypy in a population of paranormal believers and experients'. *Personality and Individual Differences*, 38, 1069–83.

Goulding, A. (2005b). 'Participant variables associated with psi ganzfeld results'. *European Journal of Parapsychology*, 20, 50–64.

Goulding A. & Parker, A. (2001). 'Finding psi in the paranormal: Psychometric measures used in research on paranormal beliefs/experiences and in research on psi-ability'. *European Journal of Parapsychology*, 16, 73–101.

Gow, K., Lane, A., & Chant, D. (2003). 'Personality characteristics, beliefs and the near-death experience'. *Australian Journal of Clinical and Experimental Hypnosis*, 31, 128–52.

Gow, K., Lang, T., & Chant, D. (2004). 'Fantasy proneness, paranormal beliefs and personality features in out-of-body experiences'. *Contemporary Hypnosis*, 21, 107–25.

Granqvist, P., Fredrikson, M., Unge, P., Hagenfeldt, A., Valind, S., Larhammar, D., & Larsson, M. (2005). 'Sensed presence and mystical experiences are predicted by suggestibility, not by the application of transcranial weak complex magnetic fields'. *Neuroscience Letters*, 379, 1–6.

Granqvist, P. & Hagekull, B. (2001). 'Seeking security in the new age: On attachment and emotional compensation'. *Journal for the Scientific Study of Religion*, 40, 527–45.

Gray, T. (1990). 'Gender differences in belief in scientifically unsubstantiated phenomena'. *Canadian Journal of Behavioural Science*, 22, 181–90.

Gray, T. & Mill, D. (1990). 'Critical abilities, graduate education (Biology vs. English), and belief in unsubstantiated phenomena'. *Canadian Journal of Behavioural Science*, 22, 162–72.

Green, J. P. & Lynn, S. J. (2009). 'Fantasy proneness and hypnotizability: Another look'. *Contemporary Hypnosis*, 25, 156–64.

Greyson, B. (2000a). 'Dissociation in people who have near-death experiences: Out of their bodies or out of their minds?' *Lancet,* 355, 460–3.

Greyson, B. (2000b). 'Near-death experiences'. In E. Cardeña, S. J. Lynn, & S. Krippner (eds), *Varieties of anomalous experience: Examining the scientific evidence* (pp. 315–52). Washington: American Psychological Association.

Greyson, B. (2003). 'Incidence and correlates of near-death experiences in a cardiac care unit'. *General Hospital Psychiatry*, 25, 269–76.

Greyson, B. & Bush, N. E. (1992). 'Distressing near-death experiences'. *Psychiatry,* 55, 95–110.

Grimmer, M. R. & White, K. D. (1992). 'Nonconventional beliefs among Australian science and non-science students'. *Journal of Psychology*, 126, 521–8.

Groth-Marnat, G. & Pegden, J. (1998). 'Personality correlates of paranormal belief: Locus of control and sensation seeking'. *Social Behaviour and Personality*, 26, 291–6.

Groth-Marnat, G., Roberts, L., & Ollier, K. (1998–9). 'Hypnotizability, dissociation, paranormal beliefs'. *Imagination, Cognition & Personality*, 18, 127–32.

Gunnoe, M. J. & Moore, K. A. (2002). 'Predictors of religiosity among youth aged 17–22: A longitudinal survey of the National Survey of children'. *Journal for the Scientific Study of Religion*, 41, 613–22.

Guthrie, S. (1993). *Faces in the clouds: A new theory of religion*. Oxford: Oxford University Press.

Hampp, A. (2010). '"Paranormal activity" wins by listening to fans' "demands"'. *Advertising Age*, 81, 48.

Hansen, G. P., Utts, J. M., & Markwick, B. (1992). 'Critique of the PEAR remote viewing experiments'. *Journal of Parapsychology*, 56, 97–113.

Haraldsson, E. (1981). 'Some determinants of belief in psychical phenomena'. *Journal of the American Society for Psychical Research*, 75, 297–309.

Haraldsson, E. (1985a). 'Representative national surveys of psychic phenomena: Iceland, Great Britain, Sweden, USA, and Gallup's multinational survey'. *Journal of the Society for Psychical Research*, 53, 145–58.

Haraldsson, E. (1985b). 'Interrogative suggestibility and its relationship with personality, perceptual defensiveness and extraordinary beliefs'. *Personality and Individual Differences*, 6, 765–7.

Haraldsson, E. (2002). *Children who speak of past-life experiences: Is there a psychological explanation?* Paper presented to the Parapsychological Association Congress, Paris, August.

Haraldsson, E., Fowler, P. C., & Periyannanpillai, V. (2000). 'Psychological characteristics of children who speak of a previous life: A further field study in Sri Lanka'. *Transcultural Psychiatry*, 37, 525–44.

Haraldsson, E. & Houtkooper, J. M. (1996). 'Traditional Christian beliefs, spiritualism, and the paranormal: An Icelandic-American comparison'. *International Journal for the Psychology of Religion*, 6, 51–64.

Harris, M. (1986). *Sorry, you've been duped! The truth behind classic mysteries of the paranormal*. London: Weidenfeld and Nicolson.

Harris, P. (1997). 'The last of the magicians? Children, scientists, and the invocation of hidden causal powers'. *Child Development*, 68, 1018–20.

Harris, P. L., Brown, E., Marriot, C., Whittal, S., & Harmer, S. (1991). 'Monsters, ghosts, and witches: Testing the limits of the fantasy–reality distinction in young children'. *British Journal of Developmental Psychology*, 9, 105–23.

Harris, S. (2012). 'Science on the brink of death'. Retrieved 13 February 2013 from http://www.samharris.org/blog/item/science-on-the-brink-of-death.

Hartman, S. E. (1999). 'Another view of the Paranormal Belief Scale'. *Journal of Parapsychology*, 63, 131–41.

Hawley, C. & Jones, M. (2010). 'Export ban for useless bomb detector'. Retrieved 2 March 2013 from http://news.bbc.co.uk/1/hi/programmes/newsnight/8471187.stm.

Heard, K. V. & Vyse, S. A. (1998–9). 'Authoritarianism and paranormal beliefs'. *Imagination, Cognition and Personality*, 18, 121–6.

Heintz, L. M. & Barušs, I. (2001). 'Spirituality in late adulthood'. *Psychological Reports*, 88, 651–4.

Hergovich, A. (2003). 'Field dependence, suggestibility, and belief in paranormal phenomena'. *Personality and Individual Differences*, 34, 195–209.

Hergovich, A. & Arendasy, A. (2005). 'Critical thinking ability and belief in the paranormal'. *Personality and Individual Differences*, 38, 1805–12.

Hergovich, A., Schott, R., & Arendasy, A. (2008). 'On the relationship between paranormal belief and schizotypy among adolescents'. *Personality and Individual Differences*, 45, 119–25.

Heriot-Maitland, C., Knight, M., & Peters, E. (2012). 'A qualitative comparison of psychotic-like phenomena in clinical and non-clinical populations'. *British Journal of Clinical Psychology*, 51, 37–53.

Higgins, S. T., Morris, E. K., & Johnson, L. M. (1989). 'Social transmission of superstitious behaviour in preschool children'. *Psychological Record*, 39, 307–23.

Hill, A. (2011). *Paranormal media: Audiences, spirits and magic in popular culture*. London and New York: Routledge.

Hines, T. (2003). *Pseudoscience and the paranormal*. 2nd edn. Amherst, NY: Prometheus.

Hodgson, R. & Davey, S. J. (1887). 'The possibilities of malobservation and lapse of memory from a practical point of view'. *Proceedings of the Society for Psychical Research*, 4, 381–404.

Holden, K. J. & French, C. C. (2002). 'Alien abduction experiences: Clues from neuropsychology and neuropsychiatry'. *Cognitive Neuropsychiatry*, 7, 163–78.

Hollinger, F. & Smith, T. B. (2002). 'Religion and esotericism among students: A cross-cultural comparative study'. *Journal of Contemporary Religion*, 17, 229–49.

Holt, N., Simmonds-Moore, C., Luke, D., & French, C. C. (2012). *Anomalistic psychology*. Basingstoke: Palgrave Macmillan.

Honorton, C. (1978). 'Psi and internal attentional states'. In B. Wolman (ed.), *Handbook of parapsychology* (pp. 435–72). Jefferson, NC: McFarland and Company.

Honorton, C. (1985). 'Meta-analysis of psi ganzfeld research: A response to Hyman'. *Journal of Parapsychology*, 49, 51–91.

Honorton, C., Ferrari, D. C., & Bem, D. J. (1992). 'Extraversion and ESP performance: Meta-analysis and a new confirmation'. In L. A. Henkel & G. R. Schmeidler (eds), *Research in parapsychology 1990* (pp. 35–8). Metuchen, NJ: Scarecrow Press.

Hood, B. (2009). *Supersense: From superstition to religion – The brain science of belief*. London: Constable.

Hopkins, B. (1987). *Intruders: The incredible visitations at Copley Woods*. New York: Random House.

Hopkins, B., Jacobs, D. M., & Westrum, R. (1992). *Unusual personal experiences: An analysis of the data from three national surveys conducted by the Roper Organisation*. Las Vegas, CA: Bigelow Holding Company.

Hough, P. & Rogers, P. (2007–8). 'Individuals who report being abducted by aliens: Core experiences and individual differences'. *Imagination, Cognition & Personality*, 27, 139–61.

Houran, J. (1997). 'Tolerance of ambiguity and the perception of UFOs'. *Perceptual and Motor Skills*, 85, 973–4.

Houran, J., Ashe, D. D., & Thalbourne, M. A. (2003). 'Encounter experiences in the context of mental boundaries and bilaterality'. *Journal of the Society for Psychical Research*, 67, 260–80.

Houran, J., Irwin, H. J., & Lange, R. (2001). 'Clinical relevance of the two-factor Rasch version of the Revised Paranormal Belief Scale'. *Personality and Individual Differences*, 31, 371–82.

Houran, J., Kumar, V. K., Thalbourne, M. A., & Lavertue, N. E. (2002). 'Haunted by somatic tendencies: Spirit infestation as psychogenic illness'. *Mental Health, Religion and Culture*, 5, 119–33.

Houran, J. & Lange, R. (1996). 'Hauntings and poltergeist-like episodes as a confluence of conventional phenomena: A general hypothesis'. *Perceptual and Motor Skills*, 83, 1307–16.

Houran, J. & Lange, R. (1997). 'Hallucinations that comfort: Contextual mediation of deathbed visions'. *Perceptual and Motor Skills*, 84, 1491–504.

Houran, J. & Lange, R. (1998). 'Modelling precognitive dreams as meaningful coincidences'. *Psychological Reports*, 83, 1411–14.

Houran, J. & Lange, R. (2001). 'Support for the construct validity of the two-factor conceptualisation of paranormal belief: A complement to Thalbourne'. *European Journal of Parapsychology*, 16, 53–61.

Houran, J. & Lange, R. (2004). 'Redefining delusion based on studies of subjective paranormal ideation'. *Psychological Reports*, 93, 501–13.

Houran, J. & Lange, R. (2009). 'Searching for an optimal level of transliminality in relation to putative psi'. *Journal of the Society for Psychical Research*, 73, 92–102.

Houran, J. & Thalbourne, M. A. (2001). 'Further study and speculation on the psychology of alien encounter experiences'. *Journal of the Society for Psychical Research*, 65, 26–37.

Houran, J., Thalbourne, M. A., & Lange, R. (2003). 'Methodological note: Erratum and comment on the use of the Revised Transliminality Scale'. *Consciousness and Cognition*, 12, 140–4.

Houran, J. & Williams, C. (1998). 'Relation of tolerance of ambiguity to global and specific paranormal experience'. *Psychological Reports*, 83, 807–18.

Houran, J., Wiseman, R., & Thalbourne, M. A. (2002). 'Perceptual-personality characteristics associated with naturalistic haunt experiences'. *European Journal of Parapsychology*, 17, 17–44.

Hunsberger, B. (1985). 'Parent–university student agreement on religious and non-religious issues'. *Journal for the Scientific Study of Religion*, 24, 314–20.

Hutson, M. (2012). *The 7 laws of magical thinking: How irrationality makes us happy, healthy, and sane*. Oxford: Oneworld Publications.

Hyman, R. (1977). '"Cold reading": How to convince strangers that you know all about them'. *The Zetetic*, Spring–Summer, 1, 18–37.

Hyman, R. (1981). 'The psychic reading'. *Annals of the New York Academy of Sciences*, 364, 169–81.

Hyman, R. (1985a). 'A critical historical overview of parapsychology'. In P. Kurtz (ed.), *A skeptic's handbook of parapsychology* (pp. 3–96). Buffalo, NY: Prometheus.

Hyman, R. (1985b). 'The ganzfeld psi experiment: A critical appraisal'. *Journal of Parapsychology*, 49, 3–49.

Hyman, R. (1994). 'Anomaly or artifact? Comments on Bem and Honorton'. *Psychological Bulletin*, 115, 19–24.

Hyman, R. (1996). 'Evaluation of a programme on anomalous mental phenomena'. *Journal of Scientific Exploration*, 10, 31–58.

Hyman, R. (2010). 'Meta-analysis that conceals more than it reveals: Comment on Storm et al. [2010a]'. *Psychological Bulletin*, 136, 486–90.

Hyman, R. & Honorton, C. (1986). 'A joint communiqué: The psi ganzfeld controversy'. *Journal of Parapsychology*, 50, 351–64.

Ioannidis, J. P. A. (2005). 'Why most published research findings are false'. *PLoS Medicine*, 2, 696–701.

Irwin, H. J. (1985a). 'A study of the measurement and the correlates of paranormal belief'. *Journal of the American Society for Psychical Research*, 79, 301–26.

Irwin, H. J. (1985b). *Flight of mind: A psychological study of the near-death experience*. Metuchen, NJ: Scarecrow Press.

Irwin, H. J. (1990). 'Fantasy-proneness and paranormal beliefs'. *Psychological Reports*, 66, 655–8.

Irwin, H. J. (1991a). 'A study of paranormal belief, psychological adjustment and fantasy-proneness'. *Journal of the American Society for Psychical Research*, 85, 317–31.

Irwin, H. J. (1991b). 'Reasoning skills of paranormal believers'. *Journal of Parapsychology*, 55, 281–300.

Irwin, H. J. (1992). 'Origins and functions of paranormal belief: The role of childhood trauma and interpersonal control'. *Journal of the American Society for Psychical Research*, 86, 199–208.

Irwin, H. J. (1993a). 'Belief in the paranormal: A review of the empirical literature'. *Journal of the American Society for Psychical Research*, 87, 1–39.

Irwin, H. J. (1993b). 'The near-death experience as a dissociative phenomenon: An empirical assessment'. *Journal of Near-Death Studies*, 12, 95–103.

Irwin, H. J. (1994a). 'Childhood trauma and the origins of paranormal belief: A constructive replication'. *Psychological Reports*, 74, 107–11.

Irwin, H. J. (1994b). 'Paranormal beliefs and proneness to dissociation'. *Psychological Reports*, 75, 1344–6.

Irwin, H. J. (1994c). 'Proneness to dissociation and traumatic childhood events'. *Journal of Nervous and Mental Disease*, 182, 456–60.

Irwin, H. J. (2000a). 'Age and sex differences in paranormal beliefs: A response to Vitulli, Tipton and Rowe (1999)'. *Psychological Reports*, 86, 595–6.

Irwin, H. J. (2000b). 'Belief in the paranormal and a sense of control over life'. *European Journal of Parapsychology*, 15, 68–78.

Irwin, H. J. (2000c). 'The disembodied self: An empirical study of dissociation and the out-of-body experience'. *Journal of Parapsychology*, 64, 261–76.

Irwin, H. J. (2001). 'Age and sex differences in paranormal beliefs after controlling for differential item functioning'. *European Journal of Psychology*, 16, 102–6.

Irwin, H. J. (2003). 'Paranormal beliefs and the maintenance of assumptive world views'. *Journal of the Society for Psychical Research*, 67, 18–25.

Irwin, H. J. (2009). *The psychology of paranormal belief: A researcher's handbook*. Hatfield, UK: University of Hertfordshire Press.

Irwin, H. J., Dagnall, N., & Drinkwater, K. (2012). 'Paranormal beliefs and cognitive processes underlying the formation of delusions'. *Australian Journal of Parapsychology*, 12, 107–26.

Irwin, H. J. & Green, M. J. (1998–9). 'Schizotypal processes and belief in the paranormal: A multidimensional study'. *European Journal of Parapsychology*, 14, 1–15.

Irwin, H. J. & Watt, C. (2007). *An introduction to parapsychology*. 5th edn. Jefferson, NC: McFarland & Co.

Irwin, H. J. & Young, J. M. (2002). 'Intuitive versus reflective processes in the formation of paranormal beliefs'. *European Journal of Parapsychology*, 17, 45–53.

Iverson, J. (1977). *More lives than one?* London: Pan Books.

Jacobs, D. M. (1990). 'The rock and roll theory of UFOs'. *Journal of UFO Studies*, 2, 141–3.

Jacobs, D. M. (1992). *Secret life: First-hand accounts of UFO abductions*. New York: Simon and Schuster.

Jacobs, D. M. (1998). *The threat – the secret agenda: What the aliens really want… and how they plan to get it*. New York: Simon and Schuster.

Jacobson, J. W., Mulick, J. A., & Schwartz, A. A. (1995). 'A history of facilitated communication. Science, pseudoscience, and antiscience. Science working group on facilitated communication'. *American Psychologist, 50*, 750–65.

James, W. (1902/1958). *The varieties of religious experience: A study in human nature.* Cambridge, MA: Harvard University Press.

Jang, K. L., Paris, J., Zweig-Frank, H., & Livesley, W. J. (1998). 'Twin study of dissociative experience'. *Journal of Nervous and Mental Disorders, 186*, 345–51.

Janis, I. L. (1982). *Groupthink: Psychological studies of policy decisions and fiascoes.* Boston, MA: Wadsworth.

Jansen, K. (1997). 'The ketamine model of the near-death experience: A central role for the N-Methyl-d-Aspartate receptor'. *Journal of Near-Death Studies, 16*, 5–26.

Jaspers, K. (1913). *General psychopathology.* Baltimore, MD: Johns Hopkins.

Jensen, C. G. & Cardeña, E. (2009). 'A controlled long-distance test of a professional medium'. *European Journal of Parapsychology, 24*, 53–67.

Joesting, J. & Joesting, R. (1969). 'Torrance's creative motivation inventory and its relationship to several personality variables'. *Psychological Reports, 24*, 30.

John, L. K., Loewenstein, G., & Prelec, D. (2012). 'Measuring the prevalence of questionable research practices with incentives for truth-telling'. *Psychological Science, 23*, 524–32.

Johnson, C. N. & Harris, P. L. (1994). 'Magic: Special but not excluded'. *British Journal of Developmental Psychology, 12*, 35–51.

Johnson, J. C., de Groot, H. P., & Spanos, N. P. (1995). 'The structure of paranormal belief: A factor-analytic investigation'. *Imagination, Cognition and Personality, 14*, 165–74.

Johnson, M. K., Hashtroudi, S., & Lindsay, D. S. (1993). 'Source monitoring'. *Psychological Bulletin, 114*, 3–28.

Johnson, M. K. & Raye, C. (1981). 'Reality monitoring'. *Psychological Review, 88*, 67–85.

Jones, W.H. & Russell, D. (1980). 'The selective processing of belief disconfirming information'. *European Journal of Social Psychology, 10*, 309–12.

Jones, W. H., Russell, D. W., & Nickel, T. W. (1977). 'Belief in the Paranormal Scale: An objective instrument to measure belief in magical phenomena and causes'. *Journal Supplement Abstract Service, Catalog of Selected Documents in Psychology, 7*, 100 (MS 1577).

Joukhador, J., Blaszczynski, A., & MacCallum, F. (2004). 'Superstitious beliefs in gambling among problem and non-problem gamblers: Preliminary data'. *Journal of Gambling Studies, 20*, 171–80.

Judd, C. M. & Gawronski, B. (2011). Editorial comment. *Journal of Personality and Social Psychology, 100*, 406.

Judson, I. R. & Wiltshaw, E. (1983). 'A near-death experience'. *Lancet, 8349*, 561–2.

Jung, C. G. (1959). *Flying saucers: A modern myth of things seen in the skies.* New York: Harcourt Brace.

Kahneman, D. (2011). *Thinking, fast and slow.* London: Penguin.

Kahneman, D. & Tversky, A. (1972). 'Subjective probability: A judgment of representativeness'. *Cognitive Psychology, 3*, 430–54.

Kane, M. F. (1888/1995). 'Spiritualism exposed: Margaret Fox Kane confesses to fraud'. In P. Kurtz (ed.), *A skeptic's handbook of parapsychology* (pp. 225–34). Buffalo, NY: Prometheus.

Kebbell, M. R. & Wagstaff, G. F. (1998). 'Hypnotic interviewing: The best way to interview eyewitnesses?' *Behavioral Sciences and the Law, 16*, 115–29.

Keene, M. L. (1976). *The psychic mafia*. New York: St Martin's Press.

Keinan, G. (1994). 'Effects of stress and tolerance of ambiguity on magical thinking'. *Journal of Personality and Social Psychology*, 67, 48–55.

Keinan, G. (2002). 'The effects of stress and desire for control on superstitious behavior'. *Personality and Social Psychology Bulletin*, 28, 102–8.

Kennedy, J. E. (2003). 'The polarization of psi beliefs: Rational, controlling masculine skepticism versus interconnected, spiritual feminine belief'. *Journal of the American Society for Psychical Research*, 97, 27–42.

Kennedy, J. E. (2004). 'A proposal and challenge for proponents and sceptics of psi'. *Journal of Parapsychology*, 68, 157–67.

Kennedy, J. E. (2007). 'Personality and motivations to believe, misbelieve, and disbelieve in paranormal phenomena'. *Journal of Parapsychology*, 71, 263–92.

Kennedy, J. E., Kanthamani, H., & Palmer, J. (1994). 'Psychic and spiritual experiences, health, well-being and meaning in life'. *Journal of Parapsychology*, 58, 353–83.

Killen, P., Wildman, R. W., & Wildman, R. W., II (1974). 'Superstitiousness and intelligence'. *Psychological Reports*, 34, 1158.

Kim, A. E. (2005). 'Nonofficial religion in South Korea: Prevalence of fortunetelling and other forms of divination'. *Review of Religious Research*, 46, 284–302.

King, L. A., Burton, C. M., Hicks, J. A., & Drigotas, S. M. (2007). 'Ghosts, UFOs, and magic: Positive affect and the experiential system'. *Journal of Personality and Social Psychology*, 92, 905–19.

Klare, R. (1990). 'Ghosts make news: How four newspapers report psychic phenomena'. *Skeptical Inquirer*, 14, 363–71.

Klass, P. J. (1983). *UFOs: The public deceived*. Buffalo, NY: Prometheus.

Klass, P. J. (1989). *UFO abductions: A dangerous game*. Updated edition. Buffalo, NY: Prometheus.

Klass, P. J. (1997). 'Additional comments about the "Unusual Personal Experiences Survey"'. In K. Frazier, B. Karr, & J. Nickell (eds), *The UFO invasion: The Roswell incident, alien abductions, and government coverups* (pp. 207–9). Amherst, NY: Prometheus.

Kobayashi, E., Hawco, C. S., Grova, C., Dubeau, F., & Gorman, J. (2006). 'Widespread and intense BOLD changes during brief focal electrographic seizures'. *Neurology*, 66, 1049–55.

Koole, S. L. & Lakens, D. (2012). 'Rewarding replications: A sure and simple way to improve psychological science'. *Perspectives on Psychological Science*, 7, 608–14.

Koopmans, J. R., Boomsma, D. I., Heath, A. C., & van Dooruen, L. J. P. (1995). 'A multivariate genetic analysis of sensation seeking'. *Behavior Genetics*, 25, 349–56.

Krippner, S. & Friedman, H. L. (eds). (2010). *Debating psychic experience: Human potential or human illusion?* Santa Barbara, CA: Praeger.

Kuhn, D. (1989). 'Children and adults as intuitive scientists'. *Psychological Review*, 96, 674–89.

Kuhn, G., Amlani, A. A., & Rensink, R. A. (2008). 'Towards a science of magic'. *Trends in Cognitive Sciences*, 12, 349–54.

Kumar, V. K., Pekala, R. J., & Cummings, J. (1993). 'Sensation seeking, drug use and reported paranormal beliefs and experiences'. *Personality and Individual Differences*, 14, 685–91.

Kurtz, P. (1985a). 'Spiritualists, mediums, and psychics: Some evidence of fraud'. In P. Kurtz (ed.), *A skeptic's handbook of parapsychology* (pp. 177–224). Buffalo, NY: Prometheus.

Kurtz, P. (1985b). 'The responsibilities of the media and paranormal claims'. *Skeptical Inquirer*, 9, 357–62.

Kurup, R. A. & Kurup, P. A. (2003). 'Hypothalamic digoxin, hemispheric chemical dominance, and spirituality'. *International Journal of Neuroscience*, 113, 383–93.

Lamont, P. (2007). 'Paranormal belief and the avowal of prior scepticism'. *Theory and Psychology*, 17, 681–96.

Lamont, P., Coelho, C., & McKinlay, A. (2009). 'Explaining the unexplained: Warranting disbelief in the paranormal'. *Discourse Studies*, 11, 543–59.

Lamont, P. & Wiseman, R. (1999). *Magic in theory: An introduction to the theoretical and psychological elements of conjuring*. Hatfield: University of Hertfordshire Press.

Lange, R. & Houran, J. (1998). 'Delusions of the paranormal: A haunting question of perception'. *Journal of Nervous and Mental Disease*, 186, 637–45.

Lange, R., Houran, J., Harte, T. M., & Havens, R. A. (1996). 'Contextual mediation of perceptions in hauntings and poltergeist-like experiences'. *Perceptual and Motor Skills*, 82, 755–62.

Lange, R., Irwin, H. J., & Houran, J. (2000). 'Top-down purification of Tobacyk's Revised Paranormal Belief Scale'. *Personality and Individual Differences*, 29, 131–56.

Lange, R. & Thalbourne, M. A. (2002). 'Rasch scaling paranormal belief and experience: Structure and semantics of Thalbourne's Australian Sheep-Goat scale'. *Psychological Reports*, 91, 1065–73.

Lange, R., Thalbourne, M. A., Houran, J., & Storm, L. (2000). 'The Revised Transliminality Scale: Reliability and validity data using a top-down purification procedure'. *Consciousness and Cognition*, 9, 591–617.

Langer, E. J. (1975). 'The illusion of control'. *Journal of Personality and Social Psychology*, 32, 311–28.

Langston, W. & Anderson, J. C. (2000). 'Talking back(wards): A test of the reverse speech hypothesis. Are listeners able to detect the emotional content of backward speech?' [US] *Skeptic*, 8(3), 30–5.

Launay, G. & Slade, P. (1981). 'The measurement of hallucinatory predisposition in male and female prisoners'. *Personality and Individual Differences*, 2, 221–34.

Lave, J. & Wenger, E. (1991). *Situated learning: Legitimate peripheral participation.* New York, NY: Cambridge University Press.

Lawrence, E. & Peters, E. (2004). 'Reasoning in believers in the paranormal'. *Journal of Nervous and Mental Disease*, 192, 727–33.

Lawrence, T. R. (1990–1). 'Subjective random generations and the reversed sheep-goat effect'. *European Journal of Parapsychology*, 8, 131–44.

Lawrence, T. R. (1995). 'How many factors of paranormal belief are there? A critique of the Paranormal Belief Scale'. *Journal of Parapsychology*, 59, 3–25.

Lawrence, T. R. & De Cicco, P. (1997). 'The factor structure of the Paranormal Belief Scale: More evidence in support of the Oblique Five'. *Journal of Parapsychology*, 61, 243–51.

Lawrence, T. R., Edwards, C., Barraclough, N., Church, S. & Hetherington, F. (1995). 'Modelling childhood causes of paranormal belief and experience: Childhood trauma and childhood fantasy'. *Personality and Individual Differences*, 19, 209–15.

Lawrence, T. R., Roe, C. A., & Williams, C. (1997). 'Confirming the factor structure of the Paranormal Belief Scale: Big orthogonal seven or oblique five?' *Journal of Parapsychology*, 61, 13–31.

Lawson, A. H. (1984). 'Perinatal imagery in UFO abduction reports'. *Journal of Psychohistory*, 12, 211–39.

Legare, C. H., Evans, E. M., Rosengren, K. S., & Harris, P. L. (2012). 'The coexistence of natural and supernatural explanations across cultures and development'. *Child Development*, 83, 779–93.

Lehman, D. R., Lempert, R. O., & Nisbett, R. E. (1988). 'The effects of graduate training on reasoning'. *American Psychologist*, 43, 431–22.

Leonard, H. L., Goldberger, E. L., Rapoport, J. L., Cheslow, D. L., & Swedo, S. E. (1990). 'Childhood rituals: Normal development or obsessive-compulsive symptoms?' *Journal of the American Academy of Child & Adolescent Psychiatry*, 29, 17–23.

Leonhard, D. & Brugger, P. (1998). 'Creative, paranormal, and delusional thought: A consequence of right hemisphere semantic activation?' *Neuropsychiatry, Neuropsychology, & Behavioral Neurology*, 11, 177–83.

Lesser, R. & Paisner, M. (1985). 'Magical thinking in formal operational adults'. *Human Development*, 28, 57–70.

Lester, D. (1982). 'Astrologers and psychics as therapists'. *American Journal of Psychotherapy*, 26, 56–66.

Lester, D. (1993). 'Paranormal beliefs and psychoticism'. *Personality and Individual Differences*, 14, 739.

Lester, D., Thinschmidt, J. S., & Trautman, L. A. (1987). 'Paranormal beliefs and Jungian dimensions of personality'. *Psychological Reports*, 61, 182.

Lett, J. (1992). 'The persistent popularity of the paranormal'. *Skeptical Inquirer*, 16, 381–8.

Lieberman, J. D. & Arndt, D. (2000). 'Understanding the limits of limiting instructions: Social psychological explanations for the failures of instructions to disregard pre-trial publicity and other inadmissible evidence'. *Psychology, Public Policy and Law*, 6, 677–711.

Lilienfeld, S. (2005). 'The 10 commandments of helping students distinguish science from pseudoscience in psychology'. *Observer*, 18, 39–40 & 49–51.

Lilienfeld, S., Lynn, S., & Lohr, J. (2003). 'Science and pseudoscience in clinical psychology: Initial thoughts, reflections, and considerations'. In S. Lilienfeld, S. Lynn, & J. Lohr (eds), *Science and pseudoscience in clinical psychology* (pp. 1–14). New York: Guilford Press.

Lillqvist, O. & Lindeman, M. (1998). 'Belief in astrology as a strategy for self-verification and coping with negative life events'. *European Psychologist*, 3, 202–8.

Lindeman, M. (1998). 'Motivation, cognition and pseudoscience'. *Scandinavian Journal of Psychology*, 39, 257–65.

Lindeman, M. & Aarnio, K. (2007). 'Superstitious, magical and paranormal beliefs: An integrative model'. *Journal of Research in Personality*, 41, 731–44.

Lindeman, M., Cederstrom, M., Simola, P., Simula, A., Ollikainen, S., & Riekki, T. (1998). 'Sentences with core knowledge violations increase the size of N400 among paranormal believers'. *Cortex*, 44, 1307–15.

Lindeman, M. & Saher, M. (2007). 'Vitalism, purpose and superstition'. *British Journal of Psychology*, 98, 33–44.

Loewenthal, K. M. (2000). *The psychology of religion: A short introduction*. Oxford: One World.

Loftus, E. F. (1979). *Eyewitness testimony*. Cambridge, MA: Harvard University Press.

Loftus, E. F. (1993). 'The reality of repressed memories'. *American Psychologist*, 48, 518–37.

Loftus, E. (2001). 'Imagining the past'. *The Psychologist*, 14, 584–7.

Long, G. (1990). *Examining the earthlight theory*. Chicago, IL: Center for UFO Studies.

Long, J. & Holden, J. M. (2007). 'Does the arousal system contribute to near-death and out-of-body experiences? A summary and response'. *Journal of Near-Death Studies*, 25, 135–69.

Lord, C. G., Ross, L., & Lepper, M. R. (1979). 'Biased assimilation and attitude polarization: The effects of prior theories on subsequently considered evidence'. *Journal of Personality and Social Psychology*, 37, 2098–109.

Lovatt, A., Mason, O., Brett, C., & Peters, E. (2010). 'Psychotic-like experiences, appraisals, and trauma'. *Journal of Nervous and Mental Disease*, 198, 813–19.

Luke, D. P. & Kittenis, M. (2005). 'A preliminary survey of paranormal experiences with psychoactive drugs'. *Journal of Parapsychology*, 69, 305–27.

Lynn, S. J. & Deming, A. (2010). 'The bifurcation of the self: The history and theory of dissociation and its disorders'. *Theory and Psychology*, 20, 289–91.

Lynn, S. J. & Rhue, J. W. (1986). 'The fantasy-prone person: Hypnosis, imagination, and creativity'. *Journal of Personality and Social Psychology,* 51, 404–8.

Lynn, S. J. & Rhue, J. W. (1988). 'Fantasy-proneness: Hypnosis, developmental antecedents, and psychopathology'. *American Psychologist*, 43, 35–44.

Lynn, S. J. & Rhue, J. W. (eds). (1991). *Theories of hypnosis: Current models and perspectives.* New York: Guilford Press.

MacDonald, M. (2000). 'Spirituality: Description, measurement, and relation to the five-factor model of personality'. *Journal of Personality*, 68, 153–97.

Mack, J. E. (1994). *Abduction: Human encounters with aliens.* New York: Scribner.

Macnick, S. L. & Martinez-Conde, S. (2010). *Sleights of mind: What the neuroscience of magic reveals about our everyday deceptions.* New York: Henry Holt and Co.

Mair, K. (2013). *Abused by therapy: How searching for childhood trauma can damage adult lives.* Leicester: Matador.

Makasovski, T. & Irwin, H. J. (1999). 'Paranormal belief, dissociative tendencies and parental encouragement of imagination in childhood'. *Journal of the American Society for Psychical Research*, 93, 233–47.

Malinowski, B. (1922). *Argonauts of the Western Pacific: An account of native enterprise and adventure in the Archipelagoes of Melanesian New Guinea.* London: Routledge and Kegan Paul.

Maller, J. B. & Lundeen, G. E. (1933). 'Sources of superstitious beliefs'. *Journal of Educational Research*, 26, 321–43.

Maller, J. B. & Lundeen, G. E. (1934). 'Superstition and emotional maladjustment'. *Journal of Educational Research*, 27, 592–617.

Maltby, J. & Day, L. (2001a). 'Spiritual involvement and belief: The relationship between spirituality and Eysenck's personality dimensions'. *Personality and Individual Differences*, 30, 187–92.

Maltby, J. & Day, L. (2001b). 'The relationship between spirituality and Eysenck's personality dimensions: A replication among English adults'. *Journal of Genetic Psychology*, 162, 119–22.

Margolis, J. (1998). *Uri Geller: Magician or mystic?* London: Orion.

Markle, D. T. (2010). 'The magic that binds us: Magical thinking and inclusive fitness'. *Journal of Social, Evolutionary, and Cultural Psychology*, 4, 18–33.

Markovsky, B. & Thye, S. R. (2001). 'Social influence on paranormal beliefs'. *Sociological Perspectives*, 44, 21–43.

Marks, A. D. G., Hine, D. W., Blore, R. L., & Phillips, W. J. (2008). 'Assessing individual differences in adolescents' preference for rational and experiential cognition'. *Personality and Individual Differences*, 44, 42–52.

Marks, D. (2000). *The psychology of the psychic.* 2nd edn. Amherst, NY: Prometheus.

Markwick, B. (1985). 'The establishment of data manipulation in the Soal-Shackleton experiments'. In P. Kurtz (ed.), *A skeptic's handbook of parapsychology* (pp. 287–312). Buffalo, NY: Prometheus.

Martin, T. F., White, J. M., & Perlman, D. (2003). 'Religious socialization: A test of the channelling hypothesis of parental influence on adolescent faith maturity'. *Journal of Adolescent Research*, 18, 169–87.

Masicampo, E. J. & Lalande, D. R. (2012). 'A peculiar prevalence of *p* values just below .05'. *Quarterly Journal of Experimental Psychology*, 65, 2271–9.

Maudsley, H. (1886). *Natural causes and supernatural seemings.* London: K. Paul, Trench, & Co.

Matheson, T. (1998). *Alien abductions: Creating a modern phenomenon.* Amherst, NY: Prometheus.

Matthews, R. & Blackmore, S. J. (1995). 'Why are coincidences so impressive?' *Perceptual and Motor Skills*, 80, 1121–2.

Matute, H. (1994). 'Learned helplessness and superstitious behavior as opposite effects of uncontrollable reinforcement in humans'. *Learning and Motivation*, 25, 216–32.

Matute, H. (1995). 'Human reactions to uncontrollable outcomes: Further evidence for superstitions rather than helplessness'. *Quarterly Journal of Experimental Psychology*, 48B, 142–57.

May, E. C. (1998). 'Response to "Experiment One of the SAIC remote viewing program: A critical re-evaluation"'. *Journal of Parapsychology*, 309–18.

McCauley, C. (1989). 'The nature of social influence in Groupthink: Compliance and internalisation'. *Journal of Personality and Social Psychology*, 57, 250–60.

McClenon, J. (1990). 'Chinese and American anomalous experiences: The role of religiosity'. *Sociological Analysis*, 51, 53–67.

McClenon, J. (1994). 'Surveys of anomalous experience: A cross-cultural analysis'. *Journal of the American Society for Psychical Research*, 88, 117–35.

McCreery, C. (2008). 'Dreams and psychosis: A new look at an old hypothesis'. Retrieved 21 March 2012 from http://www.celiagreen.com/charlesmccreery/dreams-and-psychosis.pdf.

McCreery, C. A. S. & Claridge, G. A. (1995). 'Out-of-body experiences and personality'. *Journal of the Society for Psychical Research*, 60, 129–48.

McCreery, C. & Claridge, G. (1996). 'A study of hallucination in normal subjects. II. Electrophysiological data'. *Personality and Individual Differences*, 21, 749–58.

McCreery, C. & Claridge, G. (2002). 'Healthy schizotypy: The case of out-of-the-body experiences'. *Personality and Individual Differences*, 32, 141–54.

McGarry, J. J. & Newberry, B. H. (1981). 'Beliefs in paranormal phenomena and locus of control'. *Journal of Personality and Social Psychology*, 41, 725–36.

McIver, T. (1988). 'Backward masking, and other backward thoughts about music'. *Skeptical Inquirer,* 13(1), 50–63.

McNally, R. J. (2003a). *Remembering trauma.* Cambridge, MA: Harvard University Press.

McNally, R. J. (2003b). 'Is the pseudoscience concept useful for clinical psychology? The demise of pseudoscience'. *The Scientific Review of Mental Health Practice*, 2, 97–101.

McNally, R. J. & Clancy, S. A. (2005). 'Sleep paralysis, sexual abuse, and space alien abduction'. *Transcultural Psychiatry*, 42, 113–22.

McNally, R. J., Lasko, N. B., Clancy, S. A., Macklin, M. L., Pitman, R. A., & Orr, S. P. (2004). 'Psychophysiological responding during script-driven imagery in people reporting abduction by space aliens'. *Psychological Science*, 15, 493–97.

Meli, S. C. & Persinger, M. A. (2009). 'Red light facilitates the sensed presence elicited by application of weak, burst-firing magnetic fields over the temporal lobes'. *International Journal of Neuroscience*, 119, 68–75.

Merckelbach, H., Horselenberg, R., & Muris, P. (2001). 'The Creative Experiences Questionnaire (CEQ): A brief self-report measure of fantasy proneness'. *Personality and Individual Differences*, 31, 987–95.

Merriam, S. B., Courtenay, B., & Baumgartner, L. (2003). 'On becoming a witch: Learning in a marginalized community of practice'. *Adult Education Quarterly*, 53, 170–88.

Messer, W. S. & Griggs, R. A. (1989). 'Student belief and involvement in the paranormal and performance in introductory psychology'. *Teaching of Psychology*, 16, 187–91.

Meyer, P. (1986). 'Ghostboosters: The press and the paranormal'. *Columbia Journalism Review*, 24, 38–41.

Michotte, A. (1962). *The perception of causality*. Andover, MA: Methuen.

Milevsky, I. M., Szuchman, L., & Milevsky, A. (2008). 'Transmission of religious beliefs in college students'. *Mental Health, Religion and Culture*, 11, 423–34.

Miller, J. G. (1940). 'The role of motivation in learning without awareness'. *American Journal of Psychology*, 53, 229–39.

Milton, J. & Wiseman, R. (1999). 'Does psi exist? Lack of replication of an anomalous process of information transfer'. *Psychological Bulletin*, 125, 387–91.

Milton, J. & Wiseman, R. (2001). 'Does psi exist? Reply to Storm and Ertel (2001)'. *Psychological Bulletin*, 127, 434–8.

Milton, J. & Wiseman, R. (2002). 'A response to Storm and Ertel (2002)'. *Journal of Parapsychology*, 62, 183–5.

Moody, R. (1975). *Life after life*. San Francisco, CA: Harper Collins.

Moon, M. L. (1975). 'Artists contrasted with non-artists concerning belief in ESP: A poll'. *Journal of the American Society for Psychical Research*, 69, 161–6.

Moore, D. W. (2005). 'Three in four Americans believe in paranormal: Little change from similar results in 2001'. Retrieved 3 October 2008 from http://www.gallup.com/poll/16915/Three-Four-Americans-Believe-Paranormal.aspx.

Morier, D. & Keeports, D. (1994). 'Normal science and the paranormal: The effect of a scientific method course on students' beliefs'. *Research in Higher Education*, 35, 443–53.

Morris, R. L. (2000). 'Parapsychology in the 21st century'. *Journal of Parapsychology*, 64, 123–37.

Morris, R. L. (2001). 'Research methods in experimental parapsychology: Problems and prospects'. *European Journal of Parapsychology*, 16, 8–18.

Mousseau, M-C. (2003a). 'Media coverage of parapsychology and the prevalence of irrational beliefs'. *Journal of Scientific Exploration*, 17, 705–14.

Mousseau, M-C. (2003b). 'Parapsychology: Science or pseudo-science?' *Journal of Scientific Exploration*, 17, 271–82.

Muller, S., Schmidt, S., & Walach, H. (2009). 'The feeling of being stared at: A parapsychological classic with a facelift'. *European Journal of Parapsychology*, 24, 117–38.

Munro, C. & Persinger, M. A. (1992). 'Relative right temporal lobe theta activity correlates with Vingiano's hemispheric quotient and the "sensed presence"'. *Perceptual and Motor Skills*, 75, 899–903.

Murphy, K. & Lester, D. (1976). 'A search for correlates of belief in ESP'. *Psychological Reports*, 38, 82.

Murray, C. D. & Fox, J. (2005). 'Dissociational body experiences: Differences between respondents with and without prior out-of-body experiences'. *British Journal of Psychology*, 96, 441–56.

Musch, J. & Ehrenberg, K. (2002). 'Probability misjudgement, cognitive ability, and belief in the paranormal'. *British Journal of Psychology*, 93, 169–77.

Myers, S. A. (1983). 'The Wilson-Barber Inventory of Childhood Memories and Imaginings: Children's form and norms for 1337 children and adolescents'. *Journal of Mental Imagery*, 7, 83–94.

Myers, S. A. & Austrin, H. R. (1985). 'Distal eidetic technology: Further characteristics of the fantasy-prone personality'. *Journal of Mental Imagery*, 9, 57–66.

Myers, S. H., Austrin, H. R., Grisso, J., & Nickeson, R. (1983). 'Personality characteristics as related to out-of-body experiences'. *Journal of Parapsychology*, 47, 131–44.

Nadon, R. & Kihlstrom, J. F. (1987). 'Hypnosis, psi, and the psychology of paranormal experience'. *Behavioural and Brain Sciences*, 10, 597–9.

Nathan, D. (2011). *Sybil exposed*. New York: Free Press.

Nelson, K., Mattingly, M., Lee, S. A., & Schmitt, F. A. (2006). 'Does the arousal system contribute to near death experience?' *Neurology*, 66, 1003–9.

Newby, R. W. & Davis, J. B. (2004). 'Relationships between locus of control and paranormal beliefs'. *Psychological Reports*, 94, 1261–6.

Newman, L. S. (1997). 'Intergalactic hostages: People who report abduction by UFOs'. *Journal of Social and Clinical Psychology*, 16, 151–77.

Newman, L. S. & Baumeister, R. F. (1996a). 'Toward an explanation of the UFO abduction phenomenon: Hypnotic elaboration, extraterrestrial sadomasochism, and spurious memories'. *Psychological Inquiry*, 7, 99–126.

Newman, L. S. & Baumeister, R. F. (1996b). 'Not just another false memory: Further thoughts on the UFO abduction phenomenon'. *Psychological Inquiry*, 7, 185–7.

Newman, L. S. & Baumeister, R. F. (1998). 'Abducted by aliens: Spurious memories of interplanetary masochism'. In S. J. Lynn & K. M. McConkey (eds), *Truth in memory* (pp. 284–303). New York: Guilford Press.

Newport, F. & Strausberg, M. (2001). 'Americans' belief in psychic and paranormal phenomena is up over last decade'. *Gallup Poll Monthly*, 429, 14–17.

Ni, H., Simile, C., & Hardy, A. M. (2002). 'Utilization of complementary and alternative medicine by United States adults'. *Medical Care*, 40, 353–8.

Nickell, J. (1996). 'A study of fantasy proneness in the thirteen cases of alleged encounters in John Mack's *Abduction*'. *Skeptical Inquirer*, 20(3), 18–20.

Nicol, J. F. (1985). 'Fraudulent children in psychical research'. In P. Kurtz (ed.), *A skeptic's handbook of parapsychology* (pp. 275–86). Buffalo, NY: Prometheus.

Nisbet, M. (2006). 'Cultural indicators of the paranormal'. Retrieved 25 March 2013 from http://www.csicop.org/specialarticles/show/cultural_indicators_of_the_paranormal/.

Nisbett, R. E., Fong, G. T., Lehman, D. R., & Cheng, P. W. (1987). 'Teaching reasoning'. *Science*, 238, 625–31.

Noyes, R. & Klett, R. (1976). 'Depersonalisation in the face of life-threatening danger: An interpretation'. *Omega*, 7, 103–14.

Oates, D. J. (1991). *Reverse speech: Hidden messages in human communication*. Indianapolis, IN: Knowledge Systems.

O'Connell, D. N., Shor, R. E., & Orne, M. T. (1970). 'Hypnotic age regression: An empirical and methodological analysis'. *Journal of Abnormal Psychology*, 76(3, Pt. 2), 1–32.

Open Science Collaboration (2012). 'An open, large-scale, collaborative effort to estimate the reproducibility of psychological science'. *Perspectives on Psychological Science*, 7, 657–60.

Orenstein, A. (2002). 'Religion and paranormal belief'. *Journal for the Scientific Study of Religion*, 41, 301–11.

Ost, J., Wright, D. B., Easton, S., Hope, L., & French, C. C. (2013). 'Experiences and beliefs regarding recovered memories, satanic abuse, dissociative identity disorder and false memories in the United Kingdom: A survey of Chartered Clinical Psychologists and Hypnotherapists'. *Psychology, Crime and Law*, 19, 1–19.

Otis, L. P. & Alcock, J. E. (1982). 'Factors affecting extraordinary belief'. *Journal of Social Psychology*, 118, 77–85.

Ozorak, E. W. (1989). 'Social and cognitive influences on the development of religious beliefs and commitment in adolescence'. *Journal for the Scientific Study of Religion*, 28, 448–63.

Pacini, R. & Epstein, S. (1999). 'The relation of rational and experiential information processing styles to personality, basic beliefs, and the ratio-bias phenomenon'. *Journal of Personality and Social Psychology*, 76, 972–87.

Padgett, V. R. & Jorgenson, D. O. (1982). 'Superstition and economic threat: Germany, 1918–1940'. *Personality and Social Psychology Bulletin*, 8, 736–41.

Palmer, J. (1979). 'A community mail survey of psychic experiences'. *Journal of the American Society for Psychical Research*, 73, 221–51.

Palmer, J. (1997). 'The challenge of experimenter psi'. *European Journal of Parapsychology*, 13, 110–25.

Palmer, J. & van der Velden, I. (1983). 'ESP and "hypnotic imagination": A group free-response study'. *European Journal of Parapsychology*, 4, 413–34.

Park, W. W. (1990). 'A review of research on groupthink'. *Behavioral Decision Making*, 3, 229–45.

Parker, A. & Brusewitz, G. (2003). 'A compendium of the evidence for psi'. *European Journal of Parapsychology*, 18, 29–48.

Parker, A., Frederiksen, A., & Johansson, H. (1997). 'Towards specifying the recipe for success with the ganzfeld: Replication of the ganzfeld findings using a manual ganzfeld with subjects reporting prior paranormal experiences'. *European Journal of Parapsychology*, 13, 15–27.

Parker, A. & Sjoden, B. (2010). 'Do some of us habituate to future emotional events?' *Journal of Parapsychology*, 74, 99–115.

Parker, M. & Gaier, E. L. (1980). 'Religion, religious beliefs and religious practices among conservative Jewish adolescents'. *Adolescence*, 15, 361–74.

Parkhomtchouk, D. V., Kotake, J., Zhang, T., Chen, W., Kokubo, H., & Yamamoto, M. (2002). 'An attempt to reproduce the presentiment EDA response'. *Journal of International Society of Life Information Science*, 20, 190–4.

Parnell, J. O. (1988). 'Measured personality characteristics of persons claiming UFO experiences'. *Psychotherapy in Private Practice*, 6, 159–65.

Parnell, J. O. & Sprinkle, R. L. (1990). 'Personality characteristics of persons who claim UFO experiences'. *Journal of UFO Studies*, 2, 45–58.

Parnia, S. & Fenwick, P. (2002). 'Near death experiences in cardiac arrest: Visions of a dying brain or visions of a new science of consciousness?' *Resuscitation*, 52, 5–11.

Pashler, H. & Wagenmakers, E-J. (2012). 'Editors' introduction to the special section on replicability in psychological science: A crisis in confidence?' *Perspectives on Psychological Science*, 7, 528–30.

Patry, A. L. & Pelletier, L. G. (2001). 'Extraterrestrial beliefs and experiences: An application of the theory of reasoned action'. *Journal of Social Psychology*, 14, 199–217.

Paulos, J. A. (1988). *Innumeracy: Mathematical illiteracy and its consequences*. New York: Hill and Wang.

Pekala, R. J. & Cardeña, E. (2000). 'Methodological issues in the study of altered states of consciousness and anomalous experiences'. In E. Cardeña, S. J. Lynn, & S. Krippner (eds), *Varieties of anomalous experience* (pp. 47–82). Washington, DC: American Psychological Association.

Pekala, R. J., Kumar, V. K., & Cummings, J. (1992). 'Types of high hypnotically susceptible individuals and reported attitudes and experiences of the paranormal and the anomalous'. *Journal of the American Society for Psychical Research*, 86, 135–50.

Pekala, R. J., Kumar, V. K., & Marcano, G. (1995). 'Anomalous/paranormal experiences, hypnotic susceptibility, and dissociation'. *Journal of the American Society for Psychical Research*, 89, 313–32.

Peltzer, K. (2002). 'Paranormal beliefs and personality among black South African students'. *Social Behavior and Personality*, 30, 391–8.

Peltzer, K. (2003). 'Magical thinking and paranormal beliefs among secondary and university students in South Africa'. *Personality and Individual Differences*, 35, 1419–26.

Perez-Navarro, J. M., Lawrence, T., & Hume, I. (2009). 'Personality, mental state, and procedure in the experimental replication of ESP: A logistic regression analysis of a successful experimental condition'. *European Journal of Parapsychology*, 24, 68–92.

Perkins, S. L. & Allen, R. (2006). 'Childhood physical abuse and differential development of paranormal belief systems'. *Journal of Nervous and Mental Disease*, 194, 349–55.

Persinger, M. A. (1989). 'Geophysical variables and behavior: LV. Predicting the details of visitor experiences and the personality of experients: The temporal lobe factor'. *Perceptual and Motor Skills*, 68, 55–65.

Persinger, M. A. (1990). 'The tectonic strain theory as an explanation for UFO phenomena: A non-technical review of the research, 1970–1990'. *Journal of UFO Studies*, 2, 105–37.

Persinger, M. A. (1993). 'Average diurnal changes in melatonin levels are associated with hourly incidence of bereavement apparitions: Support for the hypothesis of temporal (limbic) lobe microseizuring'. *Perceptual and Motor Skills*, 76, 444–6.

Persinger, M. A. (2001). 'The neuropsychiatry of paranormal experiences'. *Neuropsychiatric Practice and Opinion*, 13, 515–24.

Persinger, M. A. (2003). 'The sensed presence within experimental settings: Implications for the male and female concept of self'. *Journal of Psychology*, 137, 5–16.

Persinger, M. A. & Makarec, K. (1987). 'Temporal lobe epileptic signs and correlative behaviors displayed by normal populations'. *Journal of General Psychology*, 114, 179–95.

Persinger, M. A. & Richards, P. (1991). 'Tobacyk's Paranormal Belief Scale and temporal lobe signs: Sex differences in the experiences of ego-alien intrusions'. *Perceptual and Motor Skills*, 73, 1151–6.

Persinger, M. A. & Valliant, P. M. (1985). 'Temporal lobe signs and reports of subjective paranormal experiences in a normal population'. *Perceptual and Motor Skills,* 60, 903–9.

Phelps, K. E. & Woolley. J. D. (1994). 'The form and function of young children's magical beliefs'. *Developmental Psychology,* 30, 385–94.

Piaget, J. (2008/1972). 'Intellectual evolution from adolescence to adulthood'. *Human Development,* 51, 40–7 (reprinted from *Human Development,* 1972, 15, 1–12).

Pieper, S., Out, D., Bakermans-Kranenburg, M. J., & van IJzendoorn, M. H. (2011) 'Behavioral and molecular genetics of dissociation: The role of the serotonin transporter gene promoter polymorphism (5-HTTLPR)'. *Journal of Traumatic Stress,* 24, 373–80.

Pizzagalli, D., Lehmann, D., Gianotti, L., Koenig, T., Tanaka, H., Wackerman, J. & Brugger, P. (2000). 'Brain electric correlates of strong belief in paranormal phenomena: Intracerebral EEG source and regional Omega complexity analyses'. *Psychiatry Research: Neuroimaging Section,* 100, 139–54.

Plug, C. (1976). 'The psychology of superstition: A review'. *Psychologia Africana,* 16, 93–115.

Poole, B. (2007). *Madonna of the toast.* New York: Mark Batty Publisher.

Popper, K. (1963). *Conjectures and refutations: The growth of scientific knowledge.* New York: Basic Books.

Popper, K. R. & Eccles, J. C. (1977). *The self and its brain.* New York: Springer.

Potter, J. (1996). *Representing reality: Discourse, rhetoric and social construction.* London: Sage.

Poulton, R., Caspi, A., Moffitt, T. E., Cannon, M., Murray, R., & Harrington, H. L. (2000). 'Children's self-reported psychotic symptoms and adult schizophreniform disorder: A 15-year longitudinal study'. *Archives of General Psychiatry,* 57, 1053–8.

Powers, S. M. (1994). 'Dissociation in alleged extraterrestrial abductees'. *Dissociation,* 7, 44–50.

Powers, S. M. (1997). 'Alien abduction narratives'. In S. Krippner & S. M. Powers (eds), *Broken images, broken selves: Dissociative narratives in clinical practice* (pp. 199–215). Philadelphia, PA: Bruner/Mazel Inc.

Preece, P. F. W. & Baxter, J. H. (2000). 'Scepticism and gullibility: The superstitious and pseudo-scientific beliefs of secondary school students'. *International Journal of Science Education,* 22, 1147–56.

Presson, P. K. & Benassi, V. A. (1996). 'Illusion of control: A meta-analytic review'. *Journal of Social Behaviour and Personality,* 1996, 493–510.

Presson, P. K. & Benassi, V. A. (2003). 'Are depressive symptoms positively or negatively associated with the illusion of control?' *Social Behaviour and Personality,* 31, 483–95.

Putz, P., Gassler, M., & Wackermann, J. (2007). 'An experiment with covert ganzfeld telepathy'. *European Journal of Parapsychology,* 22, 49–72.

Pynoos, R. S. & Nader, K. (1989). 'Children's memory and proximity to violence'. *Journal of the American Academy of Child & Adolescent Psychiatry,* 28, 236–41.

Pyysiäinen, I. (2001). *How religion works: Towards a new cognitive science of religion.* Cognition and Culture Book Series, 1. Leiden: Brill.

Pyysiäinen, I. & Anttonen, V. (2002). *Current approaches in the cognitive science of religion.* London: Continuum.

Rachman, S. & de Silva, P. (1978). 'Abnormal and normal obsessions'. *Behavioural Research and Therapy,* 16, 233–48.

Radin, D. I. (1997a). 'Unconscious perception of future emotions: An experiment in presentiment'. *Journal of Scientific Exploration*, 11, 163–80.

Radin, D. I. (1997b). *The conscious universe: The scientific truth of psychic phenomena*. New York, HY: Harper Collins.

Radin, D. I. (2006). *Entangled minds: Extrasensory experiences in a quantum reality*. New York, NY: Paraview.

Radin, D. I. (2010). 'A brief history of science and psychic phenomena'. In S. Krippner & H. L. Friedman (eds), *Debating psychic experience: Human potential or human illusion?* (pp. 13–27). Santa Barbara, CA: Praeger.

Radin, D. I., Nelson, R. D., Dobyns, Y., & Houtkooper, J. (2006). 'Reexamining psychokinesis: Comment on the Bösch, Steinkamp and Boller (2006) meta-analysis'. *Psychological Bulletin*, 132, 529–32.

Radin, D. I., Taylor, R. K., & Braud, W. G. (1995). 'Remote mental influence of human electrodermal activity: A pilot replication'. *European Journal of Parapsychology*, 11, 19–34.

Radner, D. & Radner, M. (1982). *Science and unreason*. Belmont, CA: Wadsworth.

Ramsey, M. C., Venette, S. J., & Rabalais, N. (2011). 'The perceived paranormal and source credibility: The effects of narrative suggestions on paranormal belief'. *Atlantic Journal of Communication*, 19, 79–96.

Randall, T. M. (1990). 'Belief in the paranormal declines: 1977–1987'. *Psychological Reports*, 66, 1347–51.

Randall, T. M. (1997). 'Paranormal short inventory'. *Perceptual and Motor Skills*, 84, 1265–6.

Randall, T. M. & Desrosiers, M. (1980). 'Measurement of supernatural belief: Sex differences and locus of control'. *Journal of Personality Assessment*, 44, 493–8.

Randi, J. (1982a). *Flim-flam: Psychics, ESP, unicorns, and other delusions*. Buffalo, NY: Prometheus.

Randi, J. (1982b). *The truth about Uri Geller*. Buffalo, NY: Prometheus.

Randi, J. (1987). *The faith healers*. Buffalo, NY: Prometheus.

Randi, J. (1990). *The mask of Nostradamus*. New York: Scribners.

Randle, K. D., Estes, R., & Cone, W. P. (1999). *The abduction enigma: The truth behind the mass alien abductions of the late twentieth century*. New York: Forge.

Randles, J. (1988). *Abduction*. London: Robert Hale.

Rassin, E. (2008). 'Individual differences in the susceptibility to confirmation bias'. *Netherlands Journal of Psychology*, 64, 87–93.

Rattet, S. L. & Bursik, K. (2001). 'Investigating the personality correlates of paranormal belief and precognitive experience'. *Personality and Individual Differences*, 31, 433–55.

Raudive, K. (1971). *Breakthrough: An amazing experiment in electronic communication with the dead*. Gerrards Cross, Bucks: Colin Smythe Ltd.

Rees, W. D. (1971). 'The hallucinations of widowhood'. *British Medical Journal*, 4, 37–41.

Rensink, R. (2004). 'Visual sensing without seeing'. *Psychological Science*, 15, 27–32.

Rew, L. (2002). 'Relationships of sexual abuse, connectedness, and loneliness to perceived well-being in homeless youth'. *Journal for Specialists in Pediatric Nursing*, 7, 51–63.

Rhue, J. W. & Lynn, S. J. (1989). 'Fantasy proneness, absorption, and hypnosis: A re-examination'. *International Journal of Clinical and Experimental Hypnosis*, 37, 100–6.

Rice, T. W. (2003). 'Believe it or not: Religious and other paranormal beliefs in the United States'. *Journal for the Scientific Study of Religion*, 42, 95–106.

Richards, D. G. (1990). 'Hypnotic susceptibility and subjective psychic experiences'. *Journal of Parapsychology*, 54, 35–51.

Richards, D. G. (1991). 'A study of the correlations between subjective psychic experiences and dissociative experiences'. *Dissociation*, 4, 83–91.

Ridolfo, H., Baxter, A., & Lucas, J. W. (2010). 'Social influences on paranormal belief: Popular versus scientific support'. *Current Research in Social Psychology*, 15, 33–41.

Ring, K. (1980). 'The reality of death experiences: A personal perspective': Comment. *Journal of Nervous and Mental Disease*, 168, 273–4.

Ring, K. & Rosing, C. J. (1990). 'The Omega Project: A psychological survey of persons reporting abductions and other UFO encounters'. *Journal of UFO Studies*, 2, 59–98.

Ritchie, S. J., Wiseman, R., & French, C. C. (2012a). 'Failing the future: Three unsuccessful attempts to replicate Bem's "retroactive facilitation of recall" effect'. *PLoS One*, 7, e33423. doi:10.1371/journal.pone.0033423.

Ritchie, S. J., Wiseman, R., & French, C. C. (2012b). 'Replication, replication, replication'. *The Psychologist*, 25, 346–8.

Roberts, M. J. & Seager, P. B. (1999). 'Predicting belief in paranormal phenomena: A comparison of conditional and probabilistic reasoning'. *Applied Cognitive Psychology*, 13, 443–50.

Robinson, E. (2009). 'Student brief: Examining the case for dream precognition'. *European Journal of Parapsychology*, 24, 93–110.

Rodeghier, M., Goodpaster, J., & Blatterbauer, S. (1991). 'Psychosocial characteristics of abductees: Results from the CUFOS abduction project'. *Journal of UFO Studies*, 3, 59–90.

Roe, C. A. (1999). 'Critical thinking and belief in the paranormal: A re-evaluation'. *British Journal of Psychology*, 90, 85–98.

Roe, C. A. & Morgan, C. L. (2002). 'Narcissism and belief in the paranormal'. *Psychological Reports*, 90, 405–11.

Roe, C. A. & Roxburgh, E. (2013). 'An overview of cold reading strategies'. In C. Moreman (ed.), *The Spiritualist Movement: Speaking with the dead in America and around the world* (pp. 177–204). Santa Barbara, CA: ABC-CLIO, Inc.

Roediger, H. L., III & McDermott, K. B. (1995). 'Creating false memories: Remembering words not presented on lists'. *Journal of Experimental Psychology: Learning, Memory, and Cognition*, 21, 803–14.

Rofe, Y. (2008). 'Does repression exist? Memory, pathogenic, unconscious and clinical evidence'. *Review of General Psychology*, 12, 63–85.

Rogers, P., Davis, T. & Fisk, J. (2009). 'Paranormal belief and susceptibility to the conjunction fallacy'. *Applied Cognitive Psychology*, 23, 524–42.

Rogers, P., Qualter, P., & Phelps, G. (2007). 'The mediating and moderating effects of loneliness and attachment style on belief in the paranormal'. *European Journal of Parapsychology*, 22, 138–65.

Rogers, P., Qualter, P., Phelps, G., & Gardner, K. (2006). 'Belief in the paranormal, coping and emotional intelligence'. *Personality and Individual Differences*, 41, 1089–105.

Rogo, D. S. (1985). 'J. B. Rhine and the Levy scandal'. In P. Kurtz (ed.), *A skeptic's handbook of parapsychology* (pp. 313–26). Buffalo, NY: Prometheus.

Rose, N. & Blackmore, S. J. (2001). 'Are false memories psi-conducive?' *Journal of Parapsychology*, 65, 125–44.

Rosengren, K. S. & Hickling, A. K. (1994). 'Seeing is believing: Children's explanations of commonplace, magical and extraordinary transformations'. *Child Development*, 65, 1605–26.

Rosengren, K. S. & Hickling, A. K. (2000). 'Metamorphosis and magic: The development of children's thinking about possible events and plausible mechanisms'. In K. S. Rosengren, C. Johnson, & P. Harris (eds), *Imagining the impossible: Magical, scientific, and religious thinking in children* (pp. 75–98). Cambridge: Cambridge University Press.

Ross, C. A. & Joshi, S. (1992). 'Paranormal experiences in the general population'. *Journal of Nervous and Mental Disease*, 180, 357–61.

Ross, C. A., Norton, G. R., & Fraser, G. A. (1989). 'Evidence against the iatrogenesis of multiple personality disorder'. *Dissociation*, 2(2), 61–5.

Ross, C. A., Ryan, L., Voigt, H., & Eide, L. (1991). 'High and low dissociators in a college student population'. *Dissociation*, 4, 147–51.

Ross, L., Greene, D., & House, P. (1977). 'The "false consensus effect": An egocentric bias in social perception and attribution processes'. *Journal of Experimental Social Psychology*, 13, 279–301.

Rotter, J. B. (1975). 'Some problems and misconceptions related to the construct of internal versus external control of reinforcement'. *Journal of Consulting and Clinical Psychology*, 43, 56–67.

Rowland, I. (2002). *The full facts book of cold reading*. 3rd edn. London: Ian Rowland Limited.

Royalty, J. (1995). 'The generalizability of critical thinking: Paranormal beliefs versus statistical reasoning'. *Journal of Genetic Psychology*, 156, 477–88.

Rozin, P., Millman, L., & Nemeroff, C. (1986). 'Operation of the laws of sympathetic magic in disgust and other domains'. *Journal of Personality and Social Psychology*, 50, 703–12.

Rudski, J. (2003). 'The illusion of control, superstitious belief, and optimism'. *Current Psychology: Developmental, Learning, Personality, Social*, 22, 306–15.

Rudski, J. M. & Edwards, A. (2007). 'Malinowski goes to college: Factors influencing student's use of ritual and superstition'. *Journal of General Psychology*, 134, 389–403.

Russell, D. & Jones, W. H. (1980). 'When superstition fails: Reactions to disconfirmation of paranormal beliefs'. *Personality and Social Psychology Bulletin*, 6, 83–8.

Rutkowski, C. A. (1984). 'Geophysical variables and human behavior. XVI. Some criticisms'. *Perceptual and Motor Skills*, 58, 840–2.

Rutkowski, C. A. (1990). 'Critical comments about earth lights and the TST'. *Journal of UFO Studies*, 2, 144–6.

Rutkowski, C. A. (1994). 'On Persinger'. *Bulletin of Anomalous Experiences*, 5, 7.

Rutkowski, C. (2000). *Abductions and aliens: The psychology behind extra-terrestrial experience*. London: Fusion Press.

Saher, M. & Lindeman, M. (2005). 'Alternative medicine: A psychological perspective'. *Personality and Individual Differences*, 39, 1169–78.

Sancho, J. (2001). 'Beyond entertainment: Research into the acceptability of alternative beliefs, psychic and occult phenomena on television'. Retrieved 2 April 2013 from http://www.ofcom.org.uk/static/archive/bsc/pdfs/research/occult.pdf.

Sanders, B., McRoberts, G., & Tollefson, C. (1989). 'Childhood stress and dissociation in a college population'. *Dissociation*, 2, 17–23.

Sanghera, S. (2002). 'Paranormal TV: Surveys edition'. *Financial Times*, 8 October (London).

Santomauro, J. & French, C. C. (2009). 'Terror in the night: The experience of sleep paralysis'. *The Psychologist*, 22, 672–5.

Saucer, P. R., Cahoon, D. D., & Edmonds, E. M. (1992). 'The paranormal belief scale and the atheistic ideation reference scale as predictors of hypnotic suggestibility'. *Psychology: A Journal of Human Behaviour*, 29, 44–6.

Saunders, D. R. & van Arsdale, P. (1968). 'Points of view about UFOs: A multi-dimensional scaling study'. *Perceptual and Motor Skills*, 27, 1219–38.

Savva, L., Roe, C. A., & Smith, M.D. (2006). 'Further testing of the precognitive habituation effect using spider stimuli'. *Journal of the Society for Psychical Research*, 70, 225–34.

Scheidt, R. J. (1973). 'Belief in supernatural phenomena and locus of control'. *Psychological Reports*, 32, 1159–62.

Schienle, A., Vaitl, D., & Stark, R. (1996). 'Covariation bias and paranormal belief'. *Psychological Reports*, 78, 291–305.

Schlitz, M. & Braud, W. (1997). 'Distant intentionality and healing: Assessing the evidence'. *Alternative Therapies*, 3, 1–46.

Schlitz, M. J. & LaBerge, S. (1994). 'Autonomic detection of remote observation: Two conceptual replications'. *Proceedings of the Parapsychological Association 37th Annual Convention*, 352–60.

Schlitz, M., Wiseman, R., Watt, C., & Radin, D. (2006). 'Of two minds: Sceptic-proponent collaboration within parapsychology'. *British Journal of Psychology*, 97, 313–22.

Schmeidler, G. (1997). 'Psi-conducive experimenters and psi-permissive ones'. *European Journal of Parapsychology*, 13, 83–94.

Schmidt, S. (2012). 'Can we help just by good intentions? A meta-analysis of experiments on distant intention effects'. *Journal of Alternative and Complementary Medicine*, 18, 529–33.

Schmidt, S., Schneider, R., Utts, J., & Walach, H. (2004). 'Distant intentionality and the feeling of being stared at: Two meta-analyses'. *British Journal of Psychology*, 95, 235–47.

Schnabel, J. (1994). *Dark white: Aliens, abductions, and the UFO obsession*. London: Hamish Hamilton.

Schredl, M. (2009). 'Frequency of precognitive dreams: Association with dream recall and personality variables'. *Journal of the Society for Psychical Research*, 73, 81–90.

Schreiber, F. R. (1973). *Sybil*. New York: Warner.

Schriever, F. (2000). 'Are there different cognitive structures behind paranormal beliefs?' *European Journal of Parapsychology*, 15, 46–7.

Schulter, G. & Papousek, I. (2008). 'Believing in paranormal phenomena: Relations to asymmetry of body and brain'. *Cortex*, 44, 1326–35.

Schwaninger, J., Eisenberg, P. R., Schechtman, K. B., & Weiss, A. N. (2002). 'A prospective analysis of near-death experiences in cardiac arrest patients'. *Journal of Near-Death Studies*, 20, 215–32.

Schwarz, B. E. (1983). *UFO dynamics*. Moore Haven, FL: Rainbow Books.

Seligman, M. E. P. (1975). *Helplessness: On depression, development, and death*. San Francisco: W. H. Freeman.

Sheaffer, R. (1998). *UFO sightings: The evidence*. Amherst, NY: Prometheus.

Sheldrake, R. & Beharee, A. (2009). 'A rapid online telepathy test'. *Psychological Reports*, 104, 957–70.

Sheldrake, R., Godwin, H., & Rockell, S. (2004). 'A filmed experiment on telephone telepathy with the Nolan sisters'. *Journal of the Society for Psychical Research*, 68, 168–72.

Sheldrake, R. & Smart, P. (2005). 'Testing for telepathy in connection with emails'. *Perceptual and Motor Skills*, 101, 771–86.

Shermer, M. (1997). *Why people believe weird things: Pseudoscience, superstition and other confusions of our time.* London: Souvenir Press.

Shermer, M. (2008). 'How to be psychic in 10 easy steps'. Retrieved 8 November 2010 from http://www.skeptic.com/eskeptic/08-12-17.html.

Shermer, M. (2011). *The believing brain: From ghosts and gods to politics and conspiracies – How we construct beliefs and reinforce them as truths.* New York: Times Books.

Sherriff, L. (2010). 'Women are NOT from Gullibull'. In W. M. Grossman & C. C. French (eds), *Why statues weep: The best of the Skeptic* (pp. 141–2). London: The Philosophy Press.

Sherwood, S. J., Roe, C. A., Holt, N. J., & Wilson, S. (2005). 'Interpersonal psi: Exploring the role of the experimenter and the experimental climate in a Ganzfeld telepathy task'. *European Journal of Parapsychology*, 20, 150–72.

Showalter, E. (1997). *Hystories: Hysterical epidemics and modern culture.* London: Picador.

Sica, C., Novara, C., & Sanavio, E. (2002). 'Culture and psychopathology: Superstition and obsessive-compulsive cognitions and symptoms in a non-clinical Italian sample'. *Personality and Individual Differences*, 32, 1001–12.

Simmonds-Moore, C. A. & Moore, C. L. (2009). 'Exploring how gender role and boundary thinness relate to paranormal experiences, beliefs and performance on a forced-choice clairvoyance task'. *Journal of the Society for Psychical Research*, 73, 129–49.

Simmons, J. P., Nelson, L. D., & Simonsohn, U. (2011). 'False-positive psychology: Undisclosed flexibility in data collection and analysis allows presenting anything as significant'. *Psychological Science*, 22, 1359–66.

Simonds, L. M., Demetre, J. D., & Read, C. (2009). 'Relationships between magical thinking, obsessive-compulsiveness and other forms of anxiety in a sample of non-clinical children'. *British Journal of Developmental Psychology*, 27, 457–71.

Simons, D. J. (2012). 'Replication: Where do we go from here?' *The Psychologist*, 25, 349.

Singer, B. & Benassi, V. A. (1981). 'Fooling some of the people all of the time'. *Skeptical Inquirer*, 5, 17–24.

Singh, S. & Ernst, E. (2008). *Trick or treatment? Alternative medicine on trial.* London: Bantam Press.

Sjöberg, L. & Wählberg, A. (2002). 'Risk perception and New Age beliefs'. *Risk Analysis*, 22, 751–64.

Sjödin, U. (2002). 'The Swedes and the paranormal'. *Journal of Contemporary Religion*, 17, 75–85.

Skinner, B. (1948). 'Superstition in the pigeon'. *Journal of Experimental Psychology*, 38, 168–72.

Smith, C. L., Johnson, J. L., & Hathaway, W. (2009). 'Personality contributions to belief in paranormal phenomena'. *Individual Differences Research*, 7, 85–96.

Smith, E. L. (1972). 'The Raudive voices – objective or subjective? A discussion'. *Journal of the Society for Psychical Research*, 46, 192–200.

Smith, J. C. (2010). *Pseudoscience and extraordinary claims of the paranormal: A critical thinker's toolkit*. Winchester: John Wiley & Sons.

Smith, M. D. (1993). 'The effect of belief in the paranormal and prior set upon the observation of a "psychic" demonstration'. *European Journal of Parapsychology*, 9, 24–34.

Smith, M. D., Foster, C. L., & Stovin, G. (1998). 'Intelligence and paranormal belief: Examining the role of context'. *Journal of Parapsychology*, 62, 65–77.

Snyder, M. (1981). 'Seek and ye shall find: Testing hypothesis about other people'. In E. T. Higgins, C. P. Heiman, & M. P. Zanna (eds) *Social cognition: The Ontario Symposium on Personality and Social Psychology* (pp. 277–303). Hillsdate, NJ: Erlbaum.

Sosis, R. (2009). 'The adaptationist–by-product debate on the evolution of religion'. *Journal of Cognition and Culture*, 9, 315–32.

Spanos, N. P. (1996). *Multiple identities and false memories: A sociocognitive perspective*. Washington, DC: American Psychological Association.

Spanos, N. P., Burgess, C. A., & Burgess, N. F. (1994). 'Past-life identities, UFO abductions, and Satanic ritual abuse: The social construction of memories'. *International Journal of Clinical and Experimental Hypnosis*, 42, 433–46.

Spanos, N. P., Cross, P. A., Dickson, K., & DuBreuil, S. C. (1993). 'Close encounters: An examination of UFO experiences'. *Journal of Abnormal Psychology*, 102, 624–32.

Spanos, N. P., Menary, E., Gabora, N. J., DuBreuil, S. C., & Dewhirst, B. (1991). 'Secondary identity enactments during hypnotic past-life regression: A sociocognitive perspective'. *Journal of Personality and Social Psychology*, 61, 308–20.

Spanos, N. P. & Moretti, P. (1988). 'Correlates of mystical and diabolical experiences in a sample of female university students'. *Journal for the Scientific Study of Religion*, 27, 105–16.

Sparks, G. G., Hansen, T., & Shah, R. (1994). 'Do televised depictions of paranormal events influence viewers' paranormal beliefs?' *Skeptical Inquirer*, 18, 386–95.

Sparks, G. G. & Miller, W. (2001). 'Investigating the relationship between exposure to television programs that depict paranormal phenomena and beliefs in the paranormal'. *Communication Monographs*, 1, 98–113.

Sparks, G. G., Nelson, C. L., & Campbell, R. G. (1997). 'The relationship between exposure to televised messages about paranormal phenomena and paranormal beliefs'. *Journal of Broadcasting & Electronic Media*, 41, 345–58.

Sparks, G. G. & Pellechia, M. (1997). 'The effect of news stories about UFOs on readers' UFO beliefs: The role of confirming or disconfirming testimony from a scientist'. *Communication Reports*, 10, 165–72.

Sparks, G. G., Pellechia, M., & Irvine, C. (1998). 'Does television news about UFOs affect viewers' UFO beliefs? An experimental investigation'. *Communication Quarterly*, 46, 284–94.

Sparks, G. G., Sparks, C. W., & Gray, K. (1995). 'Media impact on fright reactions and belief in UFOs: The potential role of mental imagery'. *Communication Research*, 22, 3–23.

Spencer, J. (1994). *Gifts of the gods?* London: Virgin.

Sperber, D. (1990). 'The epidemiology of beliefs'. In G. Frazer & G. Gaskell (eds), *The social psychological study of widespread beliefs* (pp. 25–44). Oxford: Clarendon Press.

Spinelli, S. N., Reid, H. M., & Norvilitis, J. M. (2001–2). 'Belief in and experience with the paranormal: Relations between personality boundaries, executive functioning, gender role and academic variables'. *Imagination, Cognition and Personality*, 21, 333–46.

Spitz, H. H. (1997). *Nonconscious movements: From mystical messages to facilitated communication*. Mahwah, NJ: Erlbaum.

Spottiswoode, J. & May, E. (2003). 'Skin conductance prestimulus response: Analyses, artefacts and a pilot study'. *Journal of Scientific Exploration*, 17, 617–41.

Stanovich, K. E. & West, R. F. (2000). 'Individual differences in reasoning: Implications for the rationality debate'. *Behavioral and Brain Sciences*, 23, 645–65.

Stires, L. (1997). '3.7 million Americans kidnapped by aliens?' In K. Frazier, B. Karr, & J. Nickell (eds), *The UFO invasion: The Roswell incident, alien abductions, and government coverups* (pp. 203–6). Amherst, NY: Prometheus.

Stoel, R. D., De Geus, E. J. C., & Boomsma, D. I. (2006). 'Genetic analysis of sensation seeking with an extended twin design'. *Behavior Genetics*, 36, 229–37.

Stone-Carmen, J. (1994). 'A descriptive study of people reporting abduction by unidentified flying objects (UFOs)'. In A. Pritchard, D. E. Pritchard, J. E. Mack, P. Casey, & C. Yapp (eds), *Alien discussions: Proceedings of the Abduction Study Conference held at MIT* (pp. 309–15). Cambridge, MA: North Cambridge Press.

Storm, L. & Ertel, S. (2001). 'Does psi exist? Comments on Milton and Wiseman's (1999) meta-analysis of ganzfeld research'. *Psychological Bulletin*, 127, 424–33.

Storm, L., Tressoldi, P. E., & Di Risio, L. (2010). 'Meta-analysis of free-response studies, 1992–2008: Assessing the noise reduction model in parapsychology'. *Psychological Bulletin*, 136, 471–85.

St-Pierre, L. S. & Persinger, M. A. (2006). 'Experimental facilitation of the sensed presence is predicted by the specific patterns of the applied magnetic fields, not by suggestibility: Re-analyses of 19 experiments'. *International Journal of Neuroscience*, 116, 1079–96.

Strassman, R. (2001). *DMT: The spirit molecule*. Rochester, VT: Park Street Press.

Strieber, W. (1987). *Communion: A true story*. New York: Morrow.

Strindberg, A. (1897/1979). *'Inferno' and 'From an occult diary'*. New York: Penguin.

Stuart-Hamilton, I., Nayak, L., & Priest, L. (2006). 'Intelligence, belief in the paranormal, knowledge of probability and aging'. *Educational Gerontology*, 32, 173–84.

Subbotsky, E. (1993). *Foundations of the mind: Children's understanding of reality*. Cambridge, MA: Harvard University Press.

Subbotsky, E. (2004a). 'Magical thinking in judgments of causation: Can anomalous phenomena affect ontological causal beliefs in children and adults?' *British Journal of Developmental Psychology*, 22, 123–52.

Subbotsky, E. (2004b). 'Magical thinking – reality or illusion?' *The Psychologist*, 17, 336–9.

Subbotsky, E. (2005). 'The permanence of mental objects: Testing magical thinking on perceived and imaginary realities'. *Developmental Psychology*, 41, 301–18.

Sutherland, S. (1992). *Irrationality*. London: Pinter and Martin.

Suziedelis, A. & Potvin, R. H. (1981). 'Sex differences in factors affecting religiousness among Catholic adolescents'. *Journal for the Scientific Study of Religion*, 20, 38–51.

Svensen, S. G., White, K. D., & Caird, D. (1992). 'Replications and resolutions: Dualistic belief, personality, religiosity and paranormal belief in Australian students'. *Journal of Psychology*, 126, 445–7.

Tandy, V. (2000). 'Something in the cellar'. *Journal of the Society for Psychical Research*, 64, 129–40.

Tandy, V. & Lawrence, T. R. (1998). 'The ghost in the machine'. *Journal of the Society for Psychical Research*, 62, 360–4.

Targ, R. & Puthoff, H. (1974). 'Information transmission under conditions of sensory shielding'. *Nature*, 251, 602–7.

Taylor, M. (1997). 'The role of creative control and culture in children's fantasy/reality judgments'. *Child Development*, 68, 1015–17.

Taylor, M., Cartwright, B. S., & Carlson, B. M. (1993). 'A developmental investigation of children's imaginary companions'. *Developmental Psychology*, 29, 276–85.

Tellegen, A. & Atkinson, R. P. (1974). 'Openness to absorbing and self-altering susceptibility'. *Journal of Abnormal Psychology*, 83, 268–77.

Tellegen, A., Lykken, D. T., Bouchard, T. J., Wilcox, K. J., Segal, N. L., & Rich, S. (1988). 'Personality similarity in twins reared apart and together'. *Journal of Personality and Social Psychology*, 54, 1031–9.

Ter Keurst, A. J. (1939). 'Comparative differences between superstitious and non-superstitious children'. *Journal of Experimental Education*, 7, 261–7.

Thalbourne, M. A. (1981). 'Extraversion and the sheep-goat variable: A conceptual replication'. *Journal of the American Society for Psychical Research*, 75, 105–19.

Thalbourne, M. A. (1994a). 'The SPR century census: II. The survey of beliefs and experiences'. *Journal of the Society for Psychical Research*, 59, 420–31.

Thalbourne, M. A. (1994b). 'Belief in the paranormal and its relationship to schizophrenia-relevant measures: A confirmatory study'. *British Journal of Clinical Psychology*, 33, 78–80.

Thalbourne, M. A. (1995). 'Further studies of the measurement and correlates of belief in the paranormal'. *Journal of the American Society for Psychical Research*, 89, 233–47.

Thalbourne, M. A. (1996). 'Belief in life after death: Psychological origins and influences'. *Personality and Individual Differences*, 21, 1043–5.

Thalbourne, M. A. (1998). 'Transliminality: Further correlates and a short measure'. *Journal of the American Society for Psychical Research*, 92, 402–19.

Thalbourne, M. A. (1998–9). 'Belief in life after death and its relationship to transliminality-relevant variables'. *European Journal of Parapsychology*, 14, 16–30.

Thalbourne, M. A. (1999). 'Personality characteristics of students who believe themselves to be psychic'. *Journal of the Society for Psychical Research*, 63, 203–12.

Thalbourne, M. A. (2000). 'Transliminality: A review'. *International Journal of Parapsychology*, 11, 1–34.

Thalbourne, M. A. (2001). 'Measures of the sheep-goat variable, transliminality, and their correlates'. *Psychological Reports*, 88, 339–50.

Thalbourne, M. A. (2003). *A glossary of terms used in parapsychology*. 2nd edn. Charlottesville, VA: Puente Publications.

Thalbourne, M. A. (2009). 'Transliminality, anomalous belief and experience, and hypnotisability'. *Australian Journal of Clinical & Experimental Hypnosis*, 37, 119–30.

Thalbourne, M. A. (2010a). 'The Australian Sheep-Goat Scale: Development and empirical findings'. *Australian Journal of Parapsychology*, 10, 5–39.

Thalbourne, M. A. (2010b). 'Transliminality: A fundamental mechanism in psychology and parapsychology'. *Australian Journal of Parapsychology*, 10, 70–81.

Thalbourne, M. A., Bartemucci, L., Delin, P. S., Fox, B., & Nofi, O. (1997). 'Transliminality: Its nature and correlates'. *Journal of the American Society for Psychical Research*, 91, 305–32.

Thalbourne, M. A., Crawley, S., & Houran, J. (2003). 'Temporal lobe lability in the highly transliminal mind'. *Personality and Individual Differences*, 35, 1965–74.

Thalbourne, M. A. & Delin, P. S. (1993). 'A new instrument for measuring the sheep-goat variable: Its psychometric properties and factor structure'. *Journal of the Society for Psychical Research*, 59, 172–86.

Thalbourne, M. A. & Delin, P. S. (1994). 'A common thread underlying belief in the paranormal, mystical experience and psychopathology'. *Journal of Parapsychology*, 58, 3–38.

Thalbourne, M. A., Dunbar, K. A., & Delin, P. S. (1995). 'An investigation into correlates of belief in the paranormal'. *Journal of the American Society for Psychical Research*, 89, 215–31.

Thalbourne, M. A. & French, C. C. (1995). 'Paranormal belief, manic-depressiveness and magical ideation: A replication'. *Personality and Individual Differences*, 18, 291–2.

Thalbourne, M. A. & Haraldsson, E. (1980). 'Personality characteristics of sheep and goats'. *Personality and Individual Differences*, 1, 180–5.

Thalbourne, M. A. & Houran, J. (2000). 'Transliminality, the Mental Experience Inventory and tolerance of ambiguity'. *Personality and Individual Differences*, 28, 853–63.

Thalbourne, M. A. & Houran, J. (2003). 'Transliminality as an index of the sheep-goat variable'. *European Journal of Parapsychology*, 18, 3–14.

Thalbourne, M. A., Keogh, E., & Crawley, S. E. (1999). 'Manic-depressiveness and its correlates'. *Psychological Reports*, 85, 45–53.

Thalbourne, M. A. & Maltby, J. (2008). 'Transliminality, thin boundaries, unusual experiences, and temporal lobe lability'. *Personality and Individual Differences*, 44, 1617–23.

Thalbourne, M. A. & Nofi, O. (1997). 'Belief in the paranormal, superstitiousness and intellectual ability'. *Journal of the Society for Psychical Research*, 61, 365–71.

Tien, A. Y. (1991). 'Distributions of hallucinations in the population'. *Social Psychiatry and Psychiatric Edpidemiology*, 26, 287–92.

Toa, J. X., Ray, A., Hawes-Ebersole, S., & Ebersole, J. S. (2005). 'Intracranial EEG substrates of scalp EEG interictal spikes'. *Epilepsia*, 46, 669–76.

Tobacyk, J. J. (1985). 'Paranormal beliefs, alienation and anomie in college students'. *Psychological Reports*, 57, 844–6.

Tobacyk, J. J. (1988). *A revised paranormal belief scale*. Unpublished manuscript. Louisiana Tech University, Ruston, LA.

Tobacyk, J. J. (1995). 'What is the correct dimensionality of paranormal beliefs? A reply to Lawrence's critique of the Paranormal Belief Scale'. *Journal of Parapsychology*, 59, 27–46.

Tobacyk, J. J. (2004). 'A revised paranormal belief scale'. *International Journal of Transpersonal Studies*, 23, 94–8.

Tobacyk, J. J. & Milford, G. (1983). 'Belief in paranormal phenomena: Assessment instrument development and implications for personality functioning'. *Journal of Personality and Social Psychology*, 44, 1029–37.

Tobacyk, J., Miller, M. J., & Jones, G. (1984). 'Paranormal beliefs of high school students'. *Psychological Reports*, 55, 255–61.

Tobacyk, J. J., Miller, M. J., Murphy, P., & Mitchell, T. (1988). 'Comparisons of paranormal beliefs of black and white university students from the Southern United States'. *Psychological Reports*, 63, 492–4.

Tobacyk, J. J. & Mitchell, T. (1987). 'Out-of-body experience status as a moderator of effects of narcissism on paranormal beliefs'. *Psychological Reports*, 60, 440–2.

Tobacyk, J. J., Nagot, E., & Miller, N. (1988). 'Paranormal beliefs and locus of control: A multi-dimensional examination'. *Journal of Personality Assessment*, 52, 241–6.

Tobacyk, J. J. & Pirttila-Backman, A-M. (1992). 'Paranormal beliefs and their implications in university students from Finland and the United States'. *Journal of Cross-Cultural Psychology*, 23, 59–71.

Tobacyk, J. J., Pritchett, G., & Mitchell, T. (1988). 'Paranormal beliefs in late adulthood'. *Psychological Reports*, 62, 965–6.

Tobacyk, J. J. & Schrader, D. (1991). 'Superstition and self-efficacy'. *Psychological Reports*, 68, 1387–8.

Tobacyk, J. J., & Thomas, A. (1997). 'How the big orthogonal seven is really the oblique seven'. *Journal of Parapsychology*, 61, 337–42.

Tobacyk, J. J. & Tobacyk, Z. S. (1992). 'Comparisons of belief-based personality constructs in Polish and American university students: Paranormal beliefs, locus of control, irrational beliefs, and social interests'. *Journal of Cross-Cultural Psychology*, 23, 311–25.

Tobacyk, J. J. & Wilkinson, L.V. (1990). 'Magical thinking and paranormal beliefs'. *Journal of Social Behavior and Personality*, 5(4), 255–64.

Tobacyk, J. J. & Wilkinson, L.V. (1991). 'Paranormal beliefs and preferences for games of chance'. *Psychological Reports*, 68, 1088–90.

Todd, M. & Brown, C. (2003). 'Characteristics associated with superstitious behavior in track and field athletes: Are there NCAA divisional level differences?' *Journal of Sport Behavior*, 26, 168–87.

Torgler, B. (2007). 'The determinants of superstition'. *The Journal of Socio-Economics*, 36, 713–33.

Truzzi, M. (1996). 'Pseudoscience'. In G. Stein (ed.), *The encyclopedia of the paranormal* (pp. 560–75). Amherst, NY: Prometheus.

Tsang, E. W. K. (2004). 'Toward a scientific inquiry into superstitious business decision-making'. *Organization Studies*, 25, 923–46.

Turner, M. E. & Pratkanis, A. R. (1998) 'Twenty-five years of groupthink theory and research: Lessons from the evaluation of a theory'. *Organizational Behavior and Human Decision Processes*, 73, 105–15.

Turner, M. E., Pratkanis, A. R., Probasco, P., & Leve, C. (1992). 'Threat, cohesion and group effectiveness: Testing a social identity maintenance perspective on groupthink'. *Journal of Personality and Social Psychology*, 63, 781–96.

Tyler, K. A. (2002). 'Social and emotional outcomes of childhood sexual abuse: A review of recent research'. *Aggression and Violent Behaviour*, 7, 567–89.

Utts, J. M. (1996). 'An assessment of the evidence for psychic functioning'. *Journal of Scientific Exploration*, 10, 3–30.

Vallee, J. (1977). *UFOs: The psychic solution*. St Albans: Panther.

van Lommel, P., van Wees, R., Meyers, V., & Efferich, I. (2001). 'Near-death experience in survivors of cardiac arrest: A prospective study in the Netherlands'. *The Lancet*, 358, 2039–45.

van Os, J., Hansen, M., Bijl, R. V., & Ravelli, A. (2000). 'Strauss (1969) revisited: A psychosis continuum in the general population?' *Schizophrenia Research*, 45, 11–20.

Velmans, M. (2000). *Understanding consciousness*. London: Psychology Press.

Vikan, A. & Clausen, S. E. (1993). 'Freud, Piaget, or neither? Beliefs in controlling others by wishful thinking and magical behavior in young children'. *Journal of Genetic Psychology*, 154, 297–314.

Vitulli, W. F. & Luper, S. L. (1998). 'Sex differences in paranormal beliefs among under-graduate college students'. *Perceptual and Motor Skills*, 87, 475–84.

Vitulli, W. F., Tipton, S. M., & Rowe, J. L. (1999). 'Beliefs in the paranormal: Age and sex differences among elderly persons and undergraduate students'. *Psychological Reports*, 85, 847–55.

Voracek, M. (2009). 'Who wants to believe? Associations between digit ratio (2D:4D) and paranormal and superstitious beliefs'. *Personality and Individual Differences*, 47, 105–9.

Vyse, S. A. (1997). *Magical thinking: The psychology of superstition*. Oxford: Oxford University Press.

Wagenaar, W. A. (1972). 'Generation of random sequences by human subjects: A criti-cal survey of the literature'. *Psychological Bulletin*, 77, 65–72.

Wagenmakers, E-J., Wetzels, R., Borsboom, D., & van der Maas, H. L. J. (2011). 'Why psychologists must change the way they analyse their data: The case of psi. Comment on Bem (2011)'. *Journal of Personality and Social Psychology*, 100, 426–32.

Wagenmakers, E-J., Wetzels, R., Borsboom, D., van der Maas, H. L. J., & Kievet, R. A. (2012). 'An agenda for purely confirmatory research'. *Perspectives on Psychological Science*, 7, 632–8.

Wagner, M. W. & Ratzeburg, F. H. (1987). 'Hypnotic susceptibility and paranormal belief'. *Psychological Reports*, 60, 1069–70.

Wagstaff, G. F. (1981). *Hypnosis, compliance, and belief*. Basingstoke: Palgrave Macmillan.

Wagstaff, G. F. (1989). 'Forensic aspects of hypnosis'. In N. P. Spanos & J. F. Chaves (eds), *Hypnosis: The cognitive-behavioral perspective* (pp. 340–57). Buffalo, NY: Prometheus.

Wagstaff, G. F. (1999). 'Hypnosis'. In S. Della Sala (ed.), *Mind myths: Exploring popu-lar assumptions about the mind and brain* (pp. 187–204). Chichester: Wiley.

Walker, W. R., Hoekstra, S. J., & Vogl, R. J. (2002). 'Science education is no guarantee of scepticism'. [US] *Skeptic*, 9, 24–7.

Waller, N. G. & Ross, C. A. (1997). 'The prevalence and biometric structure of patho-logical dissociation in the general population: Taxometric and behavior genetic find-ings'. *Journal of Abnormal Psychology*, 106, 499–510.

Wason, P. C. (1960). 'On the failure to eliminate hypotheses in a conceptual task'. *Quarterly Journal of Experimental Psychology*, 12, 129–40.

Watson, D., Clark, L. A., & Tellegen, A. (1988). 'Development and validation of brief measures of positive and negative affect: The PANAS scales'. *Journal of Personality and Social Psychology*, 54, 1063–70.

Watt, C. (2005). 'Parapsychology's contribution to psychology: A view from the front line'. *Journal of Parapsychology*, 69, 215–31.

Watt, C., Watson, S., & Wilson, L. (2007). 'Cognitive and psychological mediators of anxiety: Evidence from a study of paranormal belief and perceived childhood control'. *Personality and Individual Differences*, 42, 335–43.

Watt, C. & Wiseman, R. (2002). 'Experimenter differences in cognitive correlates of paranormal belief and in psi'. *Journal of Parapsychology*, 66, 371–85.

Wegner, D. M. (2002). *The illusion of conscious will*. Cambridge, MA: Bradford Books.

Wehr, T. (2009). 'Staring nowhere? Unseen gazes remain undetected under considera-tion of three statistical methods'. *European Journal of Parapsychology*, 24, 32–52.

Wellman, H. M. & Estes, D. (1986). 'Early understanding of mental entities: A re-examination of childhood realism'. *Child Development*, 57, 910–23.

Whinnery, J. E. (1997). 'Psychophysiologic correlates of unconsciousness and near-death experiences'. *Journal of Near-Death Studies,* 15, 231–58.

Whittle, C. H. (2004). 'Development of beliefs in paranormal and supernatural phenomena'. *Skeptical Inquirer,* 28, 43–5.

Wicherts, J. M., Bakker, M., & Molenaar, D. (2011). 'Willingness to share research data is related to the strength of the evidence and the quality of reporting of statistical results'. *PLoS ONE,* 6(11), e26828.

Wickramasekera, I. (1989). 'Risk factors for parapsychological verbal reports and somatic complaints'. In B. Shapin & L. Coly (eds), *Parapsychology and human nature* (pp. 19–35). New York: Parapsychology Foundation.

Wierzbicki, M. (1985). 'Reasoning errors and belief in the paranormal'. *Journal of Social Psychology,* 125, 489–94.

Wilde, D. J. & Murray, C. D. (2009). 'An interpretative phenomenological analysis of out-of-body experiences in two cases of novice meditators'. *Australian Journal of Clinical and Experimental Hypnosis,* 37, 90–118.

Willging, B. T. & Lester, D. (1997). 'Paranormal beliefs and personality scores of high school students'. *Perceptual and Motor Skills,* 85, 938.

Williams, E., Francis, L. J., & Robbins, M. (2007). 'Personality and paranormal belief: A study among adolescents'. *Pastoral Psychology,* 56, 9–14.

Williams, L. M. (1994). 'Recall of childhood trauma: A prospective study of women's memories of child sexual abuse'. *Journal of Consulting and Clinical Psychology,* 62, 1167–76.

Williams, L. M. & Irwin, H. J. (1991). 'A study of paranormal belief, magical ideation as an index of schizotypy and cognitive style'. *Personality and Individual Differences,* 12, 1339–48.

Wilson, D. B. & Shadish, W. R. (2006). 'On blowing trumpets to the tulips: To prove or not to prove the null hypothesis – Comment on Bösch, Steinkamp, and Boller (2006)'. *Psychological Bulletin,* 132, 524–8.

Wilson, I. (1987). *The after death experience.* New York: William Morrow.

Wilson, K. & French, C. C. (2006). 'The relationship between susceptibility to false memories, dissociativity, and paranormal belief and experience'. *Personality and Individual Differences,* 41, 1493–502.

Wilson, K. & French, C. C. (2008–9). 'Misinformation effects for psychic readings and belief in the paranormal'. *Imagination, Cognition and Personality,* 28, 155–71.

Wilson, S. (2002). 'Psi, perception without awareness, and false recognition'. *Journal of Parapsychology,* 66, 271–89.

Wilson, S. (2010). 'The naturalness of weird beliefs'. *The Psychologist,* 23, 564–7.

Wilson, S. C. & Barber, T. X. (1983). 'The fantasy-prone personality: Implications for understanding imagery, hypnosis, and parapsychological phenomena'. In A. A. Sheikh (ed.), *Imagery: Current theory, research and application* (pp. 340–87). New York: John Wiley & Sons.

Windholz, G. & Diamant, L. (1974). 'Some personality traits of believers in extraordinary phenomena'. *Bulletin of the Psychonomic Society,* 3, 125–6.

Wiseman, R. (2011). *Paranormality: Why we see what isn't there.* London: Macmillan.

Wiseman, R. & Greening, E. (2005). '"It's still bending": Verbal suggestion and alleged psychokinetic ability'. *British Journal of Psychology,* 96, 115–27.

Wiseman, R. & Greening, E. (2010). 'Psychic con-men'. In W. M. Grossman & C. C. French (eds), *Why statues weep: The best of the Skeptic* (pp. 7–9). London: Philosophy Press.

Wiseman, R., Greening, E., & Smith, M. (2003). 'Belief in the paranormal and suggestion in the séance room'. *British Journal of Psychology*, 94, 285–97.
Wiseman, R. & Milton, J. (1998). 'Experiment one of the SAIC remote viewing program: A critical re-evaluation'. *Journal of Parapsychology*, 62, 297–308.
Wiseman, R. & Milton, J. (1999). 'Experiment one of the SAIC remote viewing program: A critical re-evaluation – A reply to May'. *Journal of Parapsychology*, 63, 3–14.
Wiseman, R. & Morris, R. L. (1994). 'Modelling the stratagems of psychic fraud'. *European Journal of Parapsychology*, 10, 31–44.
Wiseman, R. & Morris, R. L. (1995a). Recalling pseudo-psychic demonstrations. *British Journal of Psychology*, 86, 113–125.
Wiseman, R. & Morris, R. L. (1995b). *Guidelines for testing psychic claimants.* Hatfield: University of Hertfordshire Press.
Wiseman, R. & Schlitz, M. (1997). 'Experimenter effects and the remote detection of staring'. *Journal of Parapsychology*, 61, 197–207.
Wiseman, R. & Schlitz, M. (1999). 'Replication of experimenter effect and the remote detection of staring'. *Proceedings of the 42nd Annual Convention of the Parapsychological Association*, 471–9.
Wiseman, R. & Smith, M. D. (1994). 'A further look at the detection of unseen gaze'. *Proceedings of the 37th Annual Convention of the Parapsychological Association*, 465–78.
Wiseman, R. & Smith, M. D. (2002). 'Assessing the role of cognitive and motivational biases in belief in the paranormal'. *Journal of the Society for Psychical Research*, 66, 157–66.
Wiseman, R., Smith, M. D., Freedman, D., Wasserman, T., & Hurst, C. (1995). 'Two further experiments concerning the remote detection of an unseen gaze'. *Proceedings of the 38th Annual Convention of the Parapsychological Association*, 480–90.
Wiseman, R., Smith, M., & Wiseman, J. (1995). 'Eyewitness testimony and the paranormal'. *Skeptical Inquirer*, 19(6), 29–32.
Wiseman, R. & Watt, C. (2004). 'Measuring superstitious belief: Why lucky charms matter'. *Personality and Individual Differences*, 37, 1533–41.
Wiseman, R. & Watt, C. (2010). 'Twitter as a new research tool: Proof of principle with a mass participation test of remote viewing'. *European Journal of Parapsychology*, 25, 89–100.
Wiseman, R. & Watt, C. (submitted). *Back to the future: A pre-registry of precognition studies.* Manuscript submitted for publication.
Wiseman, R. S. (2010). 'Heads I win, tails you lose: How some parapsychologists nullify null results and what to do about it'. In S. Krippner & H. L. Friedman (eds), *Debating psychic experience: Human potential or human illusion?* (pp. 169–78). Santa Barbara, CA: Praeger.
Wolfgang, A. (2008). 'Correlations between the EEGs of two spatially separated subjects: A replication study'. *European Journal of Parapsychology*, 23, 131–46.
Wolfradt, U. (1997). 'Dissociative experiences, trait anxiety and paranormal beliefs'. *Personality and Individual Differences*, 23, 15–19.
Wolfradt, U., Oubaid, V., Straube, E. R., Bischoff, N., & Mischo, J. (1999). 'Thinking styles, schizotypal traits and anomalous experiences'. *Personality and Individual Differences*, 27, 821–30.
Wolfradt, U. & Watzke, S. (1999). 'Deliberate out-of-body-experiences, depersonalization, schizotypal traits and thinking styles'. *Journal of the American Society for Psychical Research*, 93, 249–57.

Woo, C-K. & Kwok, R. H. F. (1994). 'Vanity, superstition and auction price'. *Economics Letters*, 44, 389–95.

Wooffitt, R. (1992). *Telling tales of the unexpected: The organisation of factual discourse*. Hemel Hempstead: Harvester Wheatsheaf.

Wooffitt, R. (2000). 'Some properties of the interactional organisation of displays of paranormal cognition in psychic–sitter interaction'. *Sociology*, 34, 457–80.

Wooffitt, R. (2008). 'Observations on trouble management in psychic practitioner–sitter interaction'. *European Journal of Parapsychology*, 23, 60–89.

Woolley, J. D. (1997a). 'Initiating a dialogue'. *Child Development*, 68, 1027–30.

Woolley, J. D. (1997b). 'Thinking about fantasy: Are children fundamentally different thinkers and believers from adults?' *Child Development*, 68, 991–1011.

Woolley, J. D., Boerger, E. A., & Markman, A. B. (2004). 'A visit from the Candy Witch: Factors influencing young children's belief in a novel fantastical being'. *Developmental Science*, 7, 456–68.

Woolley, J. D., Browne, C. A., & Boerger, E. A. (2006). 'Constraints on children's judgments of magical causality'. *Journal of Cognition and Development*, 7, 253–77.

Woolley, J. D. & Phelps, K. E. (1994). 'Young children's practical reasoning about imagination'. *British Journal of Developmental Psychology*, 12, 53–67.

Woolley, J. D., Phelps, K. E., Davis, D. L., & Mandell, D. J. (1999). 'Where theories of mind meet magic: The development of children's beliefs about wishing'. *Child Development*, 70, 571–87.

Woolley, J. D. & Wellman, H. M. (1990). 'Young children's understanding of realities, nonrealities and appearances'. *Child Development*, 61, 946–61.

Woolley, J. D. & Wellman, H. M. (1993). 'Origin and truth: Young children's understanding of imaginary mental representations'. *Child Development*, 64, 1–17.

World Health Organisation (1990). *Composite International Diagnostic Interview (CIDI) Version 1.0*. Geneva: World Health Organisation.

Wulff, D. M. (1997). *Psychology of religion: Classic and contemporary*. 2nd edn. New York: Wiley.

Wuthnow, R. (1976). 'Astrology and marginality'. *Journal for the Scientific Study of Religion*, 15, 157–68.

Yapko, M. D. (1994). *Suggestions of abuse*. New York: Simon and Schuster.

Yates, G. C. R. & Chandler, M. (2000). 'Where have all the skeptics gone? Patterns of new age beliefs and anti-scientific attitudes in preservice primary teachers'. *Research in Science Education*, 30, 377–87.

Zapf, R. M. (1945). 'Relationship between belief in superstitions and other factors'. *Journal of Educational Research*, 38, 561–79.

Zebb, B. J. & Moore, M. C. (2003). 'Superstitiousness and perceived anxiety control as predictors of psychological distress'. *Anxiety Disorders*, 17, 115–30.

Zuckerman, M. (1994). *Behavioral expressions and biosocial bases of sensation seeking*. New York: Cambridge University Press.

Zusne, L. & Jones, W. H. (1982). *Anomalistic psychology: A study of extraordinary phenomena of behavior and experience*. Hillsdale, NJ: Lawrence Erlbaum Associates.

Zusne, L. & Jones, W. H. (1989). *Anomalistic psychology: A study of magical thinking*. 2nd edn. Hillsdale, NJ: Lawrence Erlbaum Associates.

Index

Note: Page numbers in bold refer to Glossary (pp. 273–81).

belief in, 6, 11, 28, 29, 31, 32, 35, 38, 43, 57, 78, 87, 142, 157
see also clairvoyance; precognition; psi; psychokinesis; telepathy
extraversion, 42–3, 51, 96–8, 236, 275
eyewitness testimony
see memory
Eysenck Personality Questionnaire (EPQ), 56

facilitated communication, 263–4, 266, 275
fairies, 9, 34, 47, 71, 73, 75, 79, 194, 222, 275
false consensus effect, 157, 275
false memories, 14–15, 22, 66, 96, 140–1, 147, 148, 149, 181–3, 205, 211–19, 222, 260, 275
falsifiability, 133, 230, 235, 250–5
fantasy-proneness, 19, 43, 46–51, 66, 69–70, 85–93, 96, 97, 112, 145, 146, 154, 171, 212–4, 218, 275
Faraday, Michael, 265
Feng Shui, 9, 178–9, 275
Forer effect, 133–4
fortune telling
see divination
Fox sisters, 53–4
fraud, 53–4, 138, 211, 227, 228, 262
fugue states, 62
Fuller, John, 204
functionalism, 257, 275

gambler's fallacy, 125
ganzfeld technique, 230–1, 232, 233, 275
Geller, Uri, 175
gender, 26–9, 36–7, 38–42, 50, 52, 82, 88, 90, 154
genetic transmission (of paranormal belief), 153–4
geomagnetism
see magnetic fields
ghosts, xii, 48–9, 96, 98–9, 104, 112, 115, 117, 125, 126, 131, 134, 136, 142, 150, 156, 163, 173, 178, 185, 196–8, 213, 245, 260, 261, 262, 275

belief in, 6, 29, 31, 38, 56, 78, 80, 90, 155, 157, 194
glossolalia, 9, 275
glutamate, 111
graphology, 126, 134, 135
gravity-induced loss of consciousness (G-LOC), 111
groupthink, 119–20, 275

habituation, 238, 275
hallucinations, 20, 22, 48, 55, 61, 63–4, 66–7, 94, 95–6, 97, 110, 111, 149, 178, 185, 211, 219–20, 221, 245, 258, 259, 260, 261, 275
hard problem, 275
see mind-body problem
hemispheric dominance, 95, 102–4, 106
heuristics, 188–9, 199, 275
see also availability heuristic; representativeness heuristic
highway hypnosis, 221
Hill, Betty and Barney, 203–4, 207, 217
hindsight bias, 115, 276
hippocampus, 259
Hopkins, Budd, 204–5, 206–7, 214, 220
horoscopes
see astrology
'hundredth monkey' phenomenon, 9, 276
Hynek, J. Allen, 202
hyperactive agency detection device (HADD), 194–6, 276
hypercarbia, 111
hypnagogic state, 95, 276
hypnopompic state, 95, 276
hypnosis, 9, 21, 149, 180–1, 204, 222, 276
hypnotic regression, 4, 96, 140–1, 182–3, 204, 205, 209, 214–19, 222, 276
hypnotic susceptibility, 46, 49–51, 66, 86, 213, 218, 276
hypoxia, 111

iatrogenic disorder, 62, 183, 276
I Ching, 9, 276
idealism, 256, 276
identity theory, 256–7, 276
ideomotor effect, 264–6, 276

Printed and bound by CPI Group (UK) Ltd, Croydon, CR0 4YY